05/07

UNIVERSITY OF
WOLVERHAMPTON

26/10

Compton Learning Centre

Compton Road West
Wolverhampton WV3 9DX

Wolverhampton (01902) 323642

foundations of
economics

ANDREW GILLESPIE

OXFORD
UNIVERSITY PRESS

OXFORD

UNIVERSITY PRESS

Great Clarendon Street, Oxford OX2 6DP

Oxford University Press is a department of the University of Oxford.
It furthers the University's objective of excellence in research, scholarship,
and education by publishing worldwide in

Oxford New York

Auckland Cape Town Dar es Salaam Hong Kong Karachi
Kuala Lumpur Madrid Melbourne Mexico City Nairobi
New Delhi Shanghai Taipei Toronto

With offices in

Argentina Austria Brazil Chile Czech Republic France Greece
Guatemala Hungary Italy Japan Poland Portugal Singapore
South Korea Switzerland Thailand Turkey Ukraine Vietnam

Oxford is a registered trade mark of Oxford University Press
in the UK and in certain other countries

Published in the United States
by Oxford University Press Inc., New York

British Library Cataloguing in Publication Data
Data available

Library of Congress Cataloging in Publication Data
Data available

Typeset by Graphicraft Limited, Hong Kong
Printed in Great Britain
on acid-free paper by
Ashford Colour Press Ltd, Gosport, Hants

ISBN 978-0-19-929637-8

3 5 7 9 10 8 6 4 2

This book is dedicated to
my family, Ali and my two beautiful
daughters Clemency and Romily.

Outline contents

Detailed contents

PART 1 Microeconomics   1

1 What is economics?   3

2 The production possibility frontier (curve): the PPF or PPC   16

PART 2 **Macroeconomics**   243

Preface

This book is intended to provide an introduction to the principles of economics and to help you to understand many issues that affect businesses and economies around the world: everything from why China has grown so fast, to the effects of the inflow of workers into the UK from Eastern Europe, to why some takeovers are prevented by the government. It will also help you to understand issues that affect your own daily life: Why are houses so expensive in the UK? What determines how much you have to pay to borrow from the bank? What are you likely to earn in your chosen career? By reading this book you will have the tools to analyse these issues from an economist's perspective, and hopefully you will soon find yourself talking and thinking like an economist as well! Going to university is an investment decision: is it worth it? Buying this book involves opportunity costs because you could have bought something else: is it worth the sacrifice? (I hope so!) Do the extra benefits from spending an extra hour on your assignment exceed the extra costs? As well as giving you an insight into economic issues, I also hope this book will help you to analyse problems logically and understand the economic consequences of any decision.

I am assuming no prior knowledge of economics at all. It does not matter if you have no background in economics (or indeed little interest!) at this stage. I aim to take you from knowing no economic theory to having a good solid foundation that gives you the knowledge and skills for further, specialised study in economics in higher education. With this background you can study the subject or parts of the subject in much more detail, but will already have an overview and insight into the key issues. I also aim to show you how relevant this subject is to everything going on around you and how valuable an understanding of economic theory can be. The examples in the book cover a range of markets from oil to cars, to chicken waste, and a range of countries from the UK to India. Do send me feedback on the book: let me know if you enjoy it and find it useful, as well as any ideas on how I can improve the next edition. You can email me at wattgill@aol.com

How to use this book

Gillespie's *Foundations of Economics* is enriched with a range of features designed to help support and reinforce your learning. This guided tour shows you how best to utilise your textbook and get the most out of your study.

LEARNING OBJECTIVES

By the end of this unit you should be able to:

✔ explain what is meant by effective demand;

✔ explain what is shown by a demand curve;

✔ understand the difference between a change in the quan demanded and a change in demand;

✔ explain the possible causes of a shift in a demand curve;

✔ appreciate the difference between marginal and total utili

Learning objectives

Each unit begins with a bulleted list of learning objectives outlining the main concepts and ideas you will encounter in the unit. These serve as helpful signposts for learning and revision.

Now you try it

Employees are hired at a wage of £200 per week. You have four employe 400 units.

What is the total cost of production?

What is the average output per employee?

You hire a fifth employee and output rises to 450 units.

What is the total cost of production?

What is the marginal product of the fifth worker?

What is the average output per employee now?

What is the average cost per unit now?

Now you try it

The text regularly offers you the opportunity to test your understanding of a concept you have just learned by trying to use the theory in a practical way. This might take the form of answering a question, working through a problem, or working with graphs.

What do you think?

What do you think are the major determinants of the demand for each

* New cars.

* Textbooks.

* Diamond rings.

* Healthcare.

What do you think?

These questions give you the opportunity to stop and reflect on the material, either on your own or in a group.

Economics in context   Influences on demand

Demand can shift for all sorts of reasons, such as the weather, a major actions. There may be particular demand patterns in a market. In the to 50% of sales are made around the Christmas period. Demand is par in the toy market because of particular 'fad' products that take off each television programmes or games, and often to the surprise of retailer Tamagochi, Furby, Teletubbies and Power Rangers are examples of po

 Question

Economics in context

Once you have understood the economic theory, it is important that you can see how it is applied to business and to everyday life. These topical illustrations also come with questions, to reinforce your understanding of the concept discussed.

Case studies

Each unit is supplemented by a short case study designed to contextualise the material in the unit and to encourage you to apply your learning to more involved analyses of real situations.

> ### Case Study
>
> Although Apple has a relatively small share of the PC market, it has with its iPod. The iPod allows users to store large quantities of music
> The product was launched in 2001 and sold over 40 million in everyday life and has radically changed the way many people listen design capabilities and the style of the iPod soon made it a major fas the growth of downloaded music and led to a levelling off of sales of the initial model Apple has continued to innovate, launching new ve version called the Shuffle. The Shuffle randomly selects music loaded

Checklist

Each unit ends with a checklist of the key topics from the unit, designed as a prompt for you to check that you have understood the important concepts. They also serve as a helpful revision tool.

> ### Checklist
>
> Now you have read this unit try to answer the following question
> ☐ Can you explain what is meant by effective demand?
> ☐ Can you explain what is shown by a demand curve?
> ☐ Do you understand the difference between a change in the change in demand?
> ☐ Can you explain the possible causes of a shift in a demand
> ☐ Do you understand the difference between marginal and to

End of unit questions

Carefully devised review questions have been provided at the end of every unit. You can use these to check your understanding of the topics before moving on to the next unit, or for group discussion or revision.

> ### End of unit questions
>
> 1 Does a demand curve show what a consumer would like to
> 2 What is the difference between a movement along and a shi
> 3 Does an increase in income always shift the demand curve t
> 4 Does the quantity demanded always fall if the price increase
> 5 To what extent do you think a supermarket can control the de

Key learning points

The author has outlined some important points for you to note at the end of every unit.

> ### Key learning points
>
> • Demand shows what customers are willing and able to pur just what they want to buy.
> • A movement along a demand curve occurs when there is a things being unchanged.
> • A shift in the demand curve occurs when more or less is der
> • A demand curve is usually downward sloping, but in some good) it can be upward sloping.

Learn more

Some more advanced concepts are introduced or are further explored on the Online Resource Centre accompanying the book. This content is referenced at the end of relevant units.

> ### Learn more
>
> A demand curve can be derived using indifference curve anal change in price and income in terms of consumers' utility. To find analysis and how a consumer maximises utility, visit our websit
>
> 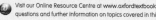 Visit our Online Resource Centre at www.oxfordtextbook questions and further information on topics covered in thi

About the online resource centre

The Online Resource Centre that accompanies this book provides students and lecturers with ready-to-use teaching and learning resources. These are free of charge and are designed to maximise the learning experience.

www.oxfordtextbooks.co.uk/orc/gillespie_econ

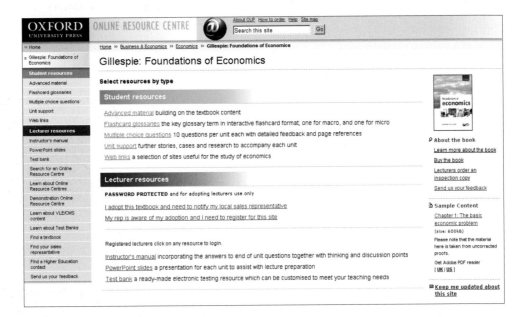

For students

Self-test questions

A suite of multiple-choice questions is provided for each unit in the book, to allow you to test your knowledge of the key themes in each unit.

Web links

A selection of annotated web links chosen by the author makes it easy for you to research those topics that are of particular interest to you. These links are checked regularly to ensure they remain up to date.

Unit support

The Online Resource Centre includes further stories, cases, and research for each unit in the book. These will help you to reinforce your understanding of topics and to further apply the theory to the real world.

Advanced material

Some advanced topics are introduced or covered in more depth, to supplement the material in the book itself.

Flashcard glossaries

Key glossary terms are available in an interactive flashcard format, to allow you to check your understanding of the important concepts.

For lecturers

PowerPoint slides

A suite of PowerPoint slides which you can customise has been included for use in lecture presentations. Arranged by unit theme, the slides may also be used as hand-outs in class.

Instructor's manual

Discussion and thinking points are included in a helpful guide for instructors. This also incorporates the answers to all of the questions set in the textbook.

Test bank

A ready-made electronic testing resource which you can customise to meet your teaching needs is included for every unit in the book.

Acknowledgements

Many thanks to everyone at OUP for their support and help putting this book together. In particular, thanks to Kirsty Reade, Fiona Loveday, Nicola Bateman, and Julie Harris.

About the book

This book is divided into the following two sections.

- **Microeconomics.** This focuses on what happens in individual markets and covers topics such as supply and demand, and market structures. When we analyse the price of oil, the salaries of merchant bankers and the power of supermarkets, this is microeconomic analysis.

- **Macroeconomics.** This focuses on the economy as a whole. Rather than examining one market, it considers the country as a whole. In macroeconomics we will cover topics such as unemployment, growth in the economy and international trade.

Whilst it is possible to read specific units in this book on their own, economics is a subject in which your understanding of a topic will often build on previous concepts and models you have studied. To analyse a monopoly or a competitive market, for example, you need a good grasp of costs and revenues. To understand the way that price adjusts to bring about equilibrium, you need to understand supply and demand. Even when it comes to macroeconomics, a lot of this relies on an understanding of microeconomic theory. Analysing the total demand in the economy and the total supply in the economy (macroeconomics) uses the same principles that are required to examine supply and demand in a particular market (microeconomics)—they are the same principles but on a much bigger scale.

The best way to read this book, therefore, is to start at the beginning and keep going until you reach the end! You will find that your understanding grows as you work your way through, and this enhances your ability to analyse new material when you come to it.

■ The structure of the units

At the beginning of each unit there is an overview of what the content of the unit involves; there are also a number of learning objectives setting out what you should gain once you have read the unit. The important issues raised by each unit are summarised in the key learning points at the end. You can see whether you have fully understood the unit or not by using the checklist and the end of unit questions. Further review tests on each unit are available online at www.oxfordtextbooks.co.uk/orc/gillespie_econ. If you would like to learn more about any of the topics in the units that you have been studying then you can go to our website for further material.

Within each unit I have included a number of features to help you in your studies. These include the following.

- **Economics in context.** This feature includes up-to-date stories that highlight how a particular economic concept relates to the 'real world'. You will find numerous interesting stories about different firms and economies throughout the book.

- **What do you think?** Every now and again it is worth sitting back and thinking about what you have read; if nothing else, this helps to make sure you have absorbed the material and reflected on it. The 'What do you think?' feature raises particular issues related to the given topic which require you to think for yourself and develop your own view. There is often no 'right' answer to economic issues, and the 'What do you think?' questions are intended to be thought-provoking and highlight that many problems can be solved in different ways.

- **Now you try it.** This feature asks you to apply your understanding—perhaps by calculating something or illustrating a change using diagrams. It is designed to help you check whether you could use the knowledge you have just acquired.

Each unit also has a case study toward the end which covers a number of the topics you have just studied, and this is intended for you to think about or discuss with other students.

Overall the book is designed to make the content relevant and accessible. I have tried to set out clearly what each unit covers and provide numerous opportunities for you to consolidate your understanding. There are also questions designed to help you apply your knowledge to other economic issues and develop your evaluative skills. This provides a modern introduction to economic theory that should develop your enthusiasm for the subject and also give you the understanding and skills for further study.

Overview of the book

■ Microeconomics Units 1 to 18

The book begins with a discussion of the basic economic problem; in Unit 1 we look at what studying economics involves and some of the key concepts and issues.

In Unit 2 we examine how resources are allocated within an economy—what determines who works where, what is produced, who earns what and who gets what. One way of solving these economic problems is to leave it to market forces of supply and demand. In Units 3 to 6 we examine supply and demand conditions and analyse how the price mechanism brings about equilibrium. Having established how the free market works, we then highlight some of the disadvantages of this approach in Units 7 and 8, and consider how the government might intervene to solve these.

Having examined the elements of a market, we then focus on market structure. We begin by developing an understanding of revenues and costs in Units 9 and 10. Once this has been covered, we analyse the different forms of market structure in detail and the implications of these in terms of price and output decisions in Units 11 to 16.

In Unit 17 we consider whether all firms do actually try to profit maximise and examine the implications of other objectives. In Unit 18 we examine the market for labour and consider how wages are determined for different jobs.

■ Macroeconomics Units 19 to 34

In the macroeconomics section we begin with an overview of the key issues in macroeconomics in Unit 19. We then analyse what causes equilibrium in the economy in Unit 20, and whether national income is a good indicator of a country's standard of living in Unit 21. In Unit 22 we consider the determinants of economic growth, before looking at aggregate demand and aggregate supply in Unit 23.

We examine the different elements of demand in the economy in turn in Units 24 to 26 when we analyse consumption, investment and government spending. After this we consider causes of, and possible cures for, unemployment in Unit 27. We then examine the money market in Unit 28 and analyse the impact of changes in money supply and interest rates on the economy. This then leads to a discussion of the causes of inflation and whether there is a relationship between inflation and unemployment in Unit 29. Following this, we move on to the international environment and examine issues such as free trade, exchange rates, the balance of payments and the European Union. These are covered in Units 30 to 32. Lastly, in Units 33 and 34 we look at the very topical issues of developing economies and globalisation.

Overall this book should provide a good introduction to the key issues in economics and provide you with the tools necessary to analyse economics problems. I hope you enjoy it.

Why study economics?

If you have ever wondered why the cost of a ticket to your favourite band's last concert was so expensive, why you are paid so little in your part-time job, why your petrol is taxed so heavily or why it is more expensive to get into a nightclub at weekends than during the week; if you have ever wondered what influences the rate at which you change your currency into another when you go on holiday, why some people seem to be so much richer than others or why some firms make more profits than others, then studying economics will be of interest to you! In fact, whether you know it or not, you are already an important part of the economic system. You are a consumer of products: every day you are out there buying and consuming goods and services, and influencing the demand for them. You may also have a job and so help to generate goods and services. If you are working, you are also paying taxes that are used to finance the provision of other products. However, just being part of an economy is one thing: studying it is another. By studying economics you can develop an analytical approach that helps you to understand a wide range of issues from what determines the price of different products, to the causes and consequences of unemployment, to the benefits of different forms of competition. By the end of this book, you should understand a whole range of economic issues such as why some people earn more than others, why some economies grow faster than others and why, if you set up in business, you might want to dominate a market.

The study of economics provides a number of models and frameworks that can be applied to a range of situations. I hope that by the end of this book you have the tools you need to examine any number of economic issues and analyse the underlying causes and consequences of any changes that have occurred.

The impact of an ageing population, price increases by your local supermarket, the returns on your investment by choosing to go to university, and the costs to society of smoking are all issues you can analyse as part of economics once you have the necessary tools.

And at the heart of economics is human behaviour: what influences it and what happens when it changes. What makes people choose one course of action rather than another? If we wanted to change behaviour, what is the best way of doing this? If we want people to be more environmentally friendly, is this best achieved by taxing environmentally unfriendly behaviour? Subsidising 'good behaviour' or legislating? Economics affects peoples' standard of living and how they live. The tax and benefits system will affect your incentive to work, your willingness to marry, to have children, to save money and to have a pension. An understanding of economics therefore provides an insight into the factors that shape society and influence the success of your business or career.

Of course, you are not the only one wanting to understand the economy and the economic impact of policy decisions. Governments would like to be able to influence the economy to achieve their objectives, such as faster economic growth and lower unemployment. Firms are interested in economic change because it will influence their ability to compete (e.g., interest rates can affect their costs and demand for their products) and determine their future strategy (e.g., what markets they should be targeting). Employees are interested in economic conditions because they affect their earnings. Consumers want to know what is likely to happen to the prices of the things they buy. Many different groups in society will therefore be interested in what influences the economy and how economies might change in the future. This probably explains why economic stories receive such media attention and why the subject has been studied so intensely over the years by economists. I hope that by the end of this book you will have a greater insight into these issues and want to explore them even further.

Microeconomics

What is economics?

In this unit we set out to explain the fundamental issues in economics. These centre on the idea of scarcity and choice. At any moment there are limited resources available and so we have to make choices about how to use them most effectively. This unit considers how these choices might be made, as well as introducing a number of key concepts.

LEARNING OBJECTIVES

By the end of this unit you should be able to:

✔ understand the basic economic problems of what is produced, how it is produced and for whom it is produced;

✔ understand the different types of economy, such as the free market economy, the command economy and the mixed economy;

✔ explain the difference between positive and normative economics;

✔ explain the difference between microeconomics and macroeconomics;

✔ understand some key terms and concepts in economics that you will need in your analysis.

▇ The basic economic problem

At the moment you are likely to have many different things that you have to do, such as write an essay, see friends or go to a film. The problem is that you do not have enough time to do them all immediately, so you are going to have to make choices. You may decide to stay in and work; by staying in and writing the essay it may help you to get a better degree and benefit you in the long run. On the other hand, maybe you should go out and enjoy yourself now, even though the consequence of this may be that your grades suffer and you do not do as well as you hoped academically. Which course of action you choose depends on your priorities and your future plans; this will affect how you use your time. Whatever you do it will involve sacrificing another option. Going out means sacrificing the better grade; staying in means sacrificing the fun of going out. Similarly, when you go shopping there are many things you could buy with your money, but with a limited income you have to make a decision about what is best for you. In fact, you are continually having to choose between alternatives, and this highlights the fundamental problem facing not only you as an individual, but also economies as a whole. At any moment in time the amount of goods and services that an economy can produce is determined by the resources it has available. These resources include the following.

- **Land**. This includes the physical land and the minerals associated with it, such as oil and diamonds.
- **Labour**. This includes the number of people willing and able to work and the skills that they have.
- **Capital**. This involves the quantity and quality of capital equipment in an economy, such as machinery and transport.
- **Entrepreneurship**. This refers to the ability of managers to think of new ideas, to manage people and to take risks.

The quantity and quality of these resources can change over time—for example, with more immigration into a country or more investment into technology—but at any given moment the amount and quality of these are known. This places a limit on what can be produced. However, whilst the amount we can produce may be limited, what we want as consumers certainly is not. We want lots of everything! Ideally, we would do our work and go to a film and see friends. When we go shopping we would like to buy everything there is. We would like to study and go out. The problem is that our resources constrain us. Like an economy, we face the problem of scarcity and choice: we would like to do and have everything, but because resources are scarce we must make choices.

Economics in context   Entrepreneurial culture

The UK is said to have a less entrepreneurial culture than America. In America it is not regarded as unusual if business people fail at some point: it is all part of the entrepreneurial learning curve. In the UK failure is looked on less favourably. Starting up again once you have been made bankrupt has been very difficult in the past in the UK. However, recent changes of legislation have enabled entrepreneurs to get started again and cancel their debts more quickly.

 Question

How can a government encourage entrepreneurship?

option is to have a government take full responsibility for the economy. This is what would happen in a 'planned economy' (also known as a 'command economy'). In this situation the government decides:

- what goods and services should be produced in the economy (for example, the government may decide that defence is a priority and allocate a significant number of resources into this area; alternatively, it might decide that greater car production is the priority);
- the combination of machines and people employed in any particular industry, including who works where and with what;
- the way in which goods and services are distributed (for example, everyone may be given access to free education and health care; prices, wages and rents may be determined by the government).

In an economy such as Cuba many economic decisions have traditionally been made by the government. Similarly, in the past the Chinese government controlled a very significant part of the economy, deciding what was produced and how it was made. A different approach is to leave the solutions to these questions to free market forces. This means that the government does not intervene and leaves all decisions to individuals and private firms to work out for themselves. If there is a demand for a particular product and firms can produce it at a profit then it will be produced. If you want to work in a particular industry, you can. If using more machinery seems to generate a high return then firms will invest in equipment. This free market approach has the advantage of not needing a central government to decide everything (which is extremely complex and may be inefficient); instead, decisions are made in many thousands of individual markets by firms and their customers. Each firm and each individual pursues their own objectives and focuses purely on what they want. There is no need for a central body to make decisions for everyone else. A free market approach also means that what is produced is definitely in demand (because if it is not demanded then firms would not produce it), whereas if a government is in control then it may order that certain things are produced only to find that they are not actually required and no one wants to buy them. In this case, there would be waste. The free market will also provide an incentive for firms to be innovative and develop new services and new ways of doing things. Being more efficient and meeting customer needs more precisely can boost profits, which firms or individuals can keep for themselves. The potential benefits from innovating mean there is likely to be greater choice for customers.

However, the free market has many potential failings and imperfections. For example, some goods or services may not be provided because they are not profitable, even if some people might think that they are things that should be provided (e.g., educational television programmes, the opera, museums and libraries). On the other hand, some products, such as guns and drugs, may be openly available because they are profitable, even though society as a whole may think they are undesirable. In the free market products are only available if people can afford them; in the case of services such as health and education this may be felt to be unacceptable. These failings of the free market mean that some intervention by a government is inevitable. The real question is how much intervention there will be. The problems with the free market and the case for intervention are examined in Unit 7.

What do you think?

Can you think of goods and services that should be available in all economies even if they are not profitable?

Can you think of goods and services that may be profitable but should not be available in a free market?

Do you think health care and education should be provided by the government? Do you think the private provision of these should be prevented or encouraged?

■ Mixed economies

In reality, no economy is completely free market or completely planned. All economies are a combination of the two (see Fig. 1.2). They are known as 'mixed economies'. In a mixed economy some goods and services are provided by the government, such as education and the police force. Other goods and services, such as fridges, cars and sofas, may be provided by private firms. However, whilst a mixed economy, in which the government steps in when the free market fails, may be the obvious solution, this still leaves open many questions, such as the following.

* To what extent should the government intervene?

* In what areas should it intervene? Should it provide public transport, energy and postal services?

* How should the government intervene: does it need to provide products itself? Can it provide products in partnership with private firms? To what extent should it regulate private businesses? Can the government effectively influence firms' and individuals' behaviour through taxing 'bad' behaviour or subsidising 'good' behaviour?

What do you think?

The government would like to reduce the number of people smoking. Should it:

Ban smoking?

Tax it more heavily?

Spend more on anti-smoking promotional campaigns?

Let people do what they want?

Focus on other issues?

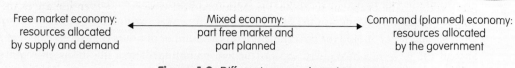

Figure 1.2 Different economic systems.

Economics in context

Social change in Venezuela

In 2005, in Venezuela, the government under Hugo Chavez initiated a huge social programme. The aim was to reduce the country's major problems of poverty and economic inequality. The programme included the following:

- a literacy campaign;
- a discounted food and household goods shopping project established in poor urban and rural areas where no supermarkets or general food stores existed before;
- a basic preventative medicine programme providing free health care and subsidised medicines to over 60% of the population who previously had no medical services at all.

Other projects, such as the creation of a huge network of 1600 businesses owned by the workers throughout the country, were aimed at creating jobs.

? Question

This programme introduced by Chavez was very interventionist. What might be the problems of such a programme?

The trend in many (but not all) economies in recent years has involved less intervention by governments in their economies. In the UK, for example, many industries have been taken out of government control and sold to private firms over the last twenty years. British Gas, British Steel and British Airways were all taken out of government control and sold in the 1990s. This process of selling government assets to private individuals and organisations is called 'privatisation'. In other sectors the government has not sold off organisations but has removed restrictions to allow more firms to compete: this is called 'deregulation'. However, in some economies, notably in South America in recent years, there has been greater government intervention as electors have felt that their societies would benefit if the government took greater responsibility for the provision of goods and services.

These decisions about the extent and method of government intervention are continually being made and reviewed by governments and their electorate. If you listen to the news then almost every day there will be discussions over the appropriate balance between private and public sector, and the extent of government intervention. Should health care be free to patients? Should the National Health Service use private hospitals to undertake some of its operations? Should the government set a minimum wage and, if so, what should it be? Should the government limit the number of hours that shops can open? Should the government regulate casinos or ban gambling? These questions all require a view about whether the free market is better at allocating resources or whether the government is needed. Your role as a voter is to elect a government which has economic policies you agree with. In part, this depends on whether you trust individuals and firms to make decisions for themselves or whether you think the government needs to intervene to make the economy work effectively.

These issues of government intervention and the benefits and limitations of the free market economy are examined in more detail in Unit 7.

What do you think?

What goods and services does the government provide in your economy? How does this differ with another economy you know?

Do you think the government should intervene more in your economy? In what way?

What do you think would happen if there was no government intervention in an economy?

■ Types of economics

This book will cover many of the essential issues in the study of economics. This includes an overview of different types of economics such as those described below.

Positive and normative economics

- **Positive economics** examines the different relationships between economic variables and provides an analysis of these that can actually be tested. For example, we may think that an increase in demand for a product will increase its price, that more government spending will lead to faster growth in the economy or that lower income taxes provide more incentive to work. These relationships can be tested over time to see whether they actually occur.

- **Normative economics**, by comparison, focuses on value judgements about what you think should happen. For example, you might think that the government should spend more money on the health service compared to defence, that it ought to divert resources away from one sector toward another sector or that it should cut taxes on profits even if it has to cut spending as a result. These are your opinions; they represent your view of what should be done or what is most important for the economy. You cannot test these ideas because they are simply opinions of what matters and what needs to be done. Not surprisingly, normative economics is the area of economics where most of the disagreements between policy makers occur! Everyone might agree that an increase in spending on health and education could improve the services in these sectors, but they may disagree enormously on which one of these is the priority or exactly how the money should be raised and used.

> **What do you think?**
>
> Normative economics is based on your views about economic issues.
> Do you think the government should regulate gambling or should it be left to the free market? Why?
> Do you think medical care should be free or should it be charged for?
> Do you think the government should tax cigarettes and alcohol more heavily?
> Why do you think the ways that governments deal with the issues above varies from country to country?

Microeconomics and macroeconomics

- **Microeconomics** focuses on the individual decisions of households and firms. It focuses on the demand and supply within a particular market, such as the market for housing or labour. It helps to explain the price of a good, your decision whether to work in a particular industry or the impact of an increase in the supply of a product. Microeconomics might analyse the determinants of the price of oil or a firm's shares, for example.

- **Macroeconomics** analyses the economy as a whole. For example, rather than focus on the price level in one market (microeconomics) it considers the general price level in the economy. Rather than examine an individual's decision whether to work (microeconomics) it considers the overall numbers employed in the economy. Macroeconomics therefore deals with topics such as inflation, unemployment, economic growth and international trade, and usually analyses these from a government's perspective.

■ Key terms and concepts in economics

In order to study economics effectively you need to learn the language of the subject. The following are some of the key terms and concepts that you will need to help you on your journey.

Goods and services

Goods are physical products such as televisions and washing machines. They are tangible —you can see them and touch them. **Services**, by comparison, are intangible; for example, education and banking are services. In reality, most organisations provide a combination of goods and services. When you visit a restaurant you buy a meal (tangible), but you also receive service and benefit from the overall environment. In this book we use the term 'product' to include goods, services and combinations of the two.

Consumer goods and capital goods

- **Consumer goods** are goods and services that are consumed by the final user; for example, magazines and sandwiches are bought by or given to the person who is going to consume them.
- **Capital goods** are goods that are bought to use in the production process, that is, they are bought to produce other goods and services. A production line is used to make products such as computers which are then sold to customers to be consumed. A fleet of lorries is bought to distribute products.

The decision by firms and governments over whether to spend money on consumption or investment has important implications for the long-term growth of an economy.

Investment, savings and consumption

The word 'investment' is often used in the media to mean money that is 'invested' into shares or banks. In economics, however, these are called '**savings**'. Savings represent the income of households that is not spent on **consumption**; for example, money put into a bank or into a pension fund. The term '**investment**' in economics refers to the purchase of capital goods; for example, firms investing in new equipment that is used in the production of products to be consumed. Firms may invest in a new factory or information technology systems, for example. Governments are often making a choice between spending on consumption goods and investment goods. Producing more capital goods enables the economy to produce more in the future, but involves sacrificing consumption today. Households also make these choices. Do you spend your bonus on a holiday (consumption) or an extension to the house (investment)? Decisions about how much to save and how much to spend have important economic implications.

> ### What do you think?
> How important do you think it is to save money for your pension?
> If the government had £10 billion to spend, do you think it should be used to invest in education or should it be given away in the form of lower taxes?

Private and public sector

The **private sector** is made up of organisations owned by individuals and firms. Companies such as Tesco plc and Barclays Bank plc are owned by private investors as opposed to the government. **Public sector** organisations are run by the government, for example the National Health Service. An important issue in economics is how much the government should intervene in an economy and in what ways it should intervene.

> **What do you think?**
>
> Do you think the objectives of private sector and public sector organisations are likely to differ? Do you think all organisations should be owned by the government?

Economic models

In order to build **economic models** we must make assumptions about how different aspects of the economy work. In many cases these are simplifications, but provided that they help to analyse what a particular outcome will be, then they remain useful. We may predict, for example, that a market will move from A to B; in reality it may move from A to C to B, but nevertheless the model has some validity because it predicts the end destination. Of course, these models of the economy are continually reviewed, and new theories and approaches are being developed. Obviously, economics does not and cannot relate to the specific decisions of a given individual or an individual firm; some people and some firms will always act differently than the majority. Economics focuses on the market, sector, region or country as a whole and seeks to explain the general behaviour within these areas. We assume, for example, that consumers are rational. If a consumer is asked to choose between something that is very good or something that is average, we assume they will choose the very good. Of course, one particular person may be perverse and may not choose this, but the vast majority will! We also assume that firms try to profit maximise. This is discussed in detail in Unit 17 and is open to some debate. However, regardless of whether all firms seek to profit maximise, and even regardless of whether all succeed, if this is what the majority are trying to do then the model has some value.

Deciding at the margin

One of the most fundamental and powerful concepts in economics is that of marginal cost and marginal benefit. Whoever you are and whatever you do, you should consider the marginal (or extra) costs and benefits of your actions. If the extra cost of doing something is less than the extra benefit, then do not do it! By doing it your welfare or happiness will fall. Equally, if the extra benefit from doing something is greater than the extra cost then do it: if you do you will gain. This concept of measuring things **at the margin** in order to work out what is best is important to remember and can be used when analysing any situation. If you do not like something then this does not mean you should stop it altogether, but you cut back to the point when marginal cost equals marginal benefit. Let us consider air travel; many people rightly claim that this has terrible environmental effects. This is true, but it also brings many benefits: it helps move supplies around for firms, it creates jobs and it provides individuals with the opportunity to do business, travel and holiday abroad. An economist would argue that air travel should be undertaken up to the point where the marginal cost equals the marginal benefit. If the marginal benefit exceeds the marginal costs, do more; if the marginal benefit is less than the marginal cost, do less.

Real and nominal

The amount of money you receive in your wage packet is a **nominal** sum. It shows how much you have been given, but does not reveal what you can actually buy with it. A '**real**' figure takes account of inflation. If, for example, you receive a pay increase of 2%, then in nominal terms you are 2% better off. However, if the prices of everything you buy have increased by 2%, then in real terms you are in the same position that you were originally; there has been no real increase. If a firm has announced a 1% increase in profits, but during the same period the price of buying materials and resources has increased by 3%, then in real terms the firm has made a loss. It is always important to think in terms of the 'real' effect, not just the nominal.

Case Study

In 2006 the National Institute for Health and Clinical Excellence (NICE) decided that there was insufficient evidence to recommend the routine use by the National Health Service (NHS) of two drugs to help treat advanced bowel cancer. These drugs are called Avastin and Erbitux.

Pressure groups said that these drugs were the best option for treating seriously ill patients whose cancer has spread. They claim that these drugs can extend life expectancy by around five months in some cases and that this has been proved in tests.

Bowel cancer kills almost fifty people per day in the UK and affects one in eighteen people during their lifetime. It is possible to treat it, but it really needs to be caught in the early stages. The problem with prescribing such drugs is that they are both expensive. Treatment using Avastin costs on average £17,655 per patient, and using Erbitux costs £11,739. The NHS has to consider how best to use its resources. It does not generate a revenue because it does not charge for its services and relies on the government for its funding. More funding for the NHS may mean less funds for other areas of government. The deputy chief executive of NICE said that neither of the two drugs represents a good use of scarce NHS resources.

? Questions

- In what ways does the NICE decision about these two drugs highlight the economic problem of scarcity and choice?
- Do you think NICE should have authorised their use in the NHS?
- Should patients be allowed to pay for these drugs themselves?

@ Web

To find out more about the work of NICE you can visit www.nice.org.uk

Checklist

Now you have read this unit try to answer the following questions.

☐ Do you understand the basic economic problems of what is produced, how it is produced and for whom it is produced?

☐ Can you distinguish between different types of economy such as the free market economy, the command economy and the mixed economy?

☐ Can you explain the difference between positive and normative economics?

☐ Can you explain the difference between microeconomics and macroeconomics?

☐ Do you understand the difference between investment and consumption goods?

End of unit questions

1 How do different economies try to solve the basic economic problem?

2 To what extent does the government intervene in your economy?

3 How does the concept of scarcity and choice affect you in your day to day life?

4 How does the concept of opportunity cost relate to your decision to go to university?

5 What do you think are the fundamental products a government should provide for its citizens?

Key learning points

• Economics considers the key economic questions of what is produced, how it is produced and who it is it produced for.

• The key economic questions can be answered by market forces of supply and demand (in a free market), by the government (in a planned economy) or by a combination of the two (in a mixed economy).

• Microeconomics focuses on what happens in a particular market.

• Macroeconomics focuses on the economy as a whole.

 Visit our Online Resource Centre at www.oxfordtextbooks.co.uk/orc/gillespie_econ for test questions and further information on topics covered in this chapter.

»2

The production possibility frontier (curve): the PPF or PPC

The starting point in our economic analysis is to consider what an economy can produce. As consumers we may want many things, but there is a limit to what our economy can actually produce. This can be analysed using the production possibility frontier (PPF). In this unit we examine the factors that determine how much an economy can produce and the implications of different output decisions.

LEARNING OBJECTIVES

By the end of this unit you should be able to:

✔ understand what is meant by a production possibility frontier;

✔ analyse the shape and the position of the production possibility frontier;

✔ understand the concept of productive efficiency.

Scarcity and choice

In Unit 1 we saw how the study of economics was based around the issue of scarcity and choice. As consumers our wants are unlimited, but there is a limit to what an economy can produce because of a scarcity of resources. As consumers and voters we are, of course, interested in what an economy can produce. What an economy is capable of producing can be shown on a production possibility frontier.

The production possibility frontier (PPF)

The **production possibility frontier** or **curve** (PPF or PPC) shows the maximum output that can be produced in an economy at any given moment, given the resources available. If an economy is fully utilising its resources then it will be producing on the PPF. To keep

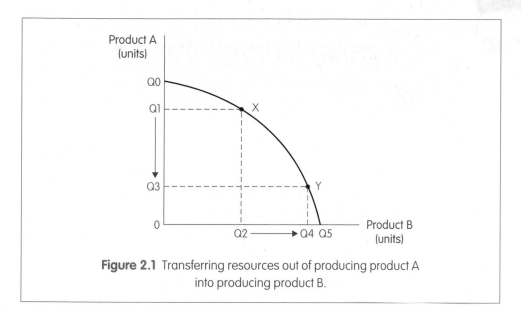

Figure 2.1 Transferring resources out of producing product A into producing product B.

our analysis simple we consider an economy that produces only two products, A and B (see Fig. 2.1). Imagine that all of an economy's resources, such as land, labour and capital, were used in industry A. Then Q0 of A would be produced and none of B would be made. Alternatively, if all resources were transferred to industry B then Q5 of B would be produced and none of A would be made. If resources were divided between the two industries then a range of combinations of products is possible. For example, at point X the economy produces Q1 of product A and Q2 of product B; alternatively, resources could be allocated differently between the two industries and it could produce at point Y, producing Q3 of A and Q4 of B. All of the points on the frontier, such as X and Y, are said to be productively efficient because they are fully utilising the economy's resources. This is attractive because it shows that resources are being used properly and not wasted. When an economy is productively efficient it can only produce more of one product by producing less of another; resources have to be shifted from one product to another. The PPF therefore illustrates the concept of opportunity costs. As more units of product B are produced this involves shifting resources into industry B and out of industry A: this will involve sacrificing product A. Some units of A will be sacrificed to produce more of product B; the amount sacrificed is the opportunity cost. For example, the opportunity cost of producing the extra Q4 – Q2 units of B is Q1 – Q3 units of A.

Now you try it

Using Fig. 2.2 calculate the opportunity cost of the 5th unit of B in terms of the number of units of A sacrificed.

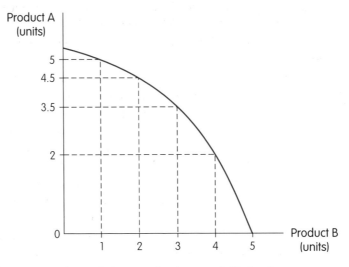

Figure 2.2 A production possibility frontier.

Economics in context

The importance of opportunity cost

The concept of opportunity cost is extremely important in economics and business. It represents the opportunities forgone. Whenever a manager makes a strategic decision he/she is deciding to lead the business in one direction rather than another. Sometimes this works; for example, Nokia's decision to move out of all of its business areas apart from mobile phones was highly successful for many years. Other times it is the wrong decision, such as Marks and Spencer's move into America and Wal-Mart's move into Germany. Any decision should be judged, not just in terms of what it achieved, but also in terms of what else could have been done with those resources.

Imagine a firm is earning a return on investment of 4%. This means the profits it earns are 4% of the amount of long-term funds in the business. This is clearly better than 0%, but is not better than the rate of interest available in most UK banks. Investors might rightly question how effectively the managers are using the resources available to them.

? Question

If you decide to invest money and buy a company's shares, what would the opportunity cost be?

Reallocation of resources

The PPF shows all the combinations of products that an economy can produce given its present resources. Any combination on the frontier is productively efficient. This shows what can be produced, but which is the right combination? What determines whether an economy should produce at X or Y? Do we want more of product A or more of product B, for example? How do we decide?

In a free market economy this decision would be taken by the market forces of supply and demand. If there was a high level of demand for product B rather than product A then it would make this industry more attractive for producers. The greater demand for B would attract firms into this industry and out of A. The firms in industry B would need more resources, such as labour and materials, to meet the higher demand. This increased demand for resources would increase the price paid for them, attracting resources into this industry and out of industry A. Market forces triggered by an increase in demand for the product would therefore lead to a reallocation of resources from one industry to another. On the PPF shown in Fig. 2.3 this can be seen as a movement from X to Y. The demand for digital cameras, for example, has grown rapidly in recent years, whilst the demand for 'traditional' film has declined. As a result, firms such as Kodak have had to move resources out of traditional film and into digital. Similarly, the music industry has experienced a rapid growth in downloading at the expense of cassettes and CDs. Companies such as EMI have had to move their resources into these newer areas.

In a planned economy the decision about what to produce is determined by government instructions and directives. For example, the government may order that more factories and employees are used to produce product B rather than A. In this case the reallocation from, say, X to Y is not determined by demand, but by government orders. This may

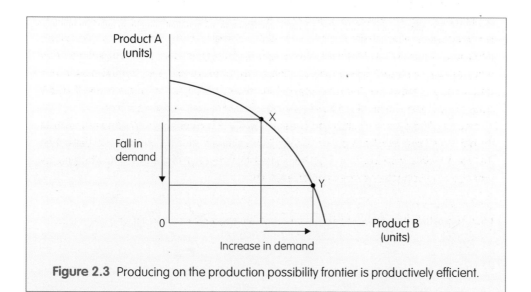

Figure 2.3 Producing on the production possibility frontier is productively efficient.

happen if the government does not trust market forces to produce what it regards as the right decision for society. For example, in a free market we may want to consume products today, but may not be very good at thinking about our health or education; the government may intervene to ensure that there is greater provision of these services.

However, what can happen is that, if the instructions given by the government do not match what people are actually demanding, then it can lead to too much of some goods being produced whilst too few of other goods are available. The government may decide that resources need to be diverted to defence or nuclear energy, for example, whereas consumers may want more houses. In democracies, political parties will set out their policies and what they intend to do if they are elected. They tell the voters what their priorities will be and then the electors can decide who they want in power.

▦ Productive inefficiency

If the economy is producing a combination of products on the production possibility frontier then it is productively efficient. However, an economy may be operating within the frontier (e.g., at the point V in Fig. 2.4), in which case it is productively inefficient. This is because it could produce more of both products by using the existing resources effectively. Imagine you were driving around a country and noticed lots of factories that were closing down, high levels of unemployment and shops with very few customers in them; this economy would be productively inefficient. This can be illustrated using a PPF diagram; for example (see Fig. 2.4), if an economy produced at point W and not V, then it would be making more of both A and B. No economy should be operating within the PPF because it is wasting its resources. However, this can happen if resources do not reallocate effectively when conditions in an economy alter. For example, demand for product B may

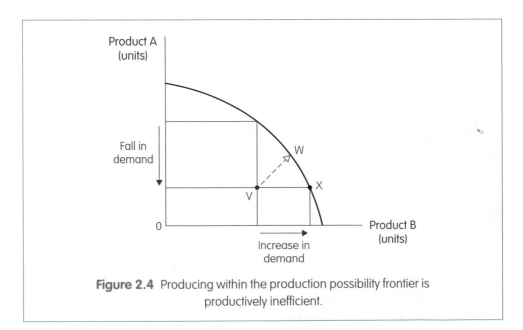

Figure 2.4 Producing within the production possibility frontier is productively inefficient.

increase, leading to firms wanting to move from A to B. Firms in industry A close down and, in theory, they and their employees would switch to B. However, if managers and employees lack the necessary skills or experience they may not be able to move easily. As a result the economy may get stuck at V. Hopefully, over the long term, employees will be trained and gain the skills required to take jobs. Firms will therefore be able to produce in industry B, enabling the economy to produce at a point such as X; however, in the short term at least, there is productive inefficiency. Alternatively, there could be a lack of demand in the economy, so that, although it can produce at W, customers can only afford the combination of products at V. Again, over time, demand will hopefully increase and the economy will end up on the frontier.

Shifting the production possibility frontier outward

Once on the production possibility frontier an economy can only produce more of both products by shifting the PPF outward, that is, increasing the amount of both products that can be produced with the economy's resources. This is what happens over time when an economy grows. Economic growth enables more goods and services to become available to consumers.

An outward shift of the frontier might be due to:

- more training of employees, enabling them to be more productive;
- greater investment in capital goods such as machines and equipment—in the short run this would mean that resources would have to be shifted from consumption goods toward capital goods, and in the long run greater investment would enable the economy to produce more products for consumption;
- an increase in the population size, for example, through immigration;
- improvements in technology providing better ways of doing things.

Most political parties put forward their policies to help an economy to grow in the future. Again, voters decide which policies they think are most likely to work. For more about economic growth see Unit 22.

What do you think?

What actions would you take if you were in government to make the UK grow faster?

Now you try it

Imagine that technological developments enabled the production of product B to increase for any given amount of other resources, such as land, labour and machinery. The technology has no impact on the production of A. Draw the new production possibility frontier that would occur following the technological development.

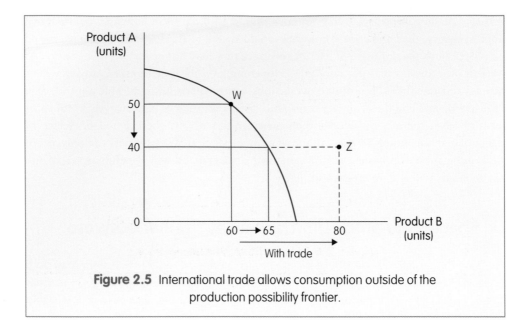

Figure 2.5 International trade allows consumption outside of the production possibility frontier.

▪ Consumption outside the production possibility frontier

The PPF shows what an economy can produce given its available resources. However, it is possible to consume outside of the frontier through international trade. It may well be that another country can produce some items more efficiently than you can, and that you can produce some products more efficiently than it can; through trade both countries can benefit.

Imagine, for example, that an economy is producing at point W and then gives up 10 units of product A (see Fig. 2.5). Within its own country it could only produce 5 units of B in return. If, however, it could find a country that was less efficient at producing A then it might be able to sell these abroad at a profit. For example, it might be able to trade these 10 units of A abroad and receive more than 5 units of B in return. For example, it may be possible to sell its 10 units of A for 20 units of B; this means the economy could operate at Z. The benefits of international trade are examined in detail in Unit 31.

Now you try it

Imagine that an economy is at the point C in Fig. 2.6. Within the domestic economy, what is the opportunity cost of 5 more units of B?

Assume that 2 units of A can be traded abroad for 12 units of B. Then, starting at C, if an economy gave up 2 units of A and traded overseas, how many units of B could it now have?

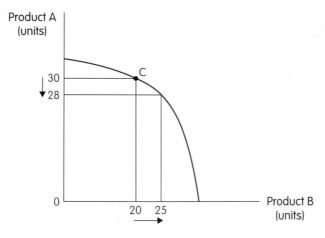

Figure 2.6 The benefits of international trade.

Present versus future decisions

The PPF is often used to illustrate the extent to which an economy is producing for the present or the future. Economies that focus on capital goods are investing for the long term: they are investing in machines and equipment that will allow the economy to produce more in the future. This will be shown over time by an outward shift of the PPF; when the machines are finished and being used the economy can produce more. Economies that focus more on the here and now will produce more consumer goods; this is likely to lead to a smaller outward shift in the PPF over time because the investment in the amount of machinery and technology is less.

> **What do you think?**
> Is it better for an economy to produce consumer goods, that is, focus on fulfilling peoples' demands today, or should it invest for the future?

The shape of the production possibility frontier

So far we have drawn the PPF as concave to the origin. This is because of the assumptions we make about what happens when resources to output are transferred from one industry to another. This depends on the returns to a factor. If there are constant returns to a factor in industries A and B then this means that every time resources are transferred from one industry to another, there is the same increase in output in B and the same decrease in

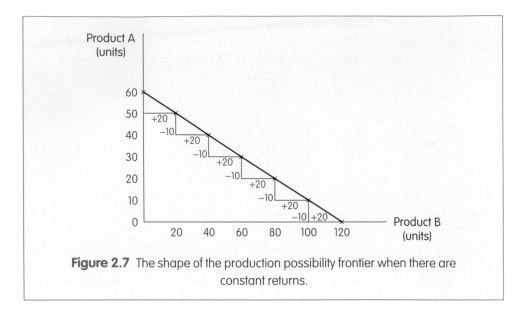

Figure 2.7 The shape of the production possibility frontier when there are constant returns.

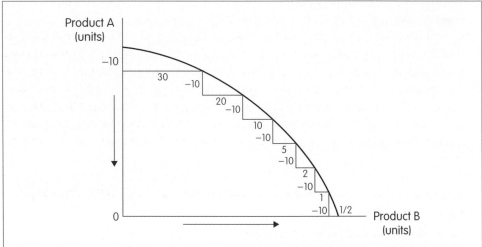

Figure 2.8 The shape of a production possibility frontier when there are diminishing returns. As resources are transferred into industry B, there are diminishing returns: successively less is produced each time.

output in industry A. This would lead to a PPF that is a straight line. For example, in the economy shown in Fig. 2.7, every time a given number of resources are shifted from industry A to B, 10 units of A are given up in return for 20 units of B.

In reality, resources are unlikely to be equally productive in both industries. Some equipment may be designed specifically for some types of production rather than others. Some employees may not be able to transfer their skills easily from one sector to another.

This may lead to diminishing returns to a factor. This means that every time a given number of resources are transferred out of industry B into industry A, successively less units of A are produced (e.g., see Fig. 2.8). This means the PPF is concave to the origin. The concept of diminishing returns to a factor is examined in Unit 9.

Case Study

The success of America over the centuries has been helped enormously by immigrants into the country. However, immigration is now a very controversial issue in the US. Many of the immigrants working in the country at the moment are illegal, for example, workers who have come over the border from Mexico. These immigrants want to be recognised and allowed to work in the US officially, and on May Day 2006 over a million of them protested in rallies held in major cities across America.

According to data from the US Department of Homeland Security, 1.1 million people became legal permanent residents of the US in 2005. Mexico was the most common country that they came from, accounting for 14% of the total. However, each year, up to a million illegal immigrants also enter the country, mostly from Latin American nations. There are now more than 11.5 million of them living in the US. Over 2.5 million are based in California and over 1.4 million are in Texas.

The immigrants mainly work in particular industries. For example, around 22% of all construction jobs in the US are held by illegal workers. Other popular sectors are farming, cleaning and preparing food. Typically, these are low-skilled, low-paid jobs. Overall, immigrants account for around 5% of the workforce. Some argue that immigrants push down wages for everyone and take jobs away from Americans. Others argue that they provide a bigger workforce and help the economy. Defenders of immigration argue that the government receives tax receipts from immigrants and that the benefits paid to them are usually low; for example, most immigrants return home and do not retire in the US, and so do not receive pensions.

❓ Questions

- How does immigration affect the production possibility frontier of an economy? Show this using a diagram.
- In what ways can immigration help an economy?
- Do you think economies should welcome immigration?

Checklist

Now you have read this unit try to answer the following questions.

- ☐ Do you understand what is meant by a production possibility frontier?
- ☐ Can you explain the shape and the position of the production possibility frontier?
- ☐ Do you understand the concept of productive efficiency?

End of unit questions

1 Can an economy produce outside the production possibility frontier? Can it consume outside?

2 Why might an economy be producing within the production possibility frontier?

3 What do you think is the best way to shift the production possibility frontier outward?

4 What do you think is the best point to be at on the production possibility frontier?

5 In what way does the production possibility frontier illustrate the concept of opportunity cost?

Key learning points

- Given the present resources of an economy, there is a maximum combination of products that can be produced. This is shown by the production possibility frontier.

- If an economy is operating within the production possibility frontier then it is productively inefficient.

- Economic growth can be seen by an outward shift of the production possibility frontier.

Learn more

If you read Unit 31 you can find out more about the principle of comparative advantage. This shows how economies can benefit from free trade and consume outside of their production possibility frontier.

 Visit our Online Resource Centre at www.oxfordtextbooks.co.uk/orc/gillespie_econ for test questions and further information on topics covered in this chapter.

Demand

In the previous unit we examined the maximum output of goods and services that an economy could produce given its resources. However, we did not analyse in detail what would determine which combination of products would be produced and consumed. What makes an economy produce more of some products and less of others? This depends on the nature of the economic system. In a free market the allocation of resources is determined by supply and demand. The next three units consider the market forces of supply and demand, and the interaction between the two. We begin with demand.

LEARNING OBJECTIVES

By the end of this unit you should be able to:

✔ explain what is meant by effective demand;

✔ explain what is shown by a demand curve;

✔ understand the difference between a change in the quantity demanded and a change in demand;

✔ explain the possible causes of a shift in a demand curve;

✔ appreciate the difference between marginal and total utility.

▓ Introduction

In a free market economy the basic economic problems of what to produce, how to produce and who gets what are solved by market forces.

• The demand and supply of goods and services determines what is produced and sold.

- The demand and supply of resources determines the combination of different resources being used, for example how much labour and how much machinery is employed in a given industry.
- The amount that people earn and the relative prices of products determines who can afford to buy different goods and services.

Imagine that changes in technology lead to a greater demand for website designers and less demand for travel agents because people can search and book direct online. This should lead to more web design companies setting up and more designers being recruited. Meanwhile, there will be less demand for travel agency services and they may have to make people redundant. Rewards will go up for the designers and down for the sales assistants as the economy adjusts to change.

An understanding of supply and demand conditions is therefore crucial to economic analysis. All markets, whether it be housing, oil, shares, labour, currencies, money, gold, silver and even university places, are underpinned by the forces of supply and demand. We shall therefore begin with an analysis of demand, then look at supply (Unit 5), and finally put the two sides of a market together to examine the concept of equilibrium (Unit 6).

▩ The demand curve

The demand for a product is the amount that customers are willing and able to buy at each and every price, all other things being unchanged. This is shown on a demand curve. A demand curve measures the quantity that households are actually able to buy at each and every price, not just the quantity they would like to buy. It therefore represents what is called 'effective demand' and depends on what they want *and* what they can afford. For example, at the price P1 the quantity Q1 is demanded (see Fig. 3.1). At a lower price P2 a greater quantity Q2 is demanded.

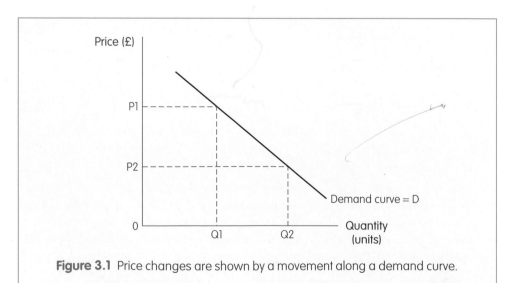

Figure 3.1 Price changes are shown by a movement along a demand curve.

Now you try it

Consider the demand curve in Fig. 3.2.

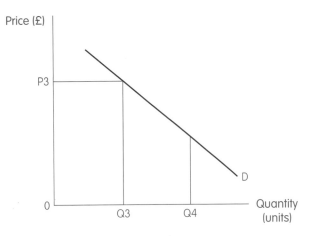

Figure 3.2 Price and quantity combinations.

What quantity is demanded at price P3?

What price is necessary for quantity Q4 to be demanded?

The level of demand for a product depends on factors such as the following.

- *The price level.* As the price changes this influences the relative value of the product and the amount customers want to buy. Higher tuition fees may deter some students from going to university, for example.

- *The customers' incomes.* This influences what customers can afford. If the economy is doing well, for example, this might lead to more spending on many goods.

- *The price of competitors' products,* that is, substitute products. For example, a change in the prices of Cadbury's chocolate may affect the sale of Mars bars.

- *The price of complementary products,* that is, products used in conjunction with each other. For example, an increase in the price of Sony Playstation consoles may affect sales of Playstation computer games, and vice versa.

- *The number of customers in the market.* For example, a product may be aimed at a new market segment (such as a new country or a new group of buyers) which can boost demand. When sports clothes manufacturers repositioned many of their products and targeted the leisurewear market this significantly increased the number of potential buyers for their products. Computer games are now being developed to help improve the memory and keep alert; this is to target the older buyer because most buyers of computer games at the moment are relatively young.

■ The shape of the demand curve

A demand curve is usually downward-sloping. This is because of the law of diminishing marginal utility. This law states that, as buyers consume additional units of a product, the extra satisfaction (or utility) they gain from each unit will fall. The second cup of tea is not as satisfying as the first; the tenth is not as satisfying as the ninth. If the extra satisfaction of a unit declines then the amount consumers are willing to pay to buy it will fall as well. For a higher quantity to be demanded the price must therefore be lower, because the satisfaction from these additional units is lower according to the law of diminishing marginal utility. Consumers may be prepared to pay the price P1 for the third unit of product A, but will only buy 10 units if the price falls to P2 because the satisfaction of the tenth unit is lower than on previous units.

■ Marginal and total utility

Marginal utility measures the extra utility (or satisfaction) from consuming an additional unit of a product. Total utility is the total satisfaction from the consumption of a product. If, for example, the extra utility from consuming another unit of the product is 6 units of utility (called utils) then the total utility will increase by 6 utils.

Notice in Table 3.1 that the law of diminishing marginal utility operates (see also Fig. 3.3). This means that the total utility increases at a diminishing rate. When the marginal utility is 0, this means there is no increase in total satisfaction from the consumption of that unit (in this case the sixth unit). It is possible that you can overconsume some items (e.g., eat too much), in which case the marginal utility might be negative (the seventh unit) and the total utility would then fall.

Table 3.1 The relationship between the marginal utility and the total utility.

Units	Marginal utility	Total utility
1	10	10
2	8	18
3	6	24
4	4	28
5	2	30
6	0	30
7	−2	28
8	−4	24

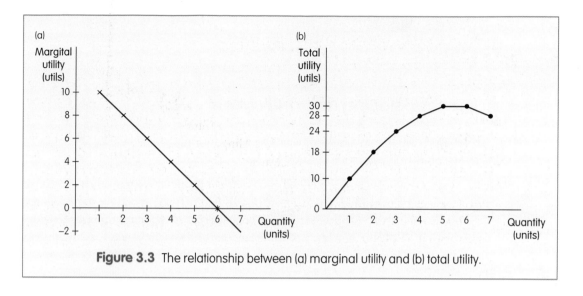

Figure 3.3 The relationship between (a) marginal utility and (b) total utility.

A movement along the demand curve

A change in the price of a product, such as P1 – P3, leads to a change in the quantity demanded (Q1 – Q3) (see Fig. 3.4). This is known as a movement along the demand curve. In the vast majority of cases a lower price will increase the quantity demanded because the customer now finds more units that provide a greater level of satisfaction than the price that has to be paid to buy them.

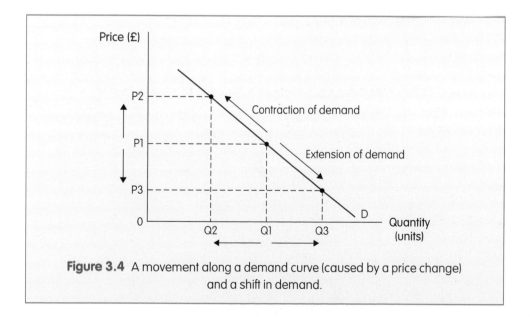

Figure 3.4 A movement along a demand curve (caused by a price change) and a shift in demand.

An increase in the quantity demanded due to a price fall is called an extension of demand (Q1 – Q3). A decrease in the quantity demanded is called a contraction of demand (Q1 – Q2).

Upward-sloping demand curves

In exceptional cases the demand curve may be upward-sloping (see Fig. 3.5). This may be due to one of the following two reasons:

- The product is a Giffen good. A Giffen good is an extremely inferior product. When the price of this type of product rises consumers find that they are spending so much on it (because they need to buy it) that they have very little left over for anything else (for example, rice in the Third World). Given the fact that consumers have so few funds left, they end up buying even more of the original product, that is, the quantity demanded increases when the price increases.

- Customers believe that the higher price reflects a better quality or has a better image and therefore want more even though it is more expensive. This type of product was described by Veblen (1899) who highlighted the desire by some customers for 'conspicuous consumption': they want to be seen to be buying more expensive items! For example, retailers sometimes find that a reduction in the price of a bottle of wine leads to a fall in sales as buyers assume that the quality is significantly worse, or do not want to be seen buying cheap wine (or giving it to their guests!).

What do you think?

Can you think of products that you buy where you tend to spend a bit more rather than buy the cheapest one? Why is that?

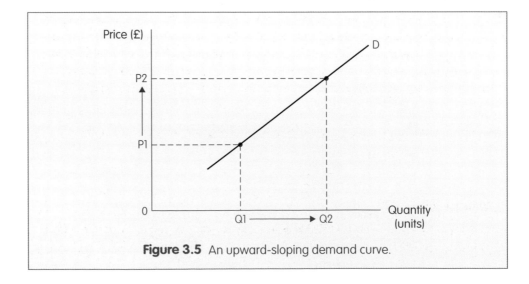

Figure 3.5 An upward-sloping demand curve.

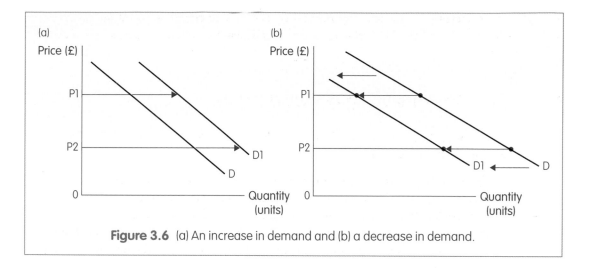

Figure 3.6 (a) An increase in demand and (b) a decrease in demand.

A shift in the demand curve

The demand curve for a product will shift if at each and every price customers are willing and able to buy more or less than they did before (see Fig. 3.6). If they demand more the curve will shift to the right. If they demand less then it will shift to the left. When the demand curve shifts this is known as a change in demand (as opposed to a change in the quantity demanded).

Economics in context Influences on demand

Demand can shift for all sorts of reasons, such as the weather, a major public event or competitors' actions. There may be particular demand patterns in a market. In the toy market, for example, over 50% of sales are made around the Christmas period. Demand is particularly difficult to estimate in the toy market because of particular 'fad' products that take off each year, often linked to films, television programmes or games, and often to the surprise of retailers. Pokemon, Thunderbirds, Tamagochi, Furby, Teletubbies and Power Rangers are examples of past Christmas hits.

? Question

What do you think the particular problems are likely to be for producers in the toy market?

What do you think?

What do you think will be the big hit in the toy market this Christmas? How would you try to estimate this?

▓ The reasons for a shift in demand

The reasons for a shift in demand include the following.

- **A change in income.** If customers have an increase in their incomes then their demand for products is likely to shift. For 'normal' goods demand will increase with more income and the demand curve will shift to the right. With more money you may go on holiday more, eat out more and go to more concerts. The amount that the demand for a particular product increases depends on how sensitive it is to changes in income. A given increase in income may lead to a relatively large increase in demand for health clubs and fine wines, for example. These goods are known as income-elastic products. For other goods demand may not increase so much. An increase in income is unlikely to boost demand for shoe polish or toothpaste very much, for example. These are known as income-inelastic products. (For more on income elasticity see Unit 4.)

  For some goods demand may actually fall when income increases because the consumers switch to something they prefer now that they have more income. These are called '**inferior goods**'. When the income of developing economies grows households usually switch from bicycles to motorbikes as a means of transport. The bicycles in this case are inferior and the motorbikes are normal products. However, the status of goods will vary for different people and over time. With even more income growth in developing economies, demand for motorbikes tends to fall as demand for cars increases. Motorbikes have then become inferior over time as consumers now choose another 'better' product.

What do you think?

Imagine you won £1 million on the lottery. What products would you buy more of? What would you buy less of?

Economics in context   Demand for cars in China

The demand for cars in China has grown very rapidly in recent years. With around 5 million cars sold each year, China is already the third largest car market in the world after America (17 million cars sold per year) and Japan (around 9 million). At the same time the Chinese government has spent heavily on the road network. By the end of 2004 the country had 21 000 miles of motorways, more than double the 2000 figure. In 1987 it had none! Only America now has more motorways than China. China's total road network is now the third longest in the world. China is aiming to put the car industry at the heart of its economy. In bigger cities consumers have gone straight from bicycles to cars, missing out motorbikes as these were banned or the use of them was severely restricted. A big boost occurred when China joined the World Trade Organization in 2001. This opened up its markets to trade, allowing foreign profits into the country, and car prices fell rapidly. Demand has also been boosted by cheap borrowing from state banks (in the past banks did not lend to individuals) and by social change. Many state-owned factories have been sold off; these have then been closed or shifted to suburban areas. Employees now have to travel much further to work and therefore need a car.

? Questions

The above passage highlights how the government is intervening in the economy to influence decisions, but that there is a free market as well. Would you describe such an economy as free market, mixed or planned?

By investing more into roads what might the opportunity cost be?

What do you think are the main factors affecting demand for new cars? Do these differ from the main factors affecting demand for other products?

Economics in context

The demand for Champagne

The UK is the largest customer for French Champagne, with British consumers drinking over 30 million bottles per year. The demand for Champagne is influenced by factors such as the following.

- The number of celebrations happening. The demand was particularly high when there were celebrations for the Millennium. During any given year sales are particularly high just before New Year.

- Income. Higher levels of disposable income stimulate demand for many alcoholic drinks. Champagne is particularly sensitive to income changes.

- Socio-economic trends. The demand for Champagne is particularly high from the higher-income groups, so as they prosper demand for Champagne grows.

? Questions

Do you think the demand for Champagne is affected by different factors than the demand for other types of alcoholic drinks? Why?

What do you think are the main factors affecting the overall demand for alcoholic drinks in a country? Do you think demand is likely to grow or fall in your country in the future? Why?

- **A change in marketing policies.** Managers of organisations will continually review their marketing strategies to try and boost the demand for their products. Changes to their marketing strategy may include new promotional campaigns or finding new distribution channels to make it easier for customers to buy the products. Effective marketing should shift the demand curve to the right.

The demand for cereal

The majority of cereals are sold through supermarkets. In the UK over 90% of sales are through stores such as Tesco and Sainsbury's. This gives the supermarkets a lot of power over the manufacturers. To increase demand, cereal manufacturers, such as Kelloggs and Cereal Partners, are always looking for new ways of getting their products to the market.

Recent efforts have included vending machines in schools and sports clubs. Also, in America the fast food chain Cereality has begun enabling customers to mix and match their cereals to tailor-make their own products.

Cereal companies have also stressed the health benefits of eating cereal in an attempt to boost demand. They highlight the vitamins in the cereal and the low level of calories. In the case of cereals, demand is influenced by both parents and children. The parents often make the final decision about what to buy as they are paying for it. They are usually interested in the health issues. The children influence this decision by making clear what they want. They are often influenced by gifts or promotional offers.

The demand for a product should not be taken as given: it will change over time. For example, in the UK fewer people have breakfast and they tend to eat on the move. Marketing managers have to respond to such changes. For example, many cereal manufacturers have moved into producing snack cereal bars or offering cereals in vending machines to be sold at work.

? Question

Cereals tend to be eaten mainly by children rather than people in their twenties and thirties. Why do you think this is, and what could you do as a marketing manager of a cereal manufacturer to boost sales to these older age groups?

- **A change in the number of buyers.** Over time more people may move into an area or a country, creating more potential buyers. Alternatively, a change in customers' tastes may lead to more demand. In recent years, for example, there has been an increasing interest in healthy foods and fitness. This has increased demand for low fat products and health clubs. At the same time it has shifted demand for many fast food restaurants to the left. Companies such as McDonald's have had to reconsider their range of products and marketing strategies.

- **A change in the price of substitute products.** Customers have choices when it comes to deciding what to buy. You may be deciding whether to go for a meal out or the cinema, or choosing between decorating the kitchen and going on holiday. This means that all products have substitutes: other products that customers may consider buying as an alternative. If these substitutes become more or less expensive then this will affect demand for the original product. For example, if the price of football tickets goes up you may decide to stop going to see the match every week and spend your money on

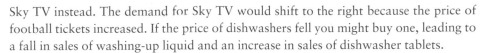

Sky TV instead. The demand for Sky TV would shift to the right because the price of football tickets increased. If the price of dishwashers fell you might buy one, leading to a fall in sales of washing-up liquid and an increase in sales of dishwasher tablets.

- **A change in the price of complements.** Complementary products are those that you tend to buy together, for example, laptops and rewritable CDs, digital cameras and photographic printing paper, and flowers and greeting cards. Changes in the price of one of these items may affect sales of the other. If the cost of filter coffee increases significantly it may decrease sales of filter coffee machines. If the price of airfares to Spain falls the sales of suncream may increase as more people go abroad.

- **Weather.** Changes in the climate can have a significant effect on the sales of some products. A hot summer boosts the demand for barbecues and lager. Amazingly, it also boosts sales of tanning lotion—office workers want to give the impression that they have been outside or on holiday, and so buy fake tan. A wet winter increases the demand for umbrellas. Rainy bank holiday weekends can have a significant effect on retailers' revenues.

- **Events.** Big events such as sporting matches can have a large impact on retail sales. In the build-up to a World Cup retail sales are high beforehand as people stock up, but low during the competition as people stay at home. In the build-up to the last World Cup sales of large flat-screen televisions soared.

- **A change in social patterns.** Over time society will change and this influences demand patterns. In the UK, for example, the average age has been increasing over the last fifty years, the typical family size has been decreasing, there are more divorces and there is a greater interest in healthy and organic foods. A noticeable development in the UK has been a change in the way we eat. Families are much less likely to sit down together and eat a family meal than they were twenty years ago; Sunday dinners are largely a thing of the past and we tend to eat now by 'grazing', that is, eating as we move about. This has helped firms such as Pret a Manger who sell sandwiches, but negatively affected others such as Waterford and Wedgwood which make traditional bone china crockery —something there is much less need for these days because formal meals are increasingly uncommon.

What do you think?

What do you think are the major determinants of the demand for each of the following?

- New cars.
- Textbooks.
- Diamond rings.
- Healthcare.

Now you try it

Using diagrams, show the effect on demand of the following.

- The effect on demand for a normal good if income decreases.
- The effect on demand for an inferior good if income increases.
- The effect of an increase in the price of a complementary product.
- The effect of a decrease in the price of a substitute product.

Economics in context **More people living alone in the UK**

By 2021 more than one-third of the UK population will be living alone. Since 1975 Britain's population has risen by 5% and the number of single-person households has risen by 31%. The proportion of income spent by single-person households on alcohol, tobacco and recreational drugs is noticeably higher than households with two or more people. The top supermarket products bought by people living alone are slimming aids; other products they are more likely to buy are Marmite and herbal tea.

Supermarkets are now trying harder to target such individuals. Sainsbury's has doubled its range of 25 cl bottles and has seen strong growth in the sale of its 2 l boxes of wine compared to its 3 l boxes. Its 'Taste the Difference' ready-meal range has also been extended to meals for one. Unilever, meanwhile, is making mini jars of Marmite and single servings of ready-made soups. The importance of people living alone can be seen in the growth of chilled ready meals. In 2005 it was worth £1.6 billion. By 2009 it is expected to be worth £2.1 billion.

❓ Question

The passage above shows how the existence of more single-person households affects the demand for some products. In the UK the population is also ageing. List five types of business that might benefit from this and five that might suffer.

▇ Individual and market demand

An individual's demand curve shows the quantity that a consumer is willing and able to buy at each and every price, others things being unchanged. The market demand is the sum of all the individual demand curves (see Fig. 3.7). To derive the market demand all the individual demands are horizontally summated: all the individual demands are added up at each price.

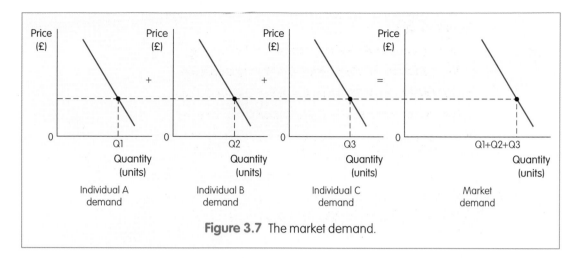

Figure 3.7 The market demand.

Case Study

Although Apple has a relatively small share of the PC market, it has a massive share of the MP3 market with its iPod. The iPod allows users to store large quantities of music and listen whilst on the move.

The product was launched in 2001 and sold over 40 million in the first five years! It is now part of everyday life and has radically changed the way many people listen to music. Apple is well known for its design capabilities and the style of the iPod soon made it a major fashion icon. Its success has stimulated the growth of downloaded music and led to a levelling off of sales of CDs in the UK. After the success of the initial model Apple has continued to innovate, launching new versions of the iPod such as the small version called the Shuffle. The Shuffle randomly selects music loaded onto it.

In 2006 the US car giant Chrysler announced that it would integrate Apple's iPod into 3 million cars and Jeeps in the US. More than 40% of US cars sold in 2006 would feature integration with the iPod.

In response to the iPod's success Microsoft launched its own portable music player, the Zune.

In 2006 the iPod accounted for more than 50% of digital music players sold, while iTunes, Apple's digital music store, has a 70% share of its market.

❓ Questions

- What factors influenced the demand for the iPod? How might these factors change over time?
- Do you think Apple was just lucky with the iPod?

Checklist

Now you have read this unit try to answer the following questions.

☐ Can you explain what is meant by effective demand?

☐ Can you explain what is shown by a demand curve?

☐ Do you understand the difference between a change in the quantity demanded and a change in demand?

☐ Can you explain the possible causes of a shift in a demand curve?

☐ Do you understand the difference between marginal and total utility?

End of unit questions

1   Does a demand curve show what a consumer would like to buy at each and every price?

2   What is the difference between a movement along and a shift in a demand curve?

3   Does an increase in income always shift the demand curve to the right? Explain your answer.

4   Does the quantity demanded always fall if the price increases?

5   To what extent do you think a supermarket can control the demand for its products?

Key learning points

- Demand shows what customers are willing and able to purchase at each and every price, not just what they want to buy.

- A movement along a demand curve occurs when there is a change in the price, all other things being unchanged.

- A shift in the demand curve occurs when more or less is demanded at each and every price.

- A demand curve is usually downward-sloping, but in some cases (such as a Veblen or Giffen good) it can be upward-sloping.

Reference

Veblen, T. (1899). *The theory of the leisure class*. Macmillan, New York.

Learn more

A demand curve can be derived using indifference curve analysis. This analyses the impact of a change in price and income in terms of consumers' utility. To find out more about indifference curve analysis and how a consumer maximises utility, visit our website at the address below.

 Visit our Online Resource Centre at www.oxfordtextbooks.co.uk/orc/gillespie_econ for test questions and further information on topics covered in this chapter.

The elasticity of demand

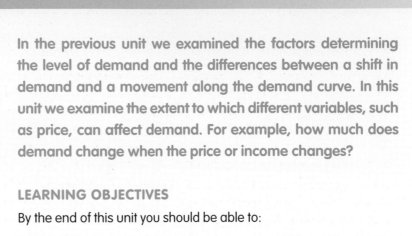

In the previous unit we examined the factors determining the level of demand and the differences between a shift in demand and a movement along the demand curve. In this unit we examine the extent to which different variables, such as price, can affect demand. For example, how much does demand change when the price or income changes?

LEARNING OBJECTIVES

By the end of this unit you should be able to:

✔ explain the meaning of the price, income and the cross price elasticity of demand;

✔ outline the determinants of the price elasticity of demand for a product;

✔ understand the difference between a normal and an inferior good;

✔ understand the difference between a substitute and a complement;

✔ understand the significance of the concept of elasticity for a firm's planning;

✔ appreciate the limitations of the concept of elasticity of demand.

▧ The elasticity of demand

The managers of a business will naturally be interested in what affects the demand for their products. If they can determine what affects their sales they can then try to plan accordingly. For example, they can estimate the staff levels they will need, the stocks they have to hold and their projected profits.

To estimate the likely demand for their products in the future, managers may use the concept of the elasticity of demand. This examines the sensitivity of demand to a number of other factors, such as price, income and the prices of other products.

The general equation for the elasticity of demand is

$$\text{Elasticity of demand} = \frac{\text{Percentage change in the quantity demanded}}{\text{Percentage change in a variable (such as price or income)}}.$$

The following are the two elements to understanding the elasticity of demand.

- *The sign of the answer*. If this is a negative answer then it means the change in the quantity demanded and the change in the variable move in opposite directions; for example, an increase in price decreases the quantity demanded or a fall in income increases the quantity demanded. A positive answer means that the variable and the quantity demanded move in the same direction, that is, both increase or both decrease; for example, an increase in income increases the quantity demanded.

- *The size of the answer*. The size of the answer shows how sensitive demand is to the variable. If the answer (ignoring the sign, i.e., ignoring whether it is positive or negative) is greater than one then it means that the quantity demanded has changed more than the variable, and demand is said to be elastic. (Looking at the equation, if the answer is greater than one then the numerator has changed more than the denominator.) If the answer (ignoring the sign) is less than one then this means that the change in the quantity demanded is less than the change in the variable. In this case demand is said to be inelastic.

◾ The price elasticity of demand

The price elasticity of demand measures the change in the quantity demanded relative to a change in price. Basically, this measures how sensitive demand is to price. If the prices at your favourite coffee shop went up would you stop going there completely? Would you go less often? Would you drink less coffee when you are there? Naturally, the coffee shop manager would be interested in the impact on sales. Would the impact be different if the price of your mortgage went up? Would you be more likely to switch to another provider? What if the price of a haircut at your local hairdresser's increased? How much would sales fall there? The answers to all of these questions are linked to the price elasticity of demand. The price elasticity of demand is calculated using the following equation:

$$\text{Price elasticity of demand} = \frac{\text{Percentage change in the quantity demanded}}{\text{Percentage change in the price of the product}}.$$

In most cases the price elasticity of demand is likely to be negative because a price increase will reduce the quantity demanded (and vice versa) (i.e., the answer is negative because the two variables move in opposite directions). Whenever the demand curve is downward sloping the price elasticity of demand will be negative (see Fig. 4.1).

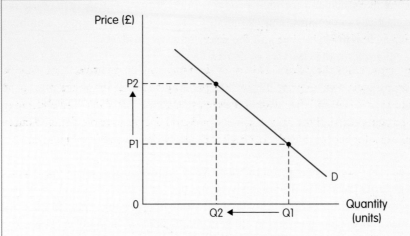

Figure 4.1 A negative price elasticity of demand. A higher price reduces the quantity demanded.

Example

Suppose that the quantity demanded of a good rises from 200 to 300 units when the price falls from £10 to £6. This means:

$$\text{Percentage change in the quantity demanded} = \left(\frac{+100}{200}\right) \times 100 = +50\%,$$

$$\text{Percentage change in price} = \left(\frac{-4}{10}\right) \times 100 = -40\%,$$

$$\text{Price elasticity of demand} = \frac{+50}{-40} = -1.25.$$

The negative sign in the price elasticity of demand shows that the quantity demanded falls as price increases. The 1.25 shows that demand is price elastic. The quantity demanded changes by 1.25 times as much as price.

NOTE Note that to calculate a percentage change we use the following expression:

$$\frac{\text{Change in value}}{\text{Original value}} \times 100.$$

It should be noted that the price elasticity of demand can also be calculated using the following equation:

$$\text{Price elasticity of demand} = \frac{\text{Change in the quantity demanded}}{\text{Change in price}} \times \frac{\text{Original price}}{\text{Original quantity demanded}}.$$

For the example above,

$$\text{Price elasticity of demand} = \frac{+100}{-4} \times \frac{10}{200} = -1.25.$$

However, in some cases the price elasticity of demand may be positive. This may be because of 'conspicuous consumption': some people may want to buy more of a good because it is more expensive and they want to be seen spending more. Alternatively, it may be a Giffen good (see Unit 3). If the price elasticity of demand is positive the demand curve is upward-sloping: a higher price leads to a higher quantity demanded (see Fig. 4.2).

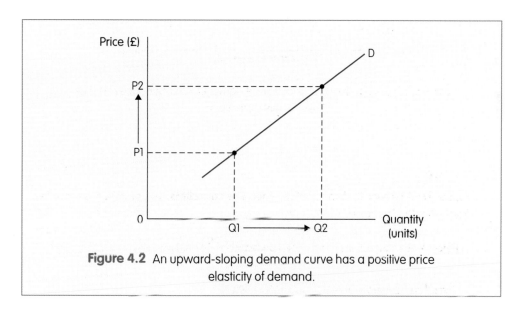

Figure 4.2 An upward-sloping demand curve has a positive price elasticity of demand.

Once the sign (positive or negative) of the price elasticity of demand has been analysed the next thing to consider is the size of the answer. This figure shows the strength of the relationship between price changes and changes in the quantity demanded. For example, if the answer is 2 (ignoring whether it is positive or negative) this means that the percentage change in the quantity demanded is twice the percentage change in price. A 1% change in price will lead to a 2% change in the quantity demanded. This means demand is sensitive to price.

If the answer is 0.5 this means that the quantity demanded changes 0.5 times as much as price (in percentages). This means that demand is not sensitive to price. A 1% change in price will lead to a 0.5% change in the quantity demanded. Again, whether it is positive or negative does not influence the strength of the relationship.

Any answer (ignoring the sign) that is greater than one is known as a price-elastic product: the quantity demanded will change by more than the price (in percentages). If a product has a price elasticity of demand of less than one (ignoring the sign) this means demand is price inelastic. The change in the quantity demanded is less than the change in price (in percentages). If a product has a price elasticity of demand equal to one this is

Table 4.1 The values of the price elasticity of demand.

	Value (ignoring the sign)	Meaning
Price inelastic	Less than one	The percentage change in the quantity demanded is less than the percentage change in price
Unitary elastic	One	The percentage change in the quantity demanded equals the percentage change in price
Price elastic	More than one	The percentage change in the quantity demanded is more than the percentage change in price

known as unitary price elasticity of demand. This means that the change in the quantity demanded is equal to the change in price (in percentages). These cases are summarised in Table 4.1.

Economics in context **High prices**

Holiday companies know that parents are increasingly being prevented by headteachers from taking their children out of school for fear of being fined or taken to court. This means that there are particular weeks of the year when families will have to go on holiday. Holiday companies respond to this by putting up prices—much to the annoyance of parents—because they know that at these times demand is not very sensitive to price: it is price inelastic.

Motorway cafes and restaurants often charge more for products than their city centre rivals. This is because, once you have decided to stop at a motorway cafe, the choice is limited and most people cannot be bothered to leave and drive somewhere else to search for a cheaper alternative. Demand is, therefore, price inelastic.

? Question
Can you think of other situations when demand is price inelastic, so that firms increase prices?

Example

Imagine that the price of a product falls from £10 to £9 and the quantity demanded rises from 400 units to 500 units. This means that the change in the quantity demanded is $(100/400) \times 100 = 25\%$, the change in price is $(-1/10) \times 100 = -10\%$, and the price elasticity of demand is $25\%/-10\% = -2.5$. This means that demand is price elastic because its value (ignoring the sign) is greater than one. The change in the quantity demanded is 2.5 times the change in price.

Example

Imagine that the price of a product falls from £20 to £10 and the quantity demanded rises from 400 units to 500 units. This means that the change in the quantity demanded is $(100/400) \times 100 = 25\%$, the change in price is $(-10/20) \times 100 = -50\%$, and the price elasticity of demand is $25\%/-50\% = -0.5$.

This means that the demand is price inelastic because the value is less than one.

Now you try it

Calculate the price elasticity of demand for the following examples.

- The price increases from £10 to £12 and the quantity demanded falls from 400 units to 300 units.

- The price increases from £10 to £12 and the quantity demanded rises from 400 units to 500 units.

- The price decreases from £40 to £30 and the quantity demanded increases from 50 units to 55 units.

What would it mean if the price elasticity of demand for a product was zero?

The price elasticity of demand will, of course, change over time as demand conditions change. For example, firms may take action to try and make demand more price inelastic.

What do you think?

Do you think firms would prefer demand for their products to be price elastic or price inelastic? What action could firms take to influence the price elasticity of demand for their products?

Determinants of the price elasticity of demand

Whether the demand for a particular product is price elastic or price inelastic (i.e., how sensitive demand is to price) depends on factors such as the following.

- **How differentiated the product is.** If a product has a strong brand image or a unique selling proposition, then customers cannot easily find substitutes, and so the impact of a price change on the quantity demanded of this product will be small relative to the price change. The demand will be price inelastic. Visiting the Eiffel Tower in Paris may be a unique experience and so demand to go up it may not be very sensitive to price.

- **The time period involved.** If a firm puts its price up then customers may find it difficult to find an alternative in the short term. Customers may be used to buying a particular brand, going to a particular restaurant or using a particular accountant, and so demand for these goods and services is price inelastic. With more time customers may be able to find other providers that are similar but cheaper, and so demand becomes more price elastic. A price increase by your insurer or gas or electricity provider may have a limited impact in the short run, but over time you are likely to search for a cheaper alternative.

- **Whether the firm has built a relationship with its customers.** Some organisations aim to develop loyalty from their customers (e.g., supermarket loyalty programmes or frequent flyer rewards); these will make the customer less sensitive to price changes because they feel loyal to the business. Internet companies such as Amazon build relationships by tracking your favourite types of books and films, and recommending other options that you might like.

- **The breadth of product category being considered.** Demand for petrol as a whole is likely to be price inelastic: car drivers cannot easily do without it. However, demand for any one garage's petrol is likely to more price elastic than for petrol as a whole; this is because drivers can switch to a competitor's garage if there is a noticeable price difference. The wider the category examined the more price inelastic demand will be. Similarly, the demand for Marlboro cigarettes is more price elastic than the demand for all cigarettes.

- **Who is paying.** If you have to pay a bill yourself you are likely to be fairly sensitive to the price. If, however, someone else is paying (e.g., your parents or your company) you are likely to be less sensitive to price. You may not be so concerned about price increases or search so hard to compare prices. Demand would therefore be more price inelastic. You can see this when travelling: first class and business seats are much more expensive because the firms are paying rather than the individuals themselves.

- **The awareness of and availability of substitutes.** If customers know that there are many similar products available then they will be more likely to switch between them if the prices are different. The demand will be more price elastic. The growth of the Internet has made it easier to compare prices (in fact, there are websites that will search for the best deal for you); this has made demand for many products more price elastic.

- **The percentage of income spent on the product.** If you spend a considerable amount of money on an item then you may be more likely to shop around for the best buy. You may be more aware of the price of a new car or a holiday, for example, than the price of a pint of milk. Demand for products that account for a high percentage of your income are therefore likely to be more price elastic than those that involve a small percentage of income.

- **The nature of the product.** If a product is habit forming or addictive, such as cigarettes, demand is likely to be price inelastic. The impact of a price increase will be relatively small. Similarly, demand for necessities such as bread, coffee, tea, electricity and gas is price inelastic. If, however, it is a 'shopping good' where people tend to look around and compare prices between stores (e.g., washing machines, dishwashers and beds), then demand is likely to be more price elastic.

What do you think?

When might a firm want demand to be price elastic?

Now you try it

What do you expect the effect on the price elasticity of demand for the product to be in the following situations?

- A competitor enters the market with a similar product.
- A firm invests in a successful advertising campaign for the product.
- A firm launches a new highly innovative product that has patent protection, meaning it cannot be copied by others for several years.

▦ The price elasticity of demand along the demand curve

The price elasticity of demand for a product changes along its demand curve (see Fig. 4.3). At the top of the demand curve the demand is price elastic (see Fig. 4.4): a price change leads to a bigger percentage change in the quantity demanded. At the bottom of the demand curve the demand is price inelastic. In the middle of the demand curve the price elasticity is unitary.

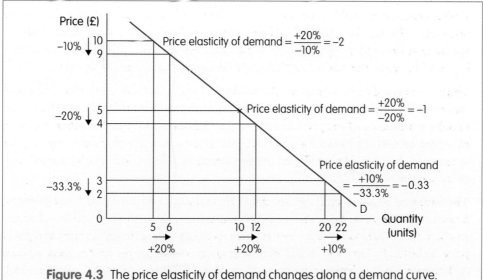

Figure 4.3 The price elasticity of demand changes along a demand curve.

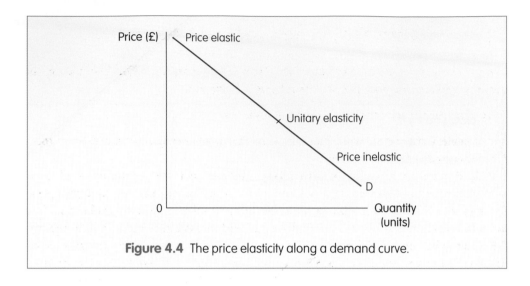

Figure 4.4 The price elasticity along a demand curve.

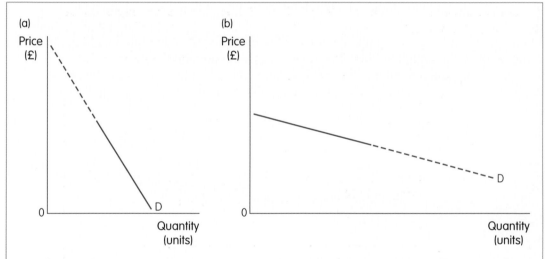

Figure 4.5 Price inelastic demand. In (a) the demand curve is price inelastic for the part of the curve indicated by the solid line, but is price elastic at higher prices. In (b) the demand curve is price elastic for the part of the curve indicated by the solid line, but is price inelastic at lower prices.

When we talk of a price-inelastic demand or a price-elastic demand curve, this is because we are focusing on a particular section of a demand curve. Demand may be insensitive to price within a given price band, for example, but if the price continues to increase then the demand will at some point become price elastic (see Fig. 4.5).

■ The price elasticity of demand and total revenue

The total revenue is the earnings generated from selling a product. This depends on the quantity sold and the price per unit, as follows (see Fig. 4.6):

Total revenue = price per unit × quantity sold.

For example, if the price of a product is £10 and the quantity sold is 20 units then the total revenue earned is £10 × 20 = £200.

   If the demand for a product is price inelastic then an increase in price will lead to an increase in revenue. Although there will be a fall in the quantity demanded, the higher price per item sold will more than compensate for the loss in the number of products sold. If demand is price inelastic then a fall in price will lead to a fall in revenue. This is because the quantity demanded will increase, but not enough to compensate for the fall in price per item. If demand is price elastic then an increase in price will lead to a fall in revenue. The fall in sales outweighs the increase in price per item. However, a fall in price will lead to an increase in revenue; this is because the increase in sales is so great that it outweighs the fall in price per unit. These statements are summarised in Table 4.2.

   If demand has a price elasticity of one then the total revenue will not change when the price changes (see Fig. 4.7).

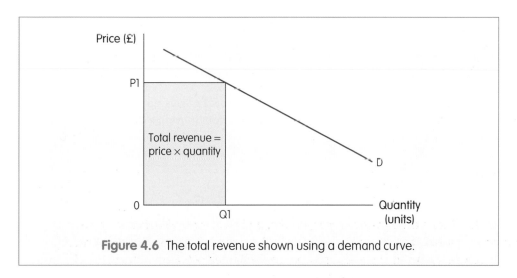

Figure 4.6 The total revenue shown using a demand curve.

Table 4.2   The impact of a price fall on revenue, depending on the price elasticity of demand.

	Value (ignoring the sign)	Impact on revenue of a price fall
Price elastic	More than one	Revenue increases
Unitary elastic	One	Revenue stays the same
Price inelastic	Less than one	Revenue decreases

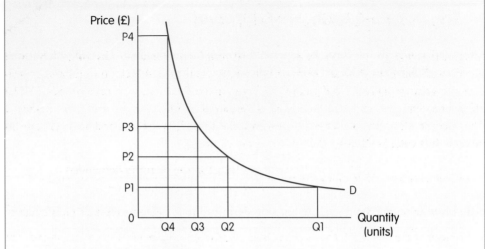

Figure 4.7 A unitary elastic demand curve. A change in price does not change the revenue (and therefore the areas P1Q1, P2Q2, P3Q3 and P4Q4 are all equal).

The estimation of the price elasticity of demand is therefore very important for firms when determining a pricing strategy. Managers will often want to increase their revenue from their business. To do this managers should:

- lower price if demand is price elastic;
- increase price if demand is price inelastic.

An understanding of price elasticity and the impact of this on pricing policies can be seen when firms price discriminate and charge different groups different prices for the same product (see Unit 15).

Now you try it

Consider the following two situations.

1 The price of a product is increased from £10 to £11. The quantity demanded falls from 50 units to 30 units.

2 The price of a product is increased from £10 to £11. The quantity demanded falls from 50 units to 49 units.

Answer the following questions for each situation.

What is the price elasticity of demand?

What is the original total revenue before the price change?

What is the new total revenue after the price change?

The conclusion is that when demand is price elastic/inelastic (*choose*) total revenue will increase/decrease (*choose*) following a price increase.

The income elasticity of demand

Imagine that you get a promotion at work and your income increases by 10%. What will you do with the money? What products will you buy more of? Which products will experience the greatest increase in demand? Will you actually buy less of some products? The effect of a change in income on demand is measured by the income elasticity of demand. The income elasticity of demand measures the sensitivity of demand to a change in income. It is calculated using the following equation:

$$\text{Income elasticity of demand} = \frac{\text{Percentage change in the quantity demanded}}{\text{Percentage change in income}}.$$

The following are the two elements to understanding the income elasticity of demand.

- *The sign of the answer.* If the income elasticity of demand is positive then this means that an increase in income leads to an increase in demand (and a fall in income leads to a fall in demand), that is, income and the quantity demanded move in the same direction. Products with a positive income elasticity of demand are known as 'normal goods'.

  If the income elasticity of demand is negative then this means that an increase in income leads to a fall in demand (and a fall in income leads to an increase in demand), that is, income and the quantity demanded move in opposite directions. These products are known as 'inferior goods'. With more income, for example, people may switch from own-brand items to more luxurious brands.

- *The size of the answer.* If the value of the income elasticity of demand (regardless of the sign) is greater than one then the product is known as a luxury product: demand is very sensitive to income. For example, a value of +3 means that the percentage increase in demand is three times as much as the percentage increase in income. A 1% increase in income will lead to a 3% increase in the quantity demanded. These may be luxury products such as health clubs, sports cars and cruise holidays.

  If the income elasticity of demand is less than one then the product is known as a necessity: demand is not particularly sensitive to income. For example, if the income elasticity of demand is +0.5 then this means that the percentage change in demand is 0.5 times as much as the percentage change in income. These may be necessity items such as yoghurts and shampoos.

The different forms of elasticity can be illustrated on an Engel curve (see Fig. 4.8).

Understanding the income elasticity of demand is important to firms because it shows what the effect of income changes might be on its demand. If, for example, an economy was expected to grow faster in the future then the income elasticity should give an insight into what might happen to sales. This in turn would influence a range of areas, such as staffing levels, cashflow and profit forecasts.

The income elasticity of demand can be shown by the extent to which the demand curve shifts when income increases; this shows the size of the income elasticity of demand. The direction of the shift (i.e., outward or inward) shows whether the good is normal or inferior (see Fig. 4.9).

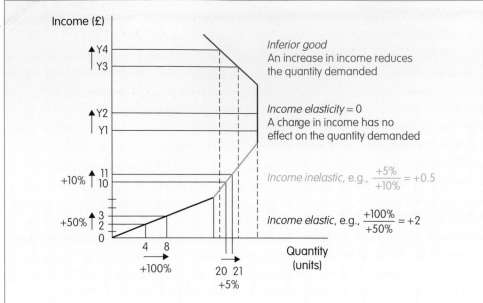

Figure 4.8 An Engel curve shows what happens to the quantity demanded when income changes.

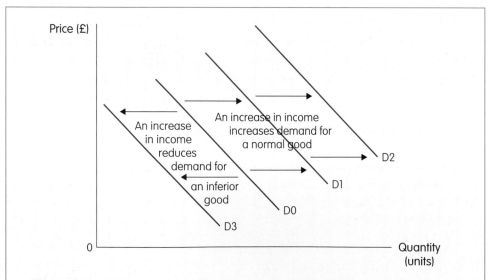

Figure 4.9 Income elasticity and shifts in demand. The greater the income elastic demand is for a product, the more it will shift following a change in income, for example, to the demand curve D2 rather than D1.

Example

The average income in an area increases from £40,000 per year to £44,000 per year. Sales of golf clubs increase by 20%.

The income elasticity of demand is defined as follows:

$$\text{Income elasticity of demand} = \frac{\text{Percentage change in the quantity demanded}}{\text{Percentage change in income}}.$$

$$\text{Percentage change in income} = \left(\frac{4000}{44{,}000}\right) \times 100 = 10\%,$$

and so

$$\text{Income elasticity of demand} = \frac{+20\%}{+10\%} = +2.$$

The demand is income elastic.

Now you try it

The average income in an area increases from £40,000 per year to £60,000 per year. Sales of digital radios increase by 10%. Calculate the income elasticity of demand. Is demand income elastic or inelastic?

What would it mean if the income elasticity of demand for a product was zero?

What do you think?

How might an understanding of income elasticity of demand affect a retailer of consumer electrical goods?

The cross price elasticity of demand

So far we have examined the sensitivity of demand to a change in price and a change in income. However, demand will also be affected by changes in the price of other products. When you are choosing a new PC or washing machine you naturally look at the prices of a range of models. Changes in the price of other products (substitutes and complements) will therefore affect demand for any given product. This effect is measured by the cross price elasticity of demand.

The cross price elasticity of demand measures the sensitivity of demand of one product to changes in the price of other goods and services. It is calculated using the following equation:

$$\text{Cross price elasticity of demand} = \frac{\text{Percentage change in demand for product A}}{\text{Percentage change in the price of product B}}.$$

If the cross price elasticity of demand is positive this means that demand for one product increases when the price of another product increases (or one falls when the other falls). These products are **substitutes**, for example two brands of coffee. An increase in the price of one brand causes customers to switch to another one.

The size of the answer shows how close the two products are as substitutes: the bigger the answer, the closer they are. For example, if the cross elasticity of demand is +2 this means that the increase in the quantity demanded of product A is twice the percentage increase in the price of product B. The easier it is for customers to switch between the two and the more similar they think the products are, the greater will be the value of the cross price elasticity.

If the cross elasticity of demand is negative this means that the products are **complements**. An increase in the price of one product leads to a fall in the quantity demanded of the other. If the price of Sony Playstation consoles increases, for example, this is likely to reduce the quantity demanded of Playstations and the demand for its computer games as well. Playstation consoles and its computer games are therefore complements.

If the cross price elasticity of demand is −3, for example, this means that a given percentage increase in the price of product B will lead to a fall in demand for product A that is three times bigger (in percentages).

The cross price elasticity of demand is important because it shows the relationship between price changes of other products and the likely impact on your demand. In most markets managers keep a close eye on competitors' pricing strategies; they will be particularly interested in those with a high cross price elasticity of demand.

What do you think?

What do you think a cross price elasticity of demand of zero would mean?
What if the value of the cross price elasticity of demand was infinity?

What do you think?

We have analysed the impact of a change in price, in income and the price of other firms on a demand curve using elasticity. There are many other factors affecting demand that could be analysed using the concept of elasticity of demand. Can you think of any?

Table 4.3 provides a summary of our discussions of price, income and cross elasticities of demand.

Table 4.3 Summary table for price, income and cross elasticities of demand.

Type of elasticity of demand	Sign	Size	Type of product
Price	Negative	More than one	Price elastic
Price	Negative	Less than one	Price inelastic
Price	Positive	–	Veblen good or Giffen good
Income	Positive	More than one	Luxury
Income	Positive	Less than one	Necessity
Income	Negative	–	Inferior
Cross	Positive	–	Complements
Cross	Negative	–	Substitutes

■ Practical limitations of the concept of elasticity of demand

In theory, the various measures of the elasticity of demand help managers to understand the impact of changes in different variables on their sales. This is important to their planning; for example, when estimating the required staffing and stock levels. However, whilst a knowledge of the price, income and cross elasticities of demand would certainly be useful, in reality using them can be difficult due to the following reasons.

• They do not show the actual cause and effect. For example, an increase in demand may be accompanied by an increase in income. It could be that the higher advertising has caused the increase in demand. However, it could be that with more demand marketing managers feel they have the funds necessary to pay for more advertising. The initial increase in demand may have been caused by something else entirely. It is not necessarily the increase in advertising that is causing the increase in demand, and so a high advertising elasticity of demand may be misleading in terms of future decision making.

• Each of the equations for the elasticity of demand measures the relationship between one specific factor and demand; for example, the price elasticity of demand analyses the impact of a change in price on the quantity demanded. In reality, many factors may be changing at the same time, such as the spending on advertising, competitors' promotional strategies and customers' incomes, as well as the firm's price. It may therefore be difficult to know what specifically has caused any change in the quantity demanded. Any change in the quantity demanded may not have been due to a price change at all, and so the value of the price elasticity of demand may be misleading.

• To know the elasticity of demand managers must either look back at what happened in the past when, for example, prices or income were changed (but the conditions are likely to have altered since then) or estimate for themselves what the values are now (in which case they may be wrong because it is an estimate). The value of elasticity is, therefore, not actually known at any moment, it is merely estimated. This means that managers should be careful about basing decisions on their estimates of the elasticity as the values will be changing all the time as demand conditions change.

Economics in context   Different types of elasticity of demand

The concept of elasticity is very flexible and can be extended to any variable. It is, after all, simply trying to quantify any correlation between a variable and the quantity demanded, which firms can then use in their planning. In some sectors the weather may have a big impact on the quantity demanded; for example, cold weather leads to fewer people going shopping, whilst increasing the number of people going into hospital. Retail and healthcare managers would be interested in the weather elasticity of demand. Umbrella manufacturers may be interested in the rainfall elasticity of demand. Managers will naturally look for the key variables that affect demand for their specific products and calculate their own forms of elasticity of demand. The advertising elasticity of demand, for example, is commonly used because it shows the relationship between advertising expenditure and the quantity demanded. This could be a very important relationship for marketing managers to understand when deciding how to allocate their marketing budget. The greater the advertising elasticity of demand, the greater the effect of any percentage change in advertising spending (see Fig. 4.10).

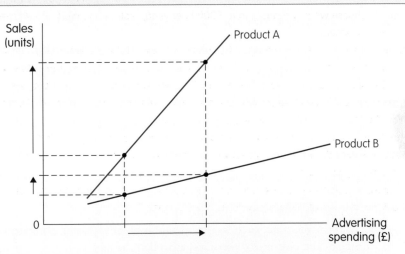

Figure 4.10 The correlation between advertising spending and sales. Product A is more sensitive to changes in advertising spending (i.e., demand is more advertising elastic). A given change in advertising spending has less impact on demand for Product B.

Questions

What might be important influences on the demand for each of the following?

- Barbecue sets.
- Skis.
- Solar panels.
- Cosmetics.
- University places.
- Dentists.

Case Study

In 2006, every university in England was able to decide what fees to charge, up to a maximum of £3000 per year. In the same year, for the first time in six years, the number of student applications to go to an English university actually fell. The number of students applying for courses went down by over 3%. The National Union of Students blamed the fall in numbers on the increased tuition fees. In the year before, applications had increased by almost 8% as students rushed to enrol before the higher charges came into effect. Before 2006 the tuition fee was set at £1175 for all students. Whilst English universities now had the freedom to choose what to charge (up to £3000 per year), Scottish and Welsh universities did not introduce this new scheme.

Figures from the University and Colleges Admissions Service (UCAS) showed that all applications to English universities were down by 3.7%, while applications to Scottish and Welsh universities were up by 1.6% and 0.5%, respectively. The largest fall was a 4.5% drop in the number of English students applying to English universities. This compared with an increase of English students applying to Scotland, which was up by 1.9%. The total number of applicants was 371 683.

The president of the National Union of Students believed that the drop suggested that higher fees had clearly put many students off and meant that society was missing out on many professionals.

Under the new system no fees were to be paid at the start and they were only to be repaid when the students started to work and earn money for themselves. Graduates had to repay the amount they owed at a rate of 9% of their income above the threshold of £15,000.

Questions

- What factors do you think influence the price elasticity of demand for students applying to university? How could this be measured?
- What actions might a university take to make the demand for its own courses more price inelastic?
- What businesses might be affected by a fall in demand for places at university?

Checklist

Now you have read this unit try to answer the following questions.

- ☐ Can you explain the meaning of the price, income and the cross price elasticity of demand?
- ☐ Can you outline the determinants of the price elasticity of demand for a product?
- ☐ Do you understand the difference between a normal and an inferior good?
- ☐ Do you understand the difference between a substitute and a complement?
- ☐ Do you understand the significance of the concept of elasticity for a firm's planning?
- ☐ Do you appreciate the limitations of the concept of elasticity of demand?

End of unit questions

1 If the price elasticity of demand equals zero then what does this mean?

2 How can a sportswear firm try to make demand for its products more price inelastic?

3 Is it better for a hotel to have a price elastic or a price inelastic demand?

4 If a firm has a high income elasticity of demand for its products how might this affect its marketing?

5 How might an understanding of the price elasticity of demand be useful to an insurance business?

Key learning points

- • The concept of elasticity measures how sensitive demand is to a change in a variable.
- • An understanding of the elasticity of demand will help a firm in its marketing activities, for example, pricing, stock levels and planning.

Learn more

The concept of elasticity can also be applied to supply. To find out about the price elasticity of supply see Unit 5.

 Visit our Online Resource Centre at www.oxfordtextbooks.co.uk/orc/gillespie_econ for test questions and further information on topics covered in this chapter.

Supply

The previous unit examined the factors that influence the demand for products. This shows what consumers are willing and able to buy. This unit examines the factors that influence the supply of a product, that is, what suppliers are willing and able to produce. We will then combine the market forces of supply and demand to find the equilibrium price and output in a market in Unit 6.

LEARNING OBJECTIVES

By the end of this unit you should be able to:

✔ explain what is shown by a supply curve;

✔ understand the difference between a change in the quantity supplied and a change in supply;

✔ explain the causes of a shift in a supply curve;

✔ understand the concept of the price elasticity of supply.

▇ Introduction to supply

The demand curve shows what consumers are willing and able to purchase at each and every price, all others things being unchanged. This is one half of a market. The other half is the supply curve. The supply of a product is the amount that producers are willing and able to produce at each and every price, all others things being unchanged. For example, it might show how many houses a construction firm might want to build at different selling prices or how many live performances a band might want to make at different appearance fees.

The supply curve is usually upward-sloping. A higher price is needed for firms to be willing and able to produce more, all other things being unchanged; as the price increases it becomes more feasible and appealing to produce more units.

◼ Movement along the supply curve

A change in the price of a product will cause a change in the quantity supplied; this is shown as a movement along the supply curve. An increase in price (P1 – P2) will usually lead to an increase in the quantity supplied (Q1 – Q2). This is known as an extension of supply (see Fig. 5.1). A fall in the quantity supplied is called a contraction of supply (see Fig. 5.2).

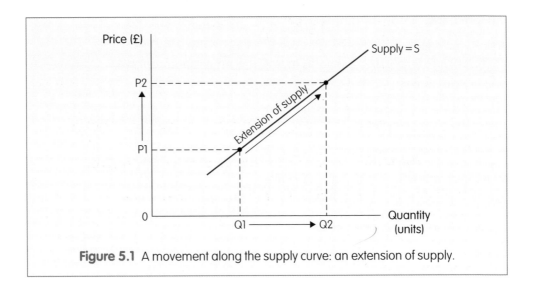

Figure 5.1 A movement along the supply curve: an extension of supply.

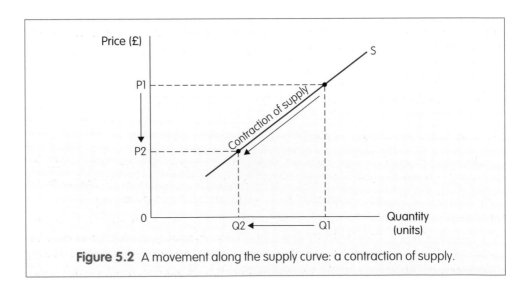

Figure 5.2 A movement along the supply curve: a contraction of supply.

Now you try it

Consider the supply curve shown in Fig. 5.3.

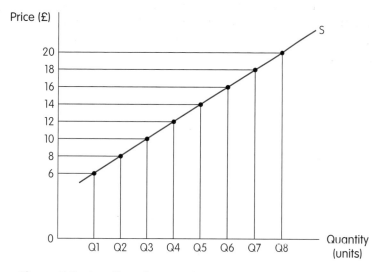

Figure 5.3 The effect of a price change on the quantity supplied.

What happens to the quantity supplied if the price increases from £6 to £20?

Shifts in supply

A shift in supply means that the supply curve shifts to the right or left (see Fig. 5.4). More (or less) products are supplied at each and every price. An increase in supply is shown by a shift of the supply curve to the right: more is supplied at each and every price. A decrease in supply shifts the supply curve to the left: less is supplied at each and every price.

The reasons for a shift in the supply curve

The reasons for a shift in the supply curve include the following.

- **A change in the number of producers.** If there is an increase in the number of producers in an industry then this should lead to an increase in supply. Producers may be attracted into an industry because they are attracted by the prospect of high returns.

- **A change in technology.** New technology should enable firms to produce more at any price, thus shifting the supply curve to the right. Technological change might also enable more firms to enter the market. For example, online trading means that new banks, estate agents or travel agents do not need to establish the same network of high street

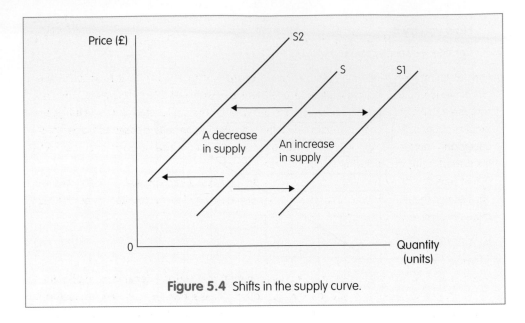

Figure 5.4 Shifts in the supply curve.

outlets that they had to have in the past. Entry into these types of market are therefore easier than they used to be.

- **A change in costs.** An increase in wages or the price of raw materials will mean that firms cannot supply as much at a given price. The supply curve will shift to the left. In recent years, increases in the price of oil have significantly increased the energy costs of many firms; this would shift their supply curves.
- **A change in indirect taxes.** If a tax such as value added tax is placed on the sale of goods then this will increase the selling price of any given output. This will have the effect of shifting the supply curve inwards as the producer adds the tax onto the selling price, so less is supplied at each price. This is analysed in more detail in Unit 6.

Now you try it

Using diagrams, illustrate the impact of the following on a supply curve.

- A decrease in price.
- A reduction in the number of producers.
- A decrease in material costs.

Economics in context

The supply of steel

Over the last fifty years the supply of steel has been increasing rapidly. In 1950 around 200 million tonnes of steel were produced worldwide. By 2005 output was over 1100 million tonnes. China is now the world's biggest steel maker, producing one-third of the global total. The next biggest producer is Japan, then the US, Russia and South Korea. Production has increased due to new producers and new technology. Increases in demand have led to more incentive to produce the product, which has increased the number of firms in the industry.

This relates back to our earlier analysis in Unit 2 about the production possibility frontier. As steel has become more attractive to produce due to increased demand, firms reallocate resources and move out of other industries and into steel production.

❓ Questions

What do you think determines the demand for steel?

If more steel is demanded at each and every price, how is this shown on a demand curve diagram?

If more steel is now supplied at each and every price, how is this shown on a supply curve diagram?

With more firms producing steel and more demand, what do you think is likely to happen to the price of steel? What might it depend on?

What do you think?

What do you think are likely to be the main determinants of the amount supplied of the following?

- Personal computers.
- Wine.
- Schools.

Economics in context

Oil

In 2005, Hurricane Katrina in America caused huge levels of damage to households and businesses in the New Orleans area. The region had many major oil production and refining facilities and was responsible for one-quarter of US oil and gas production. Over 90% of these energy production facilities were closed due to the damage caused by the hurricane. World oil prices were already high due to increased demand, but the impact of Katrina significantly reduced supply. As a result, American motorists who were already paying $3 per gallon for petrol had to pay $4—a major increase on the price of $1.86 in the year before.

❓ Question

Why do you think the fall in supply of petrol led to an increase in the price?

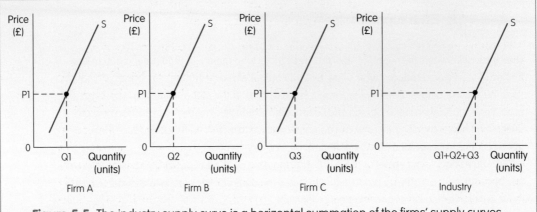

Figure 5.5 The industry supply curve is a horizontal summation of the firms' supply curves.

What do you think?

Can you think of three products in which it might be difficult to increase supply quickly? Why is it so difficult?

Industry supply

The industry supply curve is derived from the horizontal summation of all of the firms' supply curves (see Fig. 5.5). At each and every price the quantity that all of the firms are willing and able to supply are added together.

Joint supply

In some cases products may be supplied together. If we kill more cows to eat for their meat then we will also have more hides produced. Although demand conditions for leather may not have altered, the supply will shift to the right, changing the equilibrium price and output in this market.

The price elasticity of supply

The impact of any change in demand will depend on how responsive the supply is. Can supply be easily increased or not? This is analysed by the price elasticity of supply. The price elasticity of supply measures the extent to which the quantity supplied in a market varies with a change in price. It is calculated using the following equation:

$$\text{Price elasticity of supply} = \frac{\text{Percentage change in the quantity supplied}}{\text{Percentage change in price}}.$$

The following are the two elements to understanding the price elasticity of supply.

- *The sign of the answer*. The sign of the answer will usually be positive, meaning that an increase in price increases the quantity supplied (and a fall in price reduces the quantity supplied), that is, the price and the change in quantity supplied move in the same direction.

- *The size of the answer*. The size of the answer measures the strength of the relationship between price and the quantity supplied. If the answer is greater than one then this means that the percentage change in the quantity supplied is greater than the percentage change in price: supply is price elastic. For example, if the price elasticity of supply is +3 it means that a 1% increase in price increases the quantity supplied by 3%. If the price people were willing and able to pay for a soft drink went up by 10% then producers could relatively easily increase production: supply is likely to be price elastic.

   If the answer is less than one then this means that the change in the quantity supplied is less than the change in price: supply is price inelastic. For example, if the price elasticity of supply is +0.5 it means that a 1% increase in price increases the quantity supplied by 0.5%. If the price the government was willing to pay to build nuclear power stations increased by 10% then the number available could not increase overnight. It would take several years to build any more nuclear power stations and so the supply is not very sensitive to price: it is price inelastic.

Economics in context   Flexible production

Many businesses are now focusing on making their production more flexible. They are investing in the latest technology to enable them to respond rapidly to changes in orders. They are also:

- providing broad descriptions to enable managers to move staff around the business to the sections as and when help is required;

- spending more on training staff so that they are multi-skilled and can undertake a range of tasks—this means they can be moved to where they are needed;

- using flexible suppliers who can quickly increase output if required;

- employing more people on temporary contracts so that managers can increase or decrease the number of staff as needed.

? Question

By being more flexible to demand, manufacturers are trying to avoid producing and hoping that demand materialises. What are the benefits of producing in response to demand rather than in advance of demand?

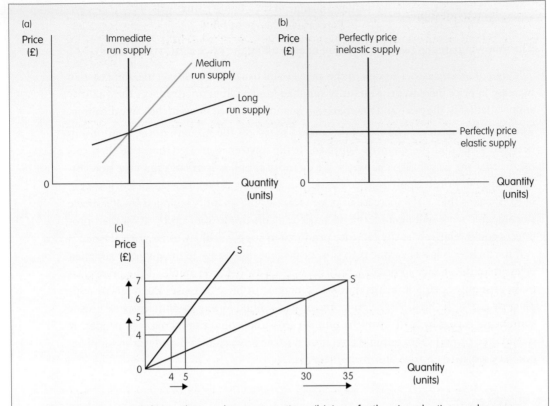

Figure 5.6 (a) Supply conditions change over time. (b) A perfectly price elastic supply curve (a change in the price leads to an infinite change in the quantity supplied; the price elasticity of supply equals infinity) and a perfectly price inelastic supply curve (a change in the price has no impact on the quantity supplied; the price elasticity of supply equals zero). (c) Supply curves that have a price elasticity equal to one are straight lines from the origin.

The price elasticity of supply for a product will depend on the following.

- *The number of firms in the industry.* The more producers there are in an industry, the more supply is likely to be able to change with price changes, that is, it is likely to be more price elastic.

- *The time period.* Over a longer period of time resources can be shifted more easily from one sector to another; this will increase or decrease supply to a greater extent than in the short term, when at least one factor of production is fixed. In the immediate run it may be impossible to change the quantity supplied at all as resources are committed to their present use. This means that the supply curve may be totally inelastic and the price elasticity of supply would have a value of zero.

The price elasticity of supply is illustrated in Fig. 5.6.

What do you think?

What problems might firms have when trying to make production more flexible?

Example

The price of a product is £10 and the quantity supplied is 200 units. The price increases to £12 and the quantity supplied increases to 300 units.

The percentage change in the quantity supplied is (100/200) × 100 = +50%.

The percentage change in price is (2/10) × 100 = +20%.

The price elasticity of supply is +50/+20 = +2.5.

This is price elastic because the value is greater than one.

Example

The price of a product is £10 and the quantity supplied is 200 units. The price increases to £12 and the quantity supplied increases to 220 units.

The percentage change in the quantity supplied is (20/200) × 100 = +10%.

The percentage change in price is (2/10) × 100 = +20%.

The price elasticity of supply is +10/+20 = +0.5.

This is price inelastic because the value is less than one.

Now you try it

- The price of a product increases from £5 to £8. The quantity supplied increases from 200 units to 400 units.

  What is the price elasticity of supply?

  Is supply price elastic or inelastic?

- The price of a product increases from £5 to £8. The quantity supplied increases from 200 units to 210 units.

  What is the price elasticity of supply?

  Is supply price elastic or inelastic?

Case Study

In 2006, water shortages in the southeast of England became so severe that the government's Environment Agency proposed that five new reservoirs needed to be built over the next twenty-five years. Reservoirs that would normally be over 90% full in February were less than 40% full after more than a year of drought conditions. Rainfall for the southeast had been less than 25% of its usual level during that time.

According to a water company spokesperson, the public were still behaving as if water was unlimited and cheap, and needed to appreciate that, in fact, it was not available in unlimited quantities. This was particularly a problem in the southeast. In mid-Kent, for example, which is in this region, consumers were using around 160 to 170 litres each per day, around 15 litres per head per day more than in the northeast.

Given the shortages, water companies tried to get customers to cut down their use of water. Hosepipe bans were brought in and then restrictions imposed on car washes and the watering of sports pitches. Bills were also increased; on average bills in England and Wales increased by 7.5%. The water companies were also keen for customers to have water meters installed. Instead of being a charged a flat fee, customers would be charged according to how much they used.

However, some analysts and pressure groups, such as the Campaign to Protect Rural England, attacked the water companies for failing to deal with the rising demand and with the effect of climate change.

The companies have also been heavily criticised for the amount of water lost through leaks. South East Water produced an extra 35 million litres per day through stopping leaks, but a large amount of water was still being wasted due to old pipes.

Problems with water shortages are forecast to get worse with the building of hundreds of thousands of homes in the southeast. New houses will be fitted with water meters.

❓ Questions

- What are the main factors influencing the supply of water to households in the UK?
- How can demand for water be reduced if supply is limited?
- Do you think water meters are a better way of charging for water than a flat fee?
- Do you think the government should provide water in the UK rather than private companies?

Checklist

Now you have read this unit try to answer the following questions.

- ☐ Can you explain what is shown by a supply curve?
- ☐ Do you understand the difference between a change in the quantity supplied and a change in supply?
- ☐ Can you explain the causes of a shift in a supply curve?
- ☐ Can you explain the meaning of the price elasticity of supply?
- ☐ Can you explain how the price elasticity of supply might change over time?

End of unit questions

1 Does a supply curve show how much producers would like to supply at each and every price?
2 Why is a change in the quantity supplied different from a change in supply?
3 What might shift the supply curve for oil to the left?
4 Why might the price elasticity of supply be price inelastic?
5 What might shift the supply curve of a product to the right?

Key learning points

- A movement along the supply curve occurs when there is a change in price.
- A shift in the supply curve occurs when there is a change in the quantity supplied at each and every price.
- An increase in supply means that more can be supplied at each and every price.
- A decrease in supply means that less is supplied at each and every price.
- The supply curve shows the decisions of producers. The demand curve shows the decisions of customers.

Learn more

A supply curve is actually derived from a marginal cost curve. To find out why see Unit 11.

 Visit our Online Resource Centre at www.oxfordtextbooks.co.uk/orc/gillespie_econ for test questions and further information on topics covered in this chapter.

6 Market equilibrium

The previous two units have considered the market forces of supply and demand. Supply shows what producers are willing and able to produce at each and every price, and demand shows what consumers are willing and able to buy at each and every price. In this unit we consider how these forces interact and how equilibrium is reached in a market via changes in the price.

LEARNING OBJECTIVES

By the end of this unit you should be able to:

✔ explain the meaning of equilibrium in a market;

✔ explain how the price adjusts in a market to bring about equilibrium;

✔ understand the impact on the equilibrium price and quantity of a shift in a supply or demand curve;

✔ understand the effect of indirect taxes and subsidies on the equilibrium price and output;

✔ understand the factors that determine the incidence of an indirect tax or subsidy on consumers and producers.

■ Markets

A market occurs when buyers and sellers interact to exchange goods and services. This can be a physical market, such as a local farmers' market, where local producers sell their goods, or a virtual market, such as eBay, where the buyers and sellers never physically meet each other. The market may be a local one with regional buyers and sellers, a national one or a global one.

■ Equilibrium

Equilibrium occurs in a market when the quantity supplied equals the quantity demanded and there is no incentive for this position to change. In a free market equilibrium is reached by changes in the price. We are all interested in the market price of products and what it is determined by. For example, if we hold shares will they go up in price? Is this a good time to sell our house or should we wait a while? Is it best to book our holiday now or nearer the time we are going? If we are applying for a job then what is a reasonable wage for that position?

How equilibrium is reached in a market is highlighted in Fig. 6.1. At P1 in this figure the price is above the equilibrium level. At this price the quantity supplied (Q1) is higher than the quantity demanded (Q3). There is excess supply (also known as a 'surplus') equal to Q1 – Q3. This puts downward pressure on the price. To get rid of their stock and boost sales firms will reduce prices. As the price falls the quantity firms are willing and able to sell falls, whilst the quantity demanded increases. This process continues until equilibrium is reached at P2.

At P3 in Fig. 6.2 the price is below the equilibrium level. At this price the quantity demanded (Q3) is above the quantity supplied (Q1). This means that there is a shortage in the market (also known as 'excess demand') equal to Q3 – Q1. This will put upward pressure on the price. As the price increases firms will be more willing to supply, whilst the quantity demanded will fall. This process continues until the equilibrium price is reached at P2 and there is no further incentive to change.

In this free market the price mechanism is acting as the following:

- *A signal and incentive.* As the price rises this acts as a signal to other producers that this is an industry that they might want to enter to earn high profits. The high price acts as an incentive for firms to enter into this industry because of the potential rewards. This

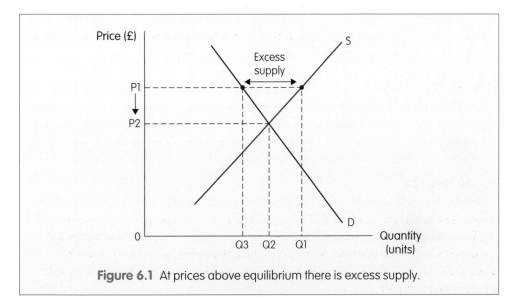

Figure 6.1 At prices above equilibrium there is excess supply.

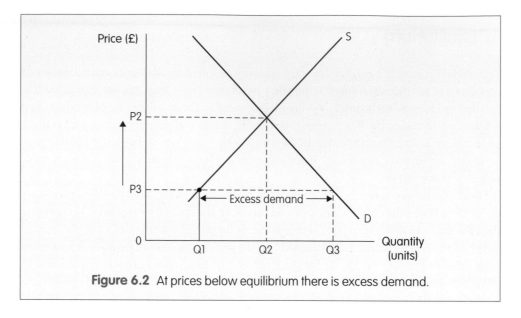

Figure 6.2 At prices below equilibrium there is excess demand.

can be seen when someone has a new idea for a type of food or cafe that proves to be successful; within months the idea is being copied as others enter the industry.

- *A rationing device.* As the price increases it reduces the quantity demanded until it equals the quantity supplied. This can be seen at an auction where the price keeps rising until only one person can afford the product for sale.

Economics in context   Demand too high at the Carphone Warehouse

In 2006, the Carphone Warehouse, Europe's largest mobile phone retailer, offered a free broadband service (although there would be a charge for some other services that you had to sign up to). Demand was much higher than expected: in the first three months the company signed up 340 000 customers, which was twice its target. Its call centres received about 20 000 calls per day, compared to the usual 7000. The company struggled to meet the level of demand. Although it had increased the amount of staff it had, it was still unable to supply the quantity being demanded. As it had committed to a price deal it could not then increase the price to ration demand, and so people had to wait to receive the new service. The price mechanism could not work because the firm had set the price in advance. This happens a lot with sports and music events, when demand turns out to be much higher or lower than expected but the price has already been set in advance.

? Questions

When firms introduce a promotional offer they must try to anticipate demand in advance to make sure that they can supply enough products.

How do you think they try to estimate demand?

Do you think it is easier to estimate future demand in some markets than others?

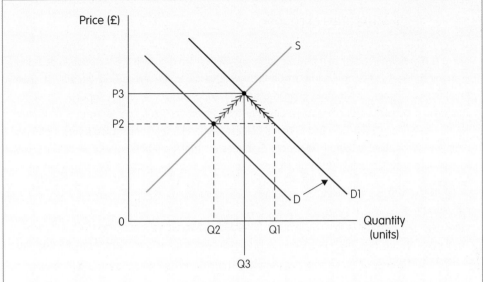

Figure 6.3 An outward shift in demand leads to a higher equilibrium price and output.

The effects on the equilibrium price and quantity of an increase in demand

Imagine a market is originally at equilibrium at the price P2 and quantity Q2 (see Fig. 6.3). If demand for this product then increases there will be excess demand at the original price. Given that there is now a shortage (equal to Q1 − Q2), there will be upward pressure on the price. The price will increase, leading to a lower quantity demanded and a higher quantity supplied until the new equilibrium is reached at the price P3 and quantity Q3. An increase in demand therefore leads to a higher equilibrium price and quantity.

Economics in context	The price of art

At Christie's in New York, £6.3 million was paid in 2006 for Andy Warhol's *Small Torn Campbell's Soup Can* (1962). A week before, £51.5 million was paid for Picasso's *Dora Maar au Chat*. Demand for art work was extremely high at the time, fuelled by investors from Russia, who had large amounts of money to spend. The increase demand pulled up prices.

❓ Questions

What do you think determines the demand for a particular artist's work?

In terms of supply and demand analysis, why do you think the price of some artist's work is so high compared to the price of a tin of paint?

The price of copper

China is a major purchaser of many products and with its rapid growth the increase in demand in many markets is having an impact on their world price. In the space of a decade Chinese purchases of copper, for example, have trebled. It now buys up 22% of all the copper in the world. This led to a massive increase in world copper prices from around $2000 per tonne in 2000 to over $8000 per tonne in 2006. One factor for the Chinese demand is the construction boom that uses copper power cables to bring in electricity. Estimates are that the urban population of China will increase from 532 million in 2006 to 970 million in 2020. If so, the demand for copper will keep on growing!

? Questions

What other products are likely to be in great demand by a fast-growing economy such as China? What effect do you think this has on the equilibrium price and quantity in these markets? Can you illustrate this?

■ The effects on equilibrium of an increase in supply

Imagine a market is originally at equilibrium at the price P2 and quantity Q2 (see Fig. 6.4). If supply of this product increases, perhaps due to improvements in technology, there will be excess supply at the original price equal to Q5 – Q2. Given that there is a surplus, there

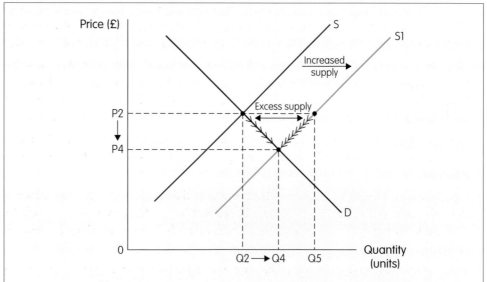

Figure 6.4 An outward shift of supply leads to a lower equilibrium price but a higher equilibrium quantity.

will be downward pressure on the price. The price will decrease, leading to a higher quantity demanded and a lower quantity supplied until the new equilibrium is reached at the price P4 and quantity Q4. An increase in supply has led to a lower equilibrium price and a higher quantity supplied.

Now you try it

Using supply and demand diagrams, illustrate the effect of each of the following.

- An increase in income for a normal good.
- An increase in material costs.
- A decrease in the price of a complementary good.
- An increase in the number of firms producing in the industry.

■ How can supply and demand analysis help us?

An understanding of supply and demand can help us to analyse many market situations and understand why the prices and quantity available in any given market are increasing or decreasing. An understanding of supply and demand will give you an insight into all kinds of markets, from diamonds to drugs. The following are some examples.

- The UK economy has been growing in recent years. This has increased demand for housing and led to an increase in house prices. Demand is particularly high in some regions such as the South East, which is why house prices are higher here than in some other parts of the country. If you find an area that has good schools, good transport links and good facilities then demand for housing is likely to be high, leading to higher house prices.

- In recent years trade between Europe and China has become much more open. This has led to a significant increase in the number of products that are produced in China now being sold in countries such as the UK. This has shifted the supply curve in markets such as clothes and footwear to the right and led to a reduction in the price of these items.

- Developments in technology in consumer electronics markets have enabled cheaper production. This has shifted supply to the right over time and reduced the price of these products.

- If the police are trying to assess the effectiveness of their anti-drugs policy they look at the street prices of drugs. If prices are falling it tells them that supply is increasing (or demand is dropping). If prices are rising it tells them that supply is falling (or demand is increasing).

- If the grades required to gain a place on a particular course at university are getting lower each year then this suggests that demand for the course is falling.

- The supply of diamonds is controlled by a few major producers. They limit the amount supplied each year to restrict supply and keep the price high.

Land prices around the world

Table 6.1 presents the land prices (£ per square foot) at different locations in 2006.

Table 6.1   The land prices (£ per square foot) in 2006.

Location	Land price
London	1744
Tokyo	1094
New York	1026
Paris	962
Moscow	916
Madrid	532
Manchester	310
Croatia	176
Bulgaria	84

Source: Knight Frank Residential Research.

? Question

Using supply and demand analysis, explain why the price of land is so much higher in London than in cities in Bulgaria.

Supply and demand analysis can also be used to analyse the impact of the introduction of indirect taxes or subsidies, and the effects of these on consumers and producers.

■ The introduction of an indirect tax

An indirect tax, such as value added tax, is one that is placed on the provider of a good or service. The producer is legally obliged to pay this tax to the government. However, the producer will try to pass this tax on to the customers and make them pay for it. The ability of the producer to do this depends on the price elasticity of demand for the product compared to the price elasticity of supply.

An indirect tax may be a fixed amount per unit (see Fig. 6.5(a)) or a percentage of the price (see Fig. 6.5(b)). The result of the imposition of an indirect tax is to shift the supply curve upward. Producers will add the indirect tax onto the price they need to supply a given output.

The effect of the imposition of an indirect tax on equilibrium is to increase the price in the market and reduce the quantity sold. In Fig. 6.6 the effect of introducing an indirect

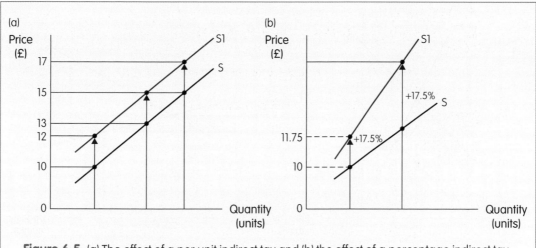

Figure 6.5 (a) The effect of a per unit indirect tax and (b) the effect of a percentage indirect tax.

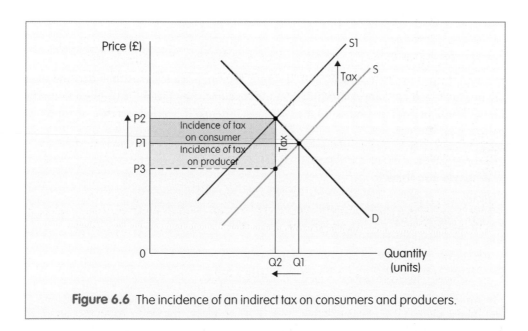

Figure 6.6 The incidence of an indirect tax on consumers and producers.

tax is to increase the equilibrium price from P1 to P2 and to reduce the equilibrium quantity supplied from Q1 to Q2. An indirect tax therefore shifts the supply curve and leads to less units being bought and sold at a higher price.

However, although the price has increased this is not usually by the full amount of the tax imposed. The producer can shift some of the tax onto the buyer, but not all of it. In Fig. 6.6 the price has risen from P1 to P2, but the tax per unit is P2 – P3. The amount of the incidence of taxation depends on the relative price elasticity of demand and supply. If demand is more price inelastic than supply then the consumer will pay more of the

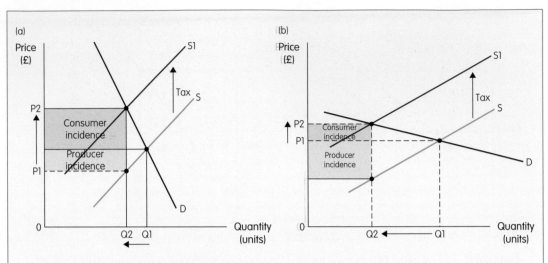

Figure 6.7 The incidence of an indirect tax on consumers and producers (a) when demand is more price inelastic than supply (the consumer pays most of the tax) and (b) when supply is more price inelastic than demand (the producer pays most of the tax).

tax than the producer (see Fig. 6.7(a)). If supply is more price inelastic than demand then the producer will pay more of the tax than the consumer (see Fig. 6.7(b)). The amount of tax will only be fully passed on to the customer if demand is price inelastic or supply is perfectly price elastic.

What do you think?

UK taxation 2006

Value added tax (VAT)

The following are the three rates of VAT:

- a standard rate, 17.5% on most goods and services;

- a reduced rate, 5% on domestic fuel;

- a zero rate—this is on goods such as children's clothing, prescription medicines, books and most food.

The duty rates on cigarettes

The duty rates on cigarettes were:

- cigarettes: an amount equal to 22% of the retail price plus £102.39 per thousand cigarettes;

- cigars: £149.12 per kilogram;

- hand-rolling tobacco: £107.18 per kilogram;

- other smoking tobacco and chewing tobacco: £65.56 per kilogram.

Alcohol

The duty rates on alcohol were:

- spirits: £19.56 per litre;
- beer: £12.92 per litre.

Do you think these tax rates are too high or too low?
Do you think they are fair?
What rates would you impose?

▧ The introduction of subsidies

Subsidies may be paid by a government to producers of particular products to reduce their costs of production. This may be to support a developing industry, to create jobs or to protect domestic firms against foreign competition. A subsidy will mean that producers can produce any given output at a lower market price (see Fig. 6.8(a)). This leads to a downward shift of the supply curve, and thus to a new equilibrium at which more is supplied at a lower price in the market. The extent to which the price falls depends on the price elasticity of supply and demand. The more price inelastic demand is relative to supply, the more the subsidy is passed on to suppliers (see Fig. 6.8(b,c)).

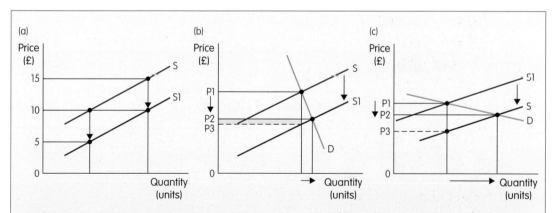

Figure 6.8 (a) The effect of a subsidy to producers on a supply curve; a subsidy means that each quantity can be supplied at a lower price. (b) The effect of a subsidy on producers and consumers when demand is more price inelastic than supply; the majority of the subsidy is passed on to the consumer (P1 – P2 out of P1 – P3). (c) The effect of a subsidy on producers and consumers when supply is more price inelastic than demand; the majority of the subsidy is kept by the producer (P2 – P3 out of P1 – P3).

> **What do you think?**
>
> What do you think might be the problems of the government subsidising producers?

■ Interrelated markets

So far we have analysed the effect of changes in supply and demand conditions on the equilibrium price and output. However, markets rarely exist in isolation; in fact, an economy is a collection of millions of different markets. Many markets are, therefore, interrelated, meaning that changes in one market will impact on others, as in the following examples.

- In 2006, the price of copper in the UK increased due to high levels of demand. This increased the costs for plumbers and therefore affected supply conditions in this market.

- Society as a whole has become more health conscious in the UK in recent years. This has reduced demand for some products such as high fat foods, but at the same time has shifted demand to the right for healthier low fat foods.

- Markets for resources such as land and labour are dependent on the demand for the final product—they are derived demands. An increase in the popularity of computer games, for example, increases demand for computer programmers. A decrease in the demand for UK coal reduces the demand for UK coal miners.

The effect of a change in one market can therefore be traced through into the impact on other markets. A change in supply or demand conditions may well benefit some, but adversely affect others, for example.

Now you try it

Can you think of examples of how changes in supply or demand benefit some groups (e.g., some firms or households), but others may be worse off?

Case Study

In 2005 and 2006, the price of oil increased dramatically and reached as much as $78 per barrel. This price increase was due to reductions in supply and growing demand. The increase in demand was linked to the growth in economies such as those of India and China. India's economy had been growing at over 7% per year and China had an annual growth rate of over 9%. There had also been continued growth due to increased demand for cars, especially fuel-guzzling sports utility vehicles (SUVs). Demand for oil increased by over 1 million barrels per year in 2006 compared to the year before. Projections for the future were that demand will increase even more in the next twenty-five years from 90 million barrels per day to around 140 million barrels.

Meanwhile, the supply of oil had been affected by local groups in Nigeria taking action to prevent production, as well as political problems between the West and oil-producing countries such as Iran and Iraq. Pressure from the shareholders of oil companies such as BP and Shell had also encouraged oil companies to run down their reserves rather than invest in new oil fields.

The resulting increase in energy prices had a significant impact on the world economy.

❓ Questions

- Identify the factors that affect demand and the factors that affect supply in the market for oil. Can you think of other factors that are not mentioned in the text?

- Illustrate separately the effect of increasing demand and the effect of falling supply on the price of oil using supply and demand diagrams.

- In what ways do you think an increase in the price of oil affects the world economy? Is a change in the price of oil likely to have a greater impact than changes in the price of other products?

Checklist

Now you have read this unit try to answer the following questions.

- ☐ Can you explain the meaning of equilibrium in a market?
- ☐ Can you explain how the price adjusts in a market to bring about equilibrium?
- ☐ Do you understand the impact of a shift in a supply or demand curve on the equilibrium price and quantity?
- ☐ Do you understand the effect of indirect taxes and subsidies on the equilibrium price and output?
- ☐ Do you understand the factors that determine the incidence of an indirect tax or a subsidy on consumers and producers?

End of unit questions

1 What might cause the equilibrium price in a market to increase?
2 What might cause the equilibrium quantity in a market to increase?
3 If the supply in a market increases what will happen to the equilibrium price?
4 How does a market return to equilibrium after an increase in demand?
5 House prices vary tremendously between regions of the UK. Explain why this might be the case by using supply and demand analysis.

Key learning points

- When an economy is in equilibrium there is no incentive to change.
- A change in supply and demand conditions will lead to a new equilibrium price and output.
- Supply and demand analysis helps to explain price and quantity changes in a wide range of markets.
- The incidence of an indirect tax or a subsidy depends on the price elasticity of demand and supply.

Learn more

To see how changes in supply and demand affect market equilibrium visit our website at the address below.

 Visit our Online Resource Centre at www.oxfordtextbooks.co.uk/orc/gillespie_econ for test questions and further information on topics covered in this chapter.

In the preceding units we have examined the workings of the free market and the influences on supply and demand. In this unit we analyse the benefits and the disadvantages of this system as a way of allocating resources within the economy.

LEARNING OBJECTIVES

By the end of this unit you should be able to:

✔ explain the advantages of the free market system;

✔ understand the meaning of consumer, producer and community surplus;

✔ analyse market failures and imperfections in the free market system;

✔ understand the difference between merit and public goods;

✔ understand the meaning of external costs and benefits;

✔ understand why a government might intervene in a free market.

■ Advantages of the free market system

The question facing all societies is the extent to which private individuals and businesses should make the economic decisions, as opposed to the government. To what extent should the basic economic questions of what to produce, how to produce and for whom be left simply to market forces? There are many arguments in favour of the market approach, at least in theory; one of these is the view that the free market can lead to the best allocation of resources from society's perspective. If this is true then the government should not intervene in a market economy.

Maximising social welfare

In a free market system the price mechanism will adjust to equalise supply and demand. At this point the welfare of society will be maximised. This is due to the following reasons.

- The demand curve is derived from the consumers' extra utility (or satisfaction) from consuming a unit; this is called the marginal utility or benefit (MB) (see Unit 3). For the moment, let us assume that the benefits to consumers of consuming a unit reflect the extra benefit to society as a whole. This means that the demand curve is derived from the social marginal benefit (SMB).

- The supply curve is derived from the extra costs of producing a unit (see Unit 11). Let us assume that this shows the extra cost to society of producing a unit, that is, the social marginal cost (SMC).

At equilibrium the quantity supplied equals the quantity demanded. This means that the extra benefit to society of the last unit produced and sold equals the extra cost to society of that unit. Therefore the welfare of society cannot be increased or decreased, so it is maximised. This is shown in Fig. 7.1.

In Fig. 7.1, on all the units up to Q1 the extra social benefit is greater than the extra social cost of providing it (SMB > SMC). Therefore society as a whole will gain from these units being produced and consumed because the benefits exceed the costs and so welfare increases.

For the units after Q1 (see Fig. 7.1) the extra social benefits are less than the extra social costs (SMB < SMC), so society would lose out if these units were produced and so welfare would fall. At Q1 the extra social benefit of consuming the unit equals the extra

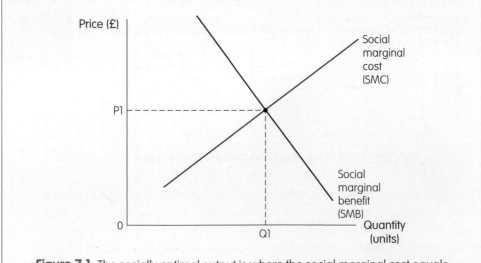

Figure 7.1 The socially optimal output is where the social marginal cost equals the social marginal benefit.

social costs of producing it; the welfare to society is therefore maximised by producing at this level of output. That is, to maximise social welfare the market should be producing at an output where

Social marginal benefit = Social marginal cost,

$$SMB = SMC.$$

This occurs at equilibrium in the free market at Q1.

Community surplus

Another way of analysing the way in which the free market brings about an optimal allocation of resources is to consider the areas of consumer surplus and producer surplus.

Consumer surplus measures the difference between what a consumer is willing to pay for a product and what he or she actually pays. It represents utility for the customer that has not been paid for.

Given the law of diminishing marginal utility, the extra satisfaction of each extra unit of a product that is consumed will fall. This means that the amount consumers are willing to pay for a unit will fall as extra units are demanded. The price paid would fall for the extra unit and all of the ones before; this creates consumer surplus (see Fig. 7.2).

For example, a consumer may be willing to pay £10 for the first unit of a product. If two units are demanded then the consumer may think that the second one is only worth £9, and so pays £9 for each of them. This means that on the first unit there is a £1 of utility that is not paid for; this is consumer surplus. Similarly, if the third unit has a utility worth £8 and the consumer buys three units at £8 each then there is a consumer surplus of £2 on the first unit and £1 on the second unit, that is, £3 in total.

Producer surplus measures the difference between the price that producers are willing to sell at and the price they actually receive. To sell more units a firm will want a higher

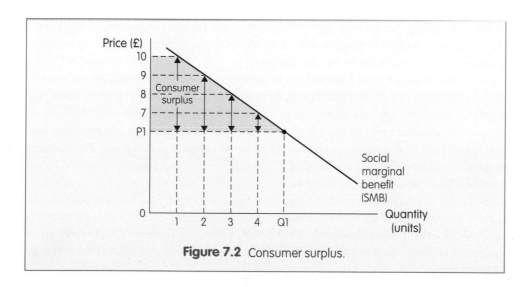

Figure 7.2 Consumer surplus.

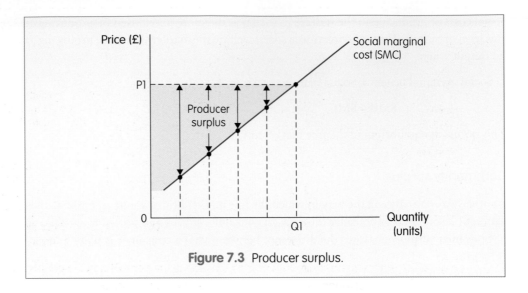

Figure 7.3 Producer surplus.

price to cover the higher additional costs. This higher price is likely to be paid on all of the units produced; this creates a producer surplus. For example, imagine that a firm is willing to sell one unit at £5 but would need £7 to sell a second unit; if it sells two units at £7 each then a surplus of £2 is created on the first one. In Fig. 7.3 the producer surplus equals the shaded area. This is the difference between the price paid for a unit and the price that firms are willing and able to supply those units at.

'Community surplus' is made up of producer surplus *and* consumer surplus. This combines the extra utility to consumers that they do not pay for and the rewards to producers over and above the price they need to supply these units. Community surplus represents welfare to consumers and producers that has not been paid for and can be written as follows:

Community surplus = Consumer surplus + Producer surplus.

In Fig. 7.4(a), in a free market equilibrium at the price P1 and the quantity Q1 the community surplus is equal to the area ABC. This area is the maximum it can be, so welfare is maximised in this situation in the free market.

No combination of price and quantity would generate as much community surplus as the free market result of the price P1 and the quantity Q1. This is why, in theory, the free market leads to the optimal allocation of resources. Imagine, for example, that the market price was forced up to P2 (see Fig. 7.4(b)). The quantity demanded and therefore sold would be Q2. The consumer surplus would be equal to the area P2AB and the producer surplus would be equal to the area P2BCF. Overall, the community surplus would be the area BEC less than it was at equilibrium.

In theory then, the free market could lead the economy to an optimal position. In reality, however, there are numerous market failures and imperfections that prevent this optimal allocation being generated. This is why there is a case for government intervention. The issues then are how much intervention is justified and what is the best way of intervening.

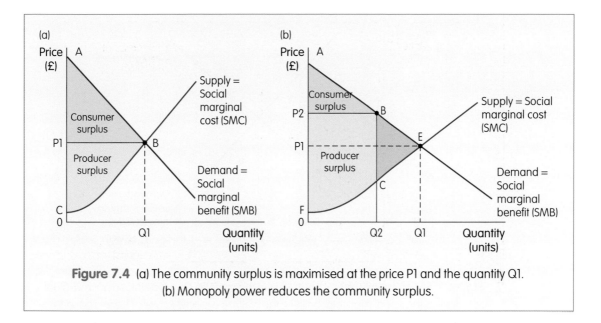

Figure 7.4 (a) The community surplus is maximised at the price P1 and the quantity Q1.
(b) Monopoly power reduces the community surplus.

The disadvantages of the market system: market failures and imperfections

As seen earlier in this unit, the socially optimal output exists when society is producing and consuming at the level where

Social marginal benefit = Social marginal cost,

$$SMB = SMC.$$

At this output society's welfare cannot be increased further.

A market failure exists if the market is selling an output where the marginal cost to society of making a product does not equal the marginal benefit to society of consuming that good or service.

If a market settles at an output where the social marginal benefit is greater than the social marginal cost (SMB > SMC) (e.g., at Q3 in Fig. 7.5) then society would benefit from an additional unit being produced. Social welfare would be increased. If, on the other hand, the social marginal benefit of a unit is less than the social marginal cost (SMB < SMC) (e.g., at Q4 in Fig. 7.5) then this unit reduces social welfare and output should be reduced.

The causes of market failures and imperfections in the free market include the following.

Monopoly power

So far we have assumed that market forces are allowed to operate and that these will lead to an equilibrium price of P1 and an output of Q1. However, in some markets a few firms may come to dominate and exert monopoly power. In this situation a monopolist is able

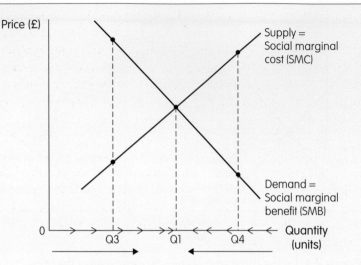

Figure 7.5 The socially optimal output is at the quantity Q1. Here the social marginal cost equals the social marginal benefit; the welfare of society cannot be increased—it is maximised. At the quantity Q3 the social marginal benefit is greater than the social marginal cost; the welfare of society would be increased if more was produced. At the quantity Q4 the social marginal benefit is less than the social marginal cost; the welfare of society would be increased if less was produced.

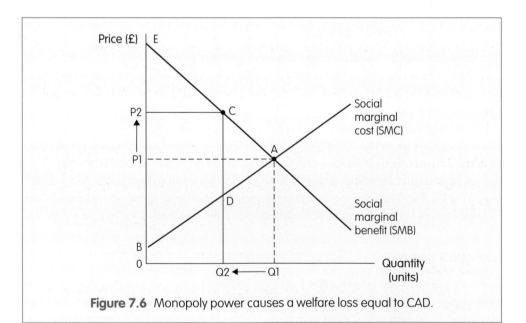

Figure 7.6 Monopoly power causes a welfare loss equal to CAD.

to determine how much output it sells and at what price. A monopolist is a price setter. For example, it may decide to restrict output and push up the price, selling the quantity Q2 at price P2 (see Fig. 7.6). This has the effect of increasing producer surplus from P1AB to P2CDB. However, the effect of this monopoly action is to reduce consumer surplus from EAP1 to ECP2; producers therefore gain at the expense of consumers (which is why they do it). There is also a reduction in the overall community surplus, which has fallen from EAB to ECDB. There is now a welfare loss equal to CAD.

On all of the units between Q2 and Q1 the extra benefit to society is greater than the extra cost of producing them. Society as a whole would therefore benefit from producing these units. However, the monopolist would not benefit because it would have to lower prices to sell these extra units; this is why it restricted output in the first place.

Monopoly power is therefore likely to lead to a lower output and higher price than a competitive market. The effect of monopoly is to reduce the overall welfare of society. This is examined in more detail in Unit 12.

Economics in context

The Competition Commission and Ottakar's

In March 2006 the government body, the Competition Commission, concluded its investigation of the proposed takeover of the book retailer Ottakar's by HMV, which also owns the Waterstone's book chain. It decided that the deal would not harm the public interest There had been concerns that the takeover would create a powerful book retailer with monopoly power that could squeeze out the smaller independent firms. The companies' stores tended to be in different geographical regions, so local competition would not be affected greatly. Also, it was felt that prices would not be forced upwards because of competition from supermarkets and online retailers.

? Question

Why do we need a body such as the Competition Commission to investigate takeovers?

@ Web

For more information on the Competition Commission visit **www.competition-commission.org.uk**

What do you think?

If monopolies can cause problems in an economy, should the government stop firms getting bigger?

Now you try it

If a market is producing where the social marginal benefit of a unit is greater than the social marginal cost, should it produce more or less units?

Externalities

In the free market the amount that customers demand and are willing to pay for products naturally depends on the benefits they personally receive. Individuals pursue their own interests. However, the benefit (or utility) that an individual customer derives from consuming a unit is not necessarily the same as the benefit that society as a whole derives from a product. This can mean that the allocation of resources in the free market is not the allocation that society as a whole would want because of the differences between private and social benefits.

For example, when you are considering whether or not to have a flu vaccination you will think of the personal benefit of not catching flu in the future. You will not think about the benefits to others if you were vaccinated. If you do not catch flu then you are not going to pass it on to others, so this will have a benefit for other people as well as yourself. The social benefits of vaccination are greater than the private benefits. This is known as a **positive consumption** externality; the social benefits are equal to the private benefits plus the external benefits to society. In this case the demand curve from society's point of view should be higher than it would be from a private perspective; this is because the social marginal benefits of each unit are greater than the private marginal benefits.

In a free market the price and output outcome would be P1 and Q1, respectively (see Fig. 7.7). However, given the additional social benefits of these units, the most socially desirable outcome is the price P2 and the quantity Q2. There is under-production and under-consumption of the product (in this case, vaccinations) in the free market. On every unit between Q1 and Q2 the extra benefit to society is greater than the extra cost to

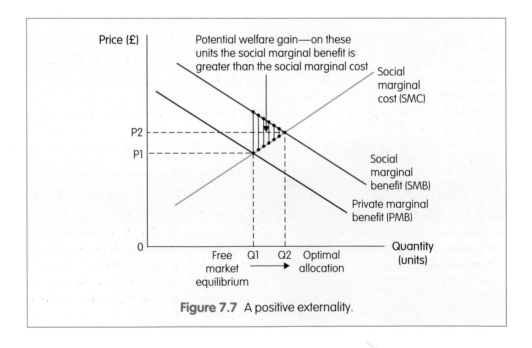

Figure 7.7 A positive externality.

society. So society would benefit if more units were provided. This means that the shaded region in Fig. 7.7 represents a potential welfare gain if there was intervention to move the market to the socially optimal price and output.

Another situation where the free market may fail is when the extra cost of producing is higher for society as a whole than the extra cost of producing for private producers. This is known as a **negative production externality**. Left to themselves, firms will only take account of the costs they have to pay for, such as labour, land and machines. These are private costs. They will not take account of other costs that affect society as a whole; for example,

- their factory may be noisy and may upset local residents,
- the production process may be generating pollution,
- when their employees come to work in the morning they may cause traffic jams and congestion.

This means that the firm's activities are generating external costs; these are costs imposed on society as a whole that a firm would not take account of in a free market. The social costs to society are equal to the private costs *plus* the external costs:

Social costs = Private costs + External costs.

If the social costs are higher than the private costs then a negative externality exists. In this case the supply curve in the free market does not fully reflect the extra costs of producing each unit because the external costs are not included. If they are included then the supply curve would move upwards. A higher price is needed for each unit to cover the additional external costs.

What do you think?

Pollution is an external cost. Left to themselves, firms and private drivers would not take account of the costs of pollution. Do you think that, if you were in government, the right thing to do would be to reduce pollution to zero?

At the moment, in the UK all private drivers pay the same road tax. Should we tax drivers per mile that they drive?

In the free market the equilibrium would be at the price P1 and the quantity Q1 (see Fig. 7.8). However, taking account of the full social costs of production, the socially desirable outcome would be at the price P2 and the quantity Q2. In the free market there is over-production and over-consumption. This is because the firm does not appreciate the full costs of providing the product. This leads to a welfare loss. On the units Q1 to Q2 the extra social cost of these units is greater than the extra benefit. This means that the welfare of society is being reduced by producing these units. A more socially efficient allocation of resources would be at the price P2 and the quantity Q2.

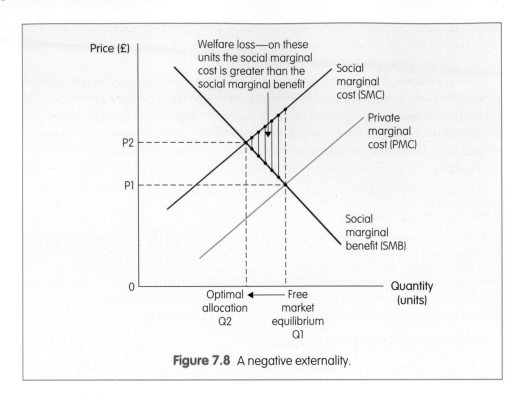

Figure 7.8 A negative externality.

Note that the optimal allocation is the price P2 and the quantity Q2. That is, just because a negative external cost exists it does not mean that we should stop production altogether: the product does provide benefits as well. What is needed is intervention to achieve the optimal allocation of resources, which would not happen in the free market.

Economics in context **Alaska**

In 2005, the US Senate blocked attempts to stop drilling for oil in Alaska's Arctic National Wildlife Refuge (ANWR). Opponents argued that this exploration would damage the environment and harm wildlife, such as birds, polar bears and caribou. The social costs appeared to be greater than the private costs of the exploration, drilling and refining. However, the government believed that the estimated 10 billion-plus barrels of crude oil was worth it because it would cut American reliance on imports, create jobs and raise revenue.

 Question

What would determine whether, in your view, drilling in Alaska was acceptable?

Economics in context

Chickens

A huge amount of toxic waste is created by poultry farms in Arkansas; this runs into streams and pollutes the water for the Illinois watershed that supplies twenty-two public water companies in eastern Oklahoma. For years, Oklahoman officials have complained about this and in 2005 they took Arkansas to court. The phosphorus from poultry is equivalent to that generated by 10.7 million people (more than the populations of Arkansas, Kansas and Oklahoma combined).

The waste is sold to farmers who use it as fertiliser and it then finds its way into the water. Poultry is a $2 billion per year business. The poultry industry has threatened to leave Arkansas and move to Mexico if the requirements become too tough.

 Question

One solution to this toxic problem would be to tax the Arkansas farmers for the external costs that they generate. How would you estimate this?

Economics in context

Chewing gum

In the UK chewing gum costs local councils well over £4 million per year to clean up from the pavements. It actually costs more to clean up the chewing gum than it does to produce it! The producers and consumers of chewing gum are generating an external cost to society which we have to pay through taxes to clean up.

 Question

Taxes are already placed on many consumers because of the external costs generated by the products that they consume. For example, drivers pay high taxes on petrol, and air travellers pay tax on their flights. Do you think a tax should be placed on chewing gum consumers?

Public goods

A public good is a product that is non-diminishable and non-excludable. This means that, once it is provided, it does not matter how many people consume it—it will still be available to everyone. The addition of extra users does not reduce the amount that others can consume. For example, a lighthouse is a public good. Once it is built, all ships can benefit from it—it does not matter how many ships are passing by, they can all gain from the light being shown. This means that the provision of this service is non-diminishable. With private goods there is a limited amount available at any moment. More consumption by one person reduces the amount left for others; for example, if you buy a pair of Nike trainers in a shop then there is one less pair available at that particular moment for others to buy.

Public goods are also 'non-excludable' because it is difficult to stop people (or ships!) benefiting from them. Any ship passing by a lighthouse will gain from it. Similarly, if you install a street light or make an area safer by having regular police patrols, then everyone can gain and it is difficult to restrict the service to those who pay. The development of wireless networks has created a form of public good in recent years. Those in the vicinity can benefit from someone else's network (unless security systems are installed).

The problem with public goods is that in a free market firms will be unwilling to provide them because they cannot restrict consumption to those who pay for it. Households will be unwilling to pay for something that others will be able to benefit from and will try to benefit from someone else providing it. This creates the 'free rider' problem: everyone will wait in the hope that someone else will pay for the service, so that they can be a free rider and benefit from it as well without actually paying for it. In this case the government has to step in to provide such products.

Instability

In the free market the price should adjust to ensure that supply equals demand. This can lead to major and sudden swings in price as supply and demand conditions change. A fall in supply can lead to a higher price and a lower quantity; a fall in demand can lead to a fall in price and sales. This instability can make it difficult for firms and consumers to plan. Price instability can be seen in many sectors, such as the markets for currency, shares

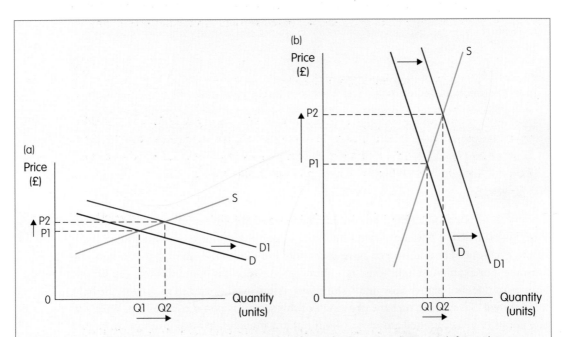

Figure 7.9 A shift in demand (a) when demand and supply are price elastic (a shift in either curve affects output more than price) and (b) when demand and supply are price inelastic (a shift in either curve affects price more than output).

and oil. If the government thinks instability is bad (e.g., unstable agricultural prices may deter farmers from continuing production) then it may intervene to bring about more stable prices. Price instability is a particular issue if supply and demand are price inelastic because any given shift in the curves has relatively more impact on price than quantity (see Fig. 7.9).

Now you try it

What should happen to the equilibrium price and quantity if the supply curve shifts to the right? What if demand shifts to the left?

Income inequality

A free market is likely to lead to income inequality. Some firms and individuals may earn very high incomes if they have products or skills that are in demand. Other people's skills may be in less demand and as a result they may have lower incomes. In terms of an economic outcome, this may actually be efficient and the result of the market mechanism; however, many people may decide it is unfair and not a desirable outcome. If this is the case, society may want a government to do something about it; for example, a government may make some products available for free to everyone so that they can all benefit from them. It may also use taxes and subsidies to redistribute income in the economy.

Economics in context   ## Income inequality in the UK

Inequality in income before taxes and benefits increased fairly steadily in the 1980s in the UK. According to the Institute for Fiscal Studies (IFS), this was partly due to an increase in the gap between the wages for skilled and unskilled workers. The reasons for this included technological change requiring particular skills and a decline in the role of trade unions.

 Question

In what ways can the government affect the distribution of income and the distribution of wealth in an economy?

What do you think?

Do you think that the government should intervene to reduce the amount of income inequality in an economy? If so, how much intervention do you think is desirable?

What do you think would be a fair tax rate on peoples' earnings?

Do you think that people should be allowed to inherit money and property?

Merit goods

A merit good is one that society believes is more beneficial than private individuals do. For example, we may not appreciate at the time how important and beneficial education or healthcare is to us as individuals. In one sense, a merit good is like a positive externality; however, they occur specifically because the government may know more than us what is good for us (as opposed to positive consumption externalities where we may know the external benefits but not care about them). Merit goods would be under-consumed in the free market because we underestimate their benefits. For example, the government might sponsor the arts, opera, museums and art galleries on the basis that these are good for society as a whole.

Demerit goods are products which we might want to consume without appreciating the harm they are doing to us, for example, cigarettes. Once again, they arise because the government may know more than we do or may know what is in our best interests, and may therefore discourage or prevent consumption of them. We may thank the government later on when we appreciate how bad these products were.

Economics in context   The price of heroin

In 2006, a bumper poppy crop in Afghanistan led to a surge in the supply of heroin in the UK. Afghanistan is the source of about 95% of the heroin in the UK and, with increased supply in that country, prices of heroin have fallen dramatically. Large investments into National Health Service schemes to combat addiction mean that the demand for heroin has not risen as fast as supply.

❓ Question
Illustrate using supply and demand diagrams why the price of heroin has fallen over time.

What do you think?
What products would you classify as merit goods?
What do you think are demerit goods?
Do you think that society's views of what are and what are not merit goods might change over time?

Missing information

Problems may occur in the free market due to a lack of information. Buyers may not know what is available or what alternatives they have. Many cinemas will be half empty some of the time and have queues outside them on other occasions. In theory, the price mechanism would adjust to make supply equal to demand. Given that there is a limited number of seats, then, when there was a lot of interest in a film, the price should increase to ration demand. On other occasions, if demand for a film was going to be low then the price should fall to stimulate more customers. However, cinema managers do not know in advance what demand will be for any particular showing. Therefore they set an average price. Sometimes this will be too high, leading to empty seats in the cinema. At other times it will be too low, leading to queues outside. For major sporting events you will usually find ticket touts trying to sell you tickets at a much higher price than they were originally sold for. This is because the initial price that was set for these events was too low. Therefore there was excess demand. Ticket touts get hold of the tickets at the original price and sell them on to others who really want them for a much higher price. In this case the ticket touts are helping the market mechanism to work because the original price was not the equilibrium one.

Case Study

The following is adapted from the Friends of the Earth website; Friends of the Earth is an environmental pressure group (© Friends of the Earth: *Heathrow briefing*, July 1997).

Heathrow Airport was built in London's green belt on top-grade farmland using wartime regulations to avoid public examination of the plan. This meant that external costs did not have to be debated. Since then Heathrow has grown so that it now comprises four terminals, two runways, roads, car parking, freight and service areas, covering close to 3000 acres of land.

Some of the statistics relating to Heathrow are staggering, such as the following, for example.

- Well over 50 million passengers travel through Heathrow—think of the impact on the environment and local areas of this many people coming to and from the airport.

- There are well over 1000 flight take-offs and landings every day.

- At peak times aircraft land and take off every 46 seconds!

- Planes start arriving at 4.30 a.m.—think of the impact of this on the neighbours.

- The noise of the airport affects over half a million people.

Clearly then, there are numerous external costs associated with operating an airport on this scale. Heathrow is now expanding and building Terminal 5. According to Friends of the Earth, this building involves the following:

- the doubling of the size and operations at Heathrow;

- further expansion, building on fields and countryside;

- 30 million more passengers per year, bringing the total to around 80 million per year;

- up to 40% more flights, leading to increased pressure for more night flights;

- more noise and air pollution, and more pollution of the local water environment;

- increased pressure on local roads, and to widen the M25 and other motorways;

- 49 000 extra car journeys every day to and from Heathrow, and 13 000 extra car parking spaces;
- up to 2000 lorries per day on local roads during construction;
- an increased threat of air traffic accidents.

Not surprisingly, Friends of the Earth is concerned about the external costs generated by this construction and whether these factors have been fully taken into account.

? Questions

- What might be the case for building Terminal 5?
- If you were in government would you shut Heathrow down?
- What other policies might you use to take account of the external effects of an airport such as Heathrow?

@ Web

BAA is the company responsible for the construction of Terminal 5. For information on the benefits of the project visit www.baa.com
For information on Friends of the Earth visit www.foe.co.uk

Checklist

Now you have read this unit try to answer the following questions.

- ☐ Can you explain the advantages of the free market system?
- ☐ Do you understand the meaning of consumer, producer and community surplus?
- ☐ Do you understand the difference between merit and public goods?
- ☐ Do you understand the meaning of external costs and benefits?
- ☐ Are you able to analyse market failures and imperfections in the free market system?

End of unit questions

1 Is a public good anything that is provided by the government?
2 Why might monopolies be undesirable?
3 Does a shift in demand have more effect on the equilibrium price or quantity if supply is relatively price elastic?
4 Should the government ban smoking because it has negative external costs?
5 Should the UK government subsidise opera? What about football?

Key learning points

- In a perfect world the free market would lead to an optimal allocation of resources. It would maximise community surplus and society would be producing at a point where the social marginal benefit equals the social marginal cost.

- There are many imperfections in the free market that move it away from the optimal allocation of resources. This is why government intervention may be necessary.

- Market failures and imperfections include public goods, externalities, monopolies, instability, and merit goods.

Learn more

Monopoly power is a major imperfection in the free market system. For a more detailed analysis of the impact of a monopoly on a market see Unit 12.

 Visit our Online Resource Centre at www.oxfordtextbooks.co.uk/orc/gillespie_econ for test questions and further information on topics covered in this chapter.

8 Intervening in the market system

In the previous unit we examined some of the advantages of the free market system as a way of allocating resources within an economy. However, we also highlighted several limitations and problems of the free market system. In this unit we consider how a government might intervene in a free market to help overcome such problems.

LEARNING OBJECTIVES

By the end of this unit you should be able to:

✔ explain how governments intervene in the free market;

✔ understand the impact of maximum and minimum prices;

✔ understand the workings of a buffer stock scheme;

✔ explain the reasons for nationalisation and privatisation;

✔ explain the problems of privatisation.

▓ Intervention in markets

In a perfect free market system the market forces of supply and demand would lead to the optimal allocation of resources where the social marginal benefit equals the social marginal cost and community surplus is maximised (see Unit 7). However, as we saw in the previous unit, a number of market failures and imperfections exist that may justify government intervention.

The ways in which the government may intervene in a market include the following.

• *The direct provision of goods and services*. For example, society may believe that education and health should be freely available to all, and therefore the government will provide these. In some countries other services such as energy, transport and telecommunications are also provided. A key political as well as economic decision is the extent to which governments should directly provide goods and services.

- *Legislation and regulation*. A government may pass laws to control certain types of behaviour. For example, if it feels that wages are too low in a free market then it may introduce a minimum wage that employers have to pay. It may also organise stabilisation schemes to prevent price instability in markets such as agriculture. Laws affect a number of areas of business behaviour such as employment, competition, health and safety, and consumer protection.

- *Subsidies and taxes*. These can be used as 'carrot' and 'stick' policies to encourage certain types of behaviour and deter other activities. This will change the allocation of resources away from the free market position toward a more socially optimal outcome. For example, undesirable behaviour may be taxed to discourage it; desirable behaviour may be subsidised to encourage it.

- *Providing information to promote particular forms of behaviour*; for example, to encourage individuals to undertake training, move to get a job, recycle or conserve energy.

What do you think?

In what ways do you think consumers need protecting from firms?

Economics in context   UK tax receipts

In 2005, the UK government received £516 billion in tax receipts. It spent £552 billion. This expenditure included:

- housing and environment, £19 billion;
- public order and safety, £32 billion;
- industry, agriculture, employment and training, £21 billion;
- debt interest, £27 billion;
- defence, £29 billion;
- education, £73 billion;
- transport, £21 billion;
- health, £96 billion.

 Question

Would you have allocated the spending differently? In what way and why?

Examples of government intervention

The following are examples of government intervention.

Regulating monopoly

Firms that dominate a market are likely to reduce the amount supplied to the market and to increase price to increase their producer surplus. The effect of this is to reduce the over-all community surplus (see Unit 7). To remedy this a government may regulate monopoly behaviour; for example, it may force the monopoly firm to reduce prices. In the UK the Competition Commission is able to investigate firms that have a market share of over 25%. It has the ability to force such firms to sell parts of their business or reduce their prices. It can also prevent one firm from buying another (a takeover) or firms joining together (a merger) if it feels that it would lead to too much market power and behaviour that would act against the public interest. UK firms are also subject to European Union legislation on competition. Article 85 states that restrictive practices (e.g., when firms collude) must be stated and these are usually prohibited. Article 86 bans the abuse of a 'dominant position' by a firm.

Economics in context   The European Commission and energy markets

In 2005, the European Commission announced that it was concerned about the possible lack of competition in the wholesale markets for oil and gas. It blamed this on the dominance of supplies by a few national gas and electricity companies. Between the start of 2003 and the end of 2005 the wholesale price of gas doubled. As a result, households in the UK experienced a 40% increase in gas prices in the same period. UK energy suppliers have blamed this situation on the fact that they have been importing increasing quantities of gas from the continent. This has been partly because of the ever-increasing demand from UK users and partly because of the declining output from the UK's own North Sea gas fields.

? Question

How might a 40% increase in gas prices affect the UK economy?

Taxing negative externalities

Negative production externalities occur when the social cost of an activity is greater than the private cost of providing it. Given that private firms do not take account of the external effects of their actions, they will overproduce these products in a free market. To remedy this the government may place indirect taxes on the products concerned. This will increase their private costs and hopefully raise them to the level of the social costs. This is known as 'internalising external costs'. Indirect taxes on products such as cigarettes, petrol and alcohol are to ensure that producers take account of external costs. However, it is often difficult to quantify external costs precisely, and therefore the government may not know exactly what level of taxes to place on selected products to achieve the optimal allocation of goods and services.

Economics in context — How to charge for road usage

Roads present a particularly interesting economic problem in many economies at the moment. The problem is not that there is a lack of capacity: most roads are empty for most of the time. The problem is that at certain times of the day, such as rush hour, or on certain days, such as bank holidays, demand is too high. Cars impose significant costs on society, such as pollution, congestion, wear and tear, and road accidents, in addition to the private costs of owning and driving a car. Without any prices directly related to where or when you drive, roads are bound to be overused. In this case queues become the rationing mechanism. A tax system whereby people pay road tax means that, in reality, rural drivers pay too much whilst drivers in urban areas, where most of the negative externalities are created, pay too little. The rural areas subsidise the cities. A different option now being proposed is road pricing, whereby people would be charged according to which roads they used and when they used them. This is certainly possible. Singapore used permits to access the city centre from 1975 to 1998 when it switched to electronic sensors. Many European countries have tolls on some of their roads. The UK government is considering a system based on satellite positioning and has set a provisional date of 2014 for this to be introduced. Politically it will be difficult. This type of scheme has been suggested before in the UK in 1964 and 1971, but on both occasions the government decided against their implementation.

❓ Questions

What other schemes can you think of, apart from tolls or the proposed car tax system, to reduce car usage in busy periods?

Can you think of any problems with or arguments against the proposed car tax system?

Creating a market in pollution

In a free market firms do not take account of the pollution they generate. To make firms take account of these external costs a government can impose a tax on firms to increase the private costs to the same level as the social costs, as has been suggested above. Alternatively, the government can regulate production by passing laws governing the levels of pollution that are allowed. For example, in the UK the Clean Air Act limits the amount of pollution that can be generated. A third option is to create a market for pollution so that firms decide for themselves how much they are willing to pollute. For example, firms are given permits allowing them to generate a certain amount of pollution. They are then allowed to trade these permits. This means that if one firm wants to increase its output then it can bid for the permit of another firm that does need to use all of its allowance. If the price is right then the permit will be sold from one firm to another. Rather than a government deciding who should be allowed to produce and pollute, it sets an overall level of pollution and then the free market decides who pollutes within this.

Coase

According to Coase (1960), the reason why externalities create a problem is because of a lack of well-defined property rights. In the case of noise pollution, for example, the following are not defined in law.

1 Whether we all have a right to silence. In this case, in a free market the people making the noise would have to pay us to be allowed to continue. The price for the noise would rise (making it less attractive to the noise makers and more attractive to the listeners) until an equilibrium level of noise was found.

2 Whether we do not have a right to silence. In this case, in a free market the people who want silence would have to pay the noise makers to reduce their noise. The price would increase, making it more attractive to the noise makers to be quieter whilst making silence less appealing to us.

According to the Coase theorem, if we could clearly establish the rights of individuals then markets could be established to set a price for things such as pollution.

Subsidising positive externalities

Positive externalities occur when the social marginal benefit is greater than the private marginal benefit. In a free market products with a positive externality are under-consumed because consumers do not realise how good they are. In this case the government would subsidise them to encourage consumption.

Minimum and maximum prices

Minimum prices

A government may intervene in a market to ensure that the price does not fall below a minimum level. For example, in the labour market the government may believe that the equilibrium wage in some industries is unacceptably low and may therefore introduce a

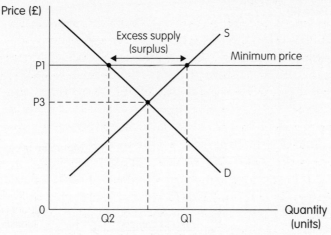

Figure 8.1 A minimum price above the equilibrium level leads to excess supply.

minimum wage to ensure that all employees must earn at least a given amount. In agricultural markets a government may want to protect farmers by preventing price from falling too low.

If a minimum price is set above equilibrium then the result is that the quantity supplied will exceed the quantity demanded (see Fig. 8.1). At price P1 the amount that suppliers are willing and able to sell exceeds the amount that buyers are willing and able to buy. This leads to a surplus equal to Q1 – Q2. In a free market the price would fall to bring back equilibrium at price P3.

Now you try it

Using supply and demand diagrams, illustrate the possible effect on overall earnings of introducing a minimum wage. What might influence the overall effect on employees' total earnings?

Maximum prices

If a government believes that the market price is too high (e.g., the rent being charged for accommodation) then it may intervene to place a maximum level in the market. If this maximum price is below the equilibrium, for example, the price P0 in Fig. 8.2, then the impact of this is to create a shortage: the quantity demanded will be greater than the quantity supplied at the given price. There is a shortage equal to Q2 – Q1.

For those who benefit from the limit on the price, they pay less than they would in a free market. However, the market as a whole has less supplied to it (e.g., less people would rent out their house). In a free market the price would rise to P1.

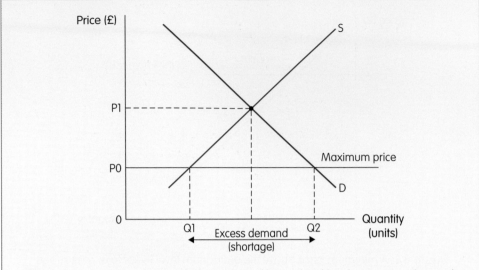

Figure 8.2 A maximum price below the equilibrium level leads to excess demand.

Now you try it

Using a supply and demand diagram, illustrate the effect of a maximum price above the equilibrium price and quantity.

Introducing price stabilisation schemes

Changes in supply and demand conditions in the free market can lead to major changes in the price level. This can be seen in agricultural markets where supply can shift significantly due to changes in weather conditions. The consequent price and income instability may discourage farmers from staying in the industry. If the government wants to maintain agriculture as a sector within the economy (perhaps to protect a way of life or, for strategic reasons, to maintain domestic control over some food supplies) then it may use price stabilisation schemes.

To stabilise prices the government can use a **buffer stock scheme** (see Fig. 8.3). If there is excess supply (perhaps due to a good harvest or developments in farming technology) then the price would fall in the free market due to a surplus being created. To stop this from happening the government can buy up the excess, so that supply equals demand at the original price. This surplus can then be stored.

When there is a fall in supply (perhaps due to a poor harvest) the government can sell the stock that it has built up in the good years (assuming there have been good years). By selling its stock the government can increase the supply of the product in the market back to its old level and thereby keep price at its original level.

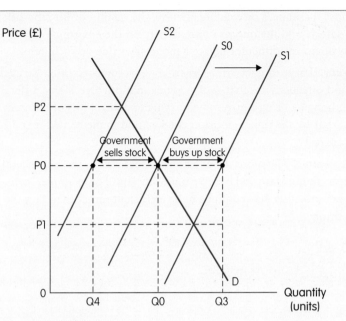

Figure 8.3 A buffer stock scheme. In a free market the price would fluctuate between P0, P1 and P2 with changes in supply. In a buffer stock scheme the government maintains the price at P0. In a good year (i.e., with an increase in supply) the government buys up the quantity Q3 – Q0; this is the buffer stock. In a bad year (i.e., when supply falls) the government sells the quantity Q4 – Q0 to increase supply and to keep the price at P0.

Such intervention does, of course, incur costs, and the government must pay to organise the stockpiling in the good years. This involves warehousing, security and possible depreciation costs. If there are continually 'good years' this means that the government will buy up more each year, creating even bigger stockpiles.

What do you think?

Do you think that the government should intervene with price stabilisation schemes?

Problems of government intervention

The following are problems which occur during government intervention.

- *Valuation problems.* When trying to take account of external costs and benefits the government will have to try and place a value on things such as the beauty of the countryside, the impact on wildlife activity, the quality of life, the risk to health and personal safety, and the impact of an activity on the environment and future generations. It is obviously difficult to place a monetary value on such items.

- *Bureaucracy*. Large organisations such as governments often struggle to respond quickly and efficiently to change. Decisions may involve many different groups and take time. Imagine being a government trying to control lots of different markets. This can mean that by the time a decision is taken and implemented it is no longer appropriate or correct.

- *Lack of incentive*. The more the government intervenes, the less incentive there is for private firms to innovate and become more efficient. For example, inefficient firms that benefit from subsidies may continue to be inefficient rather than face the harsh realities of competition.

Economics in context **From wine to fuel**

In 2006, nearly a billion bottles of wine were ordered by the European Union (EU) to be turned into fuel and disinfectant. The EU spent €131 million to distil 430 million bottles of French wine and 371 million bottles of Italian wine into fuel. Nearly one-quarter of Spanish wine was also being used for industrial purposes. The European Agriculture Commissioner said that, 'Crisis distillation is becoming a depressingly regular feature . . . Europe is producing too much wine for which there is no market.' Proposals from the EU were likely to put 400 000 hectares under the plough. Farmers would then be paid for not producing wine, but for keeping up environmental standards. One problem was that there were too many small wine makers. In France there was one worker per hectare of vineyards; in Australia there was one worker for every fifty hectares.

 Questions

In the free market how would equilibrium be reached in this market?

Why do you think that the European Union bought up the excess supply?

■ Nationalisation

If governments want to completely control a business rather than trying to influence its behaviour via legislation, taxes and subsidies then it can nationalise it. Nationalised industries are organisations whose ownership has been transferred from the private sector to the public sector; for example, if the government buys the shares of a private company and takes it into state control.

The following are arguments in favour of nationalisation.

- **Natural monopolies.** This occurs when the cost advantages of expanding are very high and therefore one firm is likely to expand and dominate the industry to benefit from lower unit costs. Other firms entering the market would find it difficult to compete if they entered at low levels of output because their unit costs would be much higher. This means that this industry is likely to be a monopoly. The government may need to nationalise to ensure that this natural monopoly does not abuse its market power.

- It is felt in a number of countries that competition in the utilities (such as gas, electricity and water) would lead to a wasteful duplication of resources and that these are better run by the state.

- **Social objectives.** Private firms will consider private benefits and costs when making output and investment decisions. The government may believe that there are significant external benefits and costs to consider, and therefore a government may want to intervene in this industry.

Economics in context   Nationalisation in Bolivia

In May 2006, President Morales of Bolivia placed the energy industry under state control. Foreign energy firms were allowed six months to sell at least 51% of their holding to the government.

His aim was to increase the government's share of revenue from gas production from $460 million to $780 million within a year. This decision affected oil companies such as Brazil's Petrobras and the UK's BP. The President stated that this decision to gain control of the energy was just the start of his nationalisation programme; mines and land were next on the agenda.

? Question
Why might there be resistance to this programme of nationalisation?

Privatisation

In fact, although nationalisation is occurring in some countries, the general trend since the 1980s has been for the government to intervene less directly in the provision of goods and services. This has led to many privatisations over the last twenty years. Privatisation occurs when resources are transferred from the public sector to the private sector.

Forms of privatisation may include the following.

- *Denationalisation.* This occurs when assets that were owned by the government are transferred into private ownership, for example, when a state-owned business is sold to private investors.

- *Contracting out.* This involves introducing private contactors to provide some services, such as food in schools and the transportation of prisoners to and from court.

- *Selling public sector assets.* For example, between 1980 and 1983 nearly 600 000 council houses and flats were sold to private individuals.

- *Selling government shares in private sector businesses.*

- *Deregulation*. This introduces competition into markets that were previously restricted (i.e., opening markets to greater competition).
- *Private finance initiative* (PFI). This occurs when projects are jointly funded by the private and public sector, for example, the expansion of the London Underground.

Economics in context   Examples of UK privatisations

The following are examples of privatisations in the UK:

- 1984 Enterprise Oil, Jaguar, British Telecom;
- 1986 British Gas;
- 1987 British Airways, British Airports Authority, BP;
- 1988 British Steel;
- 1989 ten water companies;
- 1990 twelve regional electricity companies;
- 1996 HMSO (stationery office).

? Question

What would you consider before buying a share in a privatised business?

▦ Reasons to privatise

The government may privatise an industry for the following reasons.

- *To raise revenue*. By selling shares in organisations that had previously been state owned the government will earn money. This can then be used to finance investment projects or to enable the government to reduce the taxes it charges. The government can also gain from contracting out by reducing its costs.
- *To free organisations from government control*. When firms are government run the danger is that they will be run for political means. For example, when elections are approaching, nationalised (state-run) industries may deliberately keep people employed even if it is uneconomic to do so because the government does not want to lose votes.
- *To provide more incentives*. If organisations are state owned then managers may lack the incentive to run them more efficiently. Given that the profits belong to the state, an increase in profits may simply mean that more funds go to central government rather than being invested back into this particular business or rewarding those who made them. In private sector organisations there may be more incentive to provide a better service or be more efficient because this creates more profits that are kept by the owners.
- *To create more competition*. When transferring resources into the private sector the government will often open up that market for other firms to compete in, which should provide more choice for consumers. Greater competition should encourage more

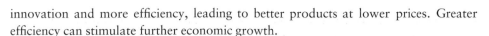

innovation and more efficiency, leading to better products at lower prices. Greater efficiency can stimulate further economic growth.

- *To provide firms with more access to finance.* Once firms are privatised they are able to sell shares to investors to raise finance. When they are nationalised they rely on the government for funding and, given that the government has many demands on its funds, they may not get the long-term investment that they need to be competitive. With access to private finance they may be able to raise more money for investment.

- *To enable firms to have access to private finance.* The government has many different demands on its funds. This may lead to under-investment in some sectors. By privatising, firms can sell shares and raise the finance needed for investment and modernisation.

- *To create more share owners in the economy and raise the general level of awareness in the economy regarding investment.* This may then lead to more investment in other firms, helping firms to finance expansion.

What do you think?

Do you think that privately-owned motorways in the UK would be a good thing?

Economics in context — Privatising the Japanese Post Office

In 2005, the Japanese government, under the Prime Minister Mr Koizumi, called and won an election in which the key issue was whether to privatise the Japanese Post Office. The Japanese Post Office did not just sell stamps; it was also a government-owned savings bank with more than $3 trillion (£1.7 trillion) in assets and the largest provider of life insurance in the country. It had 24 700 branches, many of which were in remote locations. There were concerns that, following privatisation, people in the countryside would lose its valuable services. There were also concerns that many of its 260 000 workers could lose their jobs.

 Question

Why would the government want to privatise the Post Office?

■ Problems of privatisation

The following are problems associated with privatisation.

- Privatisation may create private monopolies that abuse their power (in which case privatised organisations may need to be regulated by the government).

- Privatised firms are likely to pursue private objectives rather than social objectives. This may mean that the needs of society are not met as effectively as they were when the industry was nationalised; the socially optimal price and output decisions may not be achieved.

- Some people criticise privatisation on the basis that it is selling the nation's assets back to the nation, that is, in some ways it is selling what we already own.

- If the public sector industries were making profits then by privatising them the government will lose this income.

- The industry may be a natural monopoly. This means that the economies of scale are so great that one firm is bound to expand and dominate to benefit from the cost advantages. By splitting up this industry into smaller firms the unit costs of smaller firms will be higher, and this may lead to higher prices.

Economics in context **Railtrack goes into administration**

In 2001, Railtrack, the company that was in charge of the UK's railway infrastructure (e.g., tracks and bridges) was put into administration when the government refused to put more money into the business. The company needed £700 million to continue. The company had been successful in its first few years following the privatisation of the railways in 1996, but problems started in 1999. Firstly, there was the Ladbroke Grove rail crash in which thirty-one people died; this led to recommendations that billions of pounds should be invested in better safety systems. Then, in October 2000, there was the Hatfield crash in which four people died, caused by a broken rail. Once again, more investment was needed and there were major disruptions to the rail system as work was carried out. Railtrack simply could not afford the investment required.

Following the administration, Railtrack's core railway business was handed over to Network Rail, a not-for-profit company controlled by train operators, rail unions and passenger groups. Network Rail is 'dedicated to the interests of rail users'. Unlike Railtrack, profits are invested into the business instead of being given to shareholders as dividends. Management incentives are tied to performance targets such as safety and punctuality, rather than profits. Railtrack had been criticised for focusing too much on profits instead of safety.

❓ Question

How can a government make sure that a privatised business still acts responsibly?

@ Web

For information on Network Rail visit www.networkrail.co.uk

■ Regulatory capture

Regulatory capture occurs when the regulating body identifies so much with the industry that it is regulating that it protects its interests rather than monitoring them. Those involved in the regulated industry will devote a great deal of time, effort and resources to protecting their own interests, and may well influence the regulator to see these from their own perspective.

Economics in context

The ending of the Royal Mail monopoly

In 2005, the monopoly of the Royal Mail over the delivery of letters ended as the market was opened up to competition. The market was worth over £4.5 billion per year. The introduction of more competition created significant challenges for the Royal Mail, which had only recently become profitable. It had very old equipment and inefficient working practices: Deutsche Post sorted 95% of letters into piles for each postman by machine, whereas the Royal Mail only sorted 50%. The required investment to bring the machinery up to date was estimated at £2.2 billion. The Post Office also had low morale, with only 60% of its employees saying that they were happy to be working for the organisation. The Royal Mail provided a universal service whereby it had to deliver everywhere; new competitors were able to focus on key, profitable deliveries.

The Royal Mail is regulated by PostComm, which has placed restrictions on the price it can charge until 2010.

❓ Question

Do you think that privatising the Royal Mail is a good thing?

@ Web

For more information on PostComm visit **www.psc.gov.uk**

Case Study

Within the European Union (EU) there is a carbon emissions trading scheme. Under this scheme, governments set quotas for the level of carbon dioxide emissions that are produced by 9400 large factories and power stations. Countries are given an overall allocation of permits and these are then allocated to firms within the country. The permits can be traded with other countries and other firms. By reducing its own pollution, a country or firm can sell the remainder of its permits to another business and earn profits by doing this. The other country or business, meanwhile, can pollute more, but its costs would increase. Emissions of carbon dioxide are thought to be a major factor in global warming. By controlling the overall level of emissions governments can hopefully limit the impact on the environment.

However, according to an EU report on the position in 2005, it seems that too many permits were issued. The result was a 2.5% surplus, with 44.2 million tonnes more carbon dioxide permits being issued than were actually needed. With an excess supply of permits, the price of carbon credits fell by around 60%. Even so, the UK claimed that its own targets were too tight when they were first set.

The idea of carbon trading began to take off after the Kyoto Protocol was signed. Under this treaty—which came into effect in February 2005—industrialised countries have to reduce their total greenhouse gas emissions by an average of 5.2% compared with 1990 levels between 2008 and 2012. The World Bank estimated that the value of carbon traded in 2005 was about $10 billion. However, there are problems. Simply creating a market, for example, does not reduce carbon emissions; this depends on the amount allowed. Also, it depends what is being reduced and its effect on environmental issues. Finally, it depends on who is taking part in the scheme. The US is the world's largest carbon dioxide polluter, but did not agree to Kyoto. Meanwhile China, one of the fastest growing economies in the world, does not have to reduce its emissions. Furthermore, the scheme only extends to some industries; some sectors, such as transport, homes and the public sector, are excluded.

On the domestic front there are proposals for personal carbon allowances. Individuals would be given a carbon allowance; this would be monitored and individuals could sell on any surplus or buy extra credits. It would cover people's direct use of energy through their electricity, gas, petrol and air travel, which make up around 44% of the economy's emissions. Cards would store carbon points and when people bought energy points would be deducted from the card.

? Questions

- What factors determine the price of carbon permits?
- What factors would firms consider before buying more carbon permits?
- Do you think that the personal carbon allowance scheme will work? Is it better than taxing consumption?

Checklist

Now you have read this unit try to answer the following questions.

- ☐ Can you explain how governments intervene in the free market?
- ☐ Do you understand the impact of maximum and minimum prices?
- ☐ Do you understand the workings of a buffer stock scheme?
- ☐ Can you explain the reasons for nationalisation?
- ☐ Can you explain the reasons for privatisation?
- ☐ Can you explain the problems of privatisation?

End of unit questions

1 If a monopoly develops, what is the likely impact on the price charged and the quantity available in a market?

2 Travelling by air has a major negative environmental impact. Do you think that air travel should be stopped?

3 What action would a government that was operating a buffer stock scheme take if there was a surplus of a product?

4 Is privatising the Royal Mail a good idea?

5 Why might a government want to nationalise an industry?

Key learning points

- A government can intervene in a number of ways to try and remedy market failures and imperfections, such as legislation, price fixing and direct provision.

- A buffer stock scheme can be used to stabilise good prices.

- Nationalisation occurs when a government takes firms under its control.

- Privatisation occurs when assets and contracts are transferred to the private sector.

- Privatisation can lead to greater efficiency and innovation, but may need regulation to ensure that customers are not exploited.

Reference

Coase, R. (1960). The problem of social cost. *Journal of Law and Economics*, 3, 1.

Learn more

One of the biggest buffer stock schemes in the world was implemented by the European Union and is called the Common Agricultural Policy. You can learn more about this when you read unit 32.

 Visit our Online Resource Centre at www.oxfordtextbooks.co.uk/orc/gillespie_econ for test questions and further information on topics covered in this chapter.

Costs: short run and long run

In the previous unit we saw the importance of costs when calculating profits. In this unit we examine the determinants of a firm's costs in more detail and consider the differences between short-run and long-run costs.

LEARNING OBJECTIVES

By the end of this unit you should be able to:

✔ distinguish between short-run and long-run costs;

✔ explain the law of diminishing returns;

✔ understand the difference between marginal, average and total product;

✔ understand the difference between marginal, average and total cost;

✔ understand the significance of economies and diseconomies of scale;

✔ understand the difference between internal and external economies of scale;

✔ understand the meaning and significance of the minimum efficient scale.

▪ The importance of costs

To be able to decide on the appropriate price and output required to maximise profits managers need a detailed understanding of the level of costs at different levels of output. They will naturally be interested in factors such as the total costs of producing, the cost per unit (average cost) and the extra costs of producing another product (marginal costs).

This unit examines the factors that determine the nature of costs in both the short run and the long run. Managers will aim to achieve the lowest possible cost per unit for any given level of output, and this involves getting the correct combination of resources. Their ability to do this varies from the short run to the long run. In the short run there will be more constraints than the long run.

The pressure on firms to be efficient has generally increased with greater worldwide competition and the ability of consumers to search more easily via the Internet. This makes it even more important for firms to look for the best way of producing. The costs structure in an industry is also important because it influences the number of firms that can survive within it. If costs are very high to start up or at low levels of output, for example, then it is likely that established firms or large producers will face limited competition.

■ Short-run costs

The short run in economics is the period of time when there is at least one factor of production fixed. In the short run at least one of the resources cannot be changed; for example, a firm cannot recruit the staff it wants, cannot acquire new equipment or cannot find new premises. This means that in the short run a firm is constrained and cannot necessarily find its optimal mix of resources. This also means that there are fixed costs in the short run. For example, you may have rented premises and be committed to a contract for a period of months or years, or you may be repaying a loan on equipment for a five year period.

Short-run total costs are therefore made up of fixed costs and variable costs.

- *Fixed costs (FC)*. These are costs that a firm has to pay but which are not dependent on the level of output. For example, the interest on a loan is related to the size of the loan and the interest rate, not the level of output. Even if output is zero a firm must pay its fixed costs. High levels of fixed costs represent a high level of risk for a business because the business must still pay these costs if sales fall.

- *Variable costs (VC)*. These are costs that are directly related to the level of output, such as the costs of materials and components used in the production process. As output increases variable costs will increase as well.

How long the short run is will vary from industry to industry. If it is easy to sell and buy land and equipment, for example, the short run may be months or a year or so. If, however, expansion involves a major investment, for example, in a new airport terminal, then it may take five to ten years to expand capacity.

What do you think?

In what ways do you think that firms can 'shorten the short run' by making their resources more flexible and avoiding fixed costs?

The law of diminishing returns

In the short run a firm's ability to produce will be constrained by its fixed factors of production. For example, a business may be constrained by its production equipment or office space. Although it will be able to change these factors over time (e.g., invest in new equipment or buy new office space), in the short term it cannot. Therefore, to increase production it can change some factors of production (e.g., managers could ask employees to work overtime or recruit more employees), but not others; it must add variable factors of production to fixed factors to increase output. As a result the business will experience the law of diminishing returns. Under the law of diminishing returns, the extra output produced as more units of the variable factors are added to fixed factors will decrease. This means that the total output increases at a decreasing rate.

The extra output produced by the variable factor is known as the marginal product. If labour is the variable factor then we measure the marginal product of labour (MPL). If capital is the variable factor then we measure the marginal product of capital (MPK; K is used to represent capital).

The marginal product (MP) can be calculated using the following equation:

$$\text{Marginal product} = \frac{\text{Change in the total output}}{\text{Change in the variable factor of production}}.$$

Imagine adding additional people to an office environment with a given amount of equipment. There will simply not be enough computers or telephones for them all to use if you keep adding staff and they will begin to get in each other's way. The first person you employ could be very useful and productive; the sixth or seventh employee may add little to the overall productivity of the office if you cannot increase fixed factors such as office space and equipment.

The law of diminishing returns is illustrated in Fig. 9.1.

Short-run marginal costs (SRMC)

The marginal cost curve shows the extra cost of producing a unit. The marginal cost is calculated as follows:

$$\text{Marginal cost} = \frac{\text{Change in the total cost}}{\text{Change in output}}.$$

The short run marginal cost (SRMC) curve is the inverse (opposite) of the marginal product curve. As each additional factor is added to the business the extra output of each employee diminishes in accordance with the law of diminishing returns. Assuming that the employees are all being paid the same amount of money, this means that you are paying the same for each extra worker who is adding less extra units; therefore the extra cost of these units in terms of labour is increasing. So when a firm experiences the law of diminishing marginal returns its short-run marginal costs are increasing. This should make intuitive sense; if extra workers are less productive then the extra output they are producing is becoming more expensive. The relationship between the marginal product and the marginal cost is shown in Fig. 9.2. The marginal cost curve is usually a 'tick shape'.

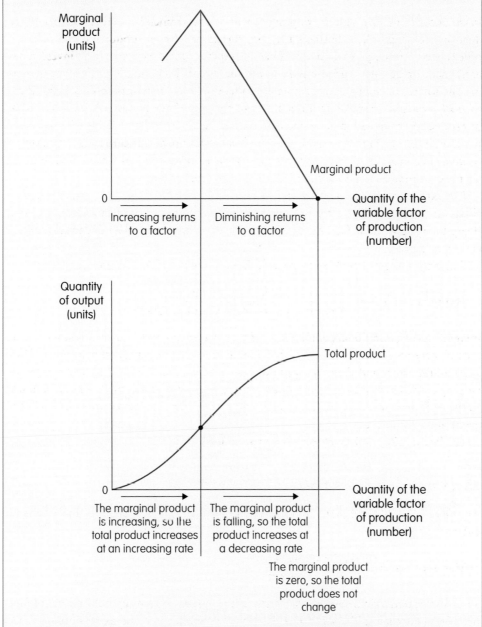

Figure 9.1 The relationship between the marginal product and the total product.

What do you think?

If the wage rate had to be increased to attract more employees, what would this do to the marginal cost curve?

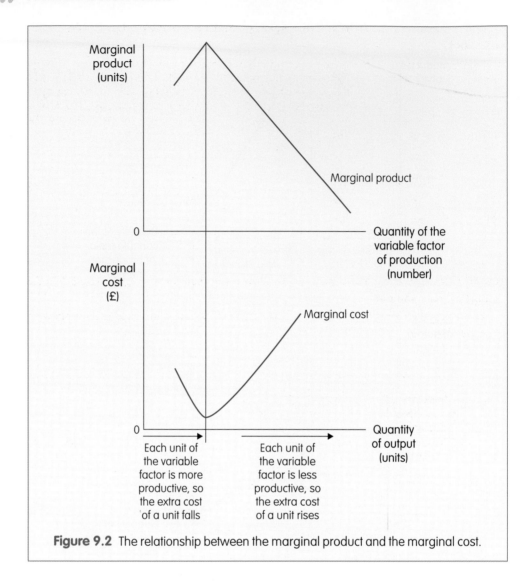

Figure 9.2 The relationship between the marginal product and the marginal cost.

Marginal product and average product of labour

The average product of labour is the output per employee (often called labour productivity).

If the marginal product of labour is greater than the average product this means that the extra employee is more productive than the employees were, on average, before. This will pull up the average; that is, if the marginal product is greater than the average product then the average product will increase.

If the marginal product of labour is less than the average product this means that the extra employee is less productive than employees were, on average, before. This will pull

Table 9.1 The relationship between the marginal product, the average product and the total output.

Number of employees	Total output (units)	Average product of labour = total output/number of employees (units)	Marginal product of labour = change in total output/change in number of employees (units)
1	10	10	–
2	30	15	20
3	60	20	30
4	76	19	16
5	80	16	4

down the average; that is, if the marginal product is less than the average product then the average product will fall.

This means that the marginal product will cross the average product at its maximum point (see Fig. 9.3).

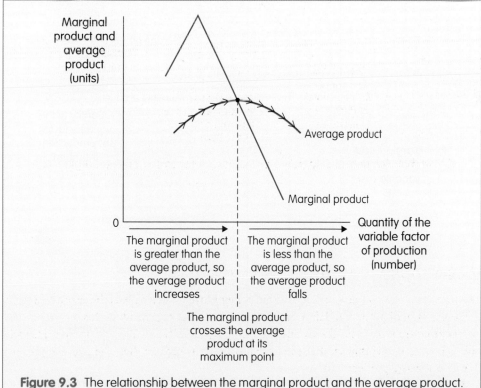

Figure 9.3 The relationship between the marginal product and the average product.

Now you try it

Employees are hired at a wage of £200 per week. You have four employees producing 400 units.

What is the total cost of production?

What is the average output per employee?

You hire a fifth employee and output rises to 450 units.

What is the total cost of production?

What is the marginal product of the fifth worker?

What is the average output per employee now?

What is the average cost per unit now?

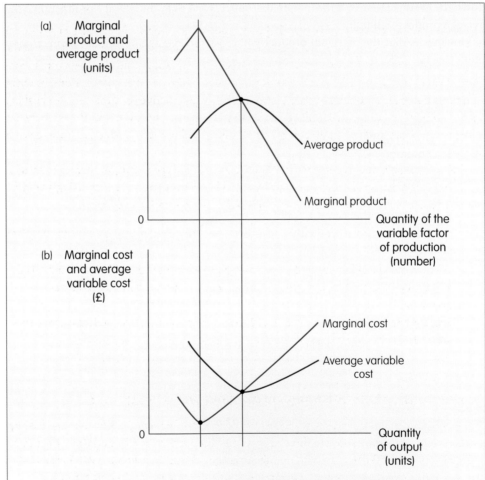

Figure 9.4 The relationship between (a) the marginal product and the average product and (b) the marginal cost and the average variable cost.

Short-run average costs (SRAC)

The short-run average cost (SRAC) curve shows the lowest cost per unit for any level of output given the fixed factor(s) of production. The short-run average cost curve is generally 'U-shaped'. It is made up of the average fixed costs and the average variable costs. From the equation

Total cost = Fixed cost + Variable cost

We divide by the output level to obtain:

$$\frac{\text{Total cost}}{\text{Output}} = \frac{\text{Fixed cost}}{\text{Output}} + \frac{\text{Variable cost}}{\text{Output}},$$

$$\frac{\text{TC}}{\text{Q}} = \frac{\text{FC}}{\text{Q}} + \frac{\text{VC}}{\text{Q}},$$

Average cost (AC) = Average fixed cost (AFC) + Average variable cost (AVC).

The average fixed cost curve will fall continuously as the fixed costs are spread over more units. The average variable cost curve is usually 'U-shaped' and is the inverse of the average product curve. Assume that the variable factor is labour and the wage rate is constant. When, on average, labour is less productive then the average cost of a unit in terms of labour will rise. When, on average, labour is more productive then the variable cost per unit in terms of labour will fall. (This is similar to the inverse relationship between marginal product and marginal cost.) The relationship between productivity and costs is shown in Fig. 9.4.

The average cost and average variable cost curves converge as output increases because the average fixed cost becomes less significant. The overall costs are increasingly dominated by variable costs as the fixed cost per unit becomes smaller (see Fig. 9.5).

Now you try it

The fixed costs of a business are £10,000. What is the average fixed cost if output is either 1 unit, 10 units or 1000 units? What is happening to the average fixed cost as output increases?

Suppose that the variable cost per unit is £2. Calculate both the total cost and the average cost for 1 unit, 10 units, 100 units and 1000 units.

The relationship between marginal cost (MC) and average cost (AC)

If the marginal cost is greater than the average cost then this will pull the average cost up. For example, if a firm produces three units at an average cost of £10 and then it produces a fourth unit for £50 then this will pull the average cost up (see Table 9.2). As the cost of the extra unit was higher than the average cost it will increase the average cost.

Conversely, if the extra cost of a unit is less than the average cost it will pull down the average cost. For example, if a firm produces three units at an average cost of £10 and then it produces a fourth unit for £6 then this will bring the average cost down.

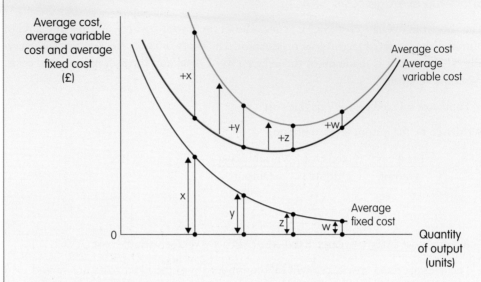

Figure 9.5 The relationship between the average cost, the average variable cost and the average fixed cost.

Table 9.2 Output and costs.

Output (units)	Total cost (£)	Marginal cost (£)	Average cost (£)
3	30	–	10
4	80	50	20
5	150	70	30

Now you try it

Fill in the ? in the table below.

Output (units)	Total cost (£)	Marginal cost (£)	Average cost (£)
3	30	–	10
4	36	6	9
5	40	?	?

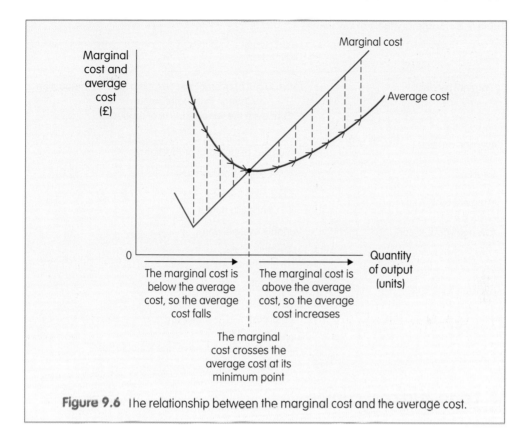

Figure 9.6 The relationship between the marginal cost and the average cost.

This relationship between marginals and averages means that the marginal cost will cross the average cost at its minimum point. This is shown in Fig. 9.6.

Now you try it

The average cost of ten units is £6. What is the total cost?

The marginal cost of the eleventh unit is £17. What is the total cost now? What is the average cost? What does this show in terms of the relationships between marginal costs and average costs?

The marginal cost of the twelfth unit is £7. What is the total cost now? What is the average cost? What does this show in terms of the relationships between marginal costs and average costs?

A summary of the key terms of covered so far is shown in Table 9.3.

Table 9.3 Summary table of key terms.

Item	Description
Marginal product	Extra output from employing an extra factor of production, $$= \frac{\text{Change in the total output}}{\text{Change in the variable factor of production}}$$
Average product	$$= \frac{\text{Total output}}{\text{Number of factors of production}}$$
Total cost	= Fixed cost + Variable cost
Marginal cost	$$= \frac{\text{Change in the total cost}}{\text{Change in output}}$$
Average variable cost	Variable cost per unit, $$= \frac{\text{Variable cost}}{\text{Output}}$$
Average fixed cost	$$= \frac{\text{Fixed cost}}{\text{Output}}$$
Average cost	$$= \frac{\text{Total cost}}{\text{Output}}$$ = Average fixed cost + Average variable cost

■ Long-run cost curves

Long-run average costs (LRAC)

The long-run average cost (LRAC) curve shows the lowest possible cost per unit for any level of output when all factors of production are variable.

In the long run firms are able to change all of their resources to find the optimal combinations. If, as a result of changing its combination of resources, the firm is able to reduce its unit costs when it produces more then this means that the firm is experiencing internal economies of scale.

Imagine that a firm has a fixed amount of machinery K1 (see Fig. 9.7). The lowest cost per unit for any level of output given this level of machinery is shown by the short-run average cost curve SRAC1. This will be the optimal amount of capital for a particular level of output, in this case Q1. With K1 the short-run unit cost is the lowest it can possibly be, and even in the long run this is the amount of capital that would be chosen. However, for any other level of output K1 would not be the optimal amount of capital. To produce Q2, for example, K2 may be the optimal amount of capital. In the short run the firm is committed to K1 capital and so the lowest unit costs is 'x'. In the long run, however, the firm is able to change the level of equipment and can find the optimal level of machinery K2. This means that it can move onto a new short-run average cost curve SRAC2 and unit costs fall to 'y'. In the long run it can produce more cheaply. The unit costs have fallen as the firm has increased the scale of production. This means that the firm is benefiting from internal economies of scale. Similar observations can be made if the firm expands further to Q3. In the short run it is now constrained by the level of equipment K2. The lowest unit

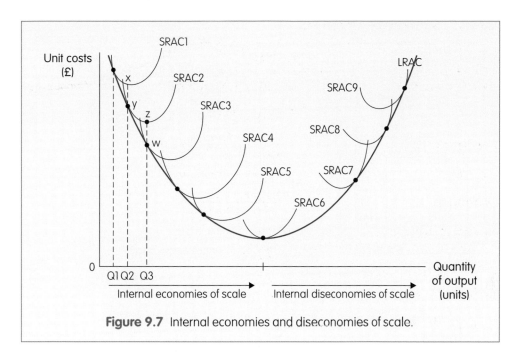

Figure 9.7 Internal economies and diseconomies of scale.

cost possible in the short run with this level of equipment is 'z'. In the long run the amount of capital can be changed, and as a result the firm moves onto a new short-run average cost curve and unit costs fall to 'w'.

Types of internal economy of scale

The reasons for internal economies of scale include 'plant economies'. These specifically refer to lower unit costs as a result of a larger size of factory. These include the following.

- *Technical economies*. With larger production levels it may be possible to adopt production techniques that are more efficient on a large scale, such as mass production. At large volumes such techniques lead to lower unit costs. These techniques require heavy investment that can be spread over high volumes to reduce the unit cost.

- *Indivisibilities*. Some machines are indivisible, that is, they can be used on a certain scale but cannot be split up or divided; so to produce on a small scale is relatively expensive. Imagine that you buy an excavator; this may be cost effective if used on a regular basis, but not if used only once a month.

- *Volume*. If you double the height, width and depth of a container (such as a lorry, warehouse or transport vessel) then the volume it contains will increase more than proportionately compared to the surface area. For example, a box that has six sides of 1 m by 1 m has six sides with an area of 1 m^2, that is, 6 m^2 overall (see Fig. 9.8). The volume is 1 m × 1 m × 1 m = 1 m^3. If the measurements are doubled then the area is now 24 m^2 (six sides of area 4 m^2) and the volume is 2 m × 2 m × 2 m = 8 m^3 (see Fig. 9.8). So a four times increase in surface area has led to an eight times increase in volume. This will reduce the average storage or transportation costs per unit. By spending four times as

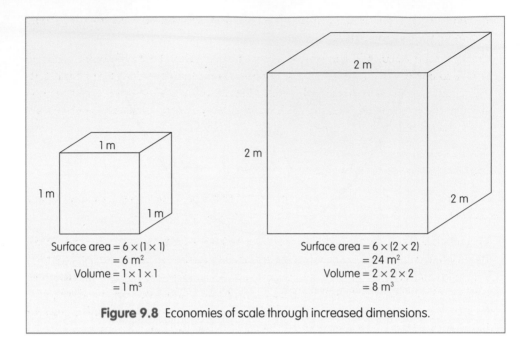

Surface area = 6 × (1 × 1)
= 6 m²
Volume = 1 × 1 × 1
= 1 m³

Surface area = 6 × (2 × 2)
= 24 m²
Volume = 2 × 2 × 2
= 8 m³

Figure 9.8 Economies of scale through increased dimensions.

much to build a container you can carry eight times as much, so the transport costs per unit will be lower.

- *Specialisation and division of labour*. As firms produce on a larger scale the production process can be divided into a series of clearly and narrowly defined jobs. This means that employees do not need extensive training. By undertaking tasks again and again they may become more productive, making production more efficient.

Other economies are known as 'firm' or 'enterprise' economies. These include the following.

- *Purchasing economies*. When a firm operates on a larger scale it will need to purchase more, such as components, materials and advertising space. Being larger puts the firm in a better bargaining position with suppliers and should mean that it is possible to negotiate better payment terms and lower prices for these resources, thereby reducing unit costs. One of the reasons for the success of Wal-Mart is its sheer size; this enables it to buy products from suppliers at much better prices than many competitors and to pass these cost savings on to consumers. This makes it difficult for smaller firms to survive.

- *Managerial economies*. As an organisation expands it may be able to employ specialist managers to undertake various functions, such as marketing, human resources and the purchasing of resources. By having specialists dedicated to these tasks this should lead to better decision making and less waste. Another managerial economy occurs because the rate of increase in the number of managers required by an organisation is not as fast as the rate of growth of the organisation itself. For example, if there is a manager of a department of eight people then it could probably grow to say twelve without a new manager being appointed; the costs of the existing manager can therefore be spread over more staff up to a point.

- *Financial economies.* A larger firm with more assets, such as land and equipment, may be able to borrow money from a bank at lower rates of interest than a new firm starting up because they have extra collateral. They are a lower risk to the banks because their assets can be seized. This greater level of security should reduce the level of interest payments that need to be made.

Internal diseconomies of scale

If a firm grows too large then it may find that the average costs begin to rise. This is because of internal diseconomies of scale. These include the following.

- *Motivation issues.* When a business is too large employees may no longer feel part of the organisation as a whole. They may lack a sense of connection to the overall business. Low motivation can lead to mistakes being made, low levels of attendance and low productivity. All of these tend to increase unit costs. Firms will try to overcome these problems in a variety of ways, such as introducing mission statements to provide a sense of direction. A mission statement sets out the purpose and values of the business.

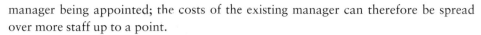

Economics in context   Unilever's mission

Unilever is an international manufacturer of leading brands in foods, home care and personal care. Its mission statement is as follows.

> Our purpose in Unilever is to meet the everyday needs of people everywhere—to anticipate the aspirations of our consumers and customers and to respond creatively and competitively with branded products and services, which raise the quality of life.

? **Question**

How useful do you think having a mission statement such as the one above would be?

- *Management problems.* Managing a larger business is a more complex process than running a small business. For example, you are likely to be controlling a wide range of products, communicating between many different sites or outlets, and coordinating many different departments. This can be very difficult and may lead to inefficiency, mistakes being made and higher unit costs. Firms may try to overcome these problems with budgets, regular meetings and review sessions called appraisals.

What do you think?

To what extent is it possible to manage growth effectively and prevent diseconomies of scale?

Returns to scale

Increasing, decreasing and constant returns to scale are described as follows.

- Increasing returns to scale occur when an increase in *all* of the factors of production leads to a more proportionate increase in output. For example, if doubling the amount of labour, land and capital leads to a tripling of output then this is known as increasing returns to scale. This leads to a fall in the average costs and is an example of internal economies of scale.

- Decreasing returns to scale occur when an increase in *all* of the factors of production leads to a less than proportionate increase in output. For example, if tripling the amount of labour, land and capital leads to a doubling of output then this is known as decreasing returns to scale. This leads to an increase in average costs and is an example of internal diseconomies of scale.

- Constant returns to scale occur when an increase in *all* of the factors of production leads to a proportionate increase in output. For example, if doubling the amount of labour, land and capital leads to a doubling of output then this is known as constant returns to scale. Average costs stay constant.

Minimum efficient scale (MES)

The long-run average cost may have a variety of shapes depending on the industry and the revelant cost conditions.

The minimum efficient scale (MES) is the first level of output at which the long-run average costs of a firm are minimised, that is, where internal economies of scale are no longer being experienced. This is illustrated in Fig. 9.9. The MES may be significant in determining the structure of an industry. If, for example, the MES is relatively high compared to demand in the industry then this suggests that only a few firms could operate efficiently within it, that is, the industry may be more likely to be an oligopoly (see Unit 13).

What do you think?

There has been huge growth by firms within the UK pharmaceutical sector. This industry is now dominated by relatively few businesses. To what extent do you think this is desirable?

If, however, the MES occurs at very low levels of output compared to the total demand in the industry then this suggests that many firms could operate efficiently. This suggests that the market may be much more competitive, with more smaller firms operating in it at the same time and providing more choice for customers.

However, the precise impact of the MES on the market structure also depends on the cost disadvantage of operating below it, that is, on what happens if a firm enters and produces below the minimum efficient scale (e.g., at one-third of the MES). If the consequences of this are that this firm would have much higher unit costs then it will clearly struggle to compete; for example, it would be likely to suffer in a price war. In this situation it is unlikely that inefficient firms will survive because the cost disadvantage is so

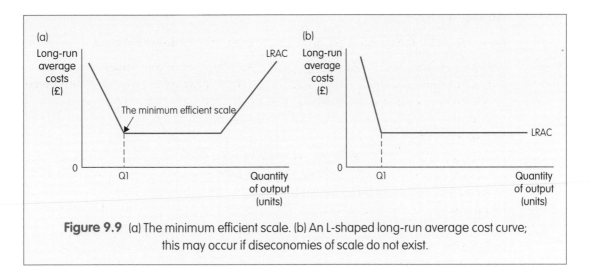

Figure 9.9 (a) The minimum efficient scale. (b) An L-shaped long-run average cost curve; this may occur if diseconomies of scale do not exist.

great. In this case the MES is a very good indicator of how many firms are likely to be in the industry.

However, if the unit costs of operating below the MES are not significant then it may be possible for many firms to be operating inefficiently. This is because they are not operating at any major disadvantage. In this case the MES may not be a good indicator of market structure as there may be many inefficient firms also operating alongside the efficient ones.

The potential impact of the MES on the market structure is illustrated in Fig. 9.10.

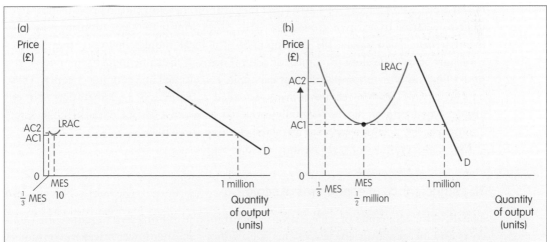

Figure 9.10 The relationship between the minimum efficient scale (MES) and market structure. (a) The MES is low relative to the market demand and the cost disadvantage of operating below the MES is also low. This means that this market is likely to be very competitive, with many firms competing. (b) The MES is high relative to the market demand, and the cost disadvantage of not operating at the MES is also high. This industry is likely to be dominated by a few firms, probably two given that the MES is half of the market demand.

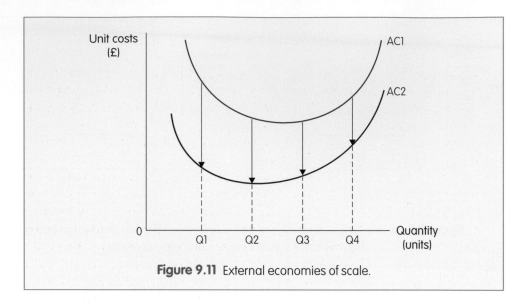

Figure 9.11 External economies of scale.

Internal versus external economies of scale

Internal economies of scale refer to cost advantages that a firm experiences when it grows, that is, the average cost per unit falls in the long run as the scale of production expands.

External economies of scale occur when changes outside the firm reduce the unit cost of operating at all output levels.

This may be because there are government subsidies in the area that reduce the costs. Governments sometimes target areas that they want to develop and so provide incentives to firms wanting to set up or grow there. Also, other firms in the same industry may have located there, encouraging the development of a local supplier network that reduces transport costs. The close proximity of several firms in the same industry may lead to a pool of labour with relevant skills that can make recruitment and training cheaper. These cost benefits of location near other firms are called 'economies of agglomeration'. For example, Northampton has traditionally attracted shoe firms, Sheffield has attracted steel companies and northern Italy has attracted clothing companies.

External economies of scale are illustrated in Fig. 9.11.

The significance of economies of scale

The drive for economies of scale is a very important one as firms seek to reduce their unit costs and increase their efficiency. This is how they can offer lower prices to consumers and/or benefit from higher profit margins. This is also how they can compete against other firms worldwide. With more free trade worldwide local producers are now facing much greater competition and need to be as efficient as they can. You will often see economies of scale given as the reason behind a takeover or merger as firms join together to benefit from shared resources and reduce the unit costs. Industries such as banking, music, insurance, car production and pharmaceuticals have seen major restructuring as firms join to gain economies of scale and be more competitive.

Case Study

In 2006, the huge American car company, General Motors, started initial talks with its rival Renault–Nissan to see if a three-way alliance was possible. In the suggested deal the other two firms would take a 20% share of General Motors. Obviously, such relationships can create major problems but they also offer numerous benefits, not least economies of scale. General Motors had already embarked on a major cost-cutting plan after it announced losses of $10.6 billion in 2005. It had been suffering from high labour costs, high pension costs and intense competition from Asia.

Renault had a 44.4% share in Nissan, which had a 15% stake in Renault. Nissan was Japan's second largest car manufacturer and the ninth largest in the world. It had had several years of profit up to 2006, having turned itself around from the 1990s. Renault was the world's tenth largest car manufacturer and was in the middle of a plan to launch twenty-six new models before 2009. In May 1999, these two companies set up a joint venture to coordinate their global product development, financial policy and corporate strategy. The two companies combined had revenues in 2005 of $327 billion, but made a loss of $1.7 billion. General Motors was the world's largest car manufacturer, with over 300 000 employees worldwide.

The proposed deal offered opportunities to share the development and production of parts, such as car engines, chassis and other parts. Shared purchasing power would also enable them to squeeze suppliers further. The deal would also give Renault more access to the huge North American market. If Nissan and Renault did take shares in General Motors then this would be a vote of confidence in the company's plans. This would probably help the General Motors credit rating and allow them to borrow more cheaply.

However, some analysts were concerned as to whether managers would be able to control and coordinate such as deal. All of the companies were involved in major strategic change and so whether this was the right time was debatable. Also, most of them would have already worked hard to get the best prices possible from their suppliers, so more cost savings there might have been unlikely.

Questions

- Analyse the possible economies of scale that could occur following a deal such as the one described above.
- How important do you think it is to gain economies of scale in the car industry?
- What problems might occur following a deal such as this?

Checklist

Now you have read this unit try to answer the following questions.

- ☐ Do you understand the difference between marginal, average and total product?
- ☐ Do you understand the difference between marginal, average and total cost?
- ☐ Do you understand the significance of economies and diseconomies of scale?
- ☐ Do you understand the difference between internal and external economies of scale?
- ☐ Do you understand the meaning and significance of the minimum efficient scale?

End of unit questions

1 If the marginal cost of producing another item is positive and increasing, what is happening to the total costs?

2 If the marginal costs are below the average costs then what will happen to the average costs?

3 What is the relationship between short-run average costs and long-run average costs?

4 Is a competitive market more likely if the minimum efficient scale is high or low relative to the level of demand in the industry? Why?

5 To what extent do you think economies of scale increase a firm's competitiveness?

Key learning points

• There is a difference between the short run and the long run; in the long run all of the factors of production are variable.

• It is important to distinguish between the marginal product (or costs) and the average product (or costs).

• Profit maximisation occurs at an output at which no extra profit can be generated.

• In the long run firms may benefit from internal economies of scale if it increases the scale of its production, but if its size increases too much then it may experience diseconomies of scale.

Learn more

Firms will want to identify the minimum cost combination of resources for any level of output. This can be analysed in more detail using what is called isoquant analysis. To learn more about this visit our website at the address below.

 Visit our Online Resource Centre at www.oxfordtextbooks.co.uk/orc/gillespie_econ for test questions and further information on topics covered in this chapter.

Revenues, costs and profits

Much of economic analysis is based on the assumption that firms want to maximise their profits. Profits occur when a firm's revenue is greater than its costs. In this unit we examine the determinants of a firm's revenue and its costs, and analyse the price and output decisions that will maximise profits. We also examine how low the price level must fall before firms shut down in the short run and the long run. An understanding of all of these issues will help us to predict how firms will behave in a particular market situation and analyse the price and outcome results in perfect competition.

LEARNING OBJECTIVES

By the end of this unit you should be able to:

✔ explain the difference between revenues and costs;

✔ outline the difference between marginal and total revenue;

✔ explain the difference between marginal and total costs;

✔ explain the difference between normal and abnormal profits;

✔ appreciate the difference between profits and profitability;

✔ explain the output level at which firms profit maximise;

✔ understand the decision of whether or not to produce in the short run and the long run.

Introduction

An important element of economic analysis is to examine the structure of a market and the behaviour of firms within it. To do this requires an understanding of revenues, costs and profits. This unit examines these different elements in detail.

Total revenue (TR)

The total revenue (TR) of a firm measures the value of its sales. If a car dealership sells ten cars at £20,000 each, then its total revenue is £200,000. The total revenue of a business equals the price of the products multiplied by the number sold:

Total revenue = Price of a unit × Quantity sold,

$$TR = P \times Q.$$

The total revenue may not be the same as the cash received at that particular moment because a sale may be on credit, but it represents what the sale is actually worth. The cash may be paid later and controlling cash flow effectively is an important business activity.

On a demand curve the total revenue is illustrated by the area under the curve for any price and quantity combination (see Fig. 10.1).

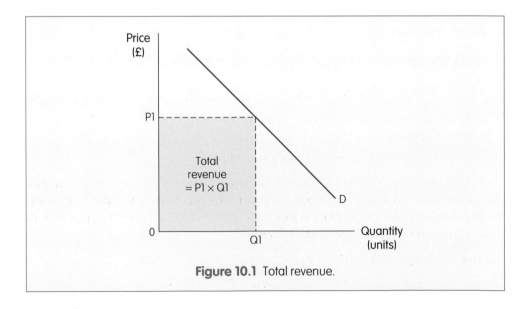

Figure 10.1 Total revenue.

Big companies

Table 10.1 shows the sizes of the five largest companies in the world, ranked according to their turnover.

Table 10.1 The five largest companies in the world in 2006.

Rank	Company	Revenue ($ millions)
1	Exxon Mobil	339,938
2	Wal-Mart Stores	315,654
3	General Motors	192,604
4	Chevron	189,481
5	Ford Motor	177,210

Source: *Fortune*.

? Question

What do you think are the benefits and problems of running such large companies?

What do you think?

Why do you think that many firms sell their products on credit rather than insisting on cash being paid?

Marginal revenue (MR)

The marginal revenue (MR) is the difference in the total revenue when an additional unit is sold:

$$\text{Marginal revenue} = \frac{\text{Change in total revenue}}{\text{Change in the number of units sold}}.$$

Assuming that the firm faces a downward-sloping demand curve, then to sell another unit it may have to reduce the price not only on the last unit, but on all of the ones before. For example, imagine that one unit is sold for £10, but to sell another the price of both must be reduced to £9. This means the following:

1 unit   Price per unit = £10   Total revenue = £10,

2 units   Price per unit = £9   Total revenue = £9 × 2 = £18.

The marginal revenue for selling the second unit is £8. Although the second unit sells for £9, the price of the first one has been reduced by £1, so the gain in revenue is £9 − £1 = £8. Thus we have

Marginal revenue = Price of the last unit − Reductions in price on the units before.

Now imagine that to sell a third unit the price is reduced to £8. This means the following:

2 units Price per unit = £9 Total revenue = £18,

3 units Price per unit = £8 Total revenue = £24.

The marginal revenue for selling the third unit is £6.

This is because the price of the last unit is £8 whilst the price of the previous two units has been reduced by £1 each. So the marginal revenue is £8 − £2 = £6.

As the number of units being sold increases, then to sell another one the price must be reduced on an increasing number of previous units. This means that the difference between the marginal revenue and the price becomes ever greater as more units are sold. The marginal revenue curve therefore diverges from the demand curve.

At some point the price cut will not change the total revenue. This means that the extra revenue (the marginal revenue) is zero. This occurs when the price elasticity of demand is equal to one (see Unit 4). This is at the midpoint of the demand curve. The relationship between the price, the marginal revenue and the total revenue is highlighted in Table 10.2.

When a relatively large number of units are being sold the total revenue can fall following a price reduction. This is because of the price cut on so many previous units that is required to sell one more. If the total revenue falls then this means that the marginal revenue is negative. It also means that the price elasticity of demand is price inelastic (see Unit 4).

The relationship between demand, the marginal revenue and the total revenue is shown in Fig. 10.2.

Table 10.2 The relationship between the marginal revenue and the total revenue.

Quantity (units)	Price (£)	Total revenue = price × quantity sold (£)	Marginal revenue = extra revenue from selling an additional unit (£)
1	10	10	–
2	9	18	8
3	8	24	6
4	7	28	4
5	6	30	2
6	5	30	0
7	4	28	−2
8	3	24	−4

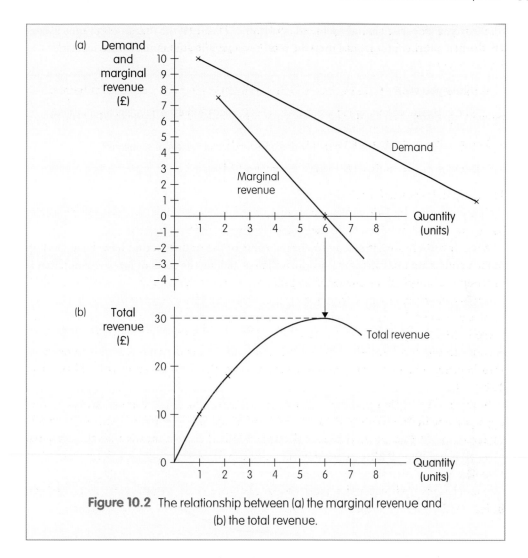

Figure 10.2 The relationship between (a) the marginal revenue and (b) the total revenue.

Now you try it

Ten units are sold at £15 each. To sell an eleventh unit the price must be reduced to £12.

Calculate the old and new total revenue.

Calculate the marginal revenue of the eleventh unit.

■ Marginal revenue and total revenue

The marginal revenue shows the change in the total revenue. If the marginal revenue is positive with a price fall and the sale of an extra unit then the total revenue increases; demand is price elastic. If the marginal revenue is zero when another unit is sold then the total revenue does not change; demand is unit price elastic. If the marginal revenue is negative when another unit is sold then the total revenue falls; demand is price inelastic.

Now you try it

The total revenue from selling twenty units is £300. Imagine that the marginal revenue from selling the twenty-first unit is either £30, £100, £0 or –£50.

What is the total revenue from twenty-one units for each of these four situations?

▨ Total costs (TC)

The total costs (TC) of a firm represent the value of the resources that have been used up in the production and sale of the products. These include the costs of labour, land, materials and machinery, and are written as follows:

Total costs = Fixed costs + Variable costs.

The total costs will increase as more output is produced because there will be more variable costs, for example, more materials will be used up.

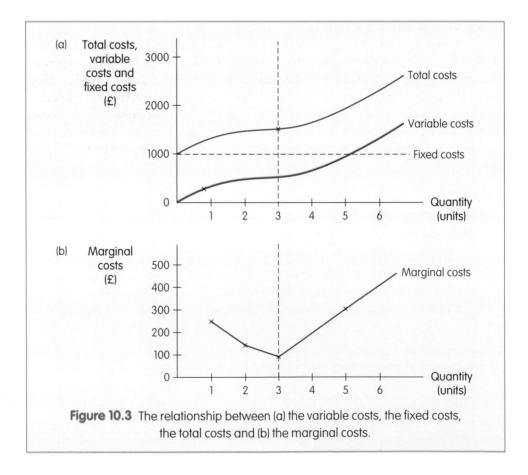

Figure 10.3 The relationship between (a) the variable costs, the fixed costs, the total costs and (b) the marginal costs.

Table 10.3 The relationship between the total costs, the marginal costs and the average costs.

Output (units)	Fixed costs (£)	Variable costs (£)	Total costs = fixed costs + variable costs (£)	Marginal costs = change in total costs/change in output (£)	Average cost (£)
0	1000	0	1000	–	–
1	1000	250	1250	250	1250
2	1000	400	1400	150	700
3	1000	500	1500	100	500
4	1000	800	1800	300	450
5	1000	1200	2200	400	440
6	1000	1700	2700	500	450

Marginal costs and total costs

The marginal cost is the extra cost of producing a unit. For example, if the cost of making four units is £1000 and the cost of making five units is £1200 then the marginal cost of the fifth unit is £200.

The relationship between the fixed costs, the variable costs, the total costs and the marginal costs is shown in Fig. 10.3.

The relationship between the different types of costs is also highlighted in Table 10.3.

If the marginal cost is positive then this means that the total costs must have increased. For example, a marginal cost of £300 means that the total costs have gone up by £300 when another unit is made. If the marginal cost is £400 then the total costs will rise by this amount. If the marginal cost is £0 then this means that the total costs do not change when an extra unit is produced. The marginal cost therefore shows the rate of change of the total costs. The relationship between the marginal costs and the total costs is shown in Fig. 10.4.

Now you try it

Complete the following table.

Output (units)	Fixed costs (£)	Variable costs (£)	Total costs = fixed costs + variable costs (£)	Marginal costs = change in total costs/change in output (£)	Average cost (£)
0	?	?	10000	–	–
1	?	1000	?	?	?
2	?	?	11500	?	?
3	?	4000	?	?	?
4	?	?	?	3000	?
5	?	?	?	?	5000
6	?	8000	?	?	?

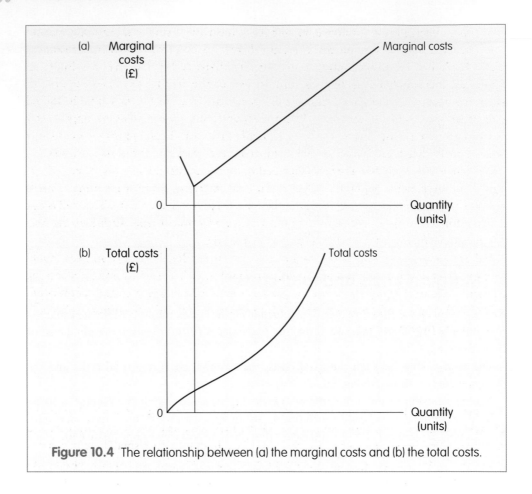

Figure 10.4 The relationship between (a) the marginal costs and (b) the total costs.

Profit

The profit of a firm measures the difference between the value of what has been sold and the value of what has been used up to provide these goods, that is,

Profit = Total revenue − Total costs.

The difference between accounting profit and economists' profits: normal and abnormal profit

When an accountant thinks of costs he or she measures the costs of items used up to produce and sell the products; these include labour, materials, components, land and equipment. An economist, however, will add opportunity costs to this list. This means that an economist will estimate how much a firm's inputs could have earned if used in another industry and include this as a cost of being in business in a particular market. As a result, in economics, when a firm is just covering its costs it is earning a sum of money that it could earn elsewhere with these resources. Therefore there is no incentive to move these resources into other industries. In accounting terms, a profit will be declared to investors, but to an economist this simply means that the firm has earned the amount of money required to keep resources where they are; if less than this was earned then resources should be shifted into other sectors of the economy. When revenue equals costs (including opportunity cost) an economist calls this 'normal profit'; if all of the firms in an industry were earning normal profit then there is no incentive to move resources into or out of this industry.

If a firm earns more than the costs included by an economist then this is called 'abnormal profit' or 'supernormal profit'. This means that the resources are generating rewards that are higher than those needed to keep them in this particular industry. This will act as a signal for resources to shift into this sector to try and benefit from such high returns. Abnormal profit will attract other firms into this sector.

If the revenue does not cover the economist's costs then a loss is made; resources should be moved out of this sector and into a more profitable one. The resources are not earning enough to justify keeping them in their present use. In accounting terms, the firm could still be declaring a profit, but to an economist if this does not justify the resources being in this industry then it is a loss.

Profits versus profitability

The profit made by a firm is measured as an absolute amount, such as £X million. However, this does not show an analyst what funds were invested to generate such a return. A £3 million profit earned in a year may be a high sum for a small business, but is not so impressive for a very large organisation such as Tesco plc. We may therefore want to measure profit in relation to the amount of long-term funds invested in the business. This is known as the return on capital employed (ROCE).

The return on capital employed is a very common measure of a firm's financial performance, and can be written as follows:

$$\text{Return on capital employed} = \frac{\text{Profit}}{\text{Capital employed}} \times 100\%.$$

Economics in context   The profitability of UK firms

The overall profitability of UK private non-financial organisations in 2005 was around 13%. For oil and gas companies it was 36%. For manufacturing firms it was around 7%. For services it was over 16%.

❓ Questions

Why do you think the rates of return differ so much?

Why are there not more firms moving out of the lower return sectors and into the higher return sectors?

Managers and investors will usually seek to generate the highest possible return on capital employed. This will mean that they are using their resources to generate a relatively high level of profit.

Profit maximisation: the marginal condition

To maximise their profits firms must sell the number of units for which there is the largest positive difference between the total revenue and the total costs. To identify this level of sales economists often use the marginal condition. This means that they look for the level of sales at which the marginal revenue from selling an extra unit equals the marginal cost of producing and selling another unit.

If the marginal revenue from selling a product is greater than the marginal cost of producing it then the extra unit will make a profit. This means that by selling the extra unit the total profits will go up. The extra revenue is greater than the extra costs, and so profits increase by producing and selling it. The firm should therefore produce all of the units for which the marginal revenue is greater than the marginal costs because, by doing so, profits will rise.

The profit maximising firm should stop producing when the marginal revenue equals the marginal costs. At this point no extra profit can be made, which means that profits must be maximised. They cannot be increased further. A firm will therefore profit maximise if the marginal revenue equals the marginal costs.

If the marginal revenue is less than the marginal costs then a loss will be made on the extra unit. These units should not be produced.

So the profit maximising output occurs when the marginal revenue equals the marginal costs, that is, MR = MC.

The profit maximising output in terms of the total revenue and the total costs, and the marginal revenue and the marginal costs is shown in Fig. 10.5.

Now you try it

If the extra revenue from selling an item is greater than the extra cost, would a profit maximising firm produce and sell it, or not?

If the extra cost of an item is greater than the extra revenue, does this mean that the firm is necessarily making a loss?

What do you think?

Why do you think it is important for firms to make a profit?

How else might you measure the success of a business apart from profits?

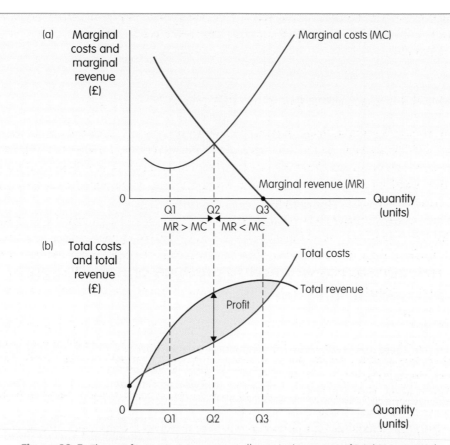

Figure 10.5 The profit maximising output, illustrated in terms of (a) the marginal revenue and the marginal costs, and (b) the total revenue and the total costs. The marginal costs fall up to Q1 and therefore the total costs rise at a decreasing rate. After Q1 the marginal costs increase, so the total costs increase at an increasing rate. At Q3 the marginal revenue is zero, so the total revenue does not increase. After Q3 the marginal revenue is negative, so the total revenue falls. Up to Q2 the marginal revenue is greater than the marginal costs, so by selling more the profits will increase. At Q2 the marginal revenue equals the marginal costs, so no extra profit can be generated; this means that profit is maximised. At output levels beyond Q2 the marginal revenue is less than the marginal costs, so the firm makes a loss on these extra units; profit would increase by cutting output back to Q2. The profit maximising output is Q2; this is also shown by the largest positive difference between the total revenue and the total costs.

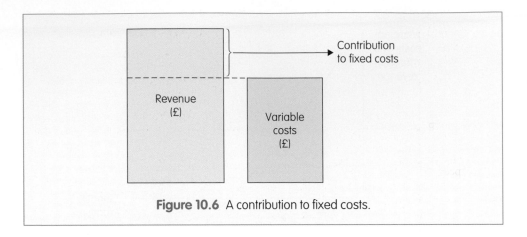

Figure 10.6 A contribution to fixed costs.

The decision of whether to produce or not: the short run and the long run

The short run

Given that there are fixed factors of production, in the short run this means that a firm must pay fixed costs even if output is zero. This means that the firm will lose an amount equal to the fixed costs even if it does not produce or sell anything. The decision of whether it is financially viable to produce will therefore depend on the variable costs (the costs incurred by producing, such as materials and components) because the fixed costs must be paid anyway. The fixed costs are 'sunk costs' and should not affect a decision about whether to continue to produce in the short run.

If the revenue earned from making and selling the units can at least cover the variable costs then this means that it is financially worth producing them. Anything earned over and above the variable costs is called a 'contribution'; it contributes towards the fixed costs. For example, if the revenue is £200 and the variable costs are £180 then there is a £20 contribution towards the fixed costs. Figure 10.6 shows a contribution being made to fixed costs. This does not mean that the firm necessarily makes a profit (this depends on the size of the fixed costs), but the loss will be less than it would be by not producing. (Remember that fixed costs must be paid anyway.) For example, imagine that the fixed costs are £100. If the firm does not produce then it makes a loss of £100. If it does produce then it gains a £20 contribution towards the fixed costs and so its losses are only £80. This means that it is better to produce than not to produce. The firm should therefore continue in production even though it makes a loss, because the revenue at least covers the variable costs. When the revenue just equals the variable costs, the loss will be the same whether producing or not producing. This is known as the shut down point. If the revenue is less than the variable costs then the firm should not produce. For example, if the revenue is £150, the variable costs are £180 and the fixed costs are £100, then by producing the firm will make a loss of £130. Not only are fixed costs being paid, but there is also another £30 of variable costs that cannot be covered by the revenue. In this situation the firm would reduce its loss by not producing.

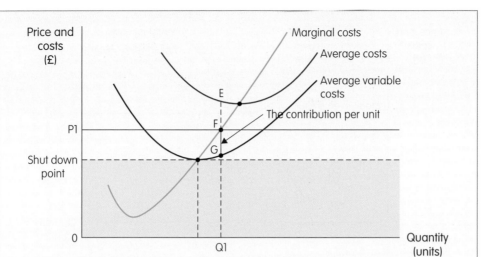

Figure 10.7 A supply curve and the shut down price. At Q1 the average fixed cost (which is the difference between the average cost and the average variable cost) is EG. By producing a loss is made. The loss per unit is shown by EF (where the price is below the average cost). However, this loss is less than if the firm did not produce because it would still pay the fixed costs in the short run. By producing the firm contributes FG per unit toward the fixed costs. The firm will not produce if the price is less than the average variable cost.

So, in the short term a firm should produce provided that its revenue at least covers its variable costs.

This analysis can also be undertaken on a 'per unit' level. If the price per unit more than covers the variable costs per unit then the sale generates a contribution per unit that can be put towards the fixed costs, and so production should continue. If the price per unit cannot cover the variable cost per unit then, not only do fixed costs have to be paid, but variable costs cannot be covered either, so the firm should shut down.

Thus, in the short run we have the following two possibilities.

- A firm should produce if the price is greater than the average variable costs. This means that a contribution is being made towards the fixed costs and so production should continue. Even if a loss is made then it is less than the loss that would be made if the firm shut down and still had to pay the fixed costs.

- A firm should not produce if the price is less than the average variable costs. This means that the firm cannot pay its variable costs and has fixed costs to pay as well. The firm should shut down. The shut down point is illustrated in Fig. 10.7.

The long run

In the long run a firm will not continue producing at a loss. It is not constrained by resources and so is not committed to fixed costs. The firm will only produce if all of its costs can be covered and at least a normal profit is made.

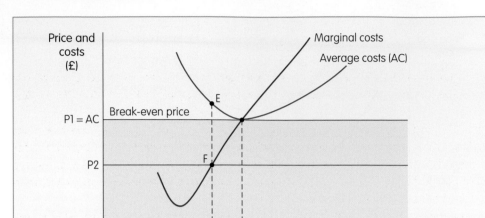

Figure 10.8 A supply curve and the break-even price. The firm will not produce below the price that equals the minimum of the average costs curve because then a loss would be made. For example, at P2 the loss per unit is EF (the price is less than the average costs). In the long run the firm will not produce if the price is below P1 as a loss is made.

Looking at this on a 'per unit' level, this means that the price per unit needs to be at least equal to the average cost per unit. If the price was less than the average cost then this means that a loss is made on each unit, and so the firm would not produce.

The break-even point is illustrated in Fig. 10.8.

Table 10.4 defines some of the key terms used in this unit.

Table 10.4 Summary table of key terms.

Term	Description
Total cost	= Fixed cost + Variable cost
Marginal cost	Extra cost of an additional unit, $= \dfrac{\text{Change in total cost}}{\text{Change in output}}$
Total revenue	Income earned from sales, $= \text{Price} \times \text{Quantity sold}$
Marginal revenue	Extra revenue from selling an extra unit, $= \dfrac{\text{Change in total revenue}}{\text{Change in the number of units sold}}$
Profit	= Total revenue − Total cost

Case Study

Increasing oil prices in 2005 helped Royal Dutch Shell to announce what was then a record annual profit for a UK-listed company. The Anglo–Dutch energy company made profits of $22.94 billion (£13.12 billion) in 2005.

The results came after a year in which the price of crude oil increased from under $45 per barrel to over $70. The majority of Shell's profits come from finding and extracting oil, and then selling it on to other firms. Very little profit comes from sales of petrol in garages; petrol is heavily taxed. Even so, pressure groups demanded that Shell reduce its prices. In 2005, Shell's profit was the equivalent of 104 300 Ferrari F430 coupés and 67 000 average UK homes.

The chief executive of Shell said that the profits would give the company 'a solid platform to build on'. The company announced that it would continue to invest heavily in new energy technologies, but some analysts think that even more needs to be diverted into this area. Shell's reserve-replacement ratio, which measures the capacity that a firm has to replace pumped oil with new oil, was 70–80%. Firms usually aim for a rate of more than 100%. In 2004, Shell's reserve-replacement ratio was less than 50%, which led to criticism from its investors.

The week before Shell's results, the American oil business Exxon Mobil announced a profit of over $33 billion, the biggest so far in corporate history. Some investors were therefore slightly disappointed with Shell's results.

In December, Shell had cut its plans for North Sea exploration, claiming that it was not viable given the Chancellor's tax increases for the move. Rather than hire three drilling rigs, this was cut to two after the UK government increased its tax on the company's profits from 10% to 20%. Instead, Shell was focusing on other areas of the world to drill in, and in November it started pumping oil from a new oil field off the Nigerian coast.

❓ Questions

- Using supply and demand analysis, illustrate why the price of oil might have increased so much.
- Why do firms often seek to make profits? What will Shell do with its profits?
- What factors influence the success of an oil business such as Shell?
- Why would an economist calculate Shell's profits differently?

Checklist

Now you have read this unit try to answer the following questions.

☐ Can you explain the difference between revenues and costs?

☐ Can you outline the difference between marginal and total revenue?

☐ Can you explain the difference between marginal and total costs?

☐ Can you explain the difference between normal and abnormal profits?

☐ Do you understand the difference between profits and profitability?

☐ Can you explain the output level at which firms profit maximise?

☐ Can you identify the price at which firms will stop producing in the short run? In the long run? Can you explain why?

End of unit questions

1 If the output of a firm was zero units, would its total costs equal its variable costs?

2 Do you think that labour is a fixed or a variable cost?

3 If the marginal cost is positive but falling, what is happening to the total costs?

4 If a firm is profit maximising, why is it impossible for the marginal revenue to be greater than the marginal cost?

5 In 2005, the oil company Shell made profits of over £13 billion. Do you think this is an acceptable level of profit or not?

Key learning points

• Profit is the difference between total revenue and total cost.

• There is a difference between an economist's view of profit and an accountant's view of profit.

• Profit is maximised at an output for which the marginal revenue equals the marginal cost.

• Normal profit occurs when the total revenue equals the total cost.

• Abnormal profit occurs when the total revenue is greater than the total cost.

• In the short run a firm will only produce if the price is equal to or greater than the average variable cost.

• In the long run a firm will only produce if the price is equal to or greater than the average cost.

Learn more

The relationship between short-run and long-run costs can be analysed in more detail using iso-quants. To learn more about this visit our website at the address below.

 Visit our Online Resource Centre at www.oxfordtextbooks.co.uk/orc/gillespie_econ for test questions and further information on topics covered in this chapter.

Perfect competition

An important part of economic analysis is to consider how firms behave in different types of markets and the impact of this on consumers. Perfect competition is one form of market structure. In this unit we examine the features of a perfectly competitive market and the consequences of this form of market structure in terms of price, output and efficiency. In the following units we then examine other market structures and compare them with perfect competition.

LEARNING OBJECTIVES

By the end of this unit you should be able to:

✔ understand the key features of a perfectly competitive market;

✔ analyse the price and output decisions in the short run and the long run in a perfectly competitive market;

✔ explain why the supply curve is the marginal cost curve in perfectly competitive markets.

■ Why study market structure?

Not all markets are the same. Some are dominated by a few firms; some have many competitors in them. In this unit and the following three units we examine different types of market to consider how the structure affects firms and consumers within them. This is an important aspect of economic analysis because it helps us to decide whether one form of market structure is better than another, and this has implications for government policy. Microsoft dominates the PC market at the moment; is this desirable or should governments intervene to limit its power? By comparison, the market for fruit and vegetables in many countries is divided between hundreds of thousands of farmers; should the government intervene to encourage the growth of a few big farmers or not? Is it better to have one business responsible for delivering the mail or many? Is it dangerous or desirable to have a few firms dominating the sale of food, petrol, banking services and insurance in the UK, or should the government leave them to it? In the following units we consider these issues as well as thinking about why markets differ in the first place. There are many providers of kennels, there are thousands and thousands of pubs in the UK, and there are lots of hairdressers, plumbers and taxi firms. There are far fewer energy companies, airlines, private medical care firms and electrical goods retailers. In the following units we examine why this might be. We begin by analysing a market structure known as perfect competition.

■ Introduction to perfect competition

A perfectly competitive market is one in which:

- there are large numbers of buyers and sellers;
- products are homogeneous (i.e., exactly the same);
- there is perfect knowledge (so buyers know what all firms are charging and firms know what profits are being made in the industry);
- there is freedom of entry into and exit from the market, so that firms can easily move into and out of the market.

■ Perfectly competitive firms as price takers

In a perfectly competitive market there are many firms. One firm's output decisions cannot influence the overall market supply to any noticeable extent. If one firm changes its output level then this has such a small effect on the industry supply that the market price does not alter.

Each firm is therefore a 'price taker'; it is so small that its actions cannot influence the market price. The firm can sell as much as it wants without bringing down the market price. This means that every unit can be sold at the market price. For example, every unit can be sold at £10, so the extra revenue generated from a sale is the same as its price. This means that the marginal revenue is the price (P = MR), as shown in Fig. 11.1.

■ Short-run equilibrium in perfect competition

In the short run firms in perfect competition are able to make abnormal profits (when the price is greater than the average cost) or losses (when the price is less than the average cost). However, this situation will not continue in the long run.

If firms are making abnormal profits then this acts as a signal for other firms to enter the market to benefit from this. The entry of more firms will lead to more being supplied and will shift the industry supply curve to the right; this will reduce the market price. (Although one firm cannot shift the industry supply on its own, the entry of many firms

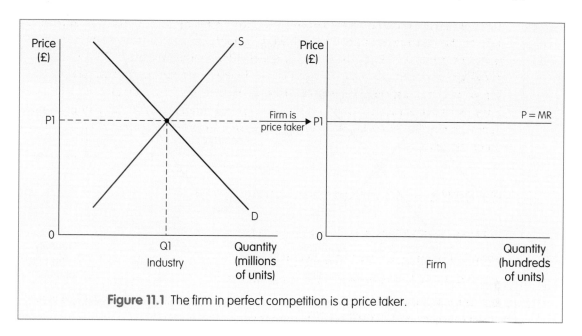

Figure 11.1 The firm in perfect competition is a price taker.

will shift the curve to the right.) This process will continue until only normal profits are being made (the price equals the average cost), as shown in Fig. 11.2. When normal profits are being made there is no incentive for more firms to enter or leave the industry.

If firms are making losses then this means that businesses will leave the industry. This shifts the industry supply curve to the left and increases the market price. This will continue until only normal profits are being made, as shown in Fig. 11.3. At this point there is no further incentive for firms to enter or leave the industry.

What do you think?

Why are the assumptions of perfect information, freedom of entry and exit, and a homogenous product important to reach the long-run equilibrium of normal profits in perfect competition?

Now you try it

Are normal profits earned in each of the following cases?

- Price equals average fixed cost.
- Price equals average variable cost.
- Price equals average total cost.
- Price equals average revenue.

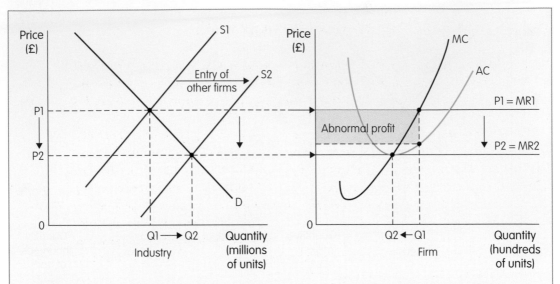

Figure 11.2 The adjustment process from short-run abnormal profits to long-run equilibrium in a perfectly competitive market. The firm is initially making abnormal profits when the price is P1. This attracts other firms into the industry, thereby shifting the industry supply curve to the right. With more firms in the industry the price falls until normal profits are made at P2.

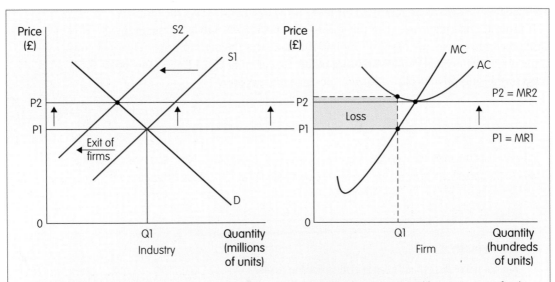

Figure 11.3 The adjustment process from short-run losses to long-run equilibrium in a perfectly competitive market. The firm originally makes a loss at the price P1 because this price is less than the average cost per unit. This leads to an exit of firms from the industry. The industry supply curve shifts to the left. This increases the price until only normal profits are made (P = AC). At this point there is no further incentive to leave the industry.

Long-run equilibrium in perfect competition

The long-run equilibrium in perfect competition is shown in Fig. 11.4. In the long run in perfect competition firms can only make normal profits. Assuming they are profit maximisers, they will produce when the marginal revenue equals the marginal costs (MR = MC) (see Unit 10).

Given that the firm is a price taker, the marginal revenue will equal the price (P = MR). This means that firms will produce when the price, the marginal revenue and the marginal cost are all equal. As a result, firms will be allocatively efficient. Allocative efficiency occurs when the extra benefit to society (as shown by the price that consumers are willing to pay) equals the extra costs, that is, the price equals the marginal cost. In the long-run equilibrium of perfect competition, firms are producing all of the units for which the price (which represents the extra benefit or utility to the consumer) is greater than the extra cost of producing it, up to the point where the extra benefit equals the extra cost. At this point the community surplus is maximised (see Unit 7).

In the long run firms in perfect competition are also productively efficient. Productive efficiency occurs when firms are producing at the minimum of the average cost curve; they have the lowest unit cost possible, and therefore they are not wasting resources.

To summarise, in the long run in perfect competition:

- firms earn normal profits;

- the industry is allocatively efficient (the price equals the marginal cost);

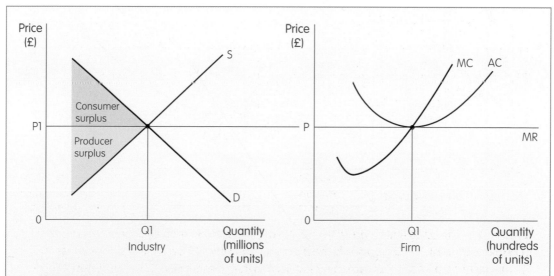

Figure 11.4 Long-run equilibrium in a perfectly competitive industry. In long-run equilibrium we have P = MR = MC = AC.

- the industry is productively efficient (firms are producing at the minimum of the average cost curve).

Now you try it

Imagine that a perfectly competitive market is in long-run equilibrium. If demand falls show the impact of this in the short run and the long run on both the industry and a firm.

■ Deriving the supply curve in perfect competition

The supply curve of a firm

A supply curve shows how much a firm is willing and able to produce at each and every price, all other things being unchanged. Assuming that a firm wants to profit maximise, it will produce when the marginal revenue equals the marginal cost (MR = MC). In perfect competition, because firms are price takers and every unit is sold at the same price, then the price equals the marginal revenue. As a result, firms will produce when the price equals the marginal costs (because the price equals the marginal revenue and the marginal revenue equals the marginal costs). Therefore, at any given price the marginal cost curve shows the quantity that will be supplied. This means that the marginal cost curve is the supply curve, as shown in Fig. 11.5.

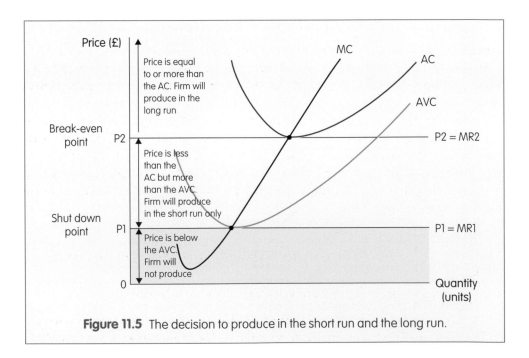

Figure 11.5 The decision to produce in the short run and the long run.

In the short run a firm will supply provided that the price is at least equal to the average variable cost (as this means that the revenue is at least making a contribution to the fixed costs), so the supply curve is the marginal cost curve above the minimum average variable cost.

In the long run a firm will only supply if the price covers the average costs (otherwise a loss would be made), so the supply curve is the marginal cost curve above the average cost curve.

The supply curve for the industry

The supply curve for the industry is the sum (or aggregate) of all the supply curves of the individuals firms. At each and every price the amount that each firm is willing and able to supply can be added together to give the quantity supplied by the industry.

■ Summary

Perfect competition may or may not exist in reality as a market structure, but it provides a benchmark against which to judge other forms of market. It highlights the benefits of competition and this may well influence government policy regarding helping start-up firms and limiting the power of firms to dominate an industry.

Case Study

Global cocoa production is over three million tonnes per year. The production of cocoa is undertaken by thousands of small producers in countries such as Ghana, the Ivory Coast and Cameroon. Although there are a few big farmers, almost 90% of production is by small producers with farms of less than five hectares.

These producers produce similar crops and have no power to control prices on the international markets. The world price is determined by the industry supply and the level of demand from the huge multinationals, such as CadburySchweppes and Mars. The small firms are often said to be exploited by the larger confectionery companies. Fair Trade organisations attempt to rectify this by guaranteeing a reasonable price for their crops. The underlying principle of Fair Trade is that the product must have been traded in such a way that:

- the primary producer gets a fair deal;
- the primary producer receives a proportion of the price in advance to enable them to pay for their inputs;
- the Fair Trade company enters into a long-term relationship with the supplier.

The Fair Trade Labelling Organisations International standard for cocoa outlines the calculation of Fair Trade cocoa prices. The prices are calculated on the basis of world market prices plus Fair Trade premiums.

? Questions

- What factors do you think determine the supply of cocoa?
- What factors do you think determine the demand of cocoa?
- Do you think that the price of cocoa is relatively stable or unstable? Why?
- In what ways is the market for cocoa like perfect competition? In what ways is it different?
- Do you think that the Fair Trade scheme is desirable? Why is it needed?

@ Web

For more information on Fair Trade visit www.fairtrade.org.uk

Checklist

Now you have read this unit try to answer the following questions.

- ☐ Do you understand the key features of a perfectly competitive market?
- ☐ Can you explain the price and output decisions in the short run and the long run in a perfectly competitive market?
- ☐ Can you explain why the supply curve is the marginal cost curve in perfectly competitive markets?

End of unit questions

1 Why are firms in perfect competition price takers?
2 Can firms in perfect competition make abnormal profits?
3 Why is the absence of barriers to entry an important assumption in perfect competition?
4 Why is the fact that firms offer homogeneous products an important assumption in perfect competition?
5 How is the supply curve in perfect competition derived?

Key learning points

- A firm in perfect competition is a price taker.
- In the short run, in perfect competition firms can make abnormal profits or losses.
- In the long run, due to the entry and exit of firms, only normal profits are made.
- In the long run, in perfect competition firms are allocatively and productively efficient.

Learn more

 Visit our Online Resource Centre at www.oxfordtextbooks.co.uk/orc/gillespie_econ for test questions and further information on topics covered in this chapter.

» 12 Monopoly

Monopoly is a very different form of market structure compared to perfect competition. This unit outlines the nature of a monopoly and examines the price, output and efficiency outcomes in this type of market. Governments are often concerned about the effects of monopoly power; in this unit we outline the arguments for and against monopoly power.

LEARNING OBJECTIVES

By the end of this unit you should be able to:

✔ explain the key features of a monopoly;

✔ explain the price and output decisions in a monopoly;

✔ discuss the efficiency of a monopoly;

✔ explain the theory of contestable markets.

■ Introduction to monopoly

A monopoly occurs when a firm dominates a market. This means that the firm determines the price in the market rather than accepting the industry price. It is a 'price maker' rather than a 'price taker'.

A 'pure' monopoly occurs when one firm has a market share of 100%; for example, in nationalised industries the government might only allow one state-owned firm to provide a particular service such as healthcare or electricity. More generally, a monopoly exists when a firm exerts a major influence over a market. Under UK law a monopoly occurs when a firm has a market share of 25% or more, that is, its sales are over 25% of the total sales in a market.

Demand and marginal revenue for a monopolist

A monopolist faces a downward-sloping demand curve. To sell more units it must lower the price. This involves lowering the price on the additional unit and on all of the units before. As a result the marginal revenue diverges from the demand curve (see Unit 10).

Price and output decisions in a monopoly

A monopolist is assumed to be a profit maximiser. This means that it produces when the marginal revenue equals the marginal cost (see Unit 10). In Fig. 12.1 this occurs at the price P2 and the quantity Q2.

At this price and quantity combination the firm will make an abnormal profit, that is, the price is greater than the average cost at that output. This means that the firm is earning more with its resources in this industry than it could earn with them elsewhere. This

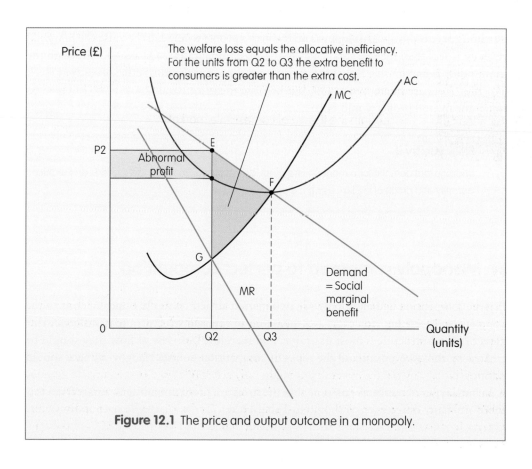

Figure 12.1 The price and output outcome in a monopoly.

abnormal profit will attract other firms into this industry from other sectors. They will want to shift resources into this industry to share the abnormal profits. However, unlike firms in a perfectly competitive industry, a monopolist can continue to make abnormal profits in the long run because it can prevent other firms from entering the market to erode its profits. This is because barriers to entry exist. (For more information on barriers to entry see Unit 15.)

Unlike the firms in the long-run equilibrium position in a perfectly competitive market, a monopoly is allocatively and productively inefficient.

It is allocatively inefficient because the price paid by consumers for a unit is greater than the marginal cost of providing it. Customers are paying more for the last unit of the product than the extra cost of producing it. Society would like more units to be produced and sold.

For the units from Q2 to Q3 the extra benefit of these units to society (as shown by the price the consumer is willing to pay) exceeds the extra cost of providing them. Therefore, if these units were produced then society's welfare would increase. The monopoly price and quantity outcome has led to a welfare loss. The triangle EFG in Fig. 12.1 is a welfare loss area that exists because the firm is allocatively inefficient.

A monopolist is also productively inefficient because the firm is not producing at the minimum average cost. To benefit from the lowest possible average costs the firm would have to sell more and produce at Q3. This would involve reducing the price because the demand curve is downward sloping and the firm's profits would fall (because the marginal revenue is less than the marginal cost on these additional Q3 – Q2 units). Although the monopolist is maximising its profits, it is not producing at the most efficient output level. The unit costs are minimised at Q3, but because the price would have to be lowered so much the overall profits would fall.

Now you try it

Imagine that demand for a monopolist's products increased. Show the effect of this on the price, quantity and profits of the firm using a diagram.

▨ Monopoly compared to perfect competition

Perfect competition and monopoly are two market structures at the opposite ends of the competitive spectrum. However, a comparison of the two structures may influence our view of which structure is most desirable, and therefore our view of how they should be treated by the government and the types of competition policies the government should adopt.

In both types of market we assume that the firms are profit maximisers. Apart from this there are many differences, as shown in Table 12.1.

Table 12.1 A comparison of perfect competition and monopoly.

	Perfect competition	Monopoly
Price taker	Yes	No
Barriers to entry	No	Yes
Long-run abnormal profits	No	Yes
Differentiated product	No	Yes
Allocatively efficient	Yes	No
Productively efficient	Yes	No

Now you try it

Can you remember the following?

- The profit maximising condition.
- The condition for allocative efficiency.
- The condition for productive efficiency.
- The difference between normal and abnormal profits

▮ Should we prevent monopolies?

There is much debate regarding monopolies. Some commentators argue that they need to be regulated and controlled due to the following reasons.

- They can abuse their market power to restrict their output and force up prices for the customer relative to a perfectly competitive situation. Given that there are limited substitutes available, the customer may be forced to pay more than he or she would in a competitive market.

- The lack of competition in a market may reduce the pressure on firms to innovate and be efficient. This may lead to a cutback in research and development spending, and less new product development.

- According to Leibenstein (1966), a monopoly situation leads to 'X inefficiency'; with less competitive pressure on firms due to barriers to entry, costs will drift upwards and this wastes resources. This means that costs in a monopoly may be higher than in a competitive market, and so monopolies are bound to be inefficient.

If monopolies do behave in the ways described above then a government may want to prevent them occurring. If they already exist it may want to regulate them.

In the UK the Competition Commission has the powers to:

- prevent takeovers or mergers that would lead to a monopoly position if it can show that it would act against the public interest;
- investigate any firm with more than 25% market share and force it to sell off parts of its business or reduce its prices.

@ **Web**

For more information on the Competition Commission and its cases visit **www.competition-commission .org.uk**

However, the following are some arguments in favour of monopolies.

- A firm may have achieved its monopoly position because it is so innovative and/or so efficient. In this case splitting it up would work against the public interest. Most governments allow firms to protect inventions with patents. These are intended to reward innovation and encourage other firms to develop new products and new ways of doing things. The patent system highlights that governments think monopoly power can be justified in certain circumstances.

- As a monopoly firm dominates the industry it may be bigger than any individual business in a more competitive industry. This means that it is more likely to benefit from internal economies of scale. Its unit costs may be lower than they would be for firms in a competitive market. This could lead to lower prices and higher output than in a competitive market situation.

- The ability to make monopoly profits provides dominant firms with the funds they need to invest in more research and development. As a result, they can afford to take risks and invest in more long-term research and development projects than firms in a competitive industry. This may lead to greater efficiency and more choice for customers.

- Any abnormal profits that are made will either be invested in the business or paid out to shareholders in the form of dividends. These shareholders will often be individuals or financial institutions, such as insurance companies and pension funds. This means that the abnormal profits of monopolies may be redistributing money from customers to investors. The money is not disappearing from society altogether, it is simply moving from one group to another.

- The fact that monopolies can make high levels of profits is an incentive for other firms to be innovative and to establish a monopoly position. This is known as the Schumpeter effect (named after Joseph Schumpeter). Monopoly profits may therefore encourage innovation as other firms try to gain control of a market for themselves. This was described as 'the perennial gale of creative destruction' by Schumpeter. Barriers to entry may exist at some point, but new firms will find ways of overcoming these to gain from the abnormal profits, that is, by creating new markets to replace the old ones. Monopoly profits therefore act as a beacon to encourage the development of new products and new ways of doing things, and this stimulates economic growth.

What do you think?

According to Schumpeter (1942), 'The fundamental impulse that sets and keeps the capitalist engine in motion comes from the new consumers, goods, the new methods of production or transportation, the new markets, the new forms of industrial organisation that capitalist enterprise creates.' What major developments in markets, technology, transportation or methods of production have occurred in your lifetime?

- In some cases the existence of a monopoly may rectify another market failure. For example, in a freely competitive market firms may create negative externalities such as pollution, and overproduce relative to the socially optimal position. A monopoly, by comparison, may cut back on output, which in this case might move the economy nearer to the socially desirable level of output. Given that the First-Best World (where there are no market failures and imperfections occur) does not exist and therefore we are operating in the Second-Best World, a monopoly may actually be desirable in some circumstances.

- Monopolies might prevent wasteful duplication. For example, if there are several gas, telecommunications, electricity or railway companies then they might simply be investing in unnecessary infrastructure that duplicates the resources of other firms.

What do you think?

Should monopolies be allowed? What do you think is the best way of regulating them?
Intel is the world's largest producer of computer processors. Do you think that governments should allow Intel to be this big?

■ Contestable markets

Traditional economic theory examines monopolies in terms of the existing market share of the dominant firm in an industry, that is, it focuses on whether a firm has a market share of over 25%. However, the theory of contestable markets considers the likelihood that other firms will enter the market in the future. This recognises that a firm that has 25% of a market with no threat of others entering is in a very different position than a firm that has 25% of a market with a high threat of others joining. In the former situation the established firm is indeed in a strong position and there is the possibility of sustained long-term abnormal profits. In the latter situation short-term abnormal profits are likely to attract more firms into the industry, and this will compete away the abnormal profits over time. To avoid this happening the established firm may deliberately avoid profit maximising in the first place.

In a **perfectly contestable market** the costs of entry and exit are zero, so any abnormal profits could quickly be eradicated by others coming in and competing them away. The threat of this happening will mean that the existing firm will:

- keep prices down so that only normal profits are made;
- have to be as efficient as possible so that entrants could not come in and undercut them.

The theory of contestable markets highlights the dynamic nature of monopolies and the importance of barriers to entry in terms of influencing monopoly behaviour.

Case Study

In 2004 Microsoft, the software giant, was fined €497 million by the European Commission under its anti-competitive legislation. This followed a five year investigation into the way Microsoft behaved. Following the investigation the company had to make elements of its programming more openly available to allow others to produce software that was compatible. At the time Microsoft had about 90% of the market for PC operating systems. It held cash of around $50 billion. Microsoft was accused of bundling its own programmes together and making it difficult for other software manufacturers to be compatible with its Windows system. Microsoft had to offer its operating system without its own MediaPlayer already installed and it had to make its codes available.

Rival software firms, such as Sun Microsystems, claimed that the punishment would lead to lower prices, greater competition and greater variety for consumers. Microsoft, however, claimed that the decision would actually harm customers. Others felt that Microsoft was being penalised for simply competing aggressively and that it might lead to less innovation in the market. This was the highest fine that the European Commission had imposed at that point. Previously the record had been €462 million, which had been imposed on the pharmaceutical group Roche after a scandal involving price fixing in the vitamin pills market.

According to the European Commissioner, 'Dominant companies have a special responsibility to ensure that the way they do business doesn't prevent competition . . . and does not harm consumers and innovation.'

❓ Questions

- Why was Microsoft fined by the European Commission?
- Do you think that the European Commission was right to fine Microsoft?
- Do you think that dominant firms have special responsibilities?

Checklist

Now you have read this unit try to answer the following questions.

- ☐ Can you explain the key features of a monopoly?
- ☐ Can you explain the price and output decisions in a monopoly?
- ☐ Can you discuss the efficiency of a monopoly?
- ☐ Do you understand the significance of barriers to entry in markets?
- ☐ Can you explain the theory of contestable markets?

End of unit questions

1   What determines the profit maximising price and output for a monopolist?

2   Can monopolies make abnormal profits in the long run?

3   What barriers to entry might exist in the car industry?

4   Why does the marginal revenue curve in a monopoly lie below and diverge from the demand curve?

5   Are monopolies good or bad for the economy?

Key learning points

- • A monopoly is a dominant firm in an industry.
- • In a monopoly it is possible to earn abnormal profits, even in the long run, due to barriers to entry.
- • A monopolist faces a downward-sloping demand curve; the marginal revenue curve is below the demand curve and diverges from the demand curve.
- • In the long run monopolies may be allocatively and productively inefficient.
- • Barriers to entry enable firms to make abnormal profits, even in the long run.
- • When analysing the market it may be important to consider the possibility of entry in the future as well as the existing levels of competition.

References

Leibenstein, H. (1966). Allocative efficiency and *X*-efficiency. *The American Economic Review*, 56, 392–415.

Schumpeter, J. A. (1942). *Capitalism, socialism and democracy*. Harper & Row, New York.

Learn more

 Visit our Online Resource Centre at www.oxfordtextbooks.co.uk/orc/gillespie_econ for test questions and further information on topics covered in this chapter.

Oligopoly

So far we have examined the market structures of perfect competition and monopoly. Another type of market is oligopoly. This has elements of monopoly power but also involves some degree of competition. An oligopoly is a relatively common form of market structure and therefore an important one to study and understand. In particular, governments are interested in the impact of an oligopoly on price and output, and whether there is a need for intervention.

LEARNING OBJECTIVES

By the end of this unit you should be able to:

✔ explain the meaning of an oligopoly;

✔ understand the significance of interdependence in an oligopoly;

✔ outline different models of behaviour in an oligopoly;

✔ explain the meaning of cartels.

■ Introduction

An oligopoly occurs when a few firms dominate a market. This is a common occurrence in the UK; for example, the car industry, the petrol market, the airline industry, the banking sector and the supermarket sector are all oligopolies. In these industries the largest few firms have a large market share. Economists often measure the four or five firm **concentration ratio**; this shows the combined market share of the largest four or five firms.

What do you think?

Figure 13.1 illustrates the market share of the UK's leading food retailers.

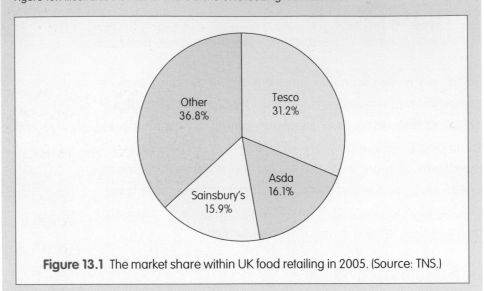

Figure 13.1 The market share within UK food retailing in 2005. (Source: TNS.)

The main supermarkets have a large share of the grocery market in the UK. Do you think this matters? Why?

The market share of the main supermarkets in the UK has been increasing. What significance do you think this has for suppliers and customers?

How might the UK government intervene to reduce the supermarkets' market share?

Oligopolies are particularly interesting markets to analyse because the firms involved are interdependent. The actions of one business will clearly affect the others. As a result of this interdependence, oligopolistic firms have to decide on how they want to behave in relation to others in a market. In a monopoly one firm dominates and so it does not have

Competitive ←		→ Uncompetitive	
Perfect competition	Monopolistic competition	**Oligopoly**	Monopoly
Many firms producing identical products	Many firms producing differentiated products	**A few firms dominating a market**	A single firm dominating a market

Figure 13.2 Different forms of market structure.

to consider what others might do; in perfect competition and monopolistic competition there are so many other firms that it is impossible to take into account how they might all react. Only in an oligopoly is the number of firms competing so few that decisions have to be made regarding how to work with them. For example, before cutting the price of its major brands Cadbury's will consider how Nestlé might react. The relationship between oligopoly and other forms of market structure is shown in Fig. 13.2.

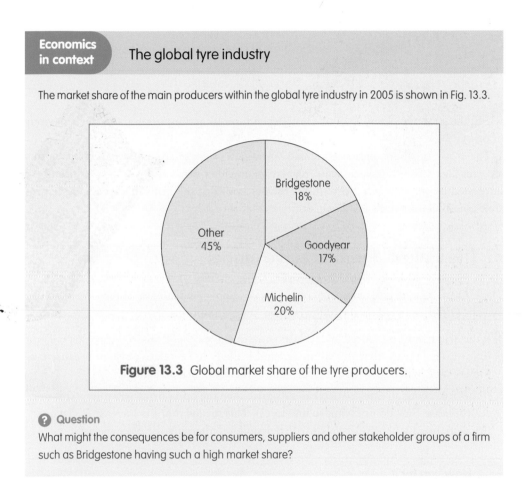

Economics in context

The global tyre industry

The market share of the main producers within the global tyre industry in 2005 is shown in Fig. 13.3.

Figure 13.3 Global market share of the tyre producers.

? Question

What might the consequences be for consumers, suppliers and other stakeholder groups of a firm such as Bridgestone having such a high market share?

One strategy that the major firms in an oligopoly might adopt is for all those involved to join together and act as if they were a monopoly. When this happens it is called a cartel; the firms collude to set the price and agree how much each one is going to produce (this is called a quota). Alternatively, the firms may decide to compete against each other, in which case this is likely to drive prices down. In between these two extremes of cartel and price war there are many different possible outcomes, depending on how firms decide to act. The range of options open to firms in oligopoly are shown in Fig. 13.4. The importance of the interdependence of firms has led to the development of game theory, in

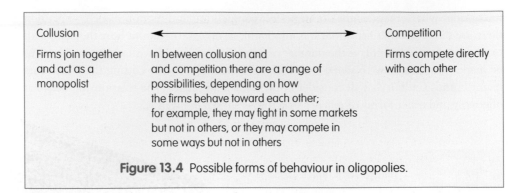

Figure 13.4 Possible forms of behaviour in oligopolies.

which the strategic planning of one firm depends on its assumptions about the behaviour of others.

The study of oligopolies is extremely important because so many markets have this structure; as a result, governments, regulators, member firms and would-be entrants are interested in knowing what determines the behaviour of the firms involved and the possible consequences of the different strategies that they adopt.

■ The kinked demand curve model

The kinked demand curve model of oligopoly developed by Hall and Hitch (1939) and by Sweezy (1939) is based on the following two key assumptions.

- If the firm being considered increases its price then the other firms in the market will not follow. This means that the fall in demand is likely to be relatively high because customers will switch to other firms; demand is therefore price elastic.

- If the firm being considered decreases its price then the other firms will follow this price cut (because they do not want to lose sales). This means that the increase in the quantity demanded will be relatively small; demand will therefore be price inelastic.

Now you try it

Can you remember the following?

- The equation for the price elasticity of demand.

- The difference between price elastic demand and price inelastic demand.

These assumptions take a pessimistic view of how others might react (i.e., it assumes that you will not get away with a price cut and that if you increase price then you will be on your own!). Given these assumptions, the firm being examined is likely to leave price where it is. An increase in price will lead to such a fall in demand that the overall revenue will fall. A decrease in price will lead to such a small increase in sales that again revenue will fall. If revenue is going to fall whatever you do with the price then why not leave it where it is?

The kinked demand curve

The demand curve D2 in Fig. 13.5 is price inelastic; it assumes that a price change will have relatively little effect on the quantity demanded because any price change by one firm will be followed by the others, and so there will be little difference between them. By comparison, the demand curve D1 is price elastic (see Fig. 13.5); it assumes that a price change will have a relatively large effect on the quantity demanded because any price change by one firm will be not followed by the others, and so the difference between them is significant.

In the kinked demand curve model it is assumed that a price increase will not be followed—so D1 is relevant—but a price decrease will be followed—D2 is relevant. This gives the kinked demand curve indicated by the thicker line in Fig. 13.5.

The marginal revenue linked to this kinked demand curve is also indicated by a thicker line. You will notice a gap in this curve; marginal costs can move between F and G and the profit maximising output (where the marginal revenue equals the marginal costs) is still at the price P1 and the quantity Q1. This shows that costs can change without affecting the profit maximising price and quantity in this model of oligopoly.

The kinked demand curve that is derived from the two demand curves in Fig. 13.5 is shown in Fig. 13.6.

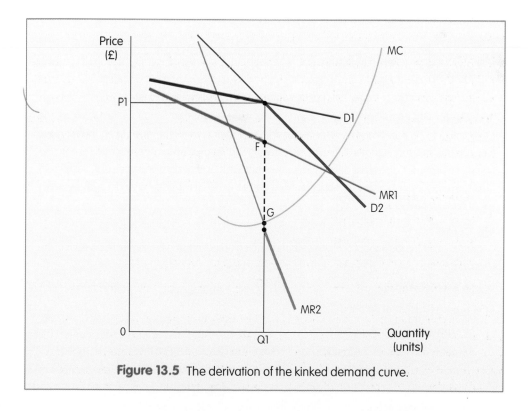

Figure 13.5 The derivation of the kinked demand curve.

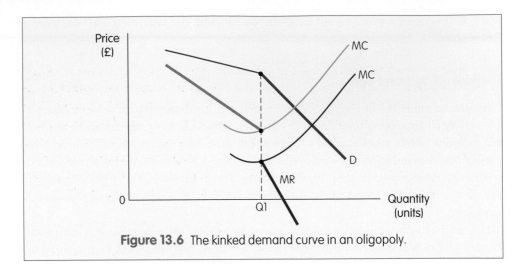

Figure 13.6 The kinked demand curve in an oligopoly.

The kinked demand curve model provides an explanation of why prices in oligopolistic markets are often 'sticky'—they do not change very much. Price competition is not common in many markets because it is relatively easy for a firm to copy another firm's price cut. Many firms prefer to try and differentiate their products, for example, by building a brand or developing some unique selling point and using this as a means of competing rather than the price. It is much more difficult for competitors to imitate a brand image than it is to copy a price cut.

Economics in context   Bottled water

In 2003, Evian, Highland Spring and Volvic had over 35% of the bottled water market. The top ten brands had 68% of sales in the same year.

Typically firms in this market spend around 1.5% of their revenue on advertising, pushing the value of the product in terms of health, rehydration and detoxification, and obviously promoting their own brands. Companies often try to link their brands to sports stars and particular lifestyles. In 2002, over £10 million was spent on promoting bottled water in advertising media such as television, radio or newspapers.

❓ Questions

What do you think the impact of high levels of spending on advertising is likely to be on each of the following?

• The level of demand.

• The price elasticity of demand.

• The cross price elasticity of demand.

How would you measure the impact of an increase in such spending on the level of demand?

◼ Cartels

A cartel occurs when the firms in an oligopoly work together to agree on the price and output that is set in a market. This agreement may be explicit (i.e., they formally agree) or implicit (i.e., both sides agree without anything actually being said or written down). The aim of a cartel is to maximise the profits of its members by restricting the amount available and pushing up price. Cartels may decide on who sells to who, and what the terms and conditions are, as well as price and output levels. Cartels also occur between countries as well as firms. OPEC (Organization of the Petroleum Exporting Countries) is a cartel of petroleum exporting countries and has a huge influence on the price of oil.

Economics in context   The Office of Fair Trading and price fixing

In 2004, the Office of Fair Trading (OFT) fined nine roofing contractors over £330,000 in total for having agreed to fix the prices of repair, maintenance and improvement services for flat roofing in the West Midlands.

On investigation, the OFT found that the contractors had reached agreement to set their tender prices so that when certain purchasers in the West Midlands area (a number of schools, a community library, a shopping centre and a car park) tendered for bids they were unable to obtain competitive prices.

The OFT operates a whistle-blowing policy to encourage businesses involved in illegal arrangements to come forward with information. In line with this policy, one contractor was granted 100% exemption from the fine and another one was given 50% exemption.

❓ Question

Can you think of any circumstances when a cartel might be acceptable?

What do you think?

What factors might influence whether a member of a cartel decides to 'blow the whistle'?

However, the basic problem with cartels is that it is in the interest of individual firms to cheat! By producing more than the amount agreed (the quota) with the other members of the cartel and selling at a slightly lower price, individual firms can make more profit at the expense of their 'associates'. On the other hand, if everyone is cheating then the market supply gets ever higher and this brings the price down; the group as a whole therefore ends up worse off. Cartels may therefore self-destruct even if it is in their interests to keep together.

In Fig. 13.7(a), the industry profit maximises at the price P1 and the quantity Q1. This determines the price and quantity that should be set. Each member of the cartel is given a

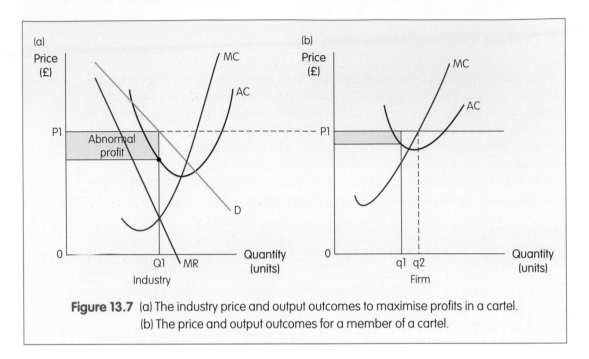

Figure 13.7 (a) The industry price and output outcomes to maximise profits in a cartel.
(b) The price and output outcomes for a member of a cartel.

quota, for example, q1 to be produced at the set price (see Fig. 13.7(b)). Each member is making an abnormal profit. However, the individual firm is not profit maximising; it would profit maximise when the price equals the marginal revenue at the quantity q2. Therefore there is an incentive to produce more to gain individually. However, if they all do this then it will drive up industry output and bring down the industry price, moving the industry as a whole away from its profit maximising position.

To make a cartel work it therefore requires the member firms to trust each other and, if necessary, to be able to check easily how much each member is producing and at what price. Policing the agreement becomes very important, otherwise it is likely to fall apart.

Economics in context   Cartel and price fixing

In 2003, the Office of Fair Trading (OFT) investigated allegations that schools acted illegally by exchanging information on each other's finances, salary increases and possible fee increases. The schools investigated included Eton, Winchester, Westminster and William Hulme's Grammar School, Manchester. Independent school fees in 2003 rose by 9% on average.

❓ **Question**
Why would schools want to exchange information on their fees?

What do you think?

What factors are likely to lead to a price fixing agreement occurring?

If you were the government, under what circumstance might you allow a price fixing agreement?

In the UK until 2001, manufacturers of certain products such as pharmaceuticals and books were allowed to set the price at which they were sold (this was called resale price maintenance). What arguments might have been used to justify such price fixing?

Under the Competition Act 1998 cartels in the UK are illegal. Any business found to be a member of a cartel can be fined up to 10% of its UK turnover. Under the Enterprise Act 2002 it is a criminal offence for individuals to dishonestly take part in the most serious types of cartels. Anyone convicted of the offence could receive a maximum of five years imprisonment and/or an unlimited fine.

■ Prisoners' dilemma

The *Prisoner's dilemma* is a famous model of game theory. In this model the decisions of a particular firm depend on what it thinks the others will do. It is called the *Prisoner's dilemma* because it is based on a scenario in which two thieves are arrested. You are interviewed separately and have to decide whether to confess or not to the crime. Your decision depends on what you think the other prisoner is going to do. Ideally you would both deny the charges and the police would not be able to prove anything. However, what if the other prisoner decides to confess to get lenient treatment? In this case the police would come down heavily on you. So should you confess just in case? But if you confess and the other prisoner does so as well then you will both be arrested; whereas if you had both said nothing then you could have got away with it. What you do depends on your view of what the other person is likely to do. This in turn depends on issues such as the degree of trust between you, the extent to which you feel you understand the other person, past behaviour and your assumptions about how rational they are.

In the economics version of this scenario there are two firms X and Y operating in a market. Each firm can decide to produce at a high level of output and sell it at a low price, or it can sell a low level of output at a high price. If they both restrict output then this is the most desirable situation because the limited amount available in the market generates high prices and profits for both. However, each firm will be worried that if it holds back then the other one will flood the market and win all the sales at a lower price. This suspicion is likely to lead both firms to flood the market because of their fear of what the other will do. The result is that the market price ends up extremely low because supply is so high, and they both do badly. If only they could trust each other and collude then they would do much better.

Table 13.1 shows the financial results of each possible outcome; the left-hand amount is the outcome for X and the right-hand amount is the outcome for Y. If they both

Table 13.1 A pay-off matrix for two firms.

		Firm Y output	
		High	Low
Firm X output	High	£1 million, £1 million	£3 million, £0
	Low	£0, £3 million	£2 million, £2 million

produce high levels of output then they will gain only £1 million each as prices will be very low with so much output; if they both restricted output then they could earn £2 million each. If one goes high whilst the other holds back, the former will win the market with lower prices and the latter will get nothing.

The interesting question here is: How could the firms get to agree to collude? One factor may be the track record of the different firms—have they stuck to their promises in the past? Secondly, is there a way of getting a commitment up front to show that they really want the agreement to work?

Price war

If the firms in an oligopolistic market do not agree to collude then they may compete. The most aggressive form of competition is a price war (also called predatory pricing) whereby one firm undercuts the others in an attempt to remove them from the market. The ability of a business to do this depends on how much the price needs to be cut and its own resources compared to the finances of its competitors. Although customers may benefit in the short term from lower prices in a price war, in the long term the firm that wins may exploit its market power and push up prices even higher than they were originally.

Economics in context   RealNetworks cuts price

In 2004, the media software firm RealNetworks halved the price of its music downloads in an attempt to boost its share of the online music market. The offer was for a limited period but was deliberately aimed at undercutting its main rival Apple. Its advertising campaign was 'Half the price of Apple. Welcome to freedom of choice.' The promotion was estimated to have cost the firm around £1 million.

? Question
What factors might a firm consider before starting a price war?

▪ Summary

Oligopolistic markets are very common. They involve a few dominant firms. The price and output outcomes in an oligopoly depend on the behaviour of the firms involved; this in turn can depend on their assumptions about what the other firms will be doing. Oligopolistic firms are often involved in complex strategic planning in which they try to determine what other firms might do.

Case Study

In 2006, it was announced that the market dominance of the major supermarkets was going to be investigated for the third time in seven years. Tesco, Asda, Sainsbury's and Morrisons control around 70% of the UK's £120 billion grocery market. The Office of Fair Trading wanted the Competition Commission to investigate how this power was being used. The concern was over the impact on other firms and on the amount of land held by these supermarkets. These firms hold a huge amount of land across the UK and this may prevent other businesses from setting up. If its findings showed that there were competition issues then the Competition Commission could force the supermarkets to sell off some of their stores. The supermarkets have come under scrutiny again because of the impact on local convenience stores. Between 2000 and 2004 over 7000 independent retailers were closed.

According to the Office of Fair Trading:

- the planning system made it expensive for new firms to enter the market;
- the major supermarkets' holdings of large areas of prime retail space prevented others from setting up;
- the supermarkets were so powerful that they could sell items below cost and distort competition.

The supermarkets claimed that there were high levels of competition in the grocery market and this benefits the consumer. According to Tesco, 'The consumer is the best regulator and there is room in a thriving market for anyone who satisfies the customer.' The Federation of Small Businesses welcomed the announcement by the Office of Fair Trading.

❓ Questions

- Explain why the Competition Commission might want to investigate the supermarkets.
- What might be the impact of the power of the supermarkets on their stakeholders?
- How might the supermarkets defend their market dominance?
- What do you think the government should do in a situation like this?

@ Web

For more information on the Office of Fair Trading visit www.oft.gov.uk

Checklist

Now you have read this unit try to answer the following questions.

☐ Can you explain the meaning of an oligopoly?

☐ Do you understand the significance of interdependence in an oligopoly?

☐ Can you outline different models of behaviour in an oligopoly?

☐ Can you explain the meaning of a cartel?

End of unit questions

1 In what ways does an oligopoly differ from perfect competition?

2 In what ways does an oligopoly differ from a monopoly?

3 Why is the kinked demand curve kinked?

4 What is meant by game theory?

5 Are firms in an oligopoly most likely to collude or compete?

Key learning points

• The price and outcome results in an oligopoly depend on the assumptions that are made regarding the way that firms behave toward each other (e.g., whether they compete or collude).

• Oligopoly highlights the significance of interdependence in business. One firm's decisions about how much to produce and what price to charge are linked to its assumptions about how other firms will behave.

References

Sweezy, P. M. (1939). Demand under conditions of oligopoly. *Journal of Political Economy*, 47, 568–73.

Hall, R. and Hitch, C. (1939). Price theory and business behaviour. *Oxford Economic Papers*, 2, 12–45.

Learn more

To learn out more about game theory and the strategies that firms might adopt visit our website at the address below. To learn more about non-price competition read unit 14.

 Visit our Online Resource Centre at www.oxfordtextbooks.co.uk/orc/gillespie_econ for test questions and further information on topics covered in this chapter.

»14 Monopolistic competition and non-price competition

We have now examined the following market structures: perfect competition, monopoly and oligopoly. Another form of market structure is monopolistic competition. In this unit we examine the features of monopolistic competition and the implications of this market structure for customers and firms.

LEARNING OBJECTIVES

By the end of this unit you should be able to:

✔ explain the key features of monopolistic competition;

✔ consider the efficiency of monopolistic competition;

✔ outline non-price forms of competition that are experienced in many markets;

✔ outline Porter's five forces analysis;

✔ understand how firms might try to influence these forces.

■ Introduction

Monopolistic competition occurs in a market when there are many firms competing and each one offers a differentiated product. There are, for example, many thousands of cafes and restaurants in the UK. Whilst they all compete in the same market there are differences between them; for example, they have different menus, different themes and different locations. These factors can influence your decision to choose between them; this means that the cafes involved have some control over their market and the ability to decide what prices to charge.

Firms in monopolistic competition face a downward-sloping demand curve. If they increase the price they will lose some customers to competitors; if they reduce prices they should gain customers from competitors. As in a monopoly, the marginal revenue is

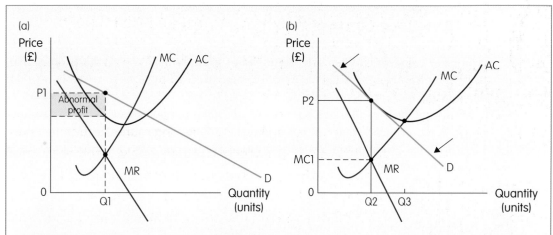

Figure 14.1 (a) Short-run abnormal profits in monopolistic competition. (b) Long-run normal profits in monopolistic competition. In the long run other firms enter the market, reducing demand for any individual firm until normal profits are made.

below the demand curve and diverging; to sell more the price has to be lowered on the last unit and all of the ones before.

Firms in monopolistic competition are assumed to be profit maximisers. This means that they will produce an output when the marginal revenue equals the marginal cost (see Fig. 14.1(a)). The difference between this type of market and a monopoly is that there are no barriers to entry. This means that if firms are making abnormal profits in the short run then this will attract other firms into the industry. This will cause the demand for any one firm's products to fall. It will cause an inward shift of the firm's demand curve until only normal profits are made (see Fig. 14.1(b)).

If losses were being made then firms would leave the industry and demand for a particular firm's products would increase until normal profits were made.

Now you try it

Draw a diagram that illustrates a firm in monopolistic competition making a loss in the short run and then, following the departure of other firms, it should show the firm making normal profits in the long run.

In the long run in monopolistic competition a firm is:

- allocatively inefficient because the price it charges is greater than the marginal cost (P2 > MC1 in Fig. 14.1(b));
- productively inefficient because the firm does not produce at the minimum of the average cost curve (Q2 not Q3 in Fig. 14.1(b)).

■ Non-price competition

Non-price competition obviously occurs when firms compete by methods other than using the price. Non-price competition is commonly used by firms to try to boost their demand and make it less price elastic.

Marketing involves all of the activities of a business to understand and fulfil customer needs. A famous marketing concept is known as the marketing mix or the four Ps (see Fig. 14.2). This describes the key elements in marketing that affect a customer's decision to purchase a product.

The four Ps are as follows.

- *The price*. This does not just involve the price but also the payment terms, for example, whether you can pay over time and how payments can occur.

- *The product*. This encompasses all of the different elements of a product, including the features, the specifications, the after-sales service and the brand. For example, Apple has long been admired for the design of its products. Dyson won a significant market share in the vacuum cleaner market with its innovative technology.

- *The promotion*. This includes all of the different ways in which a firm communicates about its product, such as advertising, the sales force, public relations activities and sales promotions (e.g. offers and competitions).

- *The place*. This refers to the distribution of the product, that is, how it gets to the market. For example, whether it is sold through wholesalers and retailers or direct to customers.

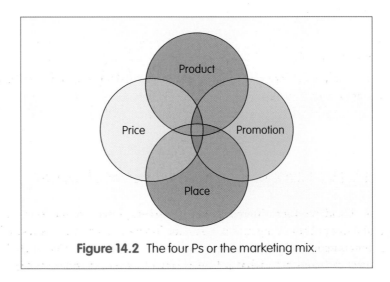

Figure 14.2 The four Ps or the marketing mix.

If a firm is not competing on price then it can use other elements of the marketing mix to win customers. For example, firms might do the following.

- Firms may use their promotional activities to develop a strong brand image. Companies such as Virgin, Microsoft, Nike and Coca Cola all have very strong brand names. Customers associate these names with certain values. This brand image has been created by the way the company advertises, the quality of its products, the way its employees behave and the type of sponsorships its undertakes. By differentiating their products firms may develop their customers' brand loyalty, that is, new entrants to the market will have to fight harder to get buyers to switch to them. Brand loyalty also means that the customer may be less sensitive to price (i.e., demand is more price inelastic) and that customers would be more likely to accept new products launched by a business. This can make their product launches cheaper and more likely to be successful.

What do you think?

How do you think the following brands differ?

- Pepsi and Coca Cola.
- French Connection and Next.
- Nike and Umbro.
- The Daily Telegraph and The Daily Mail.

- Firms may develop the product to create a unique selling point, that is, something that makes it stand out from the competition. This could be the recipe for the product or a special feature.
- Firms may develop more distribution channels to make the product more widely available and easier for customers to buy.

What do you think?

The markets for many consumer products are very competitive. Is it better to compete in these markets on price or using other factors?

■ Porter's five forces analysis of market structure

We have now considered four different types of market: perfect competition, monopoly, oligopoly and monopolistic competition. Each one has its own characteristics and its own price and output outcomes. A comparison of these helps us to predict what might happen in different markets and to consider what policies we might want to introduce as a government.

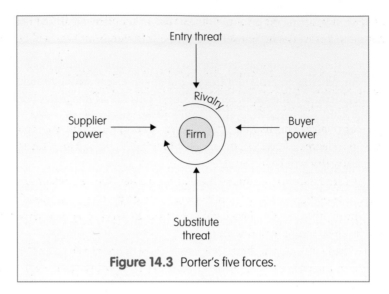

Figure 14.3 Porter's five forces.

In 1985 Michael Porter, a business analyst, produced his study of market structure. According to Porter the likelihood of making profits in an industry depends on the following five factors (see Fig. 14.3).

1 **The likelihood of new entry,** that is, the extent to which barriers to entry exist. The more difficult it is for other firms to enter a market, the more likely it is that existing firms can make relatively high profits. In a monopoly, for example, these would be high, whereas in a competitive market it would be easier to enter.

Economics in context   Audio novels

In 2006, the world's first audio-only novel was launched, responding to the fast growth of downloadable books. *Sex on Legs* was a 75 000 word novel written and read by Brian Luff, and was made available at www.audible.co.uk Mr Luff had no contract with a traditional book publisher. New technology has made the book 'publishing' industry much easier for anyone to enter.

 Question
Can you think of markets where sales via the Internet are high?

---

2 **The power of buyers.** The stronger the power of buyers in an industry, the more likely it is that they will be able to force down prices and reduce the profits of firms that provide the product. Buyer power will be higher if:
  • there are relatively few buyers;
  • the buyers can easily switch to other providers;
  • the buyers can threaten to take over the firm.

3 **The power of suppliers.** The stronger the power of suppliers to an industry, the more difficult it is for firms within that sector to make a profit. Suppliers will be more powerful if:
  • there are relatively few of them (so the buyer has few alternatives);
  • switching to another supplier is difficult and/or expensive;
  • the supplier can threaten to buy the existing firms.

4 **The degree of rivalry.** This measures the degree of competition between existing firms. The higher the degree of rivalry, the more difficult it is for existing firms to generate high profits. Rivalry will be higher if:
  • there are a large number of similar sized firms (rather than a few dominant firms);
  • the costs of leaving the industry are high (e.g., because of high levels of investment) and this means that existing firms will fight hard to survive because they cannot easily transfer their resources elsewhere;
  • the level of capacity underutilisation is high—if there are high levels of capacity being underutilised then the existing firms will be very competitive to try and win sales to boost their own demand.

5 **The substitute threat.** This measures the ease with which buyers can switch to another product that does the same thing, for example, aluminium cans rather than glass bottles.

Using Porter's analysis an industry is likely to generate higher returns if:

• the industry is difficult to enter;

• there is limited rivalry;

• buyers are relatively weak;

• suppliers are relatively weak;

• there are few substitutes.

On the other hand, returns are likely to be low if:

• the industry is easy to enter;

• there is a high degree of rivalry between firms within the industry;

• buyers are strong;

• suppliers are strong;

• it is easy to switch to alternatives.

The implication of Porter's analysis for managers of firms is that they should examine these five factors before choosing an industry to move into. They should also consider ways of changing the five factors to make them more favourable. For example:

• if firms merge together then this can reduce the degree of rivalry;

• if firms buy up distributors (this is called forward vertical integration) then they can gain more control over buyers;

• firms may differentiate their product, perhaps by trying to generate some form of unique selling proposition (USP) that makes it stand out from the competition.

The five forces will change over time as market conditions alter. For example, the Internet has made it easier for customers to compare prices, and therefore this increases buyer power in many markets, including travel and consumer products such as fridges and televisions. The Internet has also made it easier for producers to access customers, making it easier to enter many markets, such as finance, book retailing and clothes retailing. As ever, the business world is not static and the conditions in any industry will always be changing to some extent.

Case Study

The chocolate market in the UK is dominated by the three large international companies Cadburys, Mars and Nestlé, who together account for approximately 75–80% of the retail market in chocolate confectionery.

This, however, is not unusual; with the process of globalisation of markets and concentration having taken place throughout the world, in common with international markets in general, it is the case that most domestic markets for volume sales of chocolate confectionery are concentrated into a few large companies. There are concerns about the diminution of competitive pressures that this causes, but it is still the case that in the UK, as well as elsewhere, there is ongoing market competition and market opportunities. On the one hand, competition between the three large companies ensures that their products remain innovative, strongly promoted and keenly priced. On the other hand, there are continuing opportunities for smaller companies operating in niche markets, such as organic, low fat and other quality aspects of chocolate products.

Chocolate manufacturers attract and keep customers through promotion as follows.

- The manufacturers expand product ranges to meet consumers needs—for example, to meet the recent trend in demand for low fat, reduced calorie or sugarless products.
- The manufacturers use brand promotion or branding, creating a brand identity so that the brand name is recognised and understood immediately.
- Price competition ensures that the manufacturers' products offer excellent value for money compared with others, including snacks.
- The manufacturers use generic promotion, such as the ICCO/CFC project in Japan that focused on the health benefits of cocoa rather than an individual product.
- The manufacturers look for new and emerging markets, such as Asia and Eastern Europe, where chocolate consumption is low and there is potential growth.

The following are examples of the use of promotion in the chocolate market.

- Attitudes can be changed by promotion. The Chocolate Manufacturers Association of the USA strategy for promotion included: reminding consumers that chocolate fits into a healthy, happy lifestyle; maintaining a positive media atmosphere for chocolate; promoting health information on chocolate to the media; and promoting chocolate to the retail trade.
- Various promotions and surveys have taken place, aimed at people's perceptions and attitudes toward giving, receiving and eating boxed chocolate.

- Spain has seen a fall in exports and in domestic consumption due to a change in consumer habits. The promotional campaign had the slogan 'Life is short, let's make the most of it, let's learn to appreciate the full flavour of chocolate.'

- In Italy, manufacturers have benefited from a boom period with increasing chocolate consumption, and it has had various campaigns promoting the taste of chocolate, its mood-enhancing and energy-giving properties, and its efficacy against allergies, migraines and cholesterol. Producers are looking to play upon its nutritional qualities in future campaigns.

For further information on the Chocolate market please see the following articles.

Graham, L. (1997). What's going on in chocolate consumption and promotion in the United States. International Cocoa Organization, CC/14/4.

International Cocoa Organisation (1998). Faire campagne pour le chocolat. (On the campaign trail for chocolate.) *Plantations, Recherche, Développement*, 5 (5), 371. www.icco.org

International Cocoa Organisation (1999). Boxed chocolate—campaign for boxed chocolate in its second year. *The Manufacturing Confectioner*, 79 (5), 30–1. www.icco.org

❓ Questions

- Outline the ways in which chocolate companies compete through non-price competition.

- What niches do you think exist in the chocolate market?

- Do you think that such non-price competition is desirable?

- How competitive do you think the chocolate market really is?

- What do you think are substitutes for chocolate?

Checklist

Now you have read this unit try to answer the following questions.

☐ Can you explain the key features of monopolistic competition?

☐ Are you able to consider the efficiency of monopolistic competition?

☐ Can you outline non-price forms of competition that are experienced in many markets?

☐ Do you understand Porter's five forces model?

End of unit questions

1 How does monopolistic competition differ from perfect competition?

2 How efficient are firms in monopolistic competition?

3 What forms of non-price competition are common in the soft drinks market?

4   What are Porter's five forces? How do they affect the structure of an industry?

5   How can firms try to influence the five forces?

Key learning points

- In markets that are monopolistically competitive there are many competitors, but each firm attempts to differentiate its products.

- In monopolistic competition firms face a downward-sloping demand curve.

- In the short run firms in monopolistic competition may make a loss or abnormal profit; in the long run firms make normal profits due to entry and exit.

- Price changes are relatively easy for competitors to follow and therefore firms often use non-price methods of competing, such as advertising.

- The structure of a market may be analysed using Porter's five forces analysis.

Learn more

 Visit our Online Resource Centre at www.oxfordtextbooks.co.uk/orc/gillespie_econ for test questions and further information on topics covered in this chapter.

Barriers to entry and price discrimination

In the previous few units we have examined different market structures. For firms to make abnormal profits in a market in the long run, barriers to entry must exist. This unit outlines different barriers to entry that can exist. It also examines the way that firms can use their monopoly power to charge different prices to different customer groups, and this is known as price discrimination.

LEARNING OBJECTIVES

By the end of this unit you should be able to:

✔ understand the meaning and significance of barriers to entry;

✔ be able to explain the different forms of barrier to entry;

✔ explain the meaning of price discrimination;

✔ outline the conditions for effective price discrimination;

✔ analyse the benefits of price discrimination.

▉ Introduction to barriers to entry

The monopoly power of a firm or group of firms can only be sustained if there are barriers to entry. Otherwise any abnormal profits that they earn will be competed away by new firms entering the market. Firms that operate within a market with barriers to entry are protected from the effects of competition and the impact of this on price and output. In some cases the barriers may exist because the government has granted exclusive rights to provide a service. In other instances firms will set out themselves to devise ways of preventing others from coming in. In its competition policy a government must decide whether barriers to entry do exist in a market and whether customers suffer as a result. Even if barriers to entry do exist, they can be removed or reduced over time; for example,

Table 15.1   Companies with the most patents registered in the US in 2004.

	IBM	Matsushita	Canon	HP
Number of patents	3248	1934	1805	1775

with the signing of treaties opening up new markets or with new technology making it easier or cheaper to enter a market.

Types of barrier to entry include the following.

1 *Legislation*

A firm's monopoly power may be protected by law. For example, it may gain a patent. This prevents other firms from making, using or selling its inventions for a given period.

It generally takes three to five years to obtain a patent. Patent protection gives firms twenty years of protection. IBM spends over $5 billion per year on research and development to develop its products and new technology (see Table 15.1). It earns over $1.2 billion by licensing its intellectual property, for example, selling the rights to use its technology.

Alternatively, barriers to entry exist if a government controls an industry itself and passes legislation to prevent other firms from competing in it.

Economics in context

Registering a patent

The following is information from the Patent Office.

To be patentable your invention must be the following.

* *Be new*. The invention must never have been made public in any way, anywhere in the world, before the date on which an application for a patent is filed.

* *Involve an inventive step*. An invention involves an inventive step if, when compared with what is already known, it would not be obvious to someone with a good knowledge and experience of the subject.

* *Be capable of industrial application*. An invention must be capable of being made or used in some kind of industry. This means that the invention must take the practical form of an apparatus or device, a product such as some new material or substance, or an industrial process or method of operation.

❓ Question

What do you think are the benefits of the patent system?

@ Web

For more information on the Patent Office visit **www.patent.gov.uk**

2 *The learning effect*

Existing firms have the benefit of experience when operating in an industry. They know what to do, how to do it, how not to do it, and how to put things right. They have the contacts and an understanding of what works and what does not work. This means that they will benefit from this experience and tasks can be completed more effectively and efficiently. This makes it more difficult for new entrants to compete. Remember when you first learnt to drive how difficult it was and yet now you can change gears without even thinking. A learner driver will find it difficult to compete with your skill. The same is true when a firm considers entering a new market; it must be aware of the expertise of those already in it and how this can give them a competitive advantage.

3 *Technology*

Existing firms may have a technological advantage that new entrants cannot easily imitate. This may be a way of producing or organising things that others do not know how to imitate.

4 *Internal economies of scale*

If there are high levels of economies of scale in an industry then those firms that are producing on a larger scale will have much lower unit costs than new entrants, who are likely to be producing on a smaller scale. This will make it more difficult for new firms to make a profit, and therefore they may not be able to afford to enter the market. In this situation a firm is most likely to enter the market and focus on a niche; this enables it to charge a higher price for a specialist product. It will be difficult to enter a market that has a high minimum efficient scale (MES) relative to demand and there is a significant cost disadvantage in operating below the MES (see Unit 9).

5 *Entry costs*

The initial costs of starting up in an industry can be high, for example, to buy equipment or to promote the product nationally. This can make entry prohibitive for small firms. For example, imagine the costs involved in establishing a national network (or even an international network) for a mobile phone operator.

6 *Fear of retaliation*

If existing firms have reacted in a hostile way to new entrants in the past (e.g., starting a price war) then this sends out a signal to others that may deter them from entering.

7 *Brand loyalty and product differentiation*

Existing firms in an industry will try to make their products different, in the eyes of the consumer, from competitors' products. If they can do this successfully then they can generate brand loyalty; this makes it difficult for potential entrants because it will be more difficult for them to win new customers.

8 *Control supplies or distribution*

If a firm can gain control of the major supplier or a significant distributor then this can make it difficult for newcomers to get into the market. In the UK, in the 1980s the main brewers controlled most of the public houses in the UK. This made it almost impossible for new brewers to get their beers to customers. This market was later investigated by the government and brewers were forced to sell off some of their public houses and open them to 'guest beers'.

The higher the level of barriers to entry, the more protected existing firms are from competition; this means that they have more power over the market and are more likely to be able to earn large abnormal profits in the long run.

▉ Price discrimination

If barriers to entry do exist in a market then firms may have some form of monopoly power and are price makers. This may enable them to price discriminate. Price discrimination occurs when a firm offers the same product to different customers at different prices. For example, a nightclub might charge different prices depending on what time of the evening or what day you enter. The price of a train ticket may vary depending on what time of day you travel.

By price discriminating a firm can increase its own profits; at the same time it reduces the amount of consumer surplus (utility that is not paid for). In our earlier analysis of monopoly the firm profit maximised at the price P1 and the quantity Q1, when the marginal revenue equalled the marginal cost. It charged one price for all of its units. If it was able to price discriminate then it might sell some of these units for a higher price. For example, imagine that the output Q2 was sold at the price P2 whilst the remainder (Q1 – Q2) was sold at P1 (see Fig. 15.1). The firm is now earning more revenue from its sales and therefore more profits. At the same time consumer surplus has been reduced from ABP1 to the shaded areas in Fig. 15.1. Price discrimination therefore enables the firm to make more profits, but the customer is worse off.

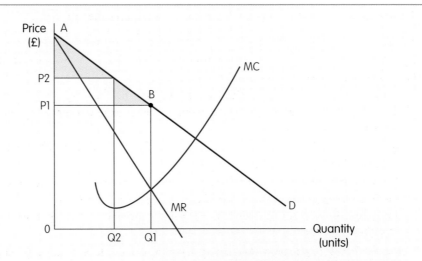

Figure 15.1 Price discrimination. A single-price monopolist would charge the price P1 for Q1 units. The consumer surplus would then be equal to the area ABP1. A price discriminator may charge the price P2 for Q2 units and the price P1 for Q1 – Q2 units. The revenue (and therefore profit) is then increased and the consumer surplus is reduced to the shaded areas.

Conditions for effective price discrimination

To price discriminate effectively a firm must be able to identify different demand conditions, for example, demand may be different between different groups of customers. It will then charge a higher price when demand is price inelastic and a lower price when demand is price elastic. This leads to different prices in different market segments.

Economics in context

The price of games characters

In the online game *EverQuest* people pay more for male games characters than females. In *EverQuest* players can become a powerful warrior, a sorcerer or a monk of either sex. More than 90% of the players of *EverQuest* are male, but only 80% of the characters in the game are male, and so some people are gender swapping. Players who want to gain powers quickly can buy high-level players. The price of male characters is greater than the price of female characters, suggesting a sexist approach. Typically a female character is worth $41 less than a male.

? Question

The insurance rates for male and female drivers are different. Why do you think this is?

To be successful a policy of price discrimination requires the following.

- The first requirement is that buyers in one market cannot switch easily to another market, that is, those being asked to pay a high price cannot switch to the low-price market (as this would undermine the policy).

  Markets can be separated in many ways, such as the following.
  - *Time*. This means that people pay different prices at different times of day (e.g., peak and off-peak travel).
  - *Age*. For example, old age pensioners or children pay less than other people on the bus; their age can be verified by travel cards.
  - *Region*. For example, charging different prices for the same model of car or the same beer in different parts of the world; the transport costs to buy the cars in the cheaper market and bring them back can ensure that it is not worth trying to buy in the lower-priced market.
  - *Status*. For example, some firms may have customer clubs or loyalty schemes and charge different rates to members and non-members.
  - *Income*. The price charged may vary according to how much you earn. Some private schools offer bursaries to subsidise students who come from low-income backgrounds. However, for this to work the business must be sure that it can tell accurately what people earn, otherwise everyone will pretend to be on a low income to try to obtain a bursary!

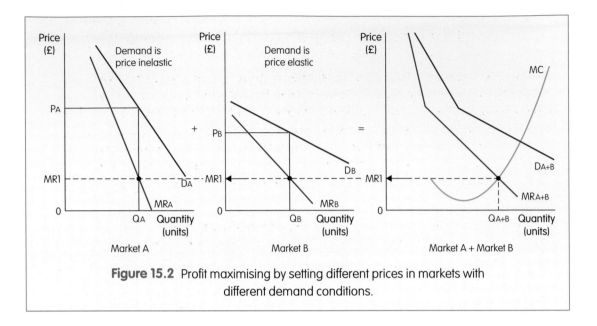

Figure 15.2 Profit maximising by setting different prices in markets with different demand conditions.

- The second requirement is that the price elasticity of demand is different, that is, demand is more price inelastic in one market segment than another, enabling prices to be increased in one market and reduced in others. The fact that demand conditions vary enables different prices to be charged. The higher price will be in the more price inelastic segment of the market as this will increase revenue (see Unit 4).

In Fig. 15.2 the demand and marginal revenue in the two markets (A and B) have been added together at each price (i.e., horizontally summated) to give the total market demand and the market marginal revenue. The profit maximising output, as ever, occurs when the marginal revenue equals the marginal cost. This determines the profit maximising output level for the market as a whole. For each market the marginal revenue must be equal to MR1. If the marginal revenue in one market is greater than in another then it would make sense to switch output to the one where the extra revenue was higher, as this would boost profit. To sell this output the price would need to fall and this would reduce the marginal revenue. This should continue until the marginal revenue is the same in both markets. Thus, to profit maximise the marginal revenue in market A must be equal to the marginal revenue in market B.

Given that the marginal revenues are equal in both markets, the relevant price and output in each one can then be identified. The price will be higher in the price inelastic market and lower in the price elastic market (PA > PB in Fig. 15.2).

Economics in context — Pricing at EasyCinema

EasyCinema was launched in May 2003 as part of easyGroup. EasyCinema operated a ten-screen multiplex cinema in Milton Keynes, showing a variety of films from first-runs and mainstream films to early classics, independent films, art house and niche productions. The price of the tickets for the films depended on when you booked and the level of demand. If you booked a long time ahead, when many seats were available, then the price would be very low. However, as you got nearer to the screening time and/or demand for seats was high then the price increased. Therefore, there would be lots of people watching the film who had paid different prices to be there.

 Questions

Would you mind if you went to the cinema and other people had paid less for a ticket?
Do you think that price-discriminating firms should worry about the reaction of their customers?

What do you think?

Is it fair to charge different prices for the same product?

Perfect price discrimination

Perfect price discrimination occurs when a different price is charged for every single unit of the product. A perfect price discriminator charges the customer the maximum that he or she is willing to pay for every single unit. In this case, the marginal revenue curve is the same as the demand curve, and consumer surplus is removed entirely. In practice, the difficulty for firms in doing this lies in identifying exactly how much customers genuinely value each item. Ask them and they may not tell you the truth!

In perfect price discrimination a firm will profit maximise when the marginal revenue equals the marginal costs; in this case, this is where the marginal cost curve crosses the demand curve. The total revenue earned is the whole area under the demand curve. In Fig. 15.3 the total costs are the area AC1EQ1O. A firm charging a single price for all of its units could not make a profit. The price could never cover the unit costs. In perfect price discrimination the revenue will be higher and could cover the costs, for example, the area OFGQ1 may be greater than AC1EQ1O.

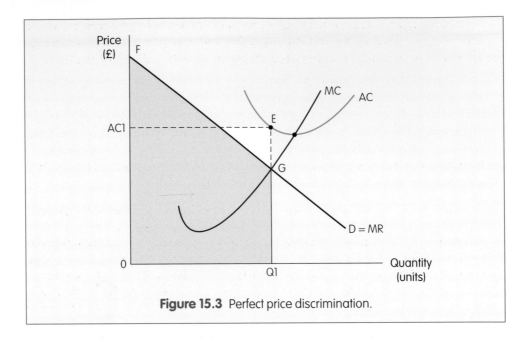

Figure 15.3 Perfect price discrimination.

Economics in context — The price of train travel

Table 15.2 gives the cost of a journey between London and Glasgow in March 2006. The price paid depends on when you book, when you want to travel and who you book with.

Table 15.2 The cost of a journey between London and Glasgow in March 2006.

	Virgin	GNER
Cheapest (advance bookings only)	£17.50 single	£13.50 single; £27 return
Saver return	£90.60	£94.10
Standard open return	£222	£222

? Question

Why do train companies have so many different fares depending on the time of day, the direction you are travelling in and the time you book?

The benefits of price discrimination

Price discrimination increases a firm's profits and reduces consumer surplus. The increase in profits may be seen as undesirable (an abuse of monopoly power); however, it may provide more funds for investment and innovation, leading to lower costs in the long term.

Price discrimination may also enable some goods and services to be produced that would not otherwise be provided. By price discriminating a firm may be able to make enough profits to want to stay in the industry when otherwise it would make a loss and leave.

Case Study

The following is an edited extract from *The undercover economist* by Tim Harford (Little, Brown Book Group Ltd, 2005).

. . . any well-run business would seek to charge each customer the maximum price he'd be willing to pay—and they do . . .

The first [strategy] is what economists call 'first-degree price discrimination', but we could call it the 'unique target' strategy: to evaluate each customer as an individual and charge according to how much he or she is willing to pay. This is the strategy of the used-car salesman or the estate agent. It usually takes skill and a lot of effort: hardly surprising, then, that it is most often seen for items that have a high value relative to the retailer's time—cars and houses, of course, but also souvenirs in African street stalls, where the impoverished merchant will find it worth bargaining for some time to gain an extra pound.

Now, however, companies are trying to automate the process of evaluating individual customers to reduce the time it takes to do so. For instance, supermarkets accumulate evidence of what you're willing to pay by giving you 'discount cards', which are needed to take advantage of sale prices. In return for getting a lower price on certain items, you allow the stores to keep records of what you buy and then in turn offer you vouchers for discounts on products. It doesn't work perfectly, because supermarkets can only send 'money off' vouchers, not 'money on' vouchers. 'Money on' vouchers have never been a success.

The second approach, the 'group target' strategy, is to offer different prices to members of distinct groups. Who could complain about reduced bus fares for children and the elderly? Surely it must be reasonable for coffee shops to offer a discount to people who work nearby, and for tourist attractions to let locals in for a lower rate? It often seems reasonable because people in groups who pay more are usually people who can afford more, and that's because people who can afford more are usually people who care less about the price. But we shouldn't forget that this is a convenient coincidence. Companies trying to increase their profits and get the maximum value out of their scarcity are interested in who is willing to pay more, rather than who can afford to pay more. For instance, when Disney World in Florida offer admission discounts of more than 50 per cent to local people, they're not making a statement about the grinding poverty of the Sunshine State. They simply know that for a reduced price, locals are more likely to come regularly. But tourists will probably come once, and once only, whether it is cheap or expensive.

. . . The same is true of discounts at coffee bars for local workers. The AMT bar in Waterloo station will knock 10 per cent off the cost of your coffee if you work locally. This isn't because the local workers are poor: they include top Whitehall mandarins and the extravagantly remunerated employees of the gigantic oil company, Shell. The discount reflects the fact that local workers are price-sensitive despite being rich. Commuters who pass through Waterloo in a hurry see only one or two coffee bars and are willing to pay high prices for convenience. Local workers pop out of the office at 11 a.m. for coffee and could walk in any direction. They can buy from several cafes, all equally convenient, all of which they will have had a chance to sample. They are bound to be more price-sensitive, even if they are rich.

The 'individual target' strategy is difficult, partly because it requires a lot of information and partly because it tends to be very unpopular. Despite the difficulties, however, it's so profitable that companies always explore new ways to do it. The 'group target' strategy of discounts for students or locals is less effective, but easier to put into action, and usually it's socially acceptable. Either will deliver more profits than simply treating all customers as a homogenous mass.

. . . Supermarkets have turned price targeting into an art, developing a vast array of strategies to that end. Above the main concourse of Liverpool Street station, there's a Marks and Spencer 'Simply Food' store, catering for busy commuters on the way in and out of London. Knowing what we do about scarcity value, we shouldn't be surprised to find that this shop isn't cheap—even compared with another branch of M&S merely 500 metres or so away, at Moorgate.

. . . Try to spot other odd mix-ups next time you're in the supermarket. Have you noticed that supermarkets often charge 10 times as much for fresh chilli peppers in a packet as for loose fresh chillies? That's because the typical customer buys such small quantities that he doesn't think to check whether they cost 4p or 40p. Randomly tripling the price of a vegetable is a favourite trick: customers who notice the mark-up just buy a different vegetable that week; customers who don't have self-targeted a whopping price rise.

? Questions

- What is meant by first-degree price discrimination? Why would this pricing approach appeal to firms? Why is it difficult for them to implement?
- What does Harford mean by the 'group target' strategy of price discrimination? Can you think of other examples of this approach?
- What other examples of price discrimination can you think of?
- Do you think that price discrimination should be allowed? Should it be encouraged?

Checklist

Now you have read this unit try to answer the following questions.

- ☐ Can you explain what is meant by barriers to entry?
- ☐ Can you outline different forms of barrier to entry?
- ☐ Can you explain the significance of barriers to entry in relation to the profits that may be earned in an industry?
- ☐ Can you explain the meaning of price discrimination?
- ☐ Can you outline the conditions for effective price discrimination?
- ☐ Can you analyse the benefits of price discrimination?

End of unit questions

1 What types of barriers to entry can you think of?
2 Are barriers to entry a good thing?

3   What is meant by a price inelastic demand?

4   Will the price be higher or lower in the more price inelastic market segment?

5   Is price discrimination a good thing?

Key learning points

- Price discrimination reduces consumer surplus but increases producer surplus.

- Price discrimination may enable some products to be produced that it would not be financially feasible to produce otherwise.

- With perfect price discrimination consumer surplus is reduced to zero.

Learn more

Effective price discrimination relies on there being different price elasticities of demand in the various markets. To make sure that you understand the determinants of the price elasticity of demand why not check your understanding of Unit 4?

 Visit our Online Resource Centre at www.oxfordtextbooks.co.uk/orc/gillespie_econ for test questions and further information on topics covered in this chapter.

»16 Integration and competition policy

The structure of a market is not static and can change as firms within it change their scale. A common objective of businesses is to grow, and one way of doing this is to join with other firms; this is known as 'integration'. This unit examines different forms of integration and considers the different reasons why firms may pursue these. We also examine the way in which the UK government regulates firms to try and ensure that firms behave in a competitive manner.

LEARNING OBJECTIVES

By the end of this unit you should be able to:

✔ explain the different forms of integration;

✔ analyse the reasons why firms integrate in different ways;

✔ outline different strategies for growth;

✔ outline the key objectives and features of competition policy.

■ Integration

Integration occurs when firms join together. This may be in one of the following forms.

- A *takeover* or an *acquisition*. This occurs when a firm or individual buys control of another business; for example, in 2005, Malcolm Glazer bought control of Manchester United.

- A *merger*. This occurs when two firms join to create one new business; for example, in 1998, Daimler Benz merged with the Chrysler Corporation to form DaimlerChrysler. In 2000, AOL joined with Time and Warner to create AOLTimeWarner.

Expanding via integration is known as 'external growth', as opposed to 'internal growth' or 'organic growth' which occurs when firms grow by developing their existing

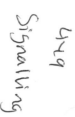 Signalling? 449

...apid and dramatic increases in the scale of a busi-
...er and therefore possibly easier to manage. Growth
...been common in many industries, particularly global
...king, car production and brewing, as firms pursue a
...ronger competitive position.

Merger ver... ...akeover

In a merger the owners of both companies become the owners of the new organisation.
In a takeover the owners of the victim company give up their shares in return for cash or
shares in the purchaser. A takeover is also called an acquisition.

A merger is a voluntary joining of two or more organisations. This has the advantage
of information being freely shared, whereas in a hostile takeover information may not be
so readily available. However, a merger may not be possible because the owners of one of
the firms may not want to join with the other. This means that the other firm may have to
buy control of the organisation. Equally, the owners of one organisation may want to
control another rather than share control of it, and so insist on a takeover.

Economics in context **The growth of General Electric**

General Electric (GE), one of the biggest companies in the world, has grown rapidly through acquisitions. Its businesses include financial services, plastics, healthcare and broadcasting. It spends
billions of dollars per year buying companies and has over 200 people working full time in its
acquisitions team. By comparison, at Procter and Gamble, another large multinational, the business development team consists of just the chief executive and his chief financial officer.

Deals at GE are judged on quantitative criteria (can they achieve a given rate of return?) and qual-
itative criteria (do they fit with the overall strategy?). The company measures performance regularly
after the deal to discover what works and what does not work.

? Question
What problems can you imagine might occur when one firm grows by taking over another one?

Types of integration

The different types of integration are shown in Fig. 16.1 and are described as follows.

- Horizontal integration occurs when two or more firms at the same stage of the same
  production process join together; for example, the Royal Bank of Scotland bought
  NatWest in 2000 (both are banks) and Morrisons bought Safeway in 2003 (both are
  supermarkets).

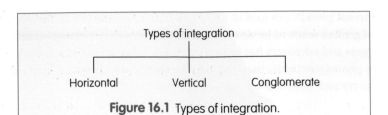

Figure 16.1 Types of integration.

Horizontal integration offers benefits such as:
- greater market share and greater market power;
- internal economies of scale; for example, the combined business will buy on a larger scale than each of the individual firms would have done before the integration, and this should lead to purchasing economies of scale.

Given that the firms are in the same industry, managing the combined business should be easier than taking over a business in a different sector entirely. Managers should understand the production process and customer needs and wants.

Economics in context   **Adidas buys Reebok**

In 1997, Adidas paid $1.4 billion for Salomon, a French maker of ski and golf equipment. In 2005, it sold this business for just $625 million. Despite this failed takeover Adidas was still looking for acquisitions. In 2005, it announced that it was going to buy Reebok, an American rival, for $3.8 billion. This joining of the number two and number three in the industry allowed it to challenge the market leader Nike, which had 35% of the market. Being larger gave Adidas more power in the market over their suppliers and retailers. Reebok was stronger in the US and Adidas was stronger in Europe, and so the takeover had a good strategic fit.

 Question
What do you think are the benefits of having a much larger market share?

- Vertical integration occurs when one firm joins with another at a different stage of the same production process. The following are some examples.
  - A film company may buy a cinema chain (this is forward integration because the firm is moving nearer to the final customer).
  - A petrol company may buy an oil refinery (this is backward integration because it goes back toward the raw materials). BP, for example, is a very vertically integrated business involved in the exploration, extraction, refining and sale of petrol.
  By vertically integrating a firm can cut out the profit margins of the other intermediaries. This may lead to a lower final price for the buyer (or higher profit margins for the firm itself). In the case of backward vertical integration a firm may be able to control

supply more effectively (e.g., more control over costs, design and delivery). With forward vertical integration the firm can ensure access to the market.

- **Conglomerate integration** occurs when one firm joins with another in a different market entirely; for example, Mars owns a food business, a vending business and a pet food company!

   This type of growth may reduce a firm's risks because if demand declines in one market then it may be increasing in another. However, from a management point of view, it will be complex managing organisations operating in different markets.

What do you think?

Is it better for a firm to specialise in one product market or to operate in several different ones?

Problems of integration

The following are some of the problems of integration.

- In the case of a takeover the buyer will have to entice shareholders to sell their shares. This can be expensive and will usually mean that the buyer has to offer more than the current market price of the shares. The buyer will therefore need to improve the performance of the business following the takeover, simply to cover the premium paid to buy the company.

- When organisations join together there may be a culture clash. The culture of an organisation refers to the values, attitudes and beliefs of the employees within it. In other words, it is 'the way we do things around here'. When firms join together their employees' views of how things should be done may be very different, and this can lead to conflict and underperformance. The problems of culture clashes are often underestimated by managers engaging in integration.

- Diseconomies of scale. When two firms join together the size of the business may make it difficult to run. Managers may struggle to control a larger scale business due to coordination and communication problems. Managing more people, producing more products and dealing with more suppliers and distributors makes the management process more complex. There are also often problems with motivation in larger firms because employees feel more distant from managers. They do not feel as noticed or as important as individuals, and this can lead to less effort and problems with attendance and work rate. To try to control the larger business companies may introduce the following.
  - Budgeting systems are used to set targets and to review financial income and expenditure. This should help to keep control of the larger business and coordinate decision making.
  - Management by objectives is a system in which all managers agree targets with their subordinates and review these regularly. This helps to ensure that everyone knows what they are trying to achieve and why.

Trouble at Vodafone

For over twenty years Vodafone was regarded as one of the most successful companies in the UK. Its strategy was to 'go global' to gain economies of scale and to focus on 'mobile only', rather than to get involved in landline telecommunications. To do this it undertook numerous takeovers. This growth made Vodafone the largest wireless firm measured by revenue. By 2006 it had over 170 million customers in over twenty-five countries. However, that year the company announced a £22 billion loss, the largest at the time in European corporate history. This was an accounting loss due to having to write off the acquisitions of companies for which too much money had been paid and which were not worth what the company had originally thought they were worth. The firm's strategy of acquisition had led to too much being paid for firms in an attempt to grow rapidly. The drive for scale led to overly rapid expansion.

❓ Question

How do you think managers decide what a business is worth when undertaking a takeover?

■ Strategies for growth

According to Ansoff (1957), the growth strategies of a business can be analysed under the following four categories (see Table 16.1).

- *Market penetration*. This occurs when firms sell more of their products within their existing markets. For example, they might advertise more, modify their products or cut the price to boost their sales. By modifying the marketing mix a firm can try to boost its sales.
- *Market development*. This occurs when a firm aims its products at new market segments. For example, a firm might try to sell its products in new countries or it might target new age ranges or new users.
- *New product development*. This involves developing new products to sell to existing customers; for example, a new variety of a brand of drinks such as Coca Cola with lemon, with lime, without caffeine and vanilla flavour.

Table 16.1 Growth strategies for a business.

		Products	
		Existing	New
Markets	Existing	Market penetration	New product development
	New	Market development	Diversification

- *Diversification*. This strategy involves moving into areas that are new to the business. This is the riskiest strategy in terms of management because it involves unknown areas for the managers.

What do you think?

Do you think it is better to grow by joining with another business or to grow independently?

Competition policy

Competition policy aims to prevent anti-competitive behaviour. For example, it is possible that if a few firms dominate a market then they will charge relatively high prices and provide a poor service to customers. There may be less investment in research and development, leading to less innovation and a fall in quality. Given that buyers do not have many alternatives, they may have to accept such behaviour. To prevent this the government may decide to intervene. Other forms of anti-competitive behaviour include:

- firms fixing prices as part of a cartel;
- firms using predatory pricing to undercut the competition and gain control over a market;
- firms controlling supply and preventing other firms from gaining access to the market.

The following is a description of competition policy according to the UK Department of Trade and Industry:

Competitive markets provide the best means of ensuring the economy's resources are put to their best use by encouraging enterprise and efficiency, and widening choice. Where markets work well they provide a strong incentive for good performance—encouraging firms to improve productivity, to reduce prices and to innovate whilst rewarding consumers with lower prices, higher quality and wider choice . . . But markets can and do fail. Competition policy is therefore used to ensure the efficient workings of markets and to avoid market failure, most notably the abuses of market power.

Competition policy aims to keep markets open to new firms. This should lead to the 'gale of creative destruction' outlined by Schumpeter (1950); the success of some firms will encourage others to enter markets and innovate. This is good news for consumers and the new entrants; it is not necessarily good news for the established firms who have to innovate themselves to survive. The rise of low-cost airlines and the rise of mobile phone firms have shaken up old established firms. Edward Luttwark, an adviser at the Centre for Strategic and International Studies, says of the old Soviet Union, 'in the absence of market competition, old and inefficient firms continued merrily along instead of releasing resources for those newer and more efficient . . . Creative destruction is the true secret of capitalism that the KGB never discovered.'

What do you think?

Do you think that greater competition in markets is a good thing?
Can monopoly power ever be justified or desirable?

In the UK, competition policy is regulated by the following.

- The Office of Fair Trading (OFT) exists to make markets work better. It deals with anti-competitive practices through enforcement and communication.

- The Competition Commission conducts enquiries into mergers, markets and the regulation of regulated markets if an issue is referred to it by, for example, the OFT or the relevant Secretary of State. The Commission can investigate if a merger or takeover leads to a market share of over 25%.

- The Restrictive Practices Court examines agreements between firms supplying goods and services in the UK, such as collusive pricing. These agreements are presumed to be unfair unless they meet one of eight possible 'gateways' or justifications; for example, that they are needed to prevent high levels of unemployment in an area.

UK competition legislation includes the Competition Act 1998 and the Enterprise Act 2002. The UK is also subject to Article 85 and Article 86 of the European Union which cover restrictive practices and monopolies.

Economics in context   Competition in the UK

The following is taken from the OECD (Organization for Economic Cooperation and Development) country report 2005 on the UK.

Competitive pressures appear to be relatively strong in the United Kingdom, with regulations inhibiting competition and barriers to trade amongst the lowest in the OECD . . . In the retail sector, market power remains a problem and the competition authorities will need to remain vigilant. The government's recent approach to planning has made new large scale entry very difficult, impeding competition and inhibiting entry. Industry regulators also need to remain vigilant in the electricity, gas and telecommunications sectors. Reforms in these sectors have led to increased productivity, though international comparisons suggest that there is scope for prices to fall.

? Question

What does this report suggest about the problems of competition in the retail, electricity, gas and telecommunications sectors? Can the government do anything about this? Should it?

@ Web

For more information on the OECD visit **www.oecd.org**

Firms found guilty of anti-competitive behaviour in the UK can face fines of up to 10% of their turnover.

Economics in context

Parisian hotels form a cartel

In 2005, several famous Paris hotels were fined for sharing commercial information and colluding to keep prices high. The Crillon, Bristol, Meurice, Piazza Athenee, Ritz and George V hotels were accused of operating a cartel by competition regulators. The six establishments were fined a total of €709,000. The establishments were in the premier division of hotels due to their central location, first-rate accommodation, high-class restaurants, facilities such as swimming pools, and high staff numbers.

 Question

To what extent do you think fines are likely to work as a deterrent to anti-competitive behaviour?

What do you think?

Do you think that there can be too much competition in a market?

Case Study

In 2006, the UK glass manufacturer Pilkington agreed to be taken over by Japan's Nippon Sheet Glass. The 180-year-old UK glassmaker employed almost 24 000 people and had factories in Birmingham and Doncaster, as well as its Head Office in St Helens in the North West. Under the cash deal Nippon Sheet offered 165 pence per share. It raised some of the money through borrowing.

The main aim of this horizontal integration was to benefit from major cost savings. For example, the head offices could be combined. It also meant that the new business would be in a stronger position to compete against the world's largest glass company, Asahi of Japan, which had around 20% of the market; Pilkington had around 19% of the market and Nippon had only 3%. The deal was also a good fit geographically, with Pilkington stronger in Europe and the US, and Nippon stronger in Asia. Nippon had focused on supplying the Japanese car industry, so the deal with Pilkington opened up new markets for it. In particular, it was hoped that it would save Nippon's contract with Toyota. Toyota had threatened to end the contract because Nippon did not have the global coverage it wanted.

? Questions

- Outline the possible benefits of this takeover deal.
- What might be the problems of a takeover such as this?
- To what extent should the UK government worry about UK firms being taken over by foreign firms?

Checklist

Now you have read this unit try to answer the following questions.

☐ Can you explain the different forms of integration?

☐ Can you analyse the reasons why firms integrate in different ways?

☐ Can you outline different strategies for growth?

☐ Can you outline the key objectives and features of UK competition policy?

End of unit questions

1 Is internal growth better than external growth?

2 Is horizontal integration better than vertical integration?

3 Should firms seek to grow via conglomerate mergers?

4 Outline the possible benefits of competitive markets.

5 Is competition policy needed?

Key learning points

- There are many forms of integration and each type may have its own motives and business logic.

- Business strategy can focus on the decision of which markets to compete in and which products to offer.

- Managing firms after external growth can be difficult due to culture clashes and difficulties in communicating and coordinating. This is why many mergers and takeovers underperform after the integration.

- Competition policy exists to protect firms and consumers from anti-competitive behaviour.

- Competition is usually assumed to lead to greater innovation, greater efficiency and lower prices.

References

Ansoff, H. I. (1957). Strategies for diversification. *Harvard Business Review*, 35 (2), 113–24.

Schumpeter, J. A. (1950). *Capitalism, socialism and democracy*, 3rd edn. Harper & Row, New York.

Learn more

To learn more about takeovers and mergers, visit our website at the address below. To learn more about monopolies you can read unit 12.

 Visit our Online Resource Centre at www.oxfordtextbooks.co.uk/orc/gillespie_econ for test questions and further information on topics covered in this chapter.

Business objectives

In this unit we examine the different forms of business in the UK and consider the advantages and disadvantages of each one. We also consider business objectives. Traditionally, economists have assumed that the overriding objective of a firm is to maximise profits. In this unit we consider some alternative objectives and the impact of these in terms of price and output decisions.

LEARNING OBJECTIVES

By the end of this unit you should be able to:

✔ analyse different business objectives and the impact of these on price and output decisions by firms;

✔ understand the idea of corporate social responsibility.

Business objectives

The classical assumption in economics is that managers will aim to maximise profits. This means that firms will produce an output where the marginal revenue equals the marginal costs. At this level of output no further profit can be made, and so there is the largest possible positive difference between the total revenue and the total costs.

Managers are expected to pursue profit due to the following reasons.

- This will generate the highest possible rewards for the owners of the business, such as the shareholders. If they fail to satisfy shareholders then they may lose their jobs.

- Profit is a source of internal finance that can be used for expansion. Alternatives to profit include borrowing (which incurs interest charges) or, if it is a company, selling more shares (which can mean that the existing shareholders lose some of their ownership).

- Profit is a common benchmark of success and so enables managers to meet their own ego needs and measure their own effectiveness relative to others.

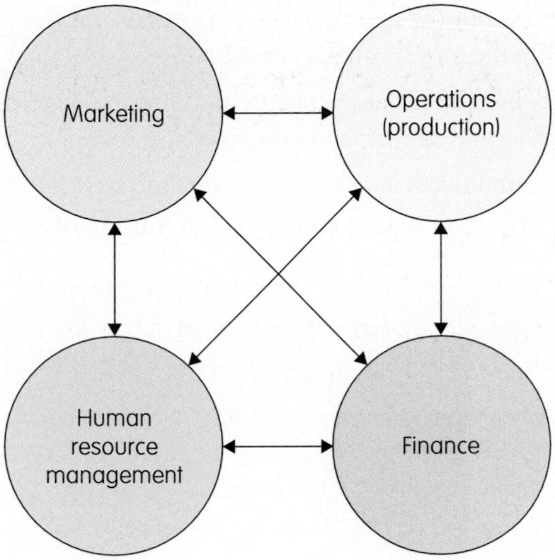

Figure 17.1 The functions of a business.

- Managers' salaries may be connected to profits. The more profits they make, the more they may earn.
- High profits may lead to more demand for the shares and an increase in the share price, which will please shareholders.

However, the profit maximising assumption has some limitations, not least the difficulties managers have knowing exactly what the revenues and costs would be at different levels of output. Without perfect knowledge it is unlikely that managers could identify the actual profit maximising price and output, even if they were trying to do so.

Furthermore, a business is actually made up of many different interest groups, all of whom may be pursuing slightly different objectives, for example, the marketing department, the production department, the human resource department, the finance department and the administrative staff (see Fig. 17.1). The finance department may well be focused on profit but the marketing team may be more concerned with the level of sales, even if boosting sales requires higher expenditure and less profits. The human resource department may be reluctant to make people redundant, even if this increases efficiency and profits.

All of these different interest groups will be bargaining and negotiating over every decision made within a business; it is therefore likely that the actual pricing and output decisions that are made are a compromise between them. A business may well 'satisfice' its different stakeholders rather than profit maximise. This idea was put forward by Simon (1947) and stems from Cyert and March (1963).

There may also be a difference between the objectives of the managers and the owners. For example, the owners may want high profits so that they can receive higher dividends whereas the managers may want the following.

- Some managers may want to control larger departments or want faster growth. They may be more interested in the scale of their operations and the power that they have rather than achieving the most profitable outputs.

- Some managers may have environmental or social concerns that lead to more expensive production methods or not producing in the least-cost location.

- Some managers and employees may be interested in job security and the quality of their working life. They may wish to be paid more, even if profits are reduced.

Economics in context

When money is not everything

Dame Anita Roddick, who made her fortune selling ethical body and beauty products, decided in 2005 to cash in her 18% share of the company and give away half of her £100 million fortune saying, 'I don't want to die rich'. Anita Roddick set up The Body Shop in 1976 in Brighton. 'The worst thing is greed, the accumulation of money. I don't know why people who are extraordinarily wealthy are not more generous.'

Microsoft founder Bill Gates has already pledged £15 billion ($26 billion) to good causes through the Bill and Melinda Gates Foundation. Set up in 2002 by Mr Gates and his wife Melinda, the foundation promotes greater equality in global health and learning, with millions of dollars being pledged to fight TB, malaria and HIV in developing countries. Bill Gates has given away more money to charity than anyone else in history. 'I think the rich have to look after the poor', said Anita Roddick.

? Question

To what extent do you think that firms should give away their profits?

■ The divorce between ownership and control

The divorce between ownership and control occurs in businesses in which the owners are not the same as the managers. In many companies, for example, the shareholders invest in the business but hire managers to run it on a day-to-day basis. This approach has advantages in that those with money hire specialists who are good at managing but who may not have the funds themselves to establish a business. A possible consequence of this may be that the objectives pursued by the managers differ from those of the owners. The owners are most likely to be interested in financial returns either through dividends or through an increase in the share price. However, they do not have perfect information and may not know at any time what would lead to the highest profits. They are likely to be guided by the managers, who may not always be seeking the maximum profit. For example, as we have seen, managers may be interested in growing the business because this makes them feel more important; or they may have particular projects that interest them, such as developing a new product. The divorce between ownership and control is also known as

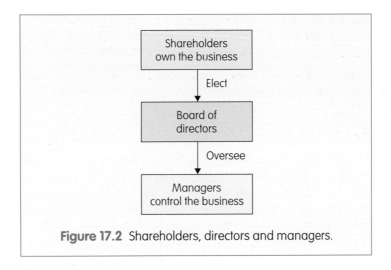

Figure 17.2 Shareholders, directors and managers.

the principal–agent problem; the principals are the shareholders and the agents are the managers they employ.

To try to control the managers, shareholders elect a Board of Directors that meets regularly and monitors the managers' behaviour. The Directors act as the watchdogs of the shareholders (see Fig. 17.2).

The divorce between ownership and control is not an issue if the owners and the managers are the same people, for example, in a sole trader. Sometimes the managers will buy up the shares in a business to gain control and remove the divorce between ownership and control. This is a called a 'management buyout'.

What do you think?

Can the problem of divorce between ownership and control ever be overcome?

| Economics in context | The divorce between ownership and control |

The dangers of the divorce between ownership and control can be seen by cases in which managers abuse their position at the expense of their owners. The following are two examples of this.

- In 2005, US prosecutors indicted Conrad Black on various charges, including racketeering, obstruction of justice and money laundering. Lord Black and three executives were accused of using almost $84 million (£49 million) of Hollinger International funds. Lord Black and three former Hollinger executives were also charged with eleven counts of fraud in the US, linked to a

$2.1 billion (£1.2 billion) sale of hundreds of Canadian newspapers. Lord Black and his co-defendants stood accused of having cheated both Hollinger International's US and Canadian shareholders, and tax authorities in Canada in three fraudulent schemes between 1998 and 2002.

- In 2001, Enron, a huge American company that went bankrupt, was investigated by the US financial regulator, the Securities Exchange Commission. It turned out that millions of dollars of debt had been hidden from investors. Some of the senior executives were taken to court on charges of fraud. Jeffrey Skilling, the former chief executive, for example, faced thirty-five charges, including conspiracy and fraud. It was alleged that he had attempted to fool investors into believing that Enron was a healthy company whilst he and other executives received high rewards. Kenneth Lay, former chairman, faced seven charges. Enron started as a producer of energy in 1985 following the merger of the two companies Internorth and Houston Natural Gas. It later became a major 'market-maker' in America, buying and selling energy. In just fifteen years it grew from very little to become America's seventh largest company, employing 21 000 staff in over forty countries. *Fortune* magazine named Enron 'America's most innovative company' for six consecutive years from 1996 to 2001. Enron ended up with $31.8 billion (£18 billion) of debts, its shares became worthless and its employees all lost their jobs.

② Question

How do you think investors ensure that managers pursue their interests?

▪ Other objectives

As we have seen, there are many groups within an organisation, all with their own agenda. In particular, managers may not necessarily pursue the objectives that shareholders want. There are a number of theories that economists have developed about possible objectives other than profit maximisation. The following are two possible alternative theories.

Sales revenue maximisation

According to Baumol (1959), managers may want to maximise the revenue earned from sales even if this reduces profits (subject to a minimum level of profit that must be made to satisfy the owners). For example, a firm may invest heavily in advertising to boost revenues and end up with lower profits than they could have achieved otherwise because of the advertising costs. Managers may want high revenues because:

- it means that the business has a higher profile, which gives the managers a sense of achievement (and may be good for their future careers if they move on to other firms);
- their salaries may be linked to the firm's income rather than its profit.

To maximise revenue a firm should produce at a level of output where the marginal revenue is zero. At this output no extra revenue can be earned. This occurs at the output Q3 in Fig. 17.3. Notice how the focus is on revenues and not costs.

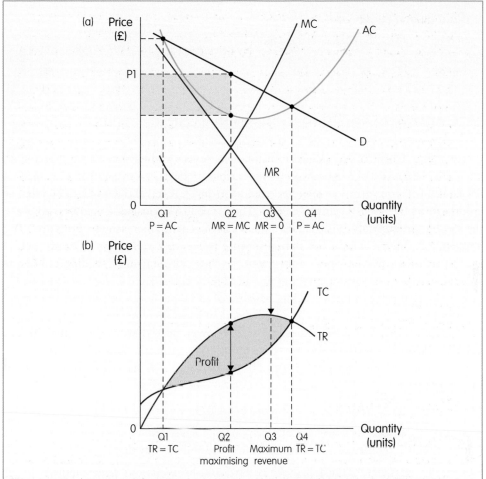

Figure 17.3 Business objectives (a) in terms of marginals and averages and (b) in terms of total costs and total revenues.

Growth maximisation

According to Marris (1964), managers may seek to make the business as large as possible in terms of its output, provided that they do not make a loss and meet some minimum profit requirement to satisfy investors. The reason why growth may be important is to make the business more difficult to take over. By increasing the size of the organisation, managers are possibly protecting their own jobs by making the firm more expensive to buy and therefore less likely to be bought. Growth also makes the business more visible because it is selling a lot of products and therefore the organisation has a higher profile. Once again, this may be good for the managers' own careers.

The highest possible level of output that a firm can produce at without making a loss is where the average revenue (price) equals the average cost. This is shown at the output Q4 in Fig. 17.3.

What do you think?

What do you think is the purpose of business?

Corporate social responsibility (CSR)

Increasingly, managers and indeed investors, employees and customers are showing an interest in the concept of corporate social responsibility (CSR). This means that when making decisions firms consider a range of 'stakeholder groups'. A stakeholder is an individual or group with an interest in the firm's activities. These stakeholders include employees, suppliers, the local community, the government and society in general. Increasingly, firms are using a much wider range of measures than just profit to measure performance. Issues such as the impact of a firm's activities on their staff, on the environment, on wildlife and on the general welfare of the community may also need to be considered. Companies such as BT now measure their performance using measures of this type. For example, they undertake and publish a 'social audit'. This is an independent assessment of the effect of the firm's activities on society, considering issues such as the representation of women and ethnic groups in the workforce, emission levels, recycling levels and their health and safety record.

This interest in non-financial measures of performance may have been brought about by the following.

- A greater interest in such issues by managers and by investors.
- A greater demand for more socially responsible behaviour by customers. Buyers are increasingly interested in issues such as Fair Trade and the way that a firm treats its staff.
- A greater awareness of the damage caused by some firms' actions, for example, in terms of environmental damage.

What do you think?

Should firms act socially responsibly? What are the possible advantages and disadvantages of this? Is this incompatible with profit maximisation?
Can you think of any examples of firms behaving socially responsibly?

Social objectives

Some organisations have very explicit social aims and do not seek to make a profit. These may be public sector organisations, charities or other non-profit organisations such as sports clubs. The National Health Service, for example, is very conscious of the costs of treatment and the opportunity costs of resources; managers also have control of huge budgets. However, because the product is not marketed and charged for, the National Health Service does not measure its success in terms of profits. Similarly, libraries, museums and galleries may need to be assessed in very different ways. And what about local football clubs, schools, social services and the defence sector? All of these have a range of performance criteria other than profits.

Case Study

There is much debate over the role of business in society. Some people think a business should focus on meeting the needs of its investors and that everything else is something of an irrelevance. This is known as the 'shareholder view'. Others believe that an organisation needs to take all of its stakeholders into account when making decisions. This is known as the 'stakeholder concept'. Organisations such as the Co-operative Bank are known to be stakeholder friendly. They regularly survey their customers to make sure that the actions of the bank fit with the customers' own values. This has led to the decision not to lend to organisations involved in animal testing or ones that produce equipment that can be used for torture. Many companies pride themselves on their donations to charity, investment in the community and environmentally friendly policies. However, a famous economist Milton Friedman believes that socially responsible actions such as this only make sense if they actually benefit the investors. According to Friedman (1970),

> In a free enterprise, private-property system, a corporate executive is an employee of the owners of the business. He has direct responsibility to his employers. That responsibility is to conduct the business in accordance with their desires, which generally will be to make as much money as possible while conforming to the basic rules of the society, both those embodied in law and those embodied in ethical custom. . . .

Whilst individual managers may wish to act socially responsibly in their own time, this is very different from using investors' money to do this. Paying more to specific suppliers that you have used for a long time may be a generous act, but does it actually help the business? Keeping on employees even when they are not needed may be the act of a kind employer rewarding loyalty, but is it profit maximising? Reducing pollution beyond the level required by law may be praiseworthy according to some environmental groups, but is it the right action of a manager who is just the 'agent' of the investors? Of course, says Friedman, if these 'socially responsible' actions do actually benefit the business in the long term (perhaps through more loyal employees or suppliers) then they should be undertaken and supported.

According to Friedman,

> It may well be in the long-run interest of a corporation that is a major employer in a small community to devote resources to providing amenities to that community or to improving its government. That may make it easier to attract desirable employees, it may reduce the wage bill or lessen losses from pilferage and sabotage or have other worthwhile effects.

Overall Friedman claims:

> There is one and only one social responsibility of business—to use its resources and engage in activities designed to increase its profits so long as it stays within the rules of the game, which is to say, engages in open and free competition without deception or fraud.

? Questions

- Summarise Friedman's views in your own words.
- To what extent do you agree with this view about the 'one and only one social responsibility' of a business?

Checklist

Now you have read this unit try to answer the following questions.

☐ Can you analyse different business objectives and the impact of these on price and output decisions by firms?

☐ Do you understand the idea of corporate social responsibility?

End of unit questions

1 Where will a firm produce if it is seeking to maximise sales revenue? Explain your answer.

2 Where will a firm produce to maximise growth without making a loss? Explain your answer.

3 How might the divorce between ownership and control affect the objectives that managers pursue?

4 Does the idea of pursuing corporate social responsibility conflict with maximising profits?

5 What other measures of business performance might you use as well as or instead of profit?

Key learning points

- Traditional economics assumes that firms profit maximise. In fact, there are a range of possible objectives (such as growth maximisation and sales revenue maximisation). Different objectives lead to different price and output outcomes.

- Corporate social responsibility occurs when firms accept obligations to society over and beyond their legal obligations, for example, obligations to the environment and the local community.

References

Baumol, W. (1959). *Business behaviour, value and growth*. Macmillan, New York.

Cyert, R. M. and March, J. G. (1963). Behavioral theory of the firm. Prentice Hall, New Jersey.

Friedman, M. (1970). The social responsibility of business is to increase profits. © 2006 *The New York Times*.

Marris, R. (1964). The economic theory of 'managerial' capitalism. Macmillan, London.

Simon, H. A. (1947). *Administrative behaviour*. Macmillan, New York.

Learn more

The issue of corporate social responsibility and the relationship between managers and an organisation's stakeholders are key issues in business today. To learn more about the issues involved in this debate visit our website at the address below.

 Visit our Online Resource Centre at www.oxfordtextbooks.co.uk/orc/gillespie_econ for test questions and further information on topics covered in this chapter.

»18 The labour market

Labour is a vital resource in business and therefore in the economy as a whole. An understanding of the labour market will help us to understand why wage levels differ between jobs and regions, and what determines the number of people working in a particular industry. In this unit we consider the determinants of supply and demand for labour and examine how changes in wages bring about equilibrium in the market.

LEARNING OBJECTIVES

By the end of this unit you should be able to:

✔ understand that labour is a derived demand;

✔ explain the factors that affect the demand and supply of labour;

✔ explain the profit maximising condition for hiring labour;

✔ understand the role of a trade union;

✔ explain the factors influencing the powers of trade unions.

▉ The labour market

Most of us are interested in the wages that are paid in different jobs. After all, we are either working now or likely to get a job fairly soon. So the rewards available matter. What is also interesting is how the wages vary between industries and why the earnings of, say, a cleaner can be so different from a merchant banker. We all think that nurses, police and firefighters do a valuable job and yet their pay is relatively low. Some footballers seem to play only a few games per season and yet earn vast sums of money. In this unit we look at the labour market and consider why wages differ so much, and examine the impact of changes in market conditions.

The supply and demand for labour

In a free market the wages of employees will be determined by the supply of and demand for labour in a given industry. In just the same way that the price adjusts to bring about equilibrium in the product market, the wage will adjust to bring about equilibrium in the labour market. So to understand why some jobs pay so much more than others we must examine the supply and demand of labour.

Labour supply

The labour force represents everyone who is in work or who is seeking work. The supply of labour depends on the number of people willing and able to work and the number of hours that they are willing to work.

The supply of labour to a particular industry will depend on the following.

- *The level of wages.* The higher the wages being paid then the more that people are likely to want to work in an industry, all other things being unchanged. This will cause a movement along the supply curve for labour (see Fig. 18.1(a)).

- *The value of the benefits available from the government if people are unemployed.* If these benefits are relatively high then there will be less incentive for people to work. This will reduce the supply of labour at any wage level and shift the supply curve of labour to the left (see Fig. 18.1(b)).

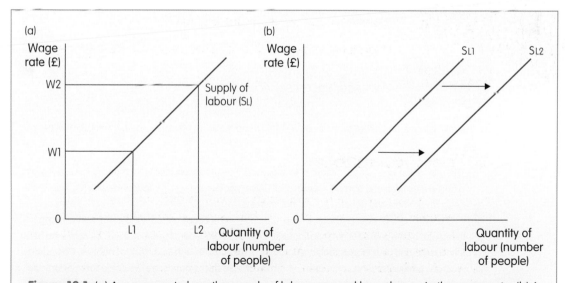

Figure 18.1 (a) A movement along the supply of labour caused by a change in the wage rate. (b) A shift in the supply of labour curve means that more (or less) is supplied at each and every wage rate.

- *The training period*. If there is a long training period for a particular industry (perhaps because the work requires highly specialist skills, such as being a surgeon) then this will reduce the number of employees who can work in this sector at any moment and shift the supply of labour to the left.

- *The overall appeal of the job*. If the job itself is unappealing (perhaps because working conditions are unpleasant or even dangerous; think of night work, working on an oil rig or being a firefighter) then this will reduce the supply of labour to it.

- *The working population*. This will determine the overall size of the labour pool and therefore the number that can work in any industry. This will depend on what the working age is (e.g., at what age people leave school and at what age they retire) and demographic factors such as birth and death rates, and migration rates.

- *Trade unions*. Trade unions represent employees and bargain with management to protect their interests. Unions may take industrial action (such as a strike) as a bargaining tool. In some countries unions can affect the supply of labour by restricting jobs to union members.

- *The time period*. In the immediate run the supply of labour will be fixed. You will have a certain number of employees available. In the short and medium term you can attract people with the right skills into your industry from other sectors. Over time, however, people can be trained to accept jobs and this will increase supply.

What do you think?

What job do you want to pursue as a career? Why?

Why might the quantity of labour supplied not increase if the wage goes up?

Economics in context

Wanted: secret service officer

The following is an extract from an advert for an operational officer for the UK Secret Intelligence Service.

The role of the Operational Officer is to plan and execute covert intelligence operations overseas. Working in London and abroad, Operational Officers gather the secret intelligence which government needs to promote and defend UK national interests.

The work calls for men and women who combine exceptional interpersonal skills with a strong intellect and a high degree of personal integrity. The successful Operational Officer will be someone able to influence and persuade others, and to do so across cultural and linguistic boundaries. Candidates who are bilingual or who come from ethnically diverse backgrounds are welcome for the particular skills and insights they bring. Regardless of their background and experience, Operational Officers will be energetic and resourceful, motivated by the challenge of solving complex problems. Resilience is important, as is the ability to deliver results under pressure, often in difficult and stressful environments. To become an Operational Officer requires a keen interest in international issues and a curiosity about other cultures, along with an appetite for living and working overseas.

Successful candidates for this special and demanding role will need a strong academic record to degree level or beyond, a history of personal achievement and influence in extra-curricular activities, and experience of independent travel. They will also have a demonstrable commitment to public service.

? Question

Do you think that the supply of labour for this position is likely to be high or low? Why?

 Economics in context — On strike for better pensions

In March 2006, many thousands of council workers stopped work for a day to protest against reforms to the government pension scheme. Many services were not provided, including schools, libraries, sports centres and public transport. The eleven trade unions involved claimed that over one million workers were involved in the dispute; this was the largest number of people stopping work in the UK since the General Strike in 1926. The employees were fighting government attempts to increase the effective retirement age from sixty to sixty-five. This change was because of the age-ing population that made the old scheme impossible to fund.

? Question

Why do you think people join trade unions?

Now you try it

What jobs would you be able to apply for tomorrow?
What jobs would you need extensive training for before you could apply?

The elasticity of supply for labour

The elasticity of supply for labour shows how responsive the supply of labour is to changes in the wage rate, all other factors being unchanged.

The elasticity of supply of labour is measured as follows:

$$\text{Elasticity of supply of labour} = \frac{\text{Percentage change in the quantity of labour supplied}}{\text{Percentage change in the wage rate}}.$$

Now you try it

Calculate the elasticity of supply of labour for the wage changes shown in Fig. 18.2.

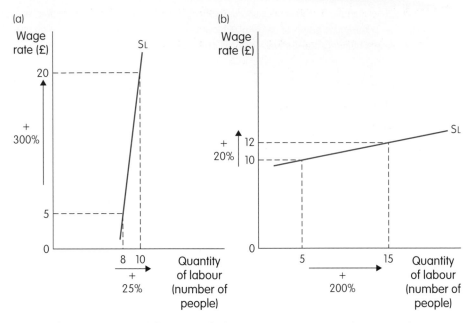

Figure 18.2 (a) A labour supply that is not responsive to changes in the wage rate: the supply of labour is wage rate inelastic. (b) A labour supply that is responsive to changes in the wage rate: the supply of labour is wage rate elastic.

The elasticity of supply of labour depends on factors such as the following.

● *The geographical mobility of labour*, that is, how easy it is for people to change location to get a job. This depends on:
  ● the availability of information (do employees know that jobs are available in the first place?);
  ● the costs of moving, for example, transport costs, removal costs and the costs of finding accommodation in different areas (house prices in some areas can be a major barrier to location);
  ● the upheaval involved in moving, for example, changing children's school, interrupting their education, and leaving friends and family;
  ● the willingness of people to take risks and move to a new area.
● *The occupational mobility of labour*, that is, how easy it is for employees to change professions if wages change. This depends on factors such as the training involved, the qualifications needed, the skills required and the awareness of the availability of jobs.

Economics in context

House prices in different areas of the UK

The house prices in different regions of the UK in 1996 and 2006 are shown in Table 18.1.

Table 18.1 Average house prices in different areas of the UK.

	1996	2006	Percentage change
Cornwall	£53,081	£195,388	268
Isle of Anglesey	£44,998	£158,527	252
Ceredigion	£48,137	£165,663	244
Carmarthenshire	£44,348	£152,049	243
Caerphilly	£37,052	£121,975	229

? Questions

Why do you think house prices differ so much between regions?

What impact do you think this has on labour supply?

What do you think?

What do you think makes people go out to work?

Economics in context

An ageing population

One of the key issues facing European business in the future is the increasing average age of the population. This means that firms will need to consider how to recruit older workers and how to retain their younger ones. It also means that many organisations will have to review their pension arrangements. Their existing pension schemes are simply not viable. In recent years nearly all large firms have ended their final salary pension scheme. This gave employees a proportion of their final salary every year of their retirement; the amount of pension they received depended on how many years they had worked. In 2005, Rentokil was the first company to end this scheme, not just for new employees but also for existing ones. It had to do this because the gap between its pension liabilities and assets was over £350 million.

? Question

How might an ageing population affect a firm's approach to recruitment and the management of staff?

■ The demand for labour

The demand for labour measures the number of employees that a firm is willing and able to employ, all other things being unchanged.

The demand for labour is a 'derived demand'. This means that employees are demanded because there is a demand for the final good or service. The demand for employees is derived from the demand for the product. Employees are needed to produce the output, so an increase in the demand for the product increases the demand for labour.

The demand for labour is determined by the value of each employee's output. This is measured by the marginal revenue product of labour (MRPL). The MRPL depends on how much output is produced by an additional employee and the value of that output when it is sold, that is,

$$MRPL = MP \times MR.$$

For example, if an additional employee produces ten units that can sell for £5 then the marginal revenue product of labour is £50.

The demand for labour will depend on the following.

- *Wages*. At higher wages less employees will be demanded because they are more expensive, all other things being unchanged. This is shown by a movement along the demand for labour curve and a change in the quantity of labour demanded.

- *The stock of capital equipment and technology*. The level of investment in capital goods will affect the productivity of employees and therefore their MRPL. Better capital equipment and technology should enable staff to produce more and this will lead to an increase in their MRPL.

- *Working practices and management approaches*. Better management and better ways of organising people can lead to improvements in the levels of output produced by employees.

- *Training*. If employees are better trained then they should be more productive and this will increase their MRPL.

- *Skills*. The more skilled employees are, the more productive they may be.

What do you think?

What do you think influences the level of investment within an industry or economy?

The MRPL is downward sloping due to the following reasons.

- The marginal product (extra output) of extra employees falls due to the law of diminishing returns (see Unit 9).

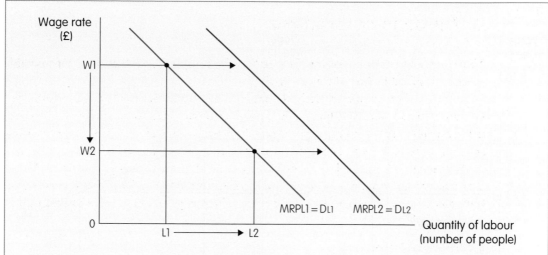

Figure 18.3 A movement along versus a shift in demand for labour. A change in the wage rate leads to a movement along the demand curve for labour. A change in other factors, such as productivity or demand for the product, shifts the demand curve.

- The marginal revenue (extra revenue) generated from selling units will either:
  - fall if the products are sold in monopoly markets (this is because the price has to be lowered to sell more; see Unit 10); or
  - be constant if the product is sold in perfectly competitive markets where the price is constant (see Unit 11).

Changes in the wage rate are shown as a movement along the demand for labour curve. Changes in any of the other factors above will lead to a shift in the curve as the value of the MRPL for any number of employees changes. The difference between a movement along and a shift in the MRPL is shown in Fig. 18.3.

■ The elasticity of demand for labour

The elasticity of demand for labour measures how sensitive the demand for labour is in relation to changes in the wage level. It is calculated as follows:

$$\text{Elasticity of demand for labour} = \frac{\text{Percentage change in the quantity demanded of labour}}{\text{Percentage change in the wage rate}}.$$

The demand for labour is wage inelastic if the percentage change in the quantity demanded in less than the percentage change in the wage level (see Fig. 18.4(a)). The demand for labour is wage elastic if the percentage change in the quantity demanded is greater than the percentage change in the wage rate (see Fig. 18.4(b)).

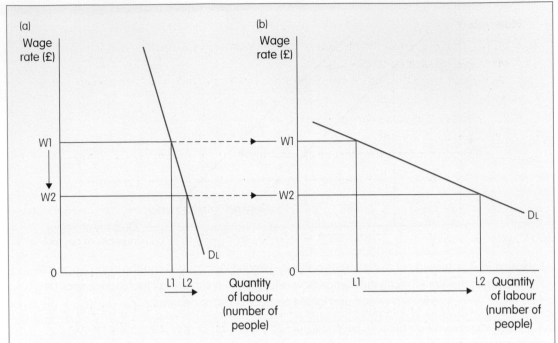

Figure 18.4 The impact of a change in wages: (a) wage inelastic demand and (b) wage elastic demand. In (a), a given percentage change in the wage rate leads to a smaller percentage change in the quantity demanded of labour. In (b), a given percentage change in the wage rate leads to a larger percentage change in the quantity demanded of labour.

The elasticity of demand for labour will depend on the following.

- *How easy it is to replace labour with other factors of production.* For example, is it easy to replace people with machines? The easier it is to replace staff, the more elastic the demand for labour will be. When economies are industrialising, the elasticity of demand for labour can be relatively high as there is plenty of scope for investment in capital equipment to do the work that people are doing at present.

- *The price elasticity of demand for the final product.* An increase in the wage rate will increase a firm's costs and therefore the price of the product. This will lead to a fall in sales. The greater the price elasticity of demand for the product, the greater the fall in sales and therefore the greater the fall in the number of staff needed, that is, the more elastic demand is for labour.

- *Wages as a proportion of total costs.* If wages are a high proportion of total costs then an increase in wages will significantly increase the overall costs. This is likely to lead to a relatively large fall in demand for labour, that is, demand for labour will be price elastic.

- *Time.* Over time it will be possible to find alternative ways of producing with less labour and so demand for labour will be more wage elastic in the long run.

Now you try it

- The wage rate increases by 10%. The quantity of labour demanded falls by 20%.
  What is the elasticity of demand for labour?
  What would happen if the elasticity of demand stayed the same and the wage rate increased by 2%?

- The price elasticity of demand for a product is –0.1.
  Is this price inelastic or elastic?
  Does this mean that demand for labour in this industry is likely to be elastic or inelastic? Why?

Wages in a perfectly competitive labour market

In a perfectly competitive labour market there are many buyers of labour. The level of wages in an industry is determined by the supply of labour and demand for labour.

If the wage was set at a wage rate above the equilibrium, for example, the wage W2 in Fig. 18.5, then this would lead to an excess supply of labour. More people are willing and able to work at this high rate than the quantity demanded. In a free market the wage rate would fall, leading to an increase in the quantity demanded and a fall in the quantity supplied. This process continues until equilibrium is reached at W1, where the quantity supplied equals the quantity demanded. At this point there is no incentive for the wage rate to change. If the wage rate was originally at W3, which is below the equilibrium rate, then there would be excess demand (see Fig. 18.5). The number of workers willing and able to

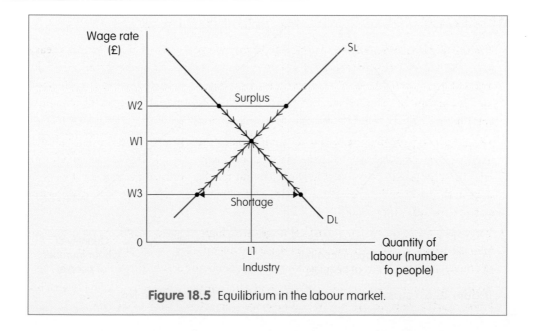

Figure 18.5 Equilibrium in the labour market.

work at this wage is less than the number demanded. In a free market this will lead to an increase in the level of wages until it reaches W1, where the market is in equilibrium.

The firm's decision to hire employees

A firm in a perfectly competitive labour market is small relative to the industry. It can hire as many employees as it wants and it will not have any noticeable impact on the overall demand for labour in the industry. This means that the firm is a wage taker: it can hire as many people as it wants at the given wage. This means that the extra cost of an employee is the wage (the marginal cost of labour equals the wage rate), as shown in Fig. 18.6.

A profit maximising firm will employ workers up until the point where the marginal revenue product of an employee is equal to the marginal cost of employing that worker, that is, the extra amount of revenue they generate is equal to the extra cost of employing them.

If the marginal revenue product of labour is greater than the marginal cost of labour then the extra revenue generated by hiring someone is greater than the extra cost of employing them, that is, profits increase by employing that person, so they will be hired.

If the marginal revenue product of labour is less than the marginal cost of labour then the extra revenue earned by hiring someone is less than the extra cost of hiring them, that is, profits will fall if that person is employed.

The area w1Bl1O in Fig. 18.6 shows the wages earned by employees. The area Aw1B represents the surplus (the difference between the marginal revenue product of labour and the marginal cost of labour) earned by the firm.

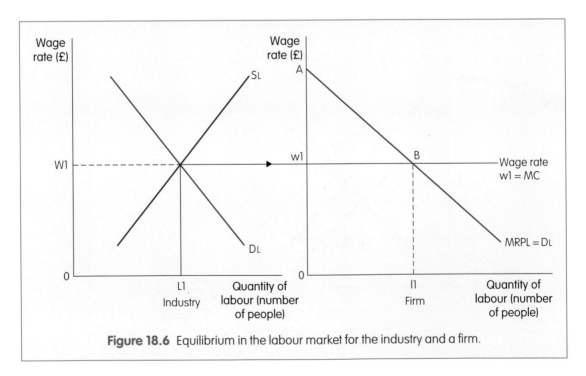

Figure 18.6 Equilibrium in the labour market for the industry and a firm.

■ Changes in demand and supply

The effect of an increase in demand for labour

Imagine that the market is at equilibrium at the wage W1 and the quantity of labour L1 (see Fig. 18.7). If there is then an outward shift in the demand for labour (perhaps due to an increase in demand for the product) then this will lead to an excess demand at the given wage. This in turn will lead to an increase in wages. As wages increase the number of people willing to work will increase (i.e., there will be an increase in quantity supplied) and the quantity of labour demanded will fall. This will continue until a new equilibrium is reached with higher wages and more people employed at the wage W2 and the quantity of labour L2 (see Fig. 18.7).

The effect of an increase in the supply of labour

Imagine that the market is at equilibrium at the wage W1 and the quantity of labour L1 (see Fig. 18.8). If there is then an outward shift in supply (perhaps due to a change in income tax rates that makes working more financially rewarding) then this will lead to an excess supply at the old wage rate. This in turn will lead to a fall in the wage rate. As this happens the quantity of labour supplied will fall whilst the quantity demanded will rise. This will continue until a new equilibrium is reached with a lower wage rate and a higher number of people employed at the wage W2 and the quantity of labour L2 (see Fig. 18.8).

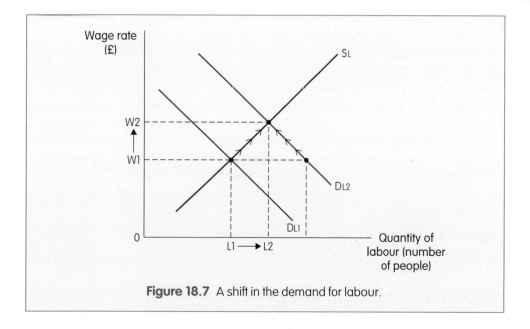

Figure 18.7 A shift in the demand for labour.

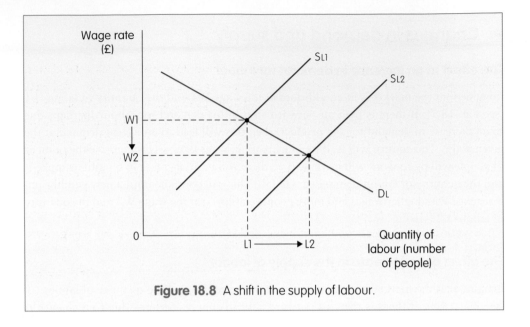

Figure 18.8 A shift in the supply of labour.

The wages of footballers

In 2003, Roman Abramovitch bought Chelsea Football Club and within a few years invested over £500 million. With his backing the club spent millions on new players. This led to football success as the club went on to win the Championship and the Carling Cup. Attendances increased by 300 000, enabling the club to fill its 42 500-seat stadium. Match day revenues reached around £1.5 million and the club had sponsorship deals with Adidas and Samsung. Even so, Chelsea Football Club struggled to break even. Following Abramovitch's investment, the plan was to start making profits by 2010. To do this it needed to control its costs, especially the wage bill. The players' wages were around 76% of the turnover. In the year to June 2004 the total payroll costs for 124 employees reached £102.5 million. This worked out as more than £826,000 per employee, according to a study by KPMG business advisers. The target at Chelsea was for wages to only account for 55% of the turnover. To achieve this, the club decided to focus more on its own youth academy. By comparison, at the League Division Two club Mansfield Town the 209 staff were paid a total of just £1.5 million in the year to June 2004, an average per person payment of £7235.

Between 1992 and 2004 the average ratio between wages and turnover in the Premier League rose from 44% to 61%.

? Question

Why do you think Chelsea players get paid so much?

Wage differentials

If all labour markets were perfectly competitive then all employees would be paid the same. This is because if the wages were higher in one industry than another then the employees in the lower-paid industry would move to the higher-paid one, attracted by the greater rewards. This would decrease the supply of labour in the lower-paid sector and bring up the equilibrium wage in that market (see Fig. 18.9(a)), whilst increasing the supply of labour in the highly-paid sector and reducing the equilibrium wage in that market (see Fig. 18.9(b)). This process continues until the wages are equal and there is no further incentive to move.

This assumes the following:

- that the movement of employees between industries is easy (i.e., no immobility);

- that employees are aware of what is being paid elsewhere and want to move to gain the highest possible wage;

- that employees have equal abilities and there are no barriers to prevent them moving and entering another industry.

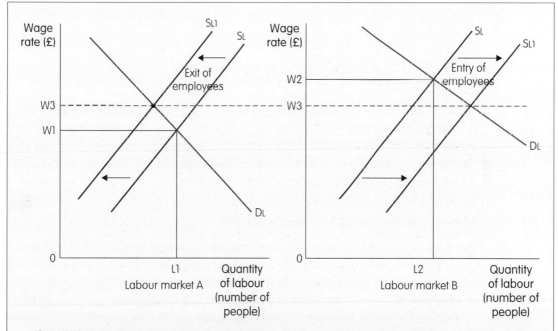

Figure 18.9 Shifts in supply bringing about equilibrium between labour markets. Consider two labour markets that are in equilibrium; market A is in equilibrium at the wage rate W1 and the quantity of labour L1, while market B is in equilibrium at the wage rate W2 and the quantity of labour L2. If there was perfect mobility then employees would leave market A and enter market B, attracted by the higher wages. The supply curve for labour in market A would shift to the left; the supply curve for labour in market B would shift to the right. This process would continue until the wages were equal and there was no further incentive for movement.

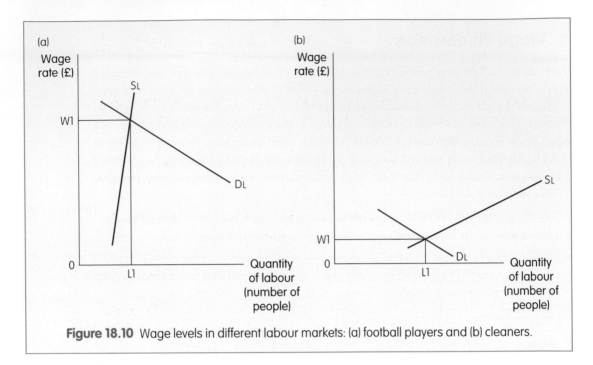

Figure 18.10 Wage levels in different labour markets: (a) football players and (b) cleaners.

In reality wage differences obviously do exist. This is due to the following reasons.

• Movement between industries is limited by geographical and occupational immobility. For example, there can be significant differences in the workforce in terms of skills and natural abilities; this can prevent employees moving easily from one market to another.

• Jobs differ significantly in terms of working conditions and job satisfaction; this naturally affects people's willingness to do them.

• Ignorance because employees may lack the information about what jobs are available elsewhere and so wage differences may continue.

These reasons mean that some people earn considerably more than others. If, for example, supply is limited (perhaps because special skills, talents or specialised training is needed) and/or demand for labour is high then the equilibrium wage rate is likely to be high (see Fig. 18.10(a)). If, however, the supply of labour is high (perhaps because it is an unskilled job) and the demand for labour is low (perhaps because it does not generate high revenues for the firm) then the wage rate will be much lower (see Fig. 18.10(b)).

What do you think?

Men and women still tend to follow very different career paths. Approximately 25% of female employees undertake administrative or secretarial work, whilst men are most likely to be managers, senior officials or in skilled trades.

Why do you think this is?

Problems with the marginal revenue product model of wage determination

Whilst using supply and demand analysis in the labour market provides some very useful insights into why certain jobs pay more than others, it does not explain all wages in a mixed economy. This is because of the following reasons.

- In some sectors, particularly the service sector, the actual productivity of an employee cannot easily be measured. What is the productivity of a receptionist, a welfare officer or a security guard?

- The output of some employees has no market value, for example, librarians, teachers and priests, and so their marginal revenue product cannot be valued.

- There are many markets. Whilst the theory of supply and demand may work, actually analysing the determinants of wages can be difficult because there are so many different markets. The demand for taxi drivers in London is very different from the demand in Dundee. The supply of motorbike couriers in the south-east of England may be different from the supply in Wales. 'The' labour market is therefore made up of millions of labour markets, each with its own supply and demand conditions.

- In the public sector the government determines the wage rate rather than market forces (although it is likely to compare public sector pay with private sector pay). In these cases the wages that are determined by supply and demand will probably influence the wages paid for these jobs, but market analysis does not effectively explain what happens.

Minimum wages

On 1 April 1999 the UK government introduced minimum wages. This set an hourly rate that employers could not go below. There are two rates: one for employees between the ages of eighteen and twenty and one for those over twenty.

The arguments for the minimum wage are the following.

- It ensures a 'living' wage, that is, one that is perceived as fair.

- It should mean that less people have to receive benefits and this should help to shift the aggregate supply function in the economy to the right.

- It should help to reduce the inequality between the low-income groups and the high-income groups.

The arguments against the minimum wage include the following.

- It raises costs and may reduce firms' profits. This may reduce funds for investment. The higher costs may also lead to higher prices for consumers.

- It creates unemployment by raising the price of labour.

In Fig. 18.11 imagine that the labour market is at equilibrium at the wage W0 and the quantity of labour L0. If a minimum wage above equilibrium is introduced then the quantity of

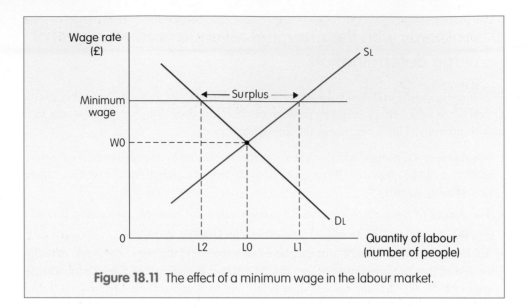

Figure 18.11 The effect of a minimum wage in the labour market.

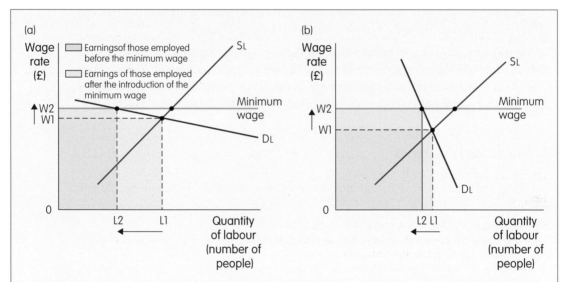

Figure 18.12 (a) The effect of a minimum wage when demand for labour is wage elastic. The introduction of a minimum wage above equilibrium leads to a fall in the overall earnings of those employed. (b) The effect of a minimum wage when demand for labour is wage inelastic. The introduction of a minimum wage above equilibrium increases the earnings of those employed.

labour supplied is L1 but the quantity demanded is L2. Those who are in work are earning more, but the total number in work is reduced.

The impact of overall earnings depends on the wage elasticity of demand for labour. If demand for labour is elastic then the higher wage leads to a proportionately higher fall in the quantity demanded and overall earnings decrease for those in jobs (see Fig. 18.12(a)).

If demand is inelastic then the higher wage leads to a proportionately lower fall in the quantity demanded and overall earnings increase for those in jobs (see Fig. 18.12(b)).

What do you think?

Should the minimum wage be higher than it is at the moment in the UK?

Case Study

The median[1] weekly pay[2] for full-time employees in the UK in 2005 was £431. For women it was £372. According to the *Annual Survey of Hours and Earnings* published by the Office of National Statistics, the top 10 per cent of the earnings distribution earned more than £851 per week, while the bottom 10 per cent earned less than £235. Obviously earnings varied between regions. Full-time weekly earnings in London were £556, significantly higher than in other regions, where they ranged from £386 in the North East to £450 in the South East.

The occupations with the highest earnings in 2005 were 'Health professionals', (median pay of full-time employees of £1021 a week), followed by 'Corporate managers' (£663) and 'Science and technology professionals' (£633). The lowest paid of all full-time employees were 'Sales occupations', at £245 a week.

Earning also differed between the public and private sectors. The monetary difference between the median level of full-time earnings in the public sector (£476 per week in April 2005) and the private sector (£412 per week) has widened over the year to April 2005; in 2004 the figures were £456 and £403, respectively.

❓ Questions

- Explain the possible reasons for the differences in earnings between regions and between jobs.
- Why do you think earnings differ between the private and public sectors?
- How could a government make earnings more equal? Do you think it should do this?

[1] The median is the value below which 50% of employees fall.
[2] Pay refers to gross pay (before tax) of full-time employees on adult rates whose pay for the survey week was unaffected by absence. Annual and weekly earnings include overtime.

Checklist

Now you have read this unit try to answer the following questions.

- ☐ Do you understand that labour is a derived demand?
- ☐ Can you explain the factors that affect the demand and supply of labour?
- ☐ Can you explain the profit maximising condition for hiring labour?
- ☐ Can you explain why wages might differ between jobs?

End of unit questions

1 Why is the demand for labour downward sloping?

2 To what extent does labour productivity determine the demand for labour?

3 What is the effect on the market wage of an increase in the supply of labour?

4 Why are merchant bankers paid so much in comparison to teachers?

5 Is having a minimum wage a good thing?

Key learning points

- The demand for labour is derived from the demand for the final product.
- Profit maximising firms employ workers up to the point where the marginal revenue product of labour equals the marginal cost of labour.
- The wage and employment decisions depend on the nature of the labour market.

Learn more

There are many different forms of labour market. In the UK, for example, the National Health Service employs a high proportion of doctors and nurses. To learn more about these labour markets visit our website at the address below.

 Visit our Online Resource Centre at www.oxfordtextbooks.co.uk/orc/gillespie_econ for test questions and further information on topics covered in this chapter.

Macroeconomics

Introduction to macroeconomics

In the previous units we have focused on microeconomic issues. For example, we have examined the demand for labour in a particular industry or the structure of a specific market. In this unit we outline the issues involved in macro-economics. These are then developed in the following units.

LEARNING OBJECTIVES

By the end of this unit you should be able to:

✔ explain the meaning of macroeconomics;

✔ explain government economic objectives;

✔ explain government policy instruments;

✔ explain the possible conflicts of government economic objectives.

■ Introduction

In the previous units we have been studying microeconomic issues. We have looked at the demand and supply of a particular product and examined the different structures that can exist in different markets. This form of analysis helps us to explain issues such as:

• why the price of a product is high or low;

• why someone working in one industry may get paid more than someone working elsewhere;

• why firms in some industries can earn more profits than others.

These are all microeconomic issues.

However, we may also want to examine the economy on a larger (or macro) scale. For example, we may be interested in the general price level in an economy rather than the price of one product. We may want to examine the average wage rate in the economy as a whole or the total amount being produced in a country rather than focus on one industry. Macroeconomics tackles all of these issues. Building on the analysis covered in microeconomics, macroeconomics takes more of an overview and focuses on big issues that affect the economy as a whole.

In microeconomics we developed an understanding of a series of concepts and models, such as supply and demand analysis, and marginal cost and marginal revenue. We were then able to apply this understanding to a range of markets and market structures. We saw how supply and demand might affect the price of oil, housing, labour, and concert tickets. Using our economic tools we could analyse many different markets to understand changes within them. The same is true in macroeconomics. We will develop an understanding of many different areas of the economy, such as households, government and firms. We will put this understanding together to build a model of the economy that includes areas such as the money market, the labour market, the capital goods market, and the market for final goods and services. We will analyse how a change in interest rates, taxation or government spending affects all of these markets and be able to trace the effect through to the impact on national income, growth, prices, employment, the government's budget and the trade position. In essence, we will be building a model of the whole economy and learning how the different elements fit together and interact with each other. The analytical tools that you gain will allow you to analyse any economy in the world and appreciate some of the fundamental issues within them. By the end of this book you should be able to form a view on the policies that any government should consider adopting given the position of its economy. However, you will also come to realise how difficult it is actually trying to control an economy made up of millions of households and firms, all with their own objectives, constraints, expectations and experiences. Sometimes policy decisions do not lead to the result that you expected, especially when you are dealing with as many different relationships as there are within any economy.

Of course, economic change has a real impact on people's lives. It affects whether they have a job, what they do, whether they can afford to buy a house, whether they have a good standard of living and whether they can afford to start a family. Economic analysis is therefore important to governments because they have a responsibility for the state of the economy and are often assessed on their economic performance. In fact, how well the economy is doing is a very important factor in determining how people vote. A government will set economic objectives and then try to influence the economy to achieve these using its policy tools.

▨ Government economic objectives

Typical government objectives include achieving the following.

- *Economic growth*. Economic growth measures how much the income of the economy is growing over time. This is often seen as a very important target for governments. This is because, with more income in the economy, people can afford more products and may have a better quality of life. Certainly, for developing countries more income can provide the healthcare needed to reduce some of the suffering. Interestingly, however, in more-developed economies there is some debate over whether having more money does necessarily lead to a better standard of living (if you work an eighty-hour week you may earn more but not enjoy life much). This debate is discussed in Unit 22. Nevertheless, most governments still try to make sure that their economies are growing. Economic growth can provide more income, more jobs and economic progress.

- *Stable prices*. In most economies prices in general increase by a small percentage each year. For most firms and people this is not a major problem; they can plan for it and take it into account when setting their own prices or bargaining for their wages. However, sometimes prices can increase at very fast rates. This can become a problem in many ways. For example, some people will find that they cannot afford products and will be worse off, and the country's products are likely to be expensive when they try to sell them abroad, which could limit sales. This is why governments usually try to keep prices relatively stable. Increases in the general price level are known as inflation and governments usually try to keep this at a low and predictable rate. The causes, consequences and possible cures of inflation are examined in Unit 29.

- *Low levels of unemployment*. If people are unemployed then they are not working. This means that they are not generating output and are not earning money. This is a waste of resources and is also a drain on a government's own income because it will probably have to pay benefits to the unemployed people. Unemployment can also lead to frustration and discontent with the government, and so, not surprisingly, the government will usually try to reduce it! The causes, consequences and cures of unemployment are examined in Unit 27.

- A *favourable balance of trade*. All countries are involved in trade. They buy goods and services from abroad (these are called imports) and they sell products overseas (these are called exports). The amount that a country buys and sells abroad depends on many factors, such as the relative price of products, the quality and the incomes in the different countries. As we shall see in Unit 31, by trading abroad a country can consume outside of its own production possibility frontier. A government is therefore likely to encourage trade but may want to make sure that the imports and exports are reasonably balanced. If there are too many imports then this leads to money leaving the economy; if there are too many exports then this may mean that foreign governments retaliate because money is flowing out of their economies. Governments will therefore monitor the balance of trade and ensure that it is at an appropriate level.

What do you think?

How well is your economy doing in terms of the economic objectives above?

Economics in context

Economic forecasts for 2007

Table 19.1 shows forecasts for a range of economic indicators for selected economies, made in 2006 for 2007.

Table 19.1 Economic forecasts for selected economies for 2007.

	National income growth 2007 (%)	Government spending-revenue (% national income)	Inflation (%)	Export revenue-import spending for goods and services (% national income)
US	3.1	−3.7	2.4	−7.6
Japan	2.2	−4.7	0.8	5.5
UK	2.9	−3.2	1.7	−2.9
China	9.5	−1.2	3.5	5.8
India	7.1	−6.8	4.3	−2.9
Russia	5.7	5.0	10.0	7.9

Source: OECD (Organization for Economic Cooperation and Development) estimates.

❓ **Question**

What do you think of the economic performance of the economies in Table 19.1?

What do you think?

Which of the four main objectives outlined above should be the government's priority? Why?

▪ Policy instruments

To achieve its objectives a government may use economic tools such as the following (see Fig. 19.1).

- *Fiscal policy*. This involves changing the level of government spending and taxation rates.
- *Monetary policy*. This involves controlling the money supply and changing interest rates.

By changing the different elements of fiscal and monetary policy the government will try to influence the total level of demand in the economy (this is called aggregate demand)

Economics in context	Indicators of economic performance

When assessing an economy there are many different indicators that can be examined. According to an OECD report, the performance of the UK economy in 2003 was as shown in Table 19.2.

Table 19.2 The performance of the UK economy in 2003 in comparison to all thirty OECD countries.

GDP per capita (i.e. income per person)	14th
Productivity (i.e. output per worker)	15th
Percentage of adults having more than low skills	17th
Intensity of research and development spending	14th
Infrastructure	17th
Extent to which product markets are liberalised (i.e. competitive)	2nd

Source: OECD (Organization for Economic Cooperation and Development) report.

? Question

What else might you measure to assess the economic performance of an economy?

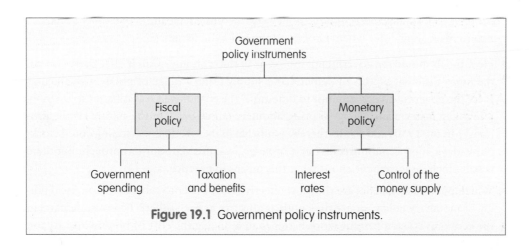

Figure 19.1 Government policy instruments.

or the total level of supply in the economy (this is called aggregate supply). For example, the government might:

- cut income tax, leaving people with more money to spend (here fiscal policy is affecting aggregate demand);
- increase its spending in areas such health and defence to generate more demand (here fiscal policy is affecting aggregate demand);

- make it cheaper for people to borrow money by lowering interest rates (here monetary policy is affecting aggregate demand);
- make it cheaper and easier for firms to borrow money to invest in new equipment (here monetary policy is affecting aggregate supply);
- reduce unemployment benefits to encourage more people to work (here fiscal policy is affecting aggregate supply).

Monetary and fiscal policy are examined in more detail in Units 28 and 26, respectively.

What do you think?

How important are changes in interest rates to you?

■ Policy debates

Inevitably, using government policy to affect the economy is quite complex and not a precise science. If you cut income tax, for example, and expect people to spend more then you may be surprised and find that they decide to save it! Instead, they may spend it much later than you thought they would, so the impact does not occur at the right time. Alternatively, at the time you cut taxes other changes in the economy may offset the expected benefits of this. Changes in economic policy can therefore have unpredictable effects.

Economists often differ when it comes to the following issues.

- How much should the government intervene in the economy? Can it effectively control the many different aspects of demand and supply using a range of policy instruments? If so, the government can attempt to 'fine-tune' the economy? Or is it better to use only a few key instruments to try to bring about broad changes in the nature of the economy? In the 1950s and 1960s there was a belief in the UK that fine-tuning could work. Nowadays, most economists favour a broader, less interventionist approach, but there is still much disagreement about what this means in practice.

- Which policy instruments are the most effective? Is it better to rely mainly on fiscal policy or monetary policy, or are they both as effective as each other? To boost demand in the economy, does a tax cut work better than reducing the cost of borrowing? Again, there is much debate here and views change over time. At the moment the UK government favours interest rates as the main policy tool to influence the economy, but obviously continues to use a range of other spending, tax and benefit programmes to support this.

The role and effectiveness of monetary and fiscal policy are examined in Units 28 and 26, respectively.

■ Policy conflicts

Even if it was clear which policy instruments were best, life would still be difficult for governments! This is because achieving all of its economic objectives at the same time may prove problematic. For example, to reduce unemployment the government may want to encourage more spending in the economy (perhaps through lower taxes and lower interest rates). However, as we saw in our microeconomic analysis, an increase in demand may lead to higher prices, causing higher inflation. Achieving one target has been at the expense of another. Similarly, if an economy was importing too much then one possible solution to this would be to slow the economy's growth; with less growth in income the amount of imported products which people were buying would probably fall. However, the consequence of this would be less demand and more unemployment within the economy. Again, achieving one goal has had a negative effect on others. Of course, by using the right combination of policies it may be possible to achieve all of the goals, or at least reach an acceptable compromise. However, the government may have to decide what the priority at any moment is, and on its general focus in terms of policy instruments.

According to the Organization for Economic Cooperation and Development (OECD), the UK economy in the decade after the mid-1990s has performed well:

> Over the last decade, macroeconomic performance has been impressive: GDP (national income) growth has been robust and cyclical fluctuations in output have proved smaller than for almost any other OECD country, while inflation has remained close to target. This performance is a testament to the strength of the institutional arrangements for setting monetary and fiscal policy as well as to the flexibility of labour and product markets.

According to the OECD, the key issues at present that are facing the government are the need for the following.

- *To raise the skill level of the workforce.* This is important to take advantage of new technology and to increase productivity.

- *To improve the innovation performance.* This is important to stimulate growth.

- *To improve the transport infrastructure.* As a result of years of under-investment there are congested roads and an unreliable rail system, which reduces productivity.

- *To increase labour participation by helping those claiming incapacity benefit into work.* This would increase the labour supply.

- *To ensure that public money is spent efficiently to contain the tax burden.*

What do you think?

Why is the transport infrastructure important to the performance of an economy?

Case Study

The following is taken from the CIA factbook.

The UK, a leading trading power and financial centre, is one of the quintet of trillion dollar economies of Western Europe. Over the past two decades the government has greatly reduced public ownership and contained the growth of social welfare programmes. . . . Services, particularly banking, insurance and business services, account by far for the largest proportion of national income while industry continues to decline in importance. The growth of the economy slipped in 2001–03 as the global downturn and the high value of the pound hurt manufacturing and exports, but partially recovered in 2004.

Despite slower growth, the economy is one of the strongest in Europe; inflation, interest rates and unemployment remain low. . . . Meanwhile the government has been speeding up the improvement of education, transport and health services at a cost in higher taxes and a widening public deficit.

❓ Questions

- How dependent do you think the UK economy is on other economies? Why is this so?
- Should the UK government spend even more on education, transport and health services?
- Why do you think services have increased in importance in the UK?
- What is meant by a 'strong' economy? How strong do you think the UK economy is now?

@ Web

For more information from the CIA on economies visit www.cia.gov/cia/publications/factbook

Checklist

Now you have read this unit try to answer the following questions.

- ☐ Can you explain the meaning of macroeconomics?
- ☐ Can you explain government economic objectives?
- ☐ Can you explain what is meant by government policy instruments?
- ☐ Can you explain possible conflicts of objectives?

End of unit questions

1 How does microeconomics differ from macroeconomics?
2 What are the four main economic objectives of a government and why do they matter?
3 Explain how the economic objectives of a government might conflict.
4 Do you think that one economic objective is more important than another?

Key learning points

- Macroeconomic analysis focuses on the economy as a whole rather than one market within it.

- Typical economic objectives include stable prices, economic growth, a favourable trade situation and low unemployment.

- The government uses policies, such as monetary and fiscal policy, to achieve its economic objectives.

- Achieving all of the government's objectives simultaneously may be difficult; at times there may be a conflict of objectives.

Learn more

To learn more about the performance of the UK economy over recent years visit our website at the address below.

 Visit our Online Resource Centre at www.oxfordtextbooks.co.uk/orc/gillespie_econ for test questions and further information on topics covered in this chapter.

Equilibrium in the economy

In this unit we examine how equilibrium in the economy is brought about. To do this we consider aggregate demand and aggregate supply. In microeconomics we examined supply and demand in one particular market. In macroeconomics we consider supply and demand for the whole economy; these are called aggregate supply and demand.

LEARNING OBJECTIVES

By the end of this unit you should be able to:

✔ distinguish between injections and withdrawals;

✔ explain the conditions necessary for equilibrium in the economy and how the economy moves toward equilibrium;

✔ explain the factors that can influence aggregate demand;

✔ analyse the multiplier effect caused by a change in aggregate demand;

✔ explain the factors that can influence aggregate supply.

▩ Introduction

We will begin our study of macroeconomics by considering how equilibrium in an economy is determined, that is, what determines how much an economy is producing and earning. This analysis will help us to understand macro issues such as economic growth, unemployment and the impact of government policy changes. Obviously, some economies are much richer than others. The USA, for example, is much richer than Papua New Guinea. This unit examines the reasons why an economy settles at a particular level of income; with this understanding, we can then consider how to increase the income of a country.

■ Equilibrium in the economy

In microeconomics we saw that equilibrium in a particular market occurs when demand equals supply. In macroeconomics equilibrium in the economy as a whole will occur when the total (or 'aggregate') planned demand in the economy for all goods and services equals the total (or 'aggregate') supply of these products. Thus, for equilibrium in the economy, we have

Aggregate demand = Aggregate supply,

$$AD = AS.$$

To analyse how and why equilibrium occurs in an economy, we first consider the circular flow of income.

■ The circular flow of income

Imagine a simple economy in which there are just firms and households. This is called a two-sector economy. In this case the value of the output produced by producers equals the income earned by households. For example, if the economy produces £100 of goods then the money for this is earned as income in some form by households (either as wages, rental on land or capital goods or profit). In the simplest of models this is then spent on buying the goods and services produced by the firms. The money flows around in what is known as a circular flow of income (see Fig. 20.1). In this situation we can see that the output of the final goods and services, the income earned and the expenditure are all equal:

Output = Income = Expenditure.

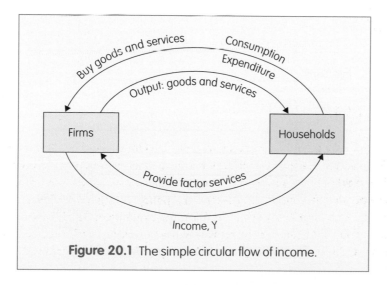

Figure 20.1 The simple circular flow of income.

Of course, this is a very limited model in which there are only two sectors and everything that is produced is sold. What we can now do is to extend the analysis by adding in other sectors of the economy (namely, the foreign sector and the government); this will introduce injections and withdrawals into the circular flow of income.

■ Injections (J)

Injections (J) into the economy represent spending on final goods and services in addition to households' spending. Injections include the following.

- *Investment*. This is spending on capital goods by firms, and is labelled 'I'. It includes the purchase of new equipment and machinery. It also includes stockbuilding; if stocks increase then firms are assumed to have invested in these (intentionally or not).

- *Government spending*. This is spending by the government on final goods and services, such as health and education, and is labelled 'G'.

- *Exports*. This represents the spending from abroad on an economy's final goods and services, and is labelled 'X'.

So, in summary, we have:

Injections (J) = I + G + X.

All of these injections are assumed to be unrelated to the level of output or income, as shown in Fig. 20.2. They are, therefore, exogeneous. This means that they are determined by factors other than the level of national income; the following are some examples.

- The level of investment in an economy (I) may be influenced by the cost of borrowing (interest rates) and expectations of future profits (which may be influenced by how the economy will do in the future) rather than the level of national income at the moment. Investment is examined in greater detail in Unit 25.

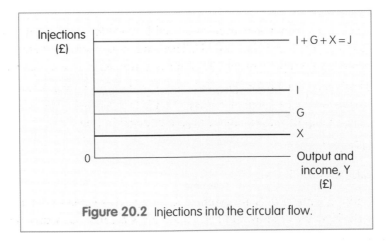

Figure 20.2 Injections into the circular flow.

- The level of government spending on final goods and services in an economy (G) may be influenced by government policy and its view about the appropriate levels of government intervention and expenditure. There is no definite, predictable relationship between the level of government spending and the level of national income. The government spending G does not include transfer payments (i.e., payments such as benefits that simply redistribute income). Government spending is examined in greater detail in Unit 26.

- The level of spending on our exports (X) may be affected by income levels abroad and the exchange rate; it is not determined by the level of UK income. The influences on a country's level of exports are examined in greater detail in Unit 31.

Planned injections refer to the amount that the government, firms and foreigners intend to spend in a given period on final goods and services in an economy.

What do you think?

What do you think the government spends money on?

What do you think are the main influences on the amount of government spending in an economy?

What do you think would make firms invest more in capital equipment?

■ Withdrawals (W)

Withdrawals (W) represent income that has been earned but which is not spent on final goods and services in this economy. Withdrawals include the following.

- *Savings*. This is income earned by households that is saved rather than spent, and is labelled 'S'. People may save by putting money in the bank, for example, or by putting some of their salary into a pension scheme. Consumption and savings are examined in greater detail in Unit 24.

- *Taxation*. This is revenue taken from firms and households by the government and therefore is not spent. This is labelled 'T'. There are many forms of taxation, such as taxes on income and company profits. Taxation is examined in greater detail in Unit 26.

- *Imports*. This is spending on foreign goods and services. This means that this spending leaves this economy to be spent elsewhere. This is labelled 'M'. The influences on a country's level of imports are examined in greater detail in Unit 31.

So, in summary, we have:

Withdrawals (W) = S + T + M.

Unlike injections, withdrawals are assumed to be directly related to income (i.e., they are a function of income), as shown in Fig. 20.3. This is because as income increases the following occurs.

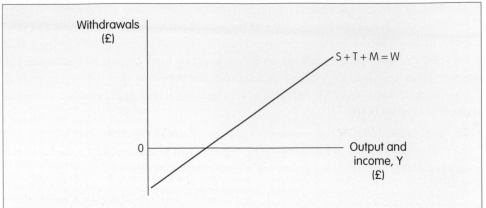

Figure 20.3 Withdrawals from the circular flow. At zero income there will still be some spending (e.g., from past savings), that is, there is dis-saving (negative savings).

- The level of savings tends to increase.
- The amount paid in tax will increase; for example, people will earn and spend more, so the government will gain more tax revenue from this.
- The amount spent on foreign goods and services will increase. With more income households will spend more, and some of this will be on foreign goods and services. This spending will therefore leave the UK economy.

Now you try it

List as many types of tax as you can.

The circular flow of income including injections and withdrawals is shown in Fig. 20.4.

■ Adding in injections and withdrawals: planned and actual

Let us now return to our simple economy with output and income of £100, but now assume that planned withdrawals are £40. This means that, of the £100 produced, £40 of this will not be demanded because households are saving, paying this in tax or spending this money abroad. The economy is clearly not in equilibrium unless there is £40 of planned injections, that is, the £40 worth of products that households do not require are wanted by someone else (e.g., the government, firms or foreigners).

If the planned injections do equal the planned withdrawals then the £40 worth of products produced but not bought by domestic households are bought by another group, such as the government. In this case, the aggregate demand in the economy will equal the

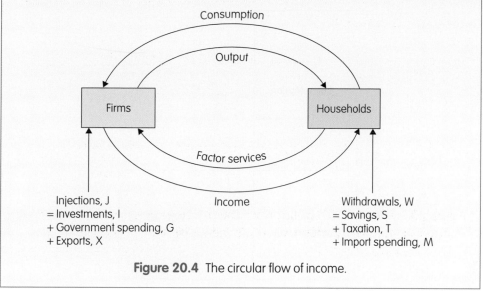

Figure 20.4 The circular flow of income.

aggregate supply, and the economy will be in equilibrium. So, for equilibrium in the economy we have:

Planned S + T + M = Planned I + G + X.

The planned injections equal the planned withdrawals, so all of the output produced is bought and the economy is in equilibrium (see Fig. 20.5).

Note that individual elements of injections and withdrawals do not need to be equal (i.e., the planned S does not have to equal the planned I), but the overall planned injections must equal the overall planned withdrawals.

■ Getting to equilibrium: the adjustment process

Imagine that planned injections are too low compared to planned withdrawals. This means that there is not enough demand in the economy. The amount that households do not buy is not completely bought by, say, the government or foreigners. Firms will have to increase their stocks unexpectedly. In the next time period they will cut back on output because the demand had been lower than expected; this means that less income is earned in the economy. This will not affect the level of injections because they are assumed to be exogeneous of income. However, with less income there will be less planned withdrawals (savings, taxation and import spending will fall with less income). This process will continue, with income falling leading to lower planned withdrawals, until the level of planned injections and planned withdrawals are equal. Changes in output and income therefore lead to a change in the level of the planned withdrawals, until the planned injections and the planned withdrawals are equal and the economy is in equilibrium, as shown in Fig. 20.6.

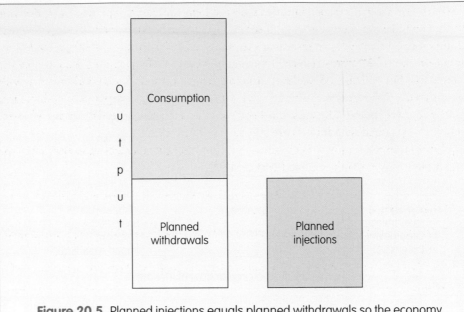

Figure 20.5 Planned injections equals planned withdrawals so the economy is in equilibrium.

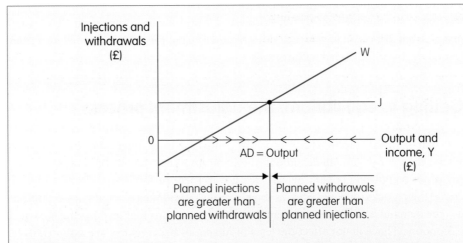

Figure 20.6 Planned injections and planned withdrawals. When planned injections are greater than planned withdrawals, there is too much demand in the economy; firms will increase their output to meet the higher levels of demand. When planned withdrawals are greater than planned injections, there is too little demand in the economy; firms will reduce their output.

On the other hand, if planned injections are too high compared to planned withdrawals then there will be too much demand in the economy. Firms will have to de-stock. In the next time period they will increase their output because demand was so high, leading to more income in the economy. This will not change the level of injections (because they are exogeneous), but will change the level of planned withdrawals. These will increase with more income. This process continues, with firms increasing output which increases income and therefore withdrawals, until equilibrium is reached where the planned injections and the planned withdrawals are equal.

Equilibrium in the economy is therefore brought about by changes in output until the planned injections equal the planned withdrawals.

Now you try it

If planned injections are £300 million and planned withdrawals are £100 million, is the economy in equilibrium or not?

If not, is equilibrium income higher or lower than the present income? Explain your answer.

From this analysis we can see that if the level of planned injections in an economy increases then the level of income will increase until the planned injections once again equal the planned withdrawals, as shown in Fig. 20.7.

Government policy that aims to increase national income might therefore focus on increasing planned injections into the economy. For example, the government may do the following:

- offer incentives to encourage investment by firms;
- increase its own government spending;
- promote UK goods and services abroad.

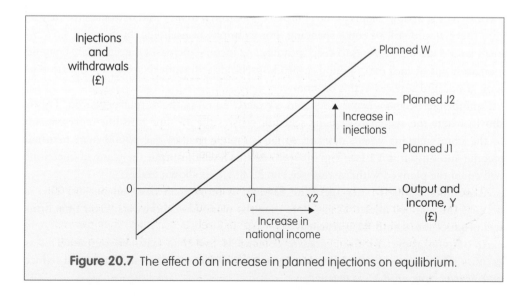

Figure 20.7 The effect of an increase in planned injections on equilibrium.

Equilibrium explained: an alternative approach

Another way of explaining equilibrium in the economy is to focus on the aggregate demand equation.

The aggregate demand (AD) is equal to the total planned demand for final goods and services in an economy, and is written as follows:

$$AD = C + I + G + X - M,$$

where C is the consumption (this is the demand for goods and services by households), I is the investment (this is the demand for goods and services by firms), G is the government spending on goods and services, and X − M equals the exports minus the imports (this represents the overall demand for goods and services resulting from international trade).

In equilibrium the aggregate demand equals the aggregate supply, that is,

$$AD = AS.$$

The aggregate demand schedule

In Fig. 20.8(a) the level of aggregate demand is shown relative to national output and income. The schedule begins at the point F; it is assumed that even if national income was zero there would still be some spending. For example, households, firms or the government would use past savings to keep spending. As income increases the aggregate demand increases; out of each extra pound earned households will want to spend a proportion of it on goods and services in this economy.

Equilibrium occurs when the demand is exactly equal to the output produced. This is shown where the aggregate demand schedule crosses the 45° line (this line represents all of the combinations where demand equals supply), that is, the equilibrium national income and output is Y1 (see Fig. 20.8(a)). At this level of output the planned injections will equal the planned withdrawals (see Fig. 20.8(b)), as shown earlier.

At outputs below Y1 the aggregate demand is more than national output. This is because the planned injections are more than the planned withdrawals. Over time firms will produce more until Y1 is reached.

At outputs above Y1 the aggregate demand is less than national output. This is because the planned injections are less than the planned withdrawals. Firms will reduce output over time until Y1 is reached.

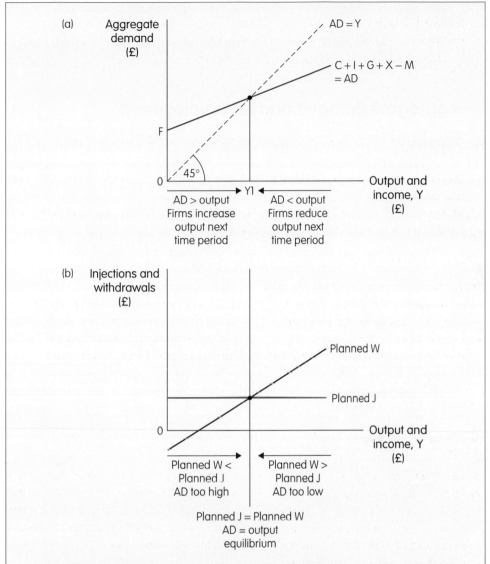

Figure 20.8 Equilibrium output (a) using aggregate demand analysis and (b) using injections and withdrawals. In (a), the aggregate demand curve slopes upwards because with more income households spend more, and so consumption increases. At zero income there will still be spending, for example, by the government.

Now you try it

Suppose that Y1 is the equilibrium output.

Below Y1 are the planned injections more or less than the planned withdrawals, or equal to them?

Above Y1 are the planned injections more or less than the planned withdrawals, or equal to them?

At Y1 are the planned injections more or less than the planned withdrawals, or equal to them?

■ Aggregate demand and full employment

Full employment occurs when all of those willing and able to work at the given real wage rate are working. Thus resources are fully employed; this represents the maximum output that the economy can produce given its existing resources.

If the aggregate demand schedule is AD1 then the economy is in equilibrium at Y1; in this case, Y1 is full employment. However, whilst the economy will always move toward equilibrium, this does not necessarily mean that this equilibrium is always at full employment. In fact, the economy will often settle in equilibrium below full employment, and therefore governments will try to boost the level of demand. If an economy is below full employment then it is operating within the production possibility frontier. When the aggregate demand is below the level required for full employment this is known as a **recessionary** or **deflationary output gap**. This means that output and income are less than they could be. The 'gap' is measured by the amount that the aggregate demand has to increase by to reach the full employment equilibrium (e.g., the vertical difference between AD2 and AD1 in Fig. 20.9).

An **inflationary output gap** occurs when the aggregate demand is above the level required for full employment. The 'gap' is measured by the amount that the aggregate

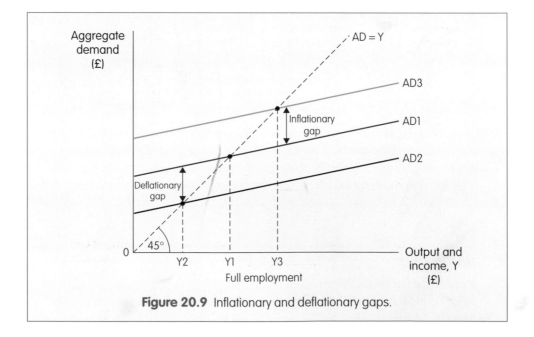

Figure 20.9 Inflationary and deflationary gaps.

demand has to decrease by to reach the full employment equilibrium (e.g., the vertical distance between AD3 and AD1 in Fig. 20.9). It is called an inflationary gap because with excess demand there will be upward pressure on prices; if prices do increase then this is called inflation. This is examined in greater detail in Unit 29.

◾ Reflationary policies

Reflationary policies occur when the government increases the level of aggregate demand in the economy. To do this a government could use demand side policies such as the following.

- The government can increase its own spending on goods and services (increasing G).
- The government can reduce taxes to increase the incomes of customers and firms; this should lead to greater spending (increasing C and I).
- The government can reduce taxes placed on goods and services; this again should encourage spending in the economy (increasing C).
- The government can reduce interest rates; this should encourage borrowing and therefore spending because loans will be cheaper to repay. It should also discourage savings because the rewards for doing so are less (increasing C and I).

An increase in the aggregate demand can be seen by an upward shift of the AD schedule. As can be seen in Fig. 20.10, this leads to a new equilibrium at Y2. The increase in the aggregate demand has led to a greater increase in national income. This is due to the multiplier effect.

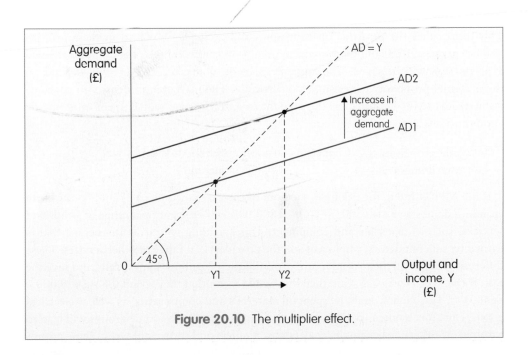

Figure 20.10 The multiplier effect.

■ The multiplier effect

The multiplier effect explains how an initial increase in the planned injections into the economy increases national income by more than the initial increase. For example, an increase in government spending by £1 million may increase national income by £5 million; in this case the multiplier is 5. The size of the multiplier shows how much output in the economy will increase relative to the initial increase in demand.

■ How does the multiplier work?

Imagine that a government decides to spend £1 million on new schools and hospitals. This means that the construction companies and architects involved in these projects will be earning £1 million. Of these earnings a proportion will be spent domestically and a proportion will be saved. The amount spent on domestic products will depend on the marginal propensity to consume domestically. The marginal propensity to consume domestically (MPCD) measures the amount of extra income that is spent on domestic goods and services:

$$\text{Marginal propensity to consume domestically} = \frac{\text{Change in consumer spending domestically}}{\text{Change in income}}.$$

If the MPCD is 0.8, for example, then out of the extra income of £1 million the extra spending domestically is £800,000. This £800,000 will be spent on a range of goods and services, such as materials and equipment. This spending will generate income that is earned by subcontractors, employees and the providers of a range of other services. These different groups will then spend a proportion of their earnings domestically and save the rest. If the MPCD was 0.8 again then this would mean that they spend 0.8 × £800,000 = £640,000. This money might be spent on materials and components, as well as electrical goods, cars, meals out, and so on. Once again, this spending by some groups will lead to earnings by others, for example, dealerships, retailers and their employees. These groups will again spend a proportion of their income, in this case $0.8 \times £640,000 = £512,000$. This process of spending leading to income, leading to further spending will be continued.

So the effect of an initial spending of £1 million will be

$$£1,000,000 + £800,000 + £640,000 + £512,000 + \ldots$$

The total effect of an increase in spending can be calculated using the following expression:

$$\frac{1}{1 - MPCD}.$$

In this case it would be $1/(1 - 0.8) = 1/0.2 = 5$. Thus any initial increase in spending will have five times the effect on the output; the multiplier has a value of 5. Therefore an initial increase in spending of £1 million will lead to an overall increase of £5 million (which is the sum of the series $£1,000,000 + £800,000 + £640,000 + £512,000 + \ldots$).

■ The size of the multiplier

The size of the multiplier depends on the size of the marginal propensity to consume domestically. The higher the marginal propensity to consume domestically, the greater will be the size of the multiplier because more of consumers' income is spent domestically at each stage of the process. For example, if the MPCD is 0.9 then the size of the multiplier will be

$$\frac{1}{1 - 0.9} = \frac{1}{0.1} = 10.$$

This means that an increase in spending of £1 million will lead to an overall increase in national income of £10 million. This is because at each stage in the process a greater proportion of income is spent, leading to a larger overall increase in demand.

A discussion of the determinants of the marginal propensity to consume domestically can be found in Unit 24.

The impact of a higher marginal propensity to consume on the multiplier can be seen in Fig. 20.11.

What do you think?

What do you think influences how much you spend out of each pound that you earn?

Now you try it

If the proportion of each pound spent in the UK was 0.6, what would the size of the multiplier be? What if only 0.5 was spent in the UK out of each pound?

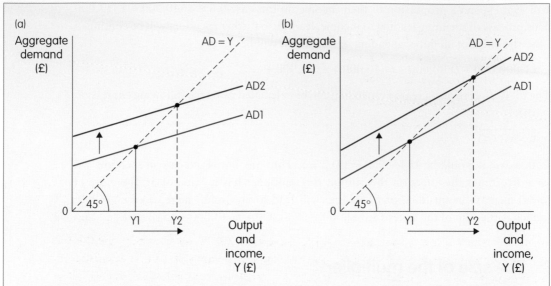

Figure 20.11 The effect of an increase in the aggregate demand (a) when the marginal propensity to consume is low and (b) when the marginal propensity to consume is high. The aggregate demand schedule in (b) is steeper than in (a) due to the higher marginal propensity to consume; the multiplier effect of a given increase in the aggregate demand is greater in (b).

■ The multiplier in an open economy

A closed economy is a theoretical situation in which there is no trade with other economies. In an 'open' economy there is trade between economies. The value of the multiplier will be less in an open economy than in a closed economy. This is because out of each pound earned a proportion will be spent on foreign goods and services. Spending will leak out of the economy. Less spending will occur within the economy, reducing the multiplier effect domestically. In a closed economy, by comparison, all of the spending will stay within the economy, thereby boosting the overall effect.

What do you think?

In recent years there has been more international trade. There are less barriers to trade between countries.

What effect do you think this has on the size of the multiplier?

Now you try it

What is the impact on the multiplier of each of the following?

- More spending out of each pound on imports.
- More saving out of each pound.
- A higher rate of income tax.

Case Study

From the 1960s onwards, Japan grew extremely fast and became a major world economic power. Close links between the government and its industry, a strong work ethic and high levels of investment in high technology gave the country a competitive edge. Japan became the third largest economy in the world after the US and China. For three decades Japan's economic growth has been spectacular: a 10% average in the 1960s, a 5% average in the 1970s and a 4% average in the 1980s. The UK average for that whole period was around 2% to 2.5% per year.

However, growth in Japan slowed considerably in the 1990s and averaged just 1.7%. This was partly due to contractionary policies by the government, such as reduced spending and higher taxation. The government was concerned that demand was growing too fast and one problem emerging was too much speculation in property. This was driving up the price of property and leading to excessive borrowing and spending by firms and households. Unfortunately, intervention by the government led to a collapse in the economy and a loss of confidence. This in turn affected investment and spending levels.

Between 2000 and 2003, the Japanese government tried to revive economic growth, but was largely unsuccessful. Growth was further hampered by the slowing of the US, European and Asian economies. This meant that Japan could not export as much. Exports are a significant element of Japanese aggregate demand. Also, households and firms seemed to be reluctant to borrow or spend because they were worried about the future. At one point the government reduced the cost of borrowing to 0% to stimulate spending. Demand was so low in Japan during these years that firms started putting their prices down in order to gain any sales. Prices in general were lower at the end of the year than at the start—an unusual occurrence for most economies.

In 2004 and 2005, growth in the economy did begin to improve. Confidence began to return, stimulating spending and investment. However, some economists remain worried about its future success. One problem is the ageing population of Japan. These people need looking after and this may require an increase in taxation, which could reduce the aggregate demand once again.

❓ Questions

- Distinguish between injections into and withdrawals from an economy. What influences each of these?
- With reference to this case study, what is the impact on an economy of a change in injections or withdrawals?

- What does the case highlight about the possible role of expectations in an economy?
- At one point interest rates were 0%; why might this be expected to stimulate spending in an economy? What are the interest rates in the UK at the moment?
- What factors do you think will determine how fast the Japanese economy grows in the future?

Checklist

Now you have read this unit try to answer the following questions.

☐ Can you explain the conditions necessary for equilibrium in the economy?

☐ Can you distinguish between injections and withdrawals?

☐ Can you explain how the economy moves toward equilibrium?

☐ Can you explain the factors that can influence aggregate demand?

☐ Can you analyse the multiplier effect caused by a change in aggregate demand?

☐ Can you explain the factors that influence the size of the multiplier?

End of unit questions

1 What are the conditions necessary for equilibrium in an economy?

2 What factors might affect the level of injections in an economy?

3 What is the effect of an increase in injections on the level of national income?

4 What factors might lead to a decrease in aggregate demand?

5 What factors would increase the size of the multiplier?

Key learning points

- Equilibrium in an economy occurs when the aggregate demand equals the aggregate supply.
- Equilibrium in an economy occurs when the planned injections equal the planned withdrawals.
- Equilibrium in an economy occurs when

    Planned $I + G + X$ = Planned $S + T + M$.

- If the planned injections are greater than the planned withdrawals then there is excess demand in the economy and national income will rise until equilibrium is restored.

- If the planned injections are less than the planned withdrawals then there is too little demand in the economy and national income will fall until equilibrium is restored.

- The aggregate demand measures the total planned expenditure on final goods and services in an economy. It is given by the expression $C + I + G + X - M$.

- An increase in the aggregate demand can set off the multiplier process, which leads to a greater increase in national income.

- The size of the multiplier depends on the marginal propensity to consume domestically.

Learn more

If you want to learn more about the relationship between injections and withdrawals, and the difference between actual and planned withdrawals, visit our website at the address below.

 Visit our Online Resource Centre at www.oxfordtextbooks.co.uk/orc/gillespie_econ for test questions and further information on topics covered in this chapter.

National income and the standard of living

In the previous unit we examined how an economy reached equilibrium. In this unit we examine how national income is actually measured and whether it can be used as a good indicator of a country's standard of living. Governments often seek to increase the income per person in their economies; this unit considers whether this is a useful objective or not.

LEARNING OBJECTIVES

By the end of this unit you should be able to:

✔ explain the meaning of national income and how it is measured;

✔ discuss the value of national income as a measure of the standard of living;

✔ explain the Gini coefficient.

■ Introduction

National income measures the value of final goods and services produced in an economy in a given period, usually a year. Naturally, there is a large amount of interest in how high the level of national income is in an economy. If national income is high then this suggests that there will be jobs and that the standard of living in a country will be high. On the other hand, a low national income will be associated with poverty and unemployment. In this unit we consider how national income is measured and whether it is, in fact, a good measure of the standard of living.

■ Measuring national income

As we saw in the previous unit, the value of what has been produced in an economy must have been earned by one or other of the factors of production. If £100 million of output has been produced then this money has been earned by one of the factors of production such as employees, owners, suppliers or landlords. Therefore we can either measure the value of the output produced or the income earned by the different factors of production. Alternatively, we can measure the amount spent in an economy (although here we have to make adjustments, e.g., if we spend less than is produced then firms will end up with unexpected stocks; provided that we include this stockbuilding as a form of spending then the total expenditure will also equal the output, which will also equal the total income).

National income can, therefore, be measured in the following different ways.

- *Output*. This can show the contribution of different sectors of the economy, such as agriculture, manufacturing and services.

- *Expenditure*. This shows the spending on final goods and services.

- *Income*. This can be broken down into, for example, income earned by companies (corporations), employees and the self-employed.

    However national income is measured, it will give the same answer, that is:

    Output = Expenditure = Income.

There are different measures of national income. These include the following.

- Gross domestic product (**GDP**). This measures the value of final goods and services produced in an economy. It shows how much has been earned within a country's national boundaries.

- Gross national product (**GNP**). This measures the value of final goods and services earned by UK nationals, as opposed to the amount of money earned within the UK. Some of the income measured by the GDP is earned by overseas producers or individuals who are not based in the UK. This money will leave the UK. At the same time, UK citizens and firms abroad will be earning money there.

    Thus we have:

    GNP = GDP

    – Income earned by overseas firms and households located within an economy
    + Income earned by the country's households and firms working abroad.

This can also be written as:

    GNP = GDP + Net property income from abroad,

where

    Net property income from abroad
    = UK earnings abroad – Foreign earnings within the UK.

- **Net national product (NNP)**. Some of the national income earned in a year is simply spent on replacing the depreciation of assets rather than genuinely adding new output to the economy. If, for example, you are buying equipment to replace old machines that have stopped working then you are not increasing the productive capacity of the economy. Depreciation refers to the wear and tear of assets.

    Thus we have:

    Net national product (NNP) = GNP – Depreciation.

- **GNP at market prices.** If we measure the value of spending on final goods and services then these prices will include taxes placed on them by the government (which increase the price) and government subsidies (which reduce the price). The prices do not therefore reflect the income of the factors of production. To measure the value of the output at 'factor cost' you need to adjust the market prices.

Thus we have:

GNP market prices − Indirect taxes + Subsidies = GNP factor cost.

■ Real national income versus nominal

If the income of an economy has increased by, say, 2% then this does not necessarily mean that firms and households are better off. This is because we need to know what is happening to the price level. If prices are growing by 2% as well then in real terms the economy is no better off. The growth in income is cancelled out by the growth in prices. Nominal increases in income simply mean that the absolute number has increased. The real GDP and the real GNP measure the national income taking account of what is happening to prices. They show the purchasing power of a given level of income.

■ National income and living standards

The standard of living in an economy is often measured by the real GDP per capita. The GDP is used (rather than the GNP) because it shows the income being earned in a region, regardless of who is earning it.

The GDP per capita measures the national income per person adjusted for inflation, that is, in real terms how much individuals earn. A higher average real income per person suggests a higher standard of living because on average people have more purchasing power.

The real GDP per capita is defined as:

$$\text{Real GDP per capita} = \frac{\text{Real GDP}}{\text{Population}}.$$

However, this measurement simply shows an average figure, for example, £20,000 per person. A more detailed examination of a country's standard of living might consider the distribution of income and wealth in an economy. It might be possible to have a relatively high average income per person, for example, but then find that most of the income is being earned by relatively few people whilst the rest live in poverty.

To analyse the distribution of income in an economy the Lorenz curve and the Gini (1921) coefficient can be used.

What do you think?

In 2004/05, the income (before taxes and benefits) of the top fifth of households in the UK was around sixteen times greater than that for the bottom fifth (£66,300 per household per year compared with £4300). After adjusting for taxes and benefits this ratio was reduced to four to one for final income, which was unchanged from previous years.

Should the government intervene to make this difference between the high-income earners and the lower-income earners more equal?

The Lorenz curve and the Gini coefficient

The Lorenz curve shows the distribution of income within an economy (see Fig. 21.1). The horizontal axis measures the percentage of the population from the poorest to the richest. The vertical axis measures the percentage of national income that they receive.

If income were distributed equally in an economy then the Lorenz curve would be a straight line: 20% of households would earn 20% of national income, 60% would earn 60%, and so on. This would lead to a 45° line from the origin and this is called the line of absolute equality. In practice, the Lorenz curve will be below the 45° line. This is because the bottom 20% of the population might only earn 5% of the country's income.

The Gini coefficient measures the ratio of the area between the Lorenz curve and the 45° line to the whole area below the 45° line (see Fig. 21.1). If the income is equally

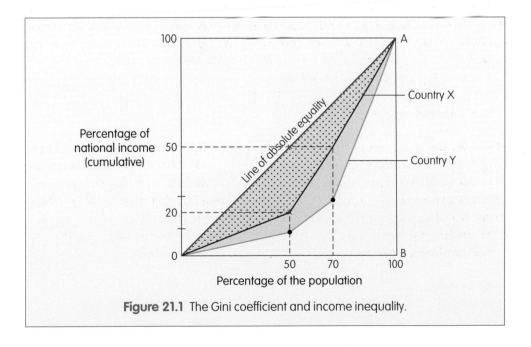

Figure 21.1 The Gini coefficient and income inequality.

distributed then the Lorenz curve would be the 45° line, and so the Gini coefficient would be equal to 0. The more unequal the distribution of income, the larger the Gini coefficient is. The largest value that the Gini coefficient can have is one.

In Fig. 21.1 the Gini coefficient would be measured as follows:

$$\text{Gini coefficient} = \frac{\text{Shaded area in Fig. 21.1}}{\text{Area OAB}}.$$

From this we can see that country Y would have a higher Gini coefficient than country X. This is because there is greater inequality; for example, in country X 70% of the population have 50% of the country's income, whereas in country Y they have a lower percentage.

Examining the distribution of income can be very revealing. In India, for example, the ratio of income of the country's richest 10% to the poorest 10% is around seven. Most South Asian economies have similar ratios. This clearly means that there is a lot of inequality, but not as much as in China which has a ratio of over eighteen and the United States which has a ratio of over fifteen.

Now you try it

If the Gini coefficient is 0.9, does this suggest that income is fairly distributed or not? Explain.

Economics in context   Income distribution in different countries

Table 21.1 shows the countries with the five most equal distributions of income in the world in 2005.

Table 21.1 The five countries with the most evenly distributed income in 2005.

Rank	Country	Gini coefficient	Ratio of richest 10% to poorest 10%	Ratio of richest 20% to poorest 20%
1	Denmark	0.247	8.1	4.3
2	Japan	0.249	4.5	3.4
3	Sweden	0.25	6.2	4.0
4	Belgium	0.25	7.8	4.5
5	Czech Republic	0.254	5.2	3.5

Source: All countries are from the United Nations 2005 Development Programme Report.

 Question

Does having an equal distribution of income within an economy matter?

Other factors affecting living standards

Many analysts do not think that the real GDP per capita provides a particularly good measure of the standard of living in economies, even if account is taken of the income distribution. There are certainly many other factors that may be important when considering a country's living standards. These include the following.

- *The quality of goods and services provided.* Over time, technology reduces the price of many goods. This may reduce the value of the output produced and the income earned in an economy, even though the quality of the products is significantly better than it used to be, and therefore the standard of living may be higher. (Simply compare the price and quality of a personal computer now compared to just ten years ago; prices have been falling whilst the power and capability of computers have been rising. A firm may produce a computer that supposedly is worth less, even though it performs at a much higher level than earlier models.)

- *The quality of life.* In recent years people have shown more interest in working less hours and having more of a life outside work. This could mean that the amount being produced and being earned is smaller, but that individuals actually prefer this situation and enjoy the quality of their lives more. More economic growth may put stress on individuals to deliver the required output and make life less enjoyable. Achieving higher levels of GDP could mean more hours at work and less holidays. This could mean that the 'work–life' balance shifts away from the home and toward the office or factory, and satisfaction falls even if the GDP per person rises.

- *Non-marketed items.* If work is undertaken but not paid for then it will not be recorded in the official statistics. For example, if you hire a plumber then this work will be paid for and will increase the recorded national income. If, however, you did the plumbing work yourself then it would not be recorded or counted. Changes in the amount of work that people do for themselves will, therefore, distort comparisons of standards of living over time and between countries.

- *The 'black economy'.* This refers to all of the work that may be done in an economy but is not declared because people want to avoid paying tax to the government. By definition, this income cannot be counted officially, even though it may be relatively high, particularly in some countries where there is a culture of not declaring earnings to the government.

- *Environmental issues.* Faster economic growth may be at the expense of damage to the environment. Although we may be richer, we may find that factors such as higher levels of pollution and global warming make growth undesirable.

- *Wealth.* Income shows the stream or flow of earnings over a given period (usually a year). Wealth measures the value of all of the assets owned by a country at a given moment. It is known as a stock concept. The income of an economy may be low during a particular year, but because of previous earnings its wealth may be high. Its citizens may benefit from this stock of assets accumulated in the past.

Traditionally, governments have been eager to increase the real GDP per person. This has been regarded as an important goal of government and a measure of its success or failure. Nowadays, some people argue that the government should not focus on increasing the real GDP per person but should look at other targets. Many economists have developed their own measures of economic welfare rather than relying on the GDP per person. For example, Nordhaus and Tobin (1972) have produced a measure called the net economic welfare (NEW). This adjusts the GNP by deducting economic 'bads' (such as pollution), adding the value of non-marketed activities and including the value of leisure. Similarly, Friends of the Earth suggest that an index of sustainable economic welfare (ISEW) is used instead. This attempts to do the following:

> . . . to measure the portion of economic activity which delivers genuine increases in our quality of life—in one sense 'quality' economic activity. For example, it makes a subtraction for air pollution caused by economic activity, and makes an addition to count unpaid household labour —such as cleaning or child-minding. It also covers areas such as income inequality, other environmental damage, and depletion of environmental assets.'

> Obviously, with these other indicators there is plenty of room for debate over what to include and the relevant weighting of the different factors.

Recently, in the UK there has been increasing interest in measuring how happy people are within a country rather than simply measuring their income.

Economics in context   ## Gross national happiness in Bhutan

The remote Himalayan kingdom of Bhutan is the only country in the world that puts happiness at the centre of government policy. The government must consider every policy for its impact, not only on gross domestic product, but also on GNH: 'gross national happiness'. For example, the capital, Thimpu, has no advertising because this is felt to promote consumerism. Bhutan has even banned plastic bags and tobacco on the grounds that they make the country less happy.

? Question

Do you think that a UK government should ban tobacco? Do you think that it would be able to?

In 1999, Tony Blair, the UK Prime Minister, stated:

> Money isn't everything. But in the past governments have seemed to forget this. Success has been measured by economic growth—GDP—alone. Delivering the best possible quality of life for us all means more than concentrating solely on economic growth. That is why sustainable development is such an important part of this Government's programme. All this depends on devising new ways of assessing how we are doing.

In 2006, David Cameron, the leader of the Conservative Party, said:

> We should be thinking not just what is good for putting money in people's pockets but what is good for putting joy in people's hearts. When politicians are looking at issues they should be saying to themselves, 'How are we going to try and make sure that we don't just make people better off but we make people happier, we make communities more stable, we make society more cohesive?'

Trying to achieve greater happiness has important implications for government policy. The following are some examples.

- Research suggests that one main reason why wealth does not lead to happiness is that we tend to compare ourselves with people who are richer than we are. Therefore, even if we become better off we do not necessarily get any happier. To produce a happier society the government would need to reduce the gap between the rich and the poor. It can do this by redistributing wealth from the rich to the poor.

- Advertising may be a major cause of unhappiness because it makes people feel less well off. Perhaps advertising should be controlled to make us feel better?

- Research suggests that happiness is likely to be higher if more people got married and stayed married. Marriage is typically so good for your happiness and general well-being that it adds an average of seven years to the life of a man and around four years for a woman. In this case the government could use the tax and benefit system to make marriage more economically attractive.

What do you think?

Do you think that people are more or less happy than they were 100 years ago? Why?

What do you think influences people's happiness?

To what extent do you think that government policy should aim to increase happiness rather than income?

If you were in government, what laws would you introduce to make people happier?

Case Study

The following information is adapted from the Office of National Statistics.

UK households have become increasingly happy to let others do the cooking for them as their incomes have increased. Spending on eating out in the UK is now greater than the amount spent on meals at home (see Table 21.2).

Spending on food and drink in pubs, clubs, takeaways and restaurants has more than doubled in the twelve years from 1992. The total amount spent on food and drink in shops for consumption at home only increased by 53% over the same period.

The total spending on health in 2004/05 was £81 billion; £6 billion less than was spent on meals out.

It is not just spending patterns that have changed as incomes have grown. The composition of the UK economy has changed dramatically since the early 1990s, i.e. how the income is being earned has changed. In the past, income was mainly generated by mining, shipbuilding and heavy industry, but this is no longer true. Income in 2004 was more than twice as likely to be created by business and financial services as manufacturing. Manufacturing still accounted for 22% of the economy in 1995, but was just 14% by 2004. Meanwhile, banks, insurers, advertising companies and estate agents made up almost one-third of the UK economy in 2004.

Table 21.2   Where we are eating out—the UK eating-out market in 2005.

Location	Percentage
Fast food	27
Pub catering	23
Hotel catering	15
Restaurant meals	14
Ethnic restaurants	7
In-store	5
Roadside	2
Other	7

Source: Mintel.

? Questions

• Why do you think UK households have been increasingly eager to spend on eating out?

• What do you think has caused the changes in the composition of the UK economy since the 1990s?

• Do you think the standard of living is higher now in the UK than in the 1990s?

@ Web

For more data on the UK economy visit **www.ons.gov.uk**

Checklist

Now you have read this unit try to answer the following questions.

☐   Can you explain the meaning of national income and how it is measured?

☐   Can you discuss the value of national income as a measure of the standard of living?

☐   Can you explain the Gini coefficient?

End of unit questions

1   How does income differ from wealth?

2   How does the gross domestic product differ from the gross national product?

3   If the Gini coefficient is close to one, is the income distribution fairly equal or not?

4   To what extent do national income figures reflect the standard of living in a country?

5   Should the government focus on increasing the happiness of its people?

Key learning points

- National income can be measured in terms of output, income or expenditure.

- The gross domestic product measures the income generated in a country. The gross national product measures the income of a country's citizens.

- Real national income adjusts the nominal income for inflation.

- The standard of living in an economy is often measured by the national income per person. However, this ignores the distribution of income.

- The Gini coefficient measures how equally income is distributed in an economy.

- The standard of living will depend on many factors apart from income, such as the quality of goods and environmental issues.

References

Gini, C. (1921). Measurement of inequality and incomes. *The Economic Journal*, 31, 124–6.

Nordhaus, W. and Tobin, J. (1972). Is growth obsolete? In *Economic growth* (ed. National Bureau of Economic Research). General Series No. 96E.

Learn more

In this unit we have focused on income rather than wealth. To learn more about the difference between these and for more information on inequality in the UK and other countries visit our website at the address below.

 Visit our Online Resource Centre at www.oxfordtextbooks.co.uk/orc/gillespie_econ for test questions and further information on topics covered in this chapter.

»22 Economic growth and the economic cycle

In Unit 20 we explained how an economy moved toward its equilibrium level. However, this level is not static and will change over time. In fact, a key government economic objective is usually to increase the country's income over time. In this unit we examine the causes of economic growth, including productivity, research and development, and entrepreneurship. We also consider the pattern of economic growth over time.

LEARNING OBJECTIVES

By the end of this unit you should be able to:

✔ outline the key stages and features of the economic cycle;

✔ explain the possible causes of the economic cycle;

✔ understand the meaning and significance of productivity;

✔ understand the meaning and significance of research and development;

✔ understand the meaning and importance of entrepreneurship;

✔ consider the possible problems of economic growth.

◼ Introduction

The level of national income is an important influence on a country's standard of living although, as we saw in the previous unit, it is not the only determinant of this. Increasing national income and achieving economic growth is a common economic objective.

Economic growth can be measured by an increase in the real output or income of an economy over time. This may be measured in terms of the whole economy or in terms of output or income per person.

Economic growth creates more income in the economy. This can lead to a higher average income per person (although the income may not actually be distributed equally). This is often linked to a higher standard of living. Greater earnings can contribute to greater welfare and a more content nation.

Remember, however, that a fast rate of growth is often achieved by economies that are industrialising quickly and starting from a relatively low base. India, for example, has grown rapidly in the last twenty years, but the average income per head was still less than $1000 per year by 2006. More mature economies may have higher incomes per person but slower economic growth.

Types of growth

When examining economic growth, it is sometimes helpful to distinguish between actual and potential growth.

- Actual growth is the rate at which the economy is actually growing. It is measured by the annual percentage increase in national income.

- Potential growth measures how much the economy could grow with all of its resources fully employed; i.e. it represents an increase in the capacity of the economy.

The difference between the two can be seen using production possibility frontiers. The movement from X to Y represents actual growth in the economy because more is produced; in this case resources are being used more fully rather than an increase in capacity (see Fig. 22.1(a)). Actual growth may be caused by a boost in aggregate demand. Potential growth is shown by an outward shift of the production possibility frontier (see Fig. 22.1(b)). This represents potential growth because the economy is increasing what it can produce whilst still utilising all of its resources fully. Potential growth may be caused by:

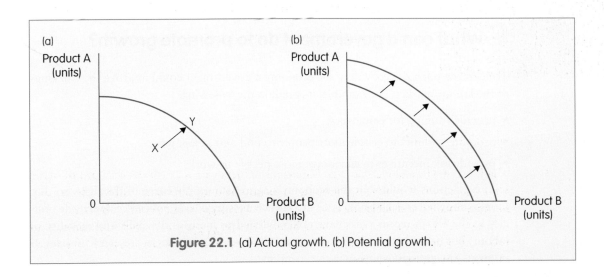

Figure 22.1 (a) Actual growth. (b) Potential growth.

- an increase in resources, such as a population increase;
- improvements in technology or the way resources are used (e.g. better management).

Economics in context

GDP forecasts

The Organization for Economic Cooperation and Development (OECD) is an organisation of thirty countries. It regularly produces economic data and forecasts for these and other economies. Table 22.1 shows estimates made by the OECD for the growth in a number of economies for 2007.

Table 22.1 Estimates of the growth in a number of economies for 2007.

	Percentage GDP growth
US	3.1
Eurozone	2.1
Japan	2.2
UK	2.9
China	9.5
India	7.1
Russia	5.7

Source: OECD estimates.

 Questions

Do you think that the differences in the growth rates shown in Table 22.1 matter? How accurate did the forecasts turn out to be? Why might forecasts be wrong?

What can a government do to promote growth?

To increase potential growth in the economy a government could improve the workings of the labour market. For example, it could do the following:

- provide training for employees;
- promote mobility to enable more people to find and accept jobs;
- provide tax incentives to encourage more people to work.

These actions would shift the economy's aggregate supply curve to the right, so that more is supplied at each price. They are known as 'supply side policies'. Supply side policies in the UK in recent years have not only tried to increase the skills and mobility of labour, but have also attempted to increase the level of productivity, research and development, and entrepreneurship in the economy.

Productivity

Productivity measures the output produced relative to the inputs used up in a production process. It can be measured in many ways, such as the output per hour or the output per worker.

Productivity is an important element of the competitiveness of a business for the following reasons.

- Productivity affects unit costs. Imagine that you want to produce ten units per week and each worker can produce five units. You obviously need to employ two people. If you could increase the productivity of your employees to ten units per person then you would only need one employee. This would cut your employment costs. With lower unit costs firms should be able to make higher profits and/or charge lower prices, making them more competitive internationally.

- The higher the productivity of any one employee, the more they are producing. This should increase the money that can be earned from selling the output they produce, thereby increasing profits.

Within the economy as a whole, greater productivity increases a country's output and contributes to economic growth. According to the UK Treasury,

> Productivity growth, alongside high and stable levels of employment, is central to long term economic performance and rising living standards. Increasing the productivity of the Economy is a key objective for the Treasury.

@ Web

For more on the UK Treasury visit www.hm-treasury.gov.uk

According to the Department of Trade and Industry,

> The Government is determined to close the UK's productivity gap with comparable international economies and is seeking to boost UK Research and Development investment to 2.5% of GDP by 2014.

@ Web

For more on the Department of Trade and Industry visit www.dti.gov.uk

The level of productivity in an economy may depend on the following.

- *The level of investment in capital goods and technology.* The better the machinery and technology available, the more productive the workforce should be.

- *The motivation of the workforce.* A more motivated workforce should be more committed and more productive.

- *The way that employees and their work are organised and managed.*

Unions boycott Vauxhall

In 2006, Vauxhall announced 900 job cuts at the firm's Cheshire factory. Trade union leaders asked the public to boycott the firm's products. The company said that it needed to make the redundancies because it was switching from three to two shifts at the factory, which makes its Astra model. It said that the move reflected the 'ongoing pressure' in the car industry to increase productivity and reduce costs. The Vauxhall chairman acknowledged the achievements of the factory but said that long-run competitiveness remained the issue. Vauxhall's parent company, General Motors, the largest US car company, was also cutting 30 000 jobs in the US on the back of falling sales and profits.

The company's European President said, 'Our industry simply cannot afford to stop continually improving productivity in its Western European car plants.'

The following is a summary of the UK car industry

- In 2005, 1.8 million cars and 3.1 million engines were produced.
- Half of all cars made in the UK are produced by Toyota, Nissan and Honda.
- Nissan's Sunderland plant is the most productive in Europe.
- Jaguar, Peugeot, TVR and MG Rover have all closed plants.

? Questions

How else could productivity be improved?

What is the likely impact of low productivity on the success of Vauxhall?

What do you think?

In 2004, UK productivity calculated as the gross domestic product per worker was lower than France and the USA, similar to that of Germany and higher than Japan. The USA continues to have the highest productivity; it is 27% higher than in the UK. (Source: Office for Notional Statistics.)

Why do you think these differences might exist? Do they matter?

Research and development (R&D)

Research and development (R&D) is defined by the Department of Trade and Industry as 'Any project to resolve scientific or technological uncertainty aimed at achieving an advance in science or technology. Advances include new or improved products, processes and services.'

R&D is important to firms and the economy as a whole to:

- develop new products;
- develop new ways of doing things;
- help firms to be more productive.

R&D can reduce costs and develop new features that add value for customers. If R&D leads to the successful commercial exploitation of an idea then this is known as innovation.

An increase in the levels of business R&D should stimulate business innovation and help to raise productivity, particularly in the manufacturing sector, which undertakes the majority of R&D in the UK. According to the Department of Trade and Industry,

> Innovation results in high quality jobs, successful businesses, better goods and services, and more efficient processes. International research has consistently demonstrated the positive correlation between R&D investment intensity and company performance measures such as sales growth and share price in the sectors where R&D is important. Businesses are in a better position to achieve and maintain competitive advantage in the increasingly global marketplace with sustained R&D and other related investment.

To try to raise awareness of levels of R&D in the UK, the DTI now publishes an R&D scoreboard reporting on levels of spending within different sectors.

Investment in R&D spending requires a long-term commitment because many projects will take years to reap rewards. One problem in the UK has been the short-termist approach of many investors. Most shares in the UK are owned by financial institutions that want quick rewards for their own investors. They are often unwilling to wait for a long-term payback. This has hindered investment in research and development in the UK in the past. However, successful innovation should bring about the following.

- Productivity should increase. This shifts the demand for resources outwards because they can generate more earnings. The marginal revenue product of labour, for example, should shift outwards. It also shifts the supply curve for a product outwards because more can be produced at any price.

- Costs could be reduced due to more efficient ways of doing things. Technological developments can lead to better and less wasteful manufacturing processes and better links with suppliers, for example.

- High quality products could be produced. Technological developments can lead to more flexible production, so firms are more able to meet customer needs. It can also help to differentiate firms by providing them with better quality and unique selling points (USPs).

This means that successful R&D can increase the aggregate demand by creating better products and also increase the aggregate supply by developing better ways of doing things. Both of these will stimulate economic growth.

Research and development spending

According to the Department of Trade and Industry:

> The major R&D nations have different R&D sector specialisations, with the USA strong in IT hardware, software and pharmaceuticals, Japan in automotive and electronics, Switzerland in pharmaceuticals and the UK in both pharmaceuticals and aerospace. The proportions of large companies in R&D-intensive sectors such as these, or in low-intensity sectors such as oil- and gas, mining, utilities and telecomms, are quite different between countries. Japan and Germany are R&D specialists: they have more than twice the proportion of companies in the R&D Global 1000 than they have in the FT Global 500 list of the world's largest companies. The US has similar proportions in both lists and the UK, with its strength in financial services, resources and retailing, has a 50% larger proportion in the FT Global 500.

? Question

Why do you think some countries are particularly strong in R&D in some sectors?

Entrepreneurship

An entrepreneur is someone who is willing to take risks in business. An entrepreneur combines resources to start up new projects and new businesses. An entrepreneur is able to see the potential rewards in providing a good or service and is willing to take the risks to do so.

Entrepreneurship is a very important resource in an economy for the following reasons.

- Entrepreneurs innovate and create more competition and better services for customers. This can also help domestic firms to be more internationally competitive, thereby boosting aggregate demand.

- Entrepreneurs create jobs and bring about growth in the economy. With more business start-ups a country's production possibility frontier will shift outwards.

There is much debate about what makes someone an entrepreneur—are entrepreneurs born or are they formed by their circumstances? Of course, the answer may be a combination of the two, and very few people would deny the importance of the culture in a country and the effect this can have on encouraging and helping entrepreneurs to develop.

To create an entrepreneurial culture in an economy a government may do the following:

- provide benefits and support for those wanting to start up in business;
- encourage banks to provide finance and to take risks by investing in start-ups;
- provide legislation that allows people who fail in business and go bankrupt to start up again more quickly.

The UK has been criticised in the past for not having an entrepreneurial culture. This is because financial institutions and indeed the media have not been very tolerant of failure. People who started a business and failed have found it difficult to get started again, whereas in some countries, such as America, failure is regarded as part of the learning process. Banks in the UK have also been rather reluctant to lend to start-ups because of the high failure rate and therefore the risk involved. If the government can encourage more entrepreneurship this should lead to more economic growth.

What do you think?

Do you think that entrepreneurs are born or made?

The zero-growth option

Although economic growth does have benefits in that people on average have more income, it also brings with it problems, as we saw in our analysis of measuring the standard of living in an economy. For example, it may lead to more stress for individuals who are pushed to work harder and may well lead to a worse quality of life. It may also damage the environment and lead to the loss of non-renewable resources, such as oil reserves. Fast growth may mean that these resources will be used up at a faster rate, leaving less for future generations. Greater growth may also lead to greater inequality as some people gain more than others, thereby widening the differences between them.

Given such problems that can result from economic growth, some economists have called for a zero-growth policy by major economies. However, this may well be too extreme a solution; typically, economists would want a marginal solution. The best level of growth would be where the social marginal benefit of growth equals the social marginal cost. The problem lies in fully identifying and measuring the social costs and benefits.

What do you think?

Do you think that zero growth is an option?

The economic cycle

The economic cycle shows the pattern of economic growth that tends to occur in economies over time. Whilst there may be an underlying steady long-run trend, most economies experience an economic cycle. This is measured by changes in national income. Over time the stages that economies go through are: growth, boom, recession and slump, as shown in Fig. 22.2. Whilst increasing national income is often an aim of government, so is stabilising its growth path. Instability and uncertainty tend to make planning difficult and deter investment. Firms may become wary of investing if they are not sure whether an economy is going to be doing well or not. Similarly, households may save more if there is greater uncertainty. If a government can provide stability then it can actually help the economy to grow faster in the long run.

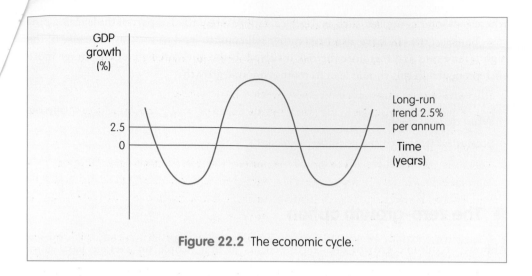

Figure 22.2 The economic cycle.

The stages of the economic cycle

The four main stages of the economic cycle are as follows.

• *A boom.* A boom is characterised by high levels of economic growth. The gross domestic product will be growing relatively fast. This should lead to relatively low levels of unemployment. Firms will have busy order books and may have to turn business away because they cannot keep up with demand. Prices may begin to rise due to demand growing so fast that output cannot keep pace.

Economics in context   Marriage and national income

In the late 1990s, the proportion of marriages ending in divorce within four years fell to around 90 in 1000. This might have been due to a change in morals and values, but was more likely due to a booming economy. Recessions put strains on marriages as couples find it hard to cope financially; in a boom relationships tend to be better, so the number of divorces is lower. Also, in a boom property prices tend to rise, making it more difficult to be able to afford to separate and have two houses.

? Question
What types of products are likely to experience most growth in a boom? Are these income elastic or income inelastic products?

• *A recession.* A recession (or downswing) occurs when there is a period of two quarters of negative economic growth. This means that the economy is shrinking. The gross domestic product is growing at a negative rate.

A recession is usually characterised by the following.

– Increasing levels of unemployment.
– Low levels of profits, reducing the amount of internal funds for investment.
– Unused capacity.
– Downward pressure on prices to try to stimulate demand.
– Less income, leading to less demand in the economy and equally less spending on imports.
– More business closures.
– Less tax revenue for the government (because less people are earning and less products are being sold). At the same time the government is likely to be paying more in subsidies and benefits, so overall the government's financial position will be weakened and this may require more government borrowing.

- *A recovery, upswing or upturn.* In the recovery phase demand begins to pick up, reducing firms' excess capacity and improving employment levels. With more demand for products, the demand for factors of production increases, which begins to pull up prices and wages. Machinery begins to be replaced or updated and business confidence picks up, leading to more investment.

- *A slump or depression.* In a slump economic growth is slow and unemployment is high. There is downward pressure on prices (deflation), and profits and business confidence are low. The point where the slump flattens out is called the 'lower turning point' of the economic cycle. The 'upper turning point' is in the boom.

Whilst this general pattern of growth outlined in the economic cycle may typically be followed, there will be differences over time in:

- how long each stage lasts;
- how large each stage is, for example, how big the slump or boom is.

In fact, different economists have identified several different economic cycles. These include the following.

- *The classical trade cycle.* This describes a pattern of boom and slump for which there is often around eight to ten years between one boom and another.

- *The Kuznets cycle.* This is named after Simon Kuznets, a Nobel prizewinner, who identified a cycle of activity in the construction industry that took between fifteen and twenty-five years.

- *The Kondratieff cycle.* This highlighted that as well as a ten-year trade there was a major underlying cycle that takes fifty to sixty years to complete, that is, there can be cycles within cycles.

What do you think?

How might different stages of the economic cycle affect a firm's marketing decisions?

■ What causes the economic cycle?

The causes of the economic cycle include the following.

- **Expectations.** Changes in the expectations of firms and households can have a major effect on the state of the economy. If an economy is growing relatively fast and confidence is high, then firms may be more likely to invest because they are more optimistic about future levels of demand. Households are more likely to spend because they are more confident about their employment and earning prospects. If expectations are positive then this is likely to generate greater spending by firms and households, and this helps to stimulate further growth in the economy. Changes in expectations may therefore exaggerate the underlying economic cycle.

What do you think?

If you were in government how could you influence people's expectations about the economy?

- **Stock levels.** Stocks include raw materials, components, semi-finished goods and finished goods waiting to be sold. They are also called inventory. Changes in stock levels can affect demand in the economy. When an economy starts to grow faster, managers may be reluctant to increase output in the short term in case the boom does not last. They will not want to invest and employ more people only to find that demand falls again. They are more likely to keep production at the same level as before and run down their stock levels. However, if demand does keep growing then firms will now have too few stocks and managers will have to expand production. They may need to increase their production capacity, not only to meet the new higher level of demand, but also to re-place their stocks that will have been run down. This leads to a relatively high increase in spending, which leads to even faster growth in the economy. This can create a boom in the economy.

  Once demand starts to grow more slowly, managers are likely to be reluctant to re-duce their production levels immediately because it may be only a temporary decline. Rather than make people redundant and reduce capacity, firms are likely to maintain the existing output level in the short term. Given that demand is lower, producing at the old level leads to increasing levels of stocks. However, if demand continues to be low then in the long run managers will cut back output. As they have been building up stocks, they can now reduce output significantly. This leads to a large fall in demand and may push the economy into a recession.

  The sluggishness of managers to react to changes in demand exaggerates the changes in demand, and creates booms and slumps.

Flexible production

A business trend in the last twenty years has been to make production more flexible so that firms can respond more quickly to changes in demand and can hold less stocks at any moment. The aim is to get demand to match supply as instantly as possible, so that producers produce 'just in time'. Toyota is famous for its just-in-time approach: it only ever starts making a car when an order is there. Zara, the fashion retailer, also produces just in time, which means that it holds much less stock of any one item. It works closely with suppliers so that it can increase the number it has of any product very quickly. However, by working just in time it does not get caught with large levels of unsold stock and can change its product range very rapidly.

? Questions

How can a firm make its production more flexible so that it can adjust quickly to demand changes? What do you think are the advantages and possible disadvantages of producing just in time? What problems might there be in introducing this approach?

• **Government policy.** Governments will often intervene to try to stabilise the economy. However, policies that are intended to stabilise the economy can actually end up destabilising it! This is because it is difficult for the government to fine-tune the economy effectively and attempts to do so may make things worse. One reason for this is that the information that the government uses to make decisions is inevitably out of date. By the time the government has determined what it thinks the level of national income actually is, the economy will have moved on. Policies intended to correct a particular problem may therefore not be relevant because the economic situation has changed.

This problem is made worse because economic policy changes take time to work through the economy and the effects are not always predictable. For example, a tax cut may not lead to an increase in spending if households decide to save the extra disposable income.

Imagine that the government thinks that the economy is at the point X in Fig. 22.3 and therefore needs a boost in aggregate demand. It might then introduce reflationary policies. However, by the time the policies begin to have an effect the economy may be at the point Y, in which case the boost to aggregate demand leads to too much demand in the economy, causing excessive growth and then demand-pull inflation. Government attempts to reduce fluctuations in demand may therefore end up exaggerating them (see Fig. 22.4).

Now you try it

If the government thought that the economy was in a recession, what type of policies would it adopt?

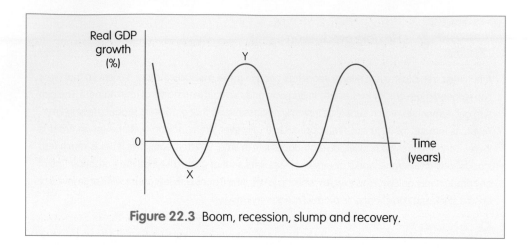

Figure 22.3 Boom, recession, slump and recovery.

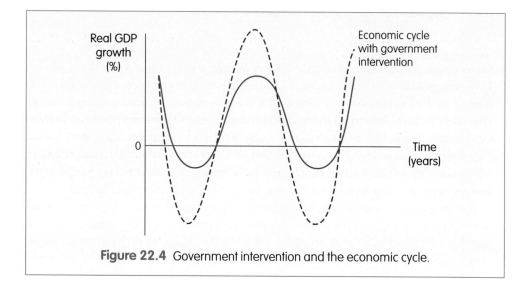

Figure 22.4 Government intervention and the economic cycle.

▨ Indicators of the economic cycle

As we have seen, one of the problems of government intervention is the difficulty of knowing when to intervene. If the government gets it wrong then intervention can actually make the economic situation worse.

Leading indicators

To help to identify how the economy is going to change, analysts examine **leading indicators**; changes in these factors may indicate future changes in the economy as a whole.

Leading indicators include the following.

- *Consumer confidence surveys*. If consumers become more confident then they are more likely to spend in the future.
- *New car registrations*. This is often an indicator of confidence as new cars are a significant expenditure.
- *Recruitment advertising*. An increase in the number of jobs being advertised highlights that firms are feeling positive and are looking to expand.
- *Mortgage applications*. Mortgages are loans that households take out to buy a house. If the number of applications for these increases then this again reveals something about the confidence of households.
- *Share prices*. An increase in share prices suggests that there is more demand to own companies. This suggests that investors believe that demand is going to be high in the future.

Coincident indicators

Coincident indicators are indicators that happen as the cycle occurs, for example, changes in the real GDP and retail sales.

Lagging indicators

Lagging indicators are indicators that alter after changes in the economic cycle. For example, unemployment tends to lag behind the cycle. When a recession starts firms are often reluctant to let staff go in case they need to re-hire them; it takes time for them to decide to make redundancies, so the number of job losses lags behind changes in the economic position.

Now you try it

Can you think of any more possible leading, coincident or lagging indicators?

Case Study

The following is adapted from *The Guardian*, 16 August 2006.

In July 1986, the number of people registered as unemployed in the UK was over 3 million and this represented around 10.6% of the workforce. Twenty years later the number of unemployed was less than 1 million, representing just 3% of the labour force. This low level of unemployment is quite an achievement given the high levels in the 1980s. When Margaret Thatcher came to power as Prime Minister in 1979, as the leader of the Conservative Party her aim was to reduce inflation. To do this she tried to limit the growth of the money supply. With restraints on the amount of spending, this was likely to reduce the rate at which prices increased. However, the result was a deep recession in the UK in the early 1980s and very high rates of unemployment. Within seven years of Thatcher coming to power, unemployment rose from

1 million to 3 million. In the late 1980s, however, the economy picked up under the Chancellor Nigel Lawson; this became known as the Lawson boom. Spending increased and property prices went up; consumers felt wealthier and more confident, which encouraged further spending. Unfortunately, this boom did not last and unemployment, having halved, went back to over 3 million in the early 1990s.

Nevertheless, in the later years of the Conservatives (who were in power from 1979 to 1997) the economy again improved, so that when Labour came to power in 1997 it inherited a claimant count of 1.35 million. One of the first major economic decisions that the Labour party made was to give independence to the Monetary Policy Committee; this was to help to control spending and inflation, and to provide some economic stability. This was very successful. Also, a number of incentives such as New Deal and Jobcentre Plus (which put benefits and job-searching together in one place) reduced unemployment to lower than had been thought possible for many years. By 2006, employment stood at nearly 29 million, which is 74.6% of the workforce—the highest rate in the leading economies of the world. Four million jobs had been created since 1986. Some of these were in the government sector (about 700 000 jobs), but the majority were in services, especially retailing. Long-term youth unemployment was nearly zero.

❓ Questions

- In the early 1980s, the UK economy was in a recession. What is the impact of a recession on an economy?

- In the late 1980s, the UK economy benefited from the Lawson boom. Why might an economy have experienced a boom?

- The above passage highlights how the UK economy goes through a series of booms and slumps over time. How might this affect firms and households?

- How do you think the government could try to stabilise the economy? Why do you think this might not work?

Checklist

Now you have read this unit try to answer the following questions.

- ☐ Can you outline the key stages and features of the economic cycle?
- ☐ Can you explain the possible causes of the economic cycle?
- ☐ Can you consider the possible problems of economic growth?
- ☐ Can you explain the meaning and significance of productivity?
- ☐ Can you analyse the factors that influence productivity?
- ☐ Can you explain the meaning of research and development, and innovation?
- ☐ Do you understand the importance of research and development, and innovation?
- ☐ Do you understand the meaning and importance of entrepreneurship?

End of unit questions

1 Why does the economic cycle matter?

2 What is the difference between actual and potential growth?

3 What is the difference between a boom and a recession? How might these stages affect a firm?

4 Can the economic cycle be controlled?

5 How can a government promote faster economic growth?

Key learning points

- National income growth does not follow a steady path but tends to occur in cycles.

- The government often intervenes to stabilise growth in the economy, but mis-timed intervention can create further instability.

- Leading indicators may be useful to identify future changes in the economy.

- Growth may bring a higher average income per person, but this does not necessarily mean that the quality of life is better or that growth is desirable.

- Growth in an economy occurs when income increases. This may lead to a higher standard of living, but there are many other factors that have to be considered to assess the quality of life.

- Potential growth in an economy can be shown by an outward shift of its production possibility frontier.

- Productivity is an important measure of efficiency.

- Productivity growth helps economies to grow.

- Entrepreneurship leads to innovation and job creation; it can stimulate economic growth.

Learn more

To learn more about the economic cycle and economic growth in the UK over the last twenty years visit our website at the address below.

 Visit our Online Resource Centre at www.oxfordtextbooks.co.uk/orc/gillespie_econ for test questions and further information on topics covered in this chapter.

»23 Aggregate demand, aggregate supply and the price level

In this unit we examine the interrelationship of aggregate supply and aggregate demand in the economy. Using supply and demand analysis we can examine the impact of changes in the aggregate demand and the aggregate supply, and consider the consequences of this in terms of the equilibrium price, output and employment.

LEARNING OBJECTIVES

By the end of this unit you should be able to:

✔ explain the shape of the aggregate demand curve relative to price;

✔ explain the shape of the aggregate supply curve relative to price;

✔ explain equilibrium in the economy in terms of aggregate supply and aggregate demand;

✔ examine the effect of changes in the aggregate supply and the aggregate demand in terms of price and output outcomes.

■ Introduction

In our earlier analysis of the aggregate demand we focused purely on the impact of changes in demand on output levels. For example, investigating the change in the aggregate demand using 45° diagrams simply showed the effect of demand changes on output. We did not consider the price level in any detail. In reality, any change in demand affects both output and prices. We now look at both aggregate supply and aggregate demand in the economy and include price analysis.

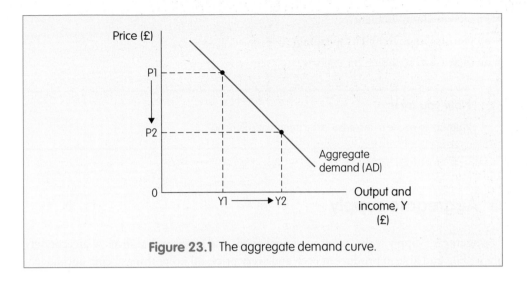

Figure 23.1 The aggregate demand curve.

Aggregate demand

The aggregate demand is the quantity of final goods and services that individuals and organisations in an economy are willing and able to buy at each and every price, all other things being unchanged.

The aggregate demand curve is downward sloping, with more products being demanded in the economy as the price falls (see Fig. 23.1). This is due to the following reasons.

- When the price level falls this increases the real wealth of households. With lower prices households and firms have more purchasing power and can buy more. Therefore the quantity demanded increases.

- When the UK price level falls there is a substitution effect. With lower prices individuals and organisations are more likely to buy UK products than foreign products, thereby increasing the quantity demanded domestically.

The level of demand at any price will depend on factors such as:

- households' incomes;
- households' and firms' expectations (which will affect their spending);
- government spending;
- the level of spending on exports and imports.

Changes in these factors will shift the aggregate demand curve; more or less will be demanded at each and every price. For example, an increase in the aggregate demand could be caused by:

- an increase in investment;
- an increase in government spending;
- an increase in spending on exports.

Now you try it

What could cause a decrease in the aggregate demand?

■ Aggregate supply

The aggregate supply is the quantity of final goods and services that firms in an economy are willing and able to produce at each and every price, all other things being unchanged. The level of aggregate supply will depend on the following.

- *The price level*. The amount supplied should increase if the price increases, as firms can afford to use less efficient methods of production and pay more for resources. This is a movement along the supply curve.
- *The level of technology in an economy*. Improvements in technology may enable more to be produced at each price. This causes an outward shift in supply.
- *The size of the labour force and its skills*. A better trained and larger workforce should be able to produce more than a smaller unskilled workforce. Immigration into an economy could increase the labour force, as could changes in the working age and retirement age.
- *The amount and state of capital equipment*. The amount of machinery, plant and equipment will clearly influence the amount that can be produced.
- *The skill of management to combine resources and use them effectively.*
- *The degree of entrepreneurship in an economy.*

An increase in price leads to a movement along the aggregate supply curve. A higher price means that firms can afford to produce more and cover their costs. This means that the aggregate supply curve will slope upwards, as shown in Fig. 23.2.

A change in the other factors will shift the aggregate supply curve; with a larger or a better-trained workforce, for example, the aggregate supply curve will shift to the right—more will be supplied at each price.

Now you try it

What factors would shift the aggregate supply curve to the left?

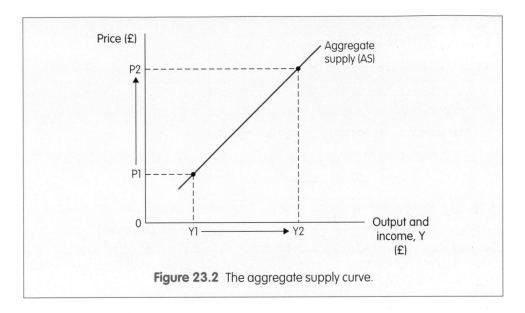

Figure 23.2 The aggregate supply curve.

■ The shape of the aggregate supply curve

The sensitivity of the aggregate supply to changes in price is likely to vary, as shown in Fig. 23.3. At low levels of output (e.g., Y1 to Y2) there are many unused resources in the economy; for example, factories are not being used and firms are working below capacity. The aggregate supply at these levels of output will be price elastic. Firms can increase output without having to put up prices significantly.

Full employment occurs when all of the resources in an economy are used efficiently. This occurs at Y3 in Fig. 23.3. This shows the maximum output that can be produced in an economy, given the existing resources in the economy. Supply will be price inelastic at full employment. Even if the price increases then, at that moment, the economy cannot produce more given its existing resources.

As the economy approaches full employment the aggregate supply in the economy becomes more price inelastic. Even with an increase in prices, supply cannot increase very much due to difficulties in recruiting employees and finding supplies. As resources become more limited the increased demand for them will bid up their prices. Bottlenecks appear in the markets for land, labour and capital. This increases firms' costs and therefore they need higher prices to be able to supply their products.

What do you think?

Where on the aggregate supply curve do you think your economy is at the moment?

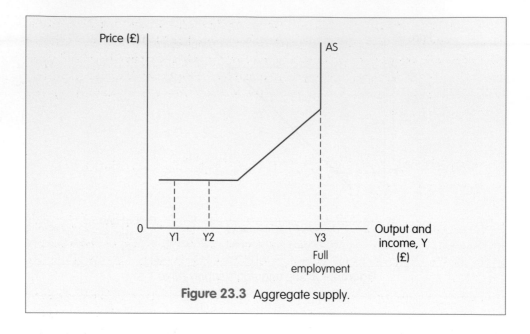

Figure 23.3 Aggregate supply.

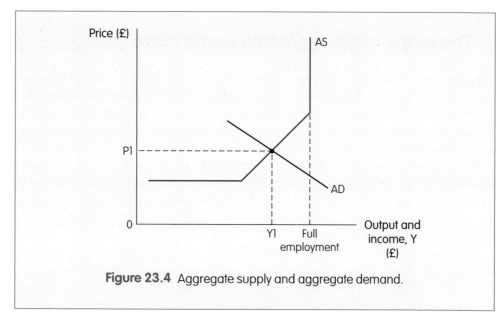

Figure 23.4 Aggregate supply and aggregate demand.

◼ Equilibrium in the economy

Equilibrium in the economy will occur at the price and output for which the aggregate demand equals the aggregate supply. This occurs at the price P1 and output Y1 in Fig. 23.4. If the price was higher than this then there would be excess supply, driving the price down to an equilibrium solution at P1. If the price was below this then there would be excess demand, pulling the price up until equilibrium is reached at P1. Just as we saw in our microeconomic analysis, the price changes to equate supply and demand. The difference here is that we are dealing with the aggregate supply, the aggregate demand and the general price level for the economy as a whole, rather than the supply, demand and price level in one specific market.

◼ The effects of a shift in the aggregate demand on the economy

When the aggregate supply is relatively price elastic then an increase in the aggregate demand will have a relatively greater effect on output and income than prices. For example, in Fig. 23.5, an increase in the aggregate demand from AD1 to AD2 increases the output from Y1 to Y2, but the price level only increases from P1 to P2.

As the aggregate supply becomes more price inelastic, a given increase in the aggregate demand has an increasingly greater effect on prices compared to output. When the aggregate demand increases from AD3 to AD4 (see Fig. 23.5) prices increase from P3 to P4 and output increases from Y3 to Y4.

When the aggregate supply is totally price inelastic at full employment, an increase in the aggregate demand increases the price level but does not change output. An increase in the aggregate demand from AD5 to AD6 leads to a price level increase from P5 to P6.

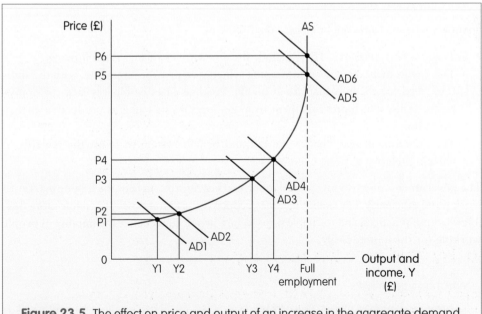

Figure 23.5 The effect on price and output of an increase in the aggregate demand.

The impact of a change in the aggregate demand (perhaps due to demand side policies) in terms of its relative effect on price and output therefore depends on the price elasticity of supply. This in turn depends on how close the economy is to full employment. The nearer an economy is to full employment, the more likely it is that expansionist demand side measures simply lead to inflation and not to increases in output. The view of how close an economy is to full employment at any moment is one area in which economists disagree quite a lot.

Now you try it

Illustrate the impact of a fall in the aggregate demand on the equilibrium price and output.

■ Supply side policies

Supply side policies focus on changing the aggregate supply rather than demand side policies that focus on the aggregate demand. Such policies could include the following.

- Increasing the quantity of resources available; for example, a lowering of the school leaving age would increase the size of the available workforce.
- Increasing the quality of those resources; for example, a better-trained workforce would be more productive.
- Increasing the efficiency in the way they are used; for example, if resources are managed more effectively then they can produce more.

Supply side measures might include the following.

- *Labour market measures*. These include fiscal incentives such as the following.
  - The government may invest in training schemes to provide employees with the skills they need for the jobs that are available. In some cases employees lack the appropriate skills, which prevents them from getting jobs or being as productive as they could be.
  - The government may change the tax and benefit system to boost the rewards of working relative to being unemployed.

The government may also introduce labour market reforms to help the labour market to work more efficiently. For example, it may reduce trade union power to enable more flexible working practices, and to enable firms to hire people and change the number of people working for them more easily.

What do you think?

Is a more flexible labour market a good thing?

- *Intervening in the capital goods market.* For example, the government may provide incentives for firms to invest in capital equipment and technology to enable firms to produce more efficiently and more effectively.
- *Intervening in the product markets to encourage competition.* For example, many governments have privatised industries and opened markets up to greater competition. The aim of such policies is to create an incentive for greater efficiency and to bring about pressure from investors to improve performance.

▧ The effects of a shift in the aggregate supply on the economy

An increase in the aggregate supply will shift this curve to the right (see Fig. 23.6). This can be caused by supply side measures. This can lead to a lower price level in the economy and an increase in the amount produced.

Economics in context — The price of oil

In the 1970s the price of oil increased significantly, making energy much more expensive. This also made many pieces of capital equipment uneconomic to run. The effect of this was to shift the aggregate supply to the left.

❓ Question

Illustrate this using a supply and demand diagram, and show the effect of this shift on the equilibrium price and output.

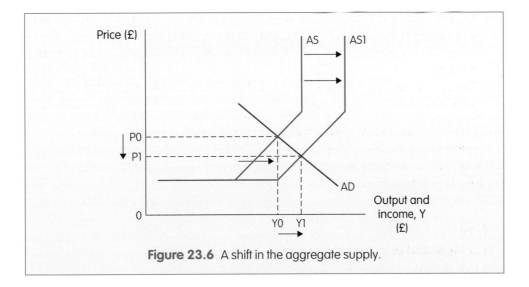

Figure 23.6 A shift in the aggregate supply.

■ Problems with supply side policies

The problems with supply side policies include the following.

- To create flexibility more employees may now have less permanent contracts and be less secure in their jobs. In an attempt to create a more flexible workforce, managers are less willing to guarantee jobs for life or offer long-term contracts. They want flexible contracts that enable them to increase or decrease supply as demand dictates. This may be good for the firm but not for employees.

- In an attempt to encourage people to work, those who are unemployed will become worse off; this will widen the gap between the rich and the poor and may be seen as unfair.

- An increase in supply is only valuable if the demand is there. Otherwise it simply creates excess capacity.

Economics in context   Supply side policies

Supply side policies focus on increasing the supply of goods and services in the economy. Supply side policies came to prominence in the 1980s when they were advocated in the UK by Margaret Thatcher and by Ronald Reagan in the US. The traditional approach to the economy of managing demand was seen to have failed, and so the emphasis was now placed on supply side issues.

? Question

Are supply side policies likely to be more of a priority than demand side policies when the economy is at, near or well below full employment?

■ Demand side versus supply side policies

Some government policies are aimed at boosting the aggregate demand. This clearly makes sense when the aggregate demand is low. For example, suppose that the aggregate demand is at AD1 in Fig. 23.5 on page 303. An increase at this point leads to an increase in output but little increase in prices because the economy has so much capacity.

If, however, the economy is at full employment then an increase in demand would lead to an increase in the price level (demand-pull inflation) without any increase in output (e.g., the aggregate demand increases from AD5 to AD6 in Fig. 23.5). If the economy was at full employment then an increase in the aggregate supply would be more effective than an increase in the aggregate demand.

As the economy approaches full employment, successive increases in the aggregate demand have successively more effect on the price level compared to output, that is, demand side polices become increasingly less attractive.

Obviously, a view of where the economy is at any moment (e.g., whether it is near full employment or not) will have a big influence on whether demand side or supply side policies are recommended.

Keynesian economists—so called because their ideas were first put forward by the economist John Maynard Keynes (1936)—believe that the economy often settles at well below full employment. In this case the aggregate supply is likely to be price elastic and increases in the aggregate demand would mainly affect output. Keynes recommended interventionist demand side policies by governments in such circumstances to boost the aggregate demand and reduce unemployment. Classical economists believe that the economy is at or near full employment, in which case demand side policies aimed at boosting demand would be most likely to increase prices and cause inflation. In these circumstances governments would be better focusing on supply side policies aimed at shifting the aggregate supply to the right.

Case Study

The following is adapted from the CIA factbook.

Russia ended 2005 with its seventh straight year of growth, averaging 6.4% annually since a financial crisis in 1998. Although high oil prices and a relatively cheap rouble are important drivers of this economic rebound, increasing aggregate demand, since 2000 investment and consumer driven demand have played a noticeably increasing role. Real fixed capital investments have averaged gains greater than 10% over the last five years and real personal incomes have realised averages over 12%. During this time poverty has declined steadily and the middle class has continued to expand . . . [It has also benefited from] strong oil exports earnings. Along with a renewed government effort to advance structural reforms [this] has raised business and investor confidence in Russia's economic prospects. Greater confidence encourages spending. Nevertheless serious problems persist. Russia's manufacturing base is dilapidated and must be replaced or modernised if the country is to achieve broad based economic growth. [At the moment] 80% of its exports are oil, natural gas, metals and timber. Other problems include a weak banking system, a poor business climate that discourages both domestic and foreign investors, corruption and widespread lack of trust in institutions.

❓ Questions

- What has caused economic growth in Russia in recent years? Illustrate this using an aggregate supply and aggregate demand diagram.
- To what extent is the Russian economy in a strong economic position?
- What policies would you recommend to the government for long-term economic stability and further growth?

@ Web

For more information from the CIA on economies visit www.cia.gov/cia/publications/factbook

Checklist

Now you have read this unit try to answer the following questions.

☐ Can you explain the shape of the aggregate demand curve relative to price?

☐ Can you explain the shape of the aggregate supply curve relative to price?

☐ Can you explain equilibrium in the economy in terms of aggregate supply and aggregate demand?

☐ Can you examine the effect of changes in the aggregate supply and the aggregate demand in terms of price and output outcomes?

End of unit questions

1 How might an increase in the aggregate demand affect the equilibrium price and output in the economy?

2 What factors cause a shift to the left in the aggregate supply curve?

3 Why might the aggregate supply be price inelastic?

4 How do supply side policies differ from demand side policies?

5 Should demand side policies always be used rather than supply side policies when a government intervenes in an economy?

Key learning points

- Equilibrium in an economy occurs when the aggregate demand equals the aggregate supply.

- The aggregate demand is downward sloping in relation to price. A higher price level for a given level of income reduces the quantity demanded.

- The aggregate supply is generally upward sloping in relation to price.

- An increase in the aggregate demand will usually lead to an increase in price and output. The relative impact on price compared to output depends on the price elasticity of the aggregate supply.

- The aggregate supply is more price elastic when the economy is well below full employment; it is price inelastic at full employment.

Reference

Keynes, J. M. (1936). *General theory of employment, interest and money*. Harcourt, Brace and Co., New York. First published by Macmillan, Cambridge University Press for the Royal Economic Society.

Learn more

Supply side policies have a significant impact on the level of income in an economy and on economic growth. To learn more about supply side policies that have been introduced in the UK visit our website at the address below.

 Visit our Online Resource Centre at www.oxfordtextbooks.co.uk/orc/gillespie_econ for test questions and further information on topics covered in this chapter.

»24 Consumption

The level of aggregate demand in an economy is made up of consumption spending, investment, government spending and net export spending. In this unit we examine the factors that affect consumption spending in particular. In the following units we examine the other elements of aggregate demand.

LEARNING OBJECTIVES

By the end of this unit you should be able to:

✔ explain the factors that influence levels of consumption;

✔ analyse the impact of a change in consumption spending.

■ Introduction

We all like to spend money, and in so doing we are consuming goods and services and creating demand in the economy. This generates output and employment. Consumption in macroeconomics measures the total planned level of demand in the economy by households for final goods and services. Consumption spending is the largest element of the aggregate demand, and so changes in households' spending can have a major impact on the economy. Economists are naturally interested in what determines the total level of consumption in the economy because this is such an important element of the aggregate demand and therefore has a big influence on how well an economy is doing.

■ The Keynesian consumption function

According to the economist John Maynard Keynes (1936), the level of consumption in an economy is given by the following equation (see Fig. 24.1):

$C = a + b\, Yd,$

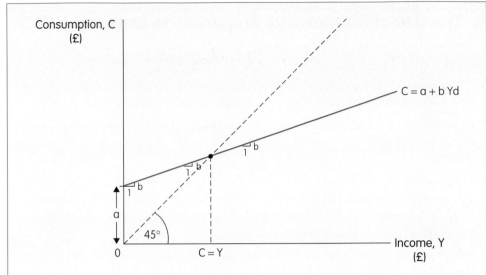

Figure 24.1 The consumption function. Here 'b' is the gradient of the consumption function; out of each extra pound 'b' is consumed.

where the notation is defined as follows.

- 'C' is the level of consumption spending.
- 'a' is the level of autonomous consumption; this is the amount of spending that there would be even if incomes were zero. This is known as dis-saving because households must be borrowing or using up past savings.
- 'b' is the marginal propensity to consume (MPC). This is the amount of extra spending out of an extra pound. For example, if the marginal propensity to consume is 0.8 then this means that eighty pence out of each extra pound is spent on the consumption of final goods and services.
- 'Yd' is the disposable income. This consists of income from employment and self-employment, pensions, investment income and cash benefits less income tax, local taxes and employees' national insurance contributions.

According to this equation, there is a direct relationship between the level of disposable income earned by households and the amount that they spend on consumption.

What do you think?

How much do you think you spend out of each extra pound you get?
Do you think this is more or less than your friends? Why?

◼ The size of the marginal propensity to consume (MPC)

The size of the marginal propensity to consume depends on the following.

- *Interest rates*. If interest rates are high then consumers may be more willing to save to earn higher returns and less willing to spend; this would reduce the MPC.

- *Expectations of future price increases*. If households expect that prices will increase in the future then they are likely to buy more now before the prices rise; this increases the MPC.

- *Expectations of the future state of the economy*. If households predict that the economy will go into a recession and that they may lose their jobs then they may save now to build up a reserve fund. In this case the marginal propensity to save may increase and the marginal propensity to consume may fall.

- *Income levels*. As income levels increase the MPC domestically is likely to fall. Consumers will already have bought many of the items they need and therefore will tend to save more out of the extra income. At low incomes, by comparison, any income earned is more likely to be spent.

- *The availability and quality of domestic goods compared to foreign goods*. This will influence the level of spending on UK products as opposed to imports.

An increase in the marginal propensity to consume will lead to more money being spent out of each extra pound and will change the slope of the consumption function (see Fig. 24.2).

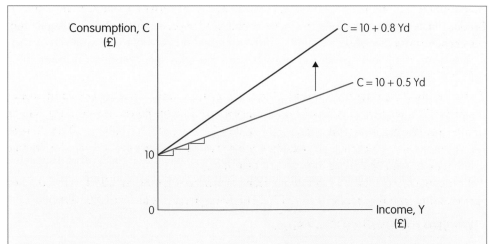

Figure 24.2 An increase in the marginal propensity to consume increases the amount spent of each extra pound; this changes the gradient of the consumption function.

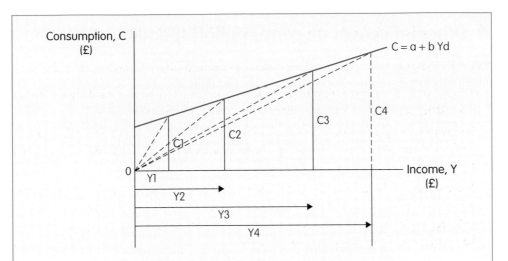

Figure 24.3 The average propensity to consume.

The average propensity to consume (APC)

The average propensity to consume (APC) measures the average spending out of every pound of income:

$$APC = \frac{C}{Yd}.$$

At any level of income the APC can be measured by the gradient of a ray drawn from the origin (see Fig. 24.3), whereas the MPC is shown by the gradient of the consumption function. Note how the APC falls as income increases (as shown by the fact that the rays become flatter); as income falls the value of the APC approaches the MPC. Imagine that the consumption function is

C = 100 + 0.8 Yd.

Out of each extra pound we spend £0.80; there is an autonomous element of spending of £100. If we earn only £1 of disposable income then the consumer spending will be £100 + £0.80, that is, a total spending of £100.80 out of £1. The APC is 100.8. Due to the autonomous element we are spending a lot even though income is low. The average spending is much higher than the marginal spending.

As income increases the autonomous element becomes far less significant and the key factor of our spending becomes the MPC. For example, if income is £10,000 then

C = £100 + (0.8 × £10,000) = £8100.

Therefore the APC = £8100/£10,000 = 0.81. The APC is now close to the MPC. The average spending is closer to the spending out of each extra pound. The autonomous element of consumption becomes almost irrelevant at high levels of income.

■ Other influences on consumption spending

Whilst Keynes may have highlighted important determinants of consumption, there are many other factors that can also influence households' spending. These may include the following.

- *The distribution of income in the economy.* Lower-income groups tend to have a higher marginal propensity to consume than higher-income groups. If you give an extra pound to a poor person then they will spend it; a rich person is more likely to save it because they have already bought many goods and services. If income is redistributed from the richer to the poorer then the MPC in the economy will rise.

- *The availability and cost of credit.* If it is easy and cheap to borrow then households are more likely to spend money, so consumption will rise even if incomes have not increased. In the UK the banks have been criticised in recent years for lending too easily to people who cannot afford to repay what they have borrowed, given their incomes. Think of all of the different ways in which you can borrow money and you will realise how much spending is financed this way and how important credit is in the UK economy.

Now you try it

There are numerous ways of borrowing money; for example, overdrafts, loans, student loans, credit cards and mortgages.

Can you think of any more?

How much do you owe?

Could you borrow more if you wanted?

How easy would it be?

Economics in context   UK consumer debt

UK consumer debt is now over £1 trillion. Consumers in the UK owe more than £1000 billion on credit cards, mortgages and loans. The amount owed by UK households is equivalent to £17,000 of debt for every person in the UK. A trillion pound debt is bigger than the whole external debt of Africa and South Africa combined.

❓ Questions

What factors are likely to determine how much consumers borrow in a country?

Does this amount of debt matter?

What do you think?

Do you think it is the banks' responsibility to check whether people can easily afford to repay a loan or not?

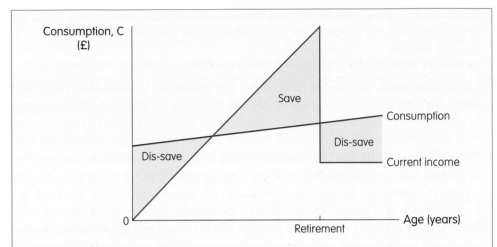

Figure 24.4 Consumption in relation to age. Over our working life our income will, hopefully, increase until retirement. Our consumption patterns may be far more stable than this, so there will be periods of dis-saving and saving.

- *Wealth effects.* If households become wealthier, perhaps due to an increase in house or share prices, then this can allow them to borrow more to spend. Often this will be spent on items such as holidays, cars and other income elastic products.

- *The age distribution in the economy.* In general, people will tend to spend more than their income when they are younger (for example, when they are just starting out in a job). We will tend to spend less than our income in our middle years (when we are building up savings) and more than our income in later life (when we are running down savings) (see Fig. 24.4). The importance of the stage in the life cycle on consumption spending was highlighted by Ando and Modigliani (1957). The UK has an ageing population, for example, which means that there may be more dis-saving.

Economics in context   **Graduate debt**

Graduates leaving university in 2006 had average debts of £13,252, a 5% increase on 2005, according to a survey by NatWest bank. Moreover, 62% of graduates left university owing more than £10,000. It is likely to be even worse in the future, with universities able to decide what to charge for their courses up to £3000 per year. Those starting university in 2006, for example, are likely to leave with debts of around £15,000. This is probably why the survey revealed that 87% of new students in 2006 expected to have to take on a part-time job to supplement their income while studying. This is almost double the number who worked part-time in 2005.

? Questions

What might be the economic effects of universities being able to set their own fees within a given band?
What might be the short-run and long-run economic implications of more students working part-time?

- *Expectations*. If consumers believe that the economy is going to grow rapidly then they may be more willing to spend now because they believe that their income is going to increase later on. This means that it is not just current income that affects spending but also future expected income.

- *The permanent income theory*. This model was developed by Friedman (1957) and states that what matters to consumers when determining spending is not their present income but their 'permanent income'. A household's permanent income depends on its view of what it will earn over its whole lifetime. Temporary unemployment may reduce the current level of income considerably (which, according to Keynes, would lead to a significant fall in spending), but its impact on the overall lifetime income is far less significant, assuming that the household thinks the unemployment will not last long. Equally, a one-off bonus would not lead to a significant increase in present spending because when this increase is spread over the whole lifetime of a household its effect is less significant. According to the permanent income hypothesis, changes in disposable income that are not expected to last will not have much effect on current spending. This has implications for government policy. A tax cut to boost spending will not affect consumers' view of their permanent income if they think the tax cut is only for the short term. To have a real effect the government would need to convince households that the tax cut would be large enough and long enough to have an impact on their average lifetime earnings.

What do you think?

What are the main influences on how much you spend?

Case Study

The level of UK retail sales in August 2005 remained unchanged compared to the previous month. According to the Office of National Statistics, demand during that month remained weak but stable. The year-on-year increase was just 0.8%.

The clothes retailer Next reported its worst like-for-like sales in ten years and the home-improvement retailer Kingfisher said it had experienced its 'toughest' trading conditions for years. Food sales also fell by the largest amount in two years.

Consumers were said to be staying away from the shops because they were worried about the housing market and feared that house prices might fall. They were also concerned whether the economy was likely to grow rapidly in the future and were affected by rising fuel prices. Another factor was that tourists seemed to be staying away from the UK, possibly because of the London bombings in July.

Analysts expected that interest rate cuts might follow the news about the flat retail sales. Interest rates at the time were 4.5%.

❓ Questions

- What does the above description suggest are the key determinants of consumer spending in the UK?
- What do you think might be the impact of a decrease in interest rates on retail sales?
- How might the fact that the level of retail sales in the UK stayed the same affect groups within the UK economy?

Checklist

Now you have read this unit try to answer the following questions.

☐ Can you explain the factors that influence levels of consumption?

☐ Can you analyse the impact of a change in consumption spending?

End of unit questions

1 Why does an understanding of consumption spending matter?

2 What, according to Keynes, is the most important determinant of consumption spending?

3 How might a fall in interest rates affect consumption spending?

4 To what extent does it matter whether consumption is mainly determined by permanent income rather than current income?

5 Why might expectations play an important role in the level of consumption in an economy?

Key learning points

- Consumption is an important element of the aggregate demand.
- The level of consumption in an economy may be influenced by a range of factors, including current income, estimates of permanent income, interest rates, expectations of the price level, the availability of credit and the age distribution.
- An increase in consumption increases the aggregate demand.

References

Ando, A. and Modigliani, F. (1957). Tests of the life cycle hypothesis of saving: comments and suggestions. *Oxford Institute of Statistics Bulletin*, xix (May), 99–124.

Friedman, M. (1957). *A theory of the consumption function*. National Bureau of Economic Research, Princeton, NJ.

Learn more

This unit has focused on the consumption function. This is clearly interrelated with the savings function. To learn more about this relationship visit our website at the address below.

 Visit our Online Resource Centre at www.oxfordtextbooks.co.uk/orc/gillespie_econ for test questions and further information on topics covered in this chapter.

Investment

Investment is an important element of the aggregate demand. It is of particular importance because it is the most volatile element of the aggregate demand, and therefore an understanding of it is vital if a government is to be able to influence the aggregate demand effectively. Investment is also important because it affects the level of aggregate supply in the economy. In this unit we examine the influences on the level of investment in an economy and the consequences of it changing on the equilibrium price, output and employment.

LEARNING OBJECTIVES

By the end of this unit you should be able to:

✔ analyse the determinants of investment spending;

✔ explain the impact of a change in investment spending on national income;

✔ explain the instability caused by the accelerator–multiplier model.

■ Introduction

Investment occurs when firms make a decision to allocate resources into projects that will generate future returns; for example, investing in a new machine or a new information technology system. Investment involves sacrificing existing, present consumption for future expected benefits.

Investment may be in the following.

- *Fixed capital*. This involves the purchase of assets that are expected to be used for a long period, for example, factories and production equipment.
- *Working capital*. These are short-term assets that will be used up in the production process; for example, stocks and materials.

Gross and net investment

The types of investment include the following.

- *Gross investment*. This measures the total investment in an economy in a period.
- *Depreciation investment*. This is investment undertaken to replace equipment or machinery that has worn out. Depreciation investment simply maintains the level and quality of the capital stock.
- *Net investment*. This is new investment that increases the capital stock in the economy.

Therefore we have:

Gross investment = Net investment + Depreciation investment.

Factors affecting the level of investment in an economy

The amount of investment in an economy will depend on the following.

- *The initial cost of projects*. Some projects may be attractive in terms of the possible rewards that they offer, but may not be affordable at the present time if firms do not have or cannot raise the necessary finance. Therefore the availability and cost of finance is an important issue. High interest rates will make it more expensive to borrow and are likely to reduce the level of investment.
- *The expected returns from the investment*. What are the expected costs and revenues from the project and, therefore, what profits does the firm expect to be earned and over what period? These estimates of revenues and costs are, of course, only a forecast of the future net inflows. Investment decisions inevitably have an element of risk and uncertainty. An investment into an oil project, for example, involves estimates of what the world oil price will be many years into the future—this involves a high degree of risk in terms of the accuracy of the forecast. However, the likely returns will depend on firms' views about the likely level of sales, which is likely to be linked to economic growth and also to the likely inflation rates.
- *The alternatives available*. A decision to invest in one project means that resources are being allocated to this area and away from something else. A decision is therefore being made about the best way to use resources and this involves an opportunity cost. If, for example, the returns available in other countries or in financial savings such as shares are high then this is likely to reduce the level of investment in the UK.
- *Risk and culture*. Any investment project will involve risk because the outcomes are not certain. Different managers and organisations may have different perceptions of the risk of any particular project and will have different attitudes to taking risks. This may affect their willingness to pursue a particular investment. If a country had a culture which was risk-taking then this might affect the level of investment in one country compared to another. National culture can also be important in other ways. In the past Japanese and German firms have tended to be more long-termist than UK firms; this

means that they were willing to wait longer for the eventual rewards. This was partly because their investors tended to be linked to the firm in some way (such as being their suppliers) and so were willing to wait for the long-term benefits in which they would share. In the UK investors do not tend to be directly linked to the business and look for short-term rewards. This has tended to reduce the number of projects that UK firms might invest in compared to Japanese firms.

- *Non-financial factors.* When considering an investment a firm may be interested in the expected profits, but it may also take into account non-financial factors. What will the investment do to the brand image? How will stakeholders in the firm react to the investment? Will it fit with any proposed policy on issues such as corporate social responsibility? Does it fit with the corporate strategy? Investing in a new product area may in itself appear profitable, for example, but may not fit with a corporate strategy that intends to focus on existing business areas. In recent years, for example, firms have generally been more concerned with the environmental impact of their activities, and this has diverted investment away from some projects that are perceived to be environmentally unfriendly. On a national scale, firms may be concerned about factors such as political stability.

- *Government policy.* Changes to the tax system can provide incentives for firms to invest. For example, tax credits may enable firms to reduce their tax bill if they invest more in research and development.

■ The importance of investment

Investment is an important element of the aggregate demand due to the following reasons.

- Investment tends to be very volatile, partly because it depends so much on expectations.
- Sudden changes in investment can lead to instability in the economy.
- Investment affects both the aggregate demand (because it involves spending) and the aggregate supply (because it increases the productive capacity of the economy and therefore, in the long run, the amount that can be produced) (see Fig. 25.1). Investment is an injection into the economy and so an increase in it will boost the level of the aggregate demand. However, more investment will also increase the productive capacity of the economy and shift the aggregate supply.

Now you try it

Using a supply and demand diagram show the effect of an increase in demand and an increase in supply due to an increase in investment.

Now you try it

Expectations are an important influence on investment decisions.
How can the government influence firms' expectations?
In what other ways do you think expectations can influence an economy?

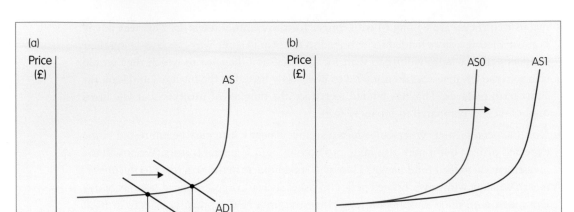

Figure 25.1 (a) The effect of an increase in investment on the aggregate demand.
(b) The effect of an increase in investment on the aggregate supply.

■ The marginal efficiency of capital (MEC)

The marginal efficiency of capital (MEC) shows the rate of return on an additional investment project. This return can be compared with the cost of borrowing to decide whether or not to invest in a project. If the return on the project (i.e., the MEC) is greater than the rate of interest then the project should go ahead on financial grounds. If the return is less than the cost of borrowing then the project should not go ahead. Therefore a profit maximising firm should invest up to the point where the marginal efficiency of capital (MEC) equals the extra costs of borrowing.

In Fig. 25.2, for example, project I1 is expected to achieve returns of 18%. Project I2 is estimated to achieve returns of 6%. If the cost of borrowing is 6% then all of the projects up to and including I2 are worth doing. The projects beyond I2 are not financially attractive because the expected return is less than the cost of borrowing.

Changes in the interest rate therefore lead to movements along the MEC schedule. Higher interest rates usually lead to less investment. The extent to which investment changes depends on the interest elasticity of demand for capital goods.

Now you try it

What do you think the equation for the interest elasticity of demand for capital goods would be? If demand for capital goods is very sensitive to interest rate changes, does this mean that it is interest elastic or interest inelastic?

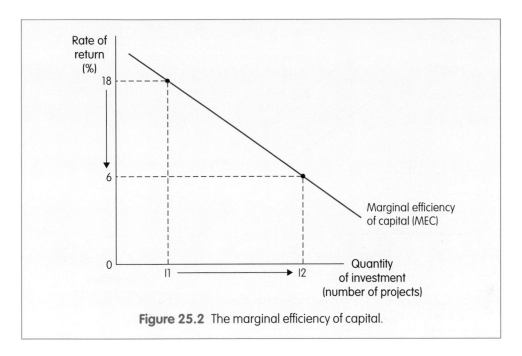

Figure 25.2 The marginal efficiency of capital.

■ Shifts in the marginal efficiency of capital

The MEC will shift if every project is expected to earn higher or lower returns. This may be due to more optimistic expectations about the level of sales; this in turn may be due to a belief that the economy is going to grow faster. This would lead to an upward shift in the MEC as higher returns are expected on each project (see Fig. 25.3). In the media you will often see reports on levels of business confidence and the views of business people about whether they think that orders will increase or not in the future. These surveys are a way of assessing business confidence. The level of business confidence is an extremely important factor in determining the level of investment in an economy. Given that people's confidence can change quite easily (e.g., if the government is having problems or if there is an external shock, such as a natural disaster or a change in the oil price), investment levels can change quite dramatically due to shifts in the MEC. This can have a large impact on the aggregate demand.

The MEC might also shift due to changes in technology or the level of capital in the economy. An increase in the expected returns on projects will lead to more investment at any level of interest rate.

What do you think?

What do you think influences firms' expectations of the future economic environment?

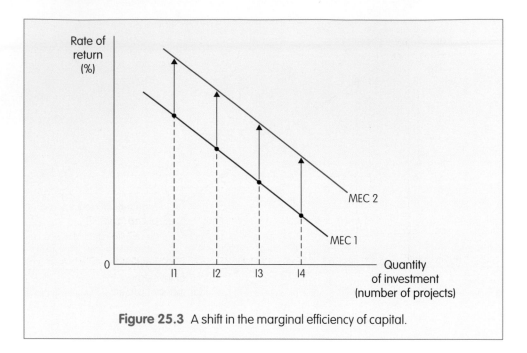

Figure 25.3 A shift in the marginal efficiency of capital.

The impact of a change in investment

If the level of investment in an economy changes then this leads to an increase or decrease in the aggregate demand. This in turn may start off the multiplier process. If, for example, investment changes by £100 million then, assuming that the marginal propensity to consume domestically is 0.8, the overall increase in national income will be £500 million (this assumes that the effect is purely on output; in reality, output may increase to some extent and prices may increase to some extent; the relative effect on output and price depends on the price elasticity of supply).

Given that investment can be quite volatile due to changes in expectations, this can lead to significant movements in the level of demand in the economy and cause instability. The instability is made greater when the multiplier interacts with the accelerator (see page 325).

Investment is also important because it affects the level of capital in an economy. This can affect the amount that can be produced and employees' productivity. This can affect the aggregate supply. To increase the aggregate supply and shift the production possibility frontier an economy needs investment over time. The effect of more investment on the production possibility frontier can be seen in Fig. 25.4.

Now you try it

What do you think is likely to determine the size of the marginal propensity to consume domestically?

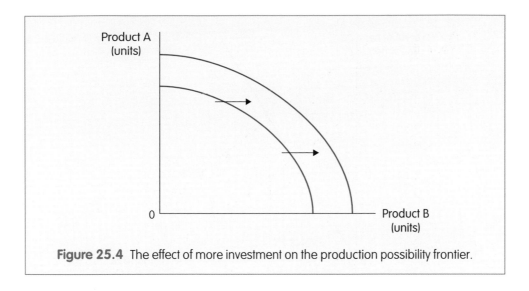

Figure 25.4 The effect of more investment on the production possibility frontier.

■ The accelerator–multiplier model

The accelerator model shows the relationship between the level of net investment in an economy and the rate of change of output. It assumes that firms will need to increase their level of capital if the rate of change of output in the economy increases. This type of investment is called induced investment because it is induced by changes in the level of output.

We assume that

Net investment = a × Change in national income,

where 'a' is the accelerator coefficient.

Imagine that demand is growing by a constant amount each year. To be able to meet this demand firms will need to invest more each year. As the growth is constant the amount of net investment remains the same each year (assuming a constant capital to output ratio).

For example, if a firm needs £2 million of capital equipment to be able to increase capacity by £1 million then, if demand grows by £5 million every year, firms will invest £10 million per year to be able to produce at this higher level. The level of net investment (i.e., ignoring spending on updating and maintaining old equipment) will be constant each year at £10 million.

If, however, demand begins to grow by more each year then, to keep pace with this increasing rate of demand, firms must increase their annual level of net investment. This in turn boosts the aggregate demand and helps to stimulate even more spending due to the multiplier process. If the spending leads to a larger increase in demand than the year before then this again increases the level of net investment to keep pace with it, and a growth spiral has been created.

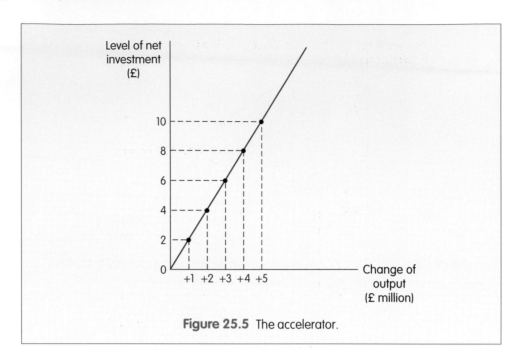

Figure 25.5 The accelerator.

For example, if demand grows by £5 million one year, £6 million in the second year, and £7 million in the third year, then firms will want to invest £10 million, then £12 million, and then £14 million. The level of net investment is increasing because the growth in demand is accelerating (see Fig. 25.5).

However, this investment–demand spiral is vulnerable to collapse. For example, if the demand grows again but by less than the year before (e.g., by £4 million rather than £5 million) then firms will need to invest to have the capacity to produce this output, but their investment will be at a lower level than the previous year. In this example investment will fall to £8 million from £10 million. As the rate at which demand has grown has slowed up, the amount of net investment will be less than before. This leads to a fall in the aggregate demand and sets off a downward multiplier. This may send the economy into a period of even slower growth and therefore another fall in net investment.

The accelerator model shows the link between net investment and the rate of growth of demand in the economy. It shows why the level of net investment in an economy may fall compared to the year before, even if the economy is still growing. It is the rate of growth that is most important. Given that changes in net investment can set off the multiplier, it also highlights how significant swings in the aggregate demand can be caused by initial changes in the rate of growth of the economy. A small fall in the rate of growth of the economy leads to a fall in net investment, which can set off a downward multiplier and create much slower long-term growth.

According to the accelerator model, an increased level of net investment can only be achieved by accelerating increases in demand in the economy, which is not sustainable.

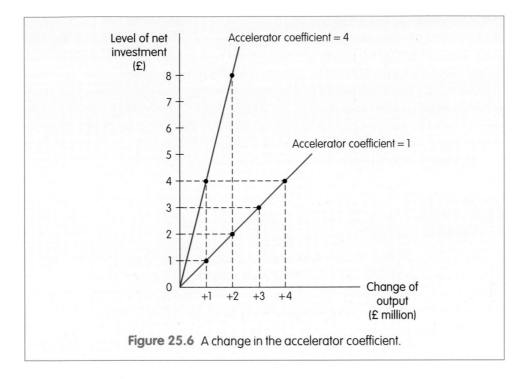

Figure 25.6 A change in the accelerator coefficient.

Limitations of the accelerator model

The limitations of the accelerator model include the following.

- Some firms will have excess capacity and therefore will not need to undertake net investment to meet an increase in demand.

- Technology may change and this will change the accelerator coefficient; for example, less net investment may be required to meet a given increase in output. The effect of a change in the accelerator coefficient can be seen in Fig. 25.6.

- There may be bottlenecks and constraints in the producer (capital goods) industry that prevent or delay the net investment going ahead.

Now you try it

Can you remember the equation for the multiplier?

Cost–benefit analysis

Cost–benefit analysis is a technique used mainly by governments when assessing an investment project. It is a technique that tries to quantify the external costs and external benefits involved in any project. It is often used by governments that are not only interested in the private costs and benefits of any activity, but also want to consider the full social impacts of any project. For example, it may be used when assessing a new council house development. The government may also ask private firms to undertake such an analysis when dealing with a major project with important social effects, such as a new airport terminal.

A cost–benefit analysis involves estimating the monetary value of external costs, such as pollution, congestion, noise and the impact of a project on wildlife. It will also try to value external benefits, such as the benefits to society of improving the public transport system. Measuring such external costs and benefits can be difficult to do, but is likely to lead to different decisions being made than a private firm would make.

Economics in context

Terminal 5 at Heathrow

The decision to go ahead with Terminal 5 at Heathrow was only reached after 27 000 letters from the general public and after forty-six months of public enquiry to consider all of the different costs and benefits. The terminal covers 26 hectares, around the same area as Hyde Park. Building it involved shifting 6.5 million cubic metres of earth and building a 13.5 km tunnel network underneath the runways.

The number of passengers using Heathrow in 2004 was 67 million; with the new terminal there will be room for 30 million more. The estimated cost of Terminal 5 is £4.2 billion.

❓ Question

What kinds of external costs and benefits might have been considered when deciding whether to invest in Terminal 5 or not?

Case Study

Dubai is a truly extraordinary city where almost anything seems possible. After all, despite being in the desert, it is home to the first ski resort in the Middle East, and it has the world's tallest building, a seven-star hotel and an underwater hotel!

Thirty years ago Dubai was little more than a fishing village, but it has now become one of the world's fastest growing cities. In 2005, its economy grew by almost 17%. This incredible growth was financed by its oil reserves and massive investment from abroad that was attracted by the lack of direct taxes. The investment has funded enormous construction projects. The city has attracted multinational companies and has also become a major tourist destination. This spending has had a multiplier effect within the economy.

However, growth has come at a price. The roads are often blocked with traffic and throughout the city there are always numerous construction projects. This growth has increased the cost of living to residents and visitors, so much so that the authorities have capped rent increases to 15% per year. Inflation in 2006 was expected to reach 15–20%.

? Questions

- Why might the lack of direct taxes attract overseas investment? What else determines the level of investment in an economy?
- Do you think economic growth can be too fast?

Checklist

Now you have read this unit try to answer the following questions.

☐   Can you analyse the determinants of investment spending?

☐   Can you explain the impact of a change in investment spending on national income?

☐   Can you explain the instability caused by the accelerator–multiplier model?

End of unit questions

1   Why are expectations such an important influence on the level of investment in an economy?

2   What is the likely effect of a fall in interest rates on the level of investment in an economy?

3   Should private firms take account of external costs and benefits when making an investment decision?

4   What is meant by the multiplier effect?

5   In what way can the accelerator–multiplier model help to explain the economic cycle?

Key learning points

- Investment depends in part on expectations of the future.
- Changes in investment lead to changes in the aggregate demand.
- The marginal efficiency of capital shows the expected return on investment projects.
- Profit maximising firms will invest up to the point where the interest rate equals the marginal efficiency of capital.
- An increase in interest rates is likely to decrease the level of investment and therefore the level of the aggregate demand in an economy, all other things being unchanged.
- The accelerator shows the relationship between net investment and the rate of change of national income. According to the accelerator, an increase in net investment requires the economy to grow at an increasing rate.

- A cost–benefit analysis uses social costs and benefits rather than private costs and benefits when assessing an investment.

Learn more

 Visit our Online Resource Centre at www.oxfordtextbooks.co.uk/orc/gillespie_econ for test questions and further information on topics covered in this chapter.

Fiscal policy

Fiscal policy refers to decisions made by the government regarding its spending, taxation and benefits policies. Changes in these can affect the level of aggregate demand and aggregate supply, and therefore the equilibrium levels of price, output and employment. In this unit we examine the elements of government fiscal policy and analyse the importance of it in terms of the economy as a whole.

LEARNING OBJECTIVES

By the end of this unit you should be able to:

✔ understand the key elements of government spending;

✔ outline the different elements of taxation;

✔ analyse the impact of changes in taxation;

✔ assess the fiscal stance of a government.

■ Introduction

Fiscal policy involves the use of changes in government spending and the taxation and benefit systems to influence the economy. Fiscal policy can be used to affect both the aggregate demand and the aggregate supply. In the past the priority of fiscal policy in the UK has been to try to fine-tune the level of the aggregate demand. More recently the government has left the control of demand to the Bank of England via interest rates; fiscal policy has been used more to influence the aggregate supply.

First of all, in this unit we examine forms of government spending and taxation, and then we consider how fiscal policy can influence demand and supply.

■ Government spending

The government in the UK is made up of central and local government. Central government is responsible for the national provision of some goods and services, such as the National Health Service and the police force. Local government is responsible for regional, city-based or town-based services, such as street cleaning and local amenities (e.g., swimming pools).

Government spending covers a wide range of goods and services, including:

- defence;
- social security benefits (e.g., government payments to people if they are ill or unemployed);
- education;
- repayments on previous borrowing.

The government will need to spend money to intervene to solve the market failures and imperfections that arise in the free market. For example, government spending may be needed to provide public and merit goods, to encourage greater production of positive externalities or to reduce instability in some markets with a buffer stock system.

To finance its spending the government raises funds from the following.

- *Taxation*.
- *Borrowing*; for example, from banks and individuals. The government sells what are called bonds or securities. These are IOUs that last for a variety of periods. Governments usually pay interest and are paid back on a specified date. Some government bonds are short term, and some are long term.

Economics in context   The US budget deficit

In 2006, the US Federal government spent about $2 trillion; the budget deficit was around $500 million.

❓ Question

Whilst these are obviously huge figures, what would you want to compare them to if you wanted to analyse their significance effectively?

An increase in government spending can increase the aggregate demand and set off the multiplier (see Fig. 26.1(a)). However, the impact of this spending on the economy will depend on how it is financed. If the funding comes from taxes then this will reduce the level of demand, thereby reducing the impact of the initial increase in spending.

Fiscal policy may also be used to provide incentives to increase the aggregate supply (see Fig. 26.1(b)).

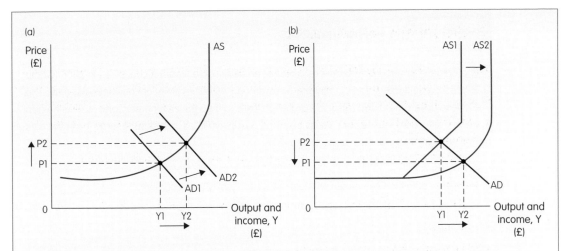

Figure 26.1 (a) Fiscal policy and the aggregate demand. An increase in government spending can increase the aggregate demand; price and output increase. (b) Fiscal policy and the aggregate supply. A change in the tax and benefit system can increase the aggregate supply (e.g., by increasing the incentive to work); this increases output and decreases the price level.

▪ Taxation

Taxes are charges levied on individuals and organisations in an economy. Taxation is used to achieve the following.

- *To raise revenue to finance government spending.*
- *To influence firms' and households' behaviour.* For example, by making some goods more expensive taxation can lead to households switching to other products or changing their consumption patterns (e.g., taxes placed on fuel may reduce energy usage).

Economics in context   Environmental taxation

The following information is from the Office for National Statistics.

In 2004, the government received £35 billion from environmental taxation. This represented about 3% of the GDP and just over 8% of total taxes and social contributions. The majority of the environmental tax was raised from duty on hydrocarbon oils, such as petrol and diesel. Other environmental taxes include landfill tax, vehicle excise duty and air passenger duty.

? Question
What products would you tax to make firms and individuals aware of the external environmental effects of their actions?

Taxing chopsticks

The Chinese government introduced a 5% tax on disposable wooden chopsticks in 2006 to help to preserve its forests. The country produces around 45 billion pairs of chopsticks per year. The Chinese government also raised consumption taxes to help the environment and reduce the gap between the rich and the poor. Taxes on yachts, luxury watches, golf clubs, energy-inefficient cars and wooden floor panels increased by 5–20%.

? Question

How else could the Chinese government reduce inequality in its country?

Types of taxes include the following.

- *Direct taxes*. These are taxes placed on households' incomes and firms' profits, for example:
  - *income tax* (this is paid on employees' income);
  - *corporation tax* (this is paid on firms' profits);
  - *capital gains tax* (this is paid when you sell an asset, such as shares and houses, that has gone up in value);
  - *inheritance tax* (this is paid when you inherit income and assets);
  - *national insurance taxes* (these are payments made by individuals and their employers to finance pensions and social security).
- *Indirect taxes*. These are incurred when items are purchased. The producer is legally obliged to pay these taxes but adds them onto the price to try to pass them on to the customer. They include:
  - *value added tax* (this is paid when most goods and services are bought);
  - *excise duties* (these are specific taxes paid on particular goods and services, such as alcohol);
  - *customs duties* (these are taxes paid on imports into the country).

▮ Marginal and average tax rates

The marginal rate of tax is the extra tax paid when an additional pound is earned. For example, forty pence may be paid on each extra pound of income earned.

The average rate of tax is calculated as follows:

$$\text{Average rate of tax} = \frac{\text{Total tax paid}}{\text{Total income}} \times 100,$$

that is, the average amount of tax paid per pound.

Example

Imagine, for example, that a tax system is 0% tax on every pound up to £999 of income and then 40% tax on every pound earned above this. This means that if £1000 is earned then:

- the marginal rate of tax (the extra tax on the last pound) is 40%;
- the average rate of tax is

$$\frac{\text{Total tax paid}}{\text{Total income}} \times 100 = \frac{£0.40}{£1000} \times 100 = 0.04\%.$$

As the amount of tax-free income relative to the actual earnings is low, the average tax rate is low. If an individual was earning £1 million then the tax paid would be 40% on the taxable amount of £999,001. The total tax paid would be £399,600.40. The average rate of tax would then be (£399,600.40/£1,000,000) × 100 = 39.96%.

What do you think?

What do you think the rate of income tax should be?

▦ Taxation systems

The following are the different types of taxation system (see Fig. 26.2).

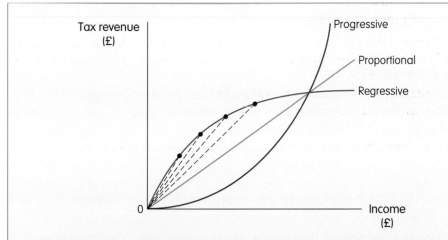

Figure 26.2 Progressive, proportional and regressive taxation systems.
In a progressive taxation system the average rate of tax increases as income increases. In a regressive taxation system the average rate of tax decreases as income increases. In a proportional taxation system the average rate of tax is constant. Note: the average rate of tax is shown by the gradient of rays from the origin. The gradient falls for a regressive system, for example.

- *Progressive*. In a progressive taxation system the average rate of tax increases as people earn more money. The income tax system in the UK is progressive; as people earn more they move into higher marginal tax brackets. The increasing marginal tax rate pulls up the average amount of tax paid per pound.

- *Regressive*. In a regressive tax system the average rate of taxation falls as income increases. This can occur if, for example, the same amount of tax is paid regardless of individuals' or firms' income levels. For example, you might pay £10 VAT on an item whether your income is £10,000 or £50,000. On average, therefore, the more income you have, the lower the tax paid per pound earned.

- *Proportional*. A proportional tax occurs when the percentage of their income that people pay in tax stays constant whatever they earn, that is, the average rate of tax is constant.

 Economics in context   **Tax Freedom Day**

Tax Freedom Day is the day on which the average UK taxpayer stops working for the government and begins earning money for themselves. In 2006 this was 3 June; for an average British taxpayer all of the money earned in the first 155 days went to the government in taxes and other deductions. Tax Freedom Day was as late as 15 June in 1982. In the US the tax burden on the average citizen is generally lower than in the UK and their Tax Freedom Day comes in May.

❓ Question
How might changes in the tax system affect people's willingness to work?

What do you think?

Some economists and politicians have argued for a flat rate of income tax rather than having different tax bands with increasing rates of tax. Would you recommend this?

An effective taxation system should be the following.

- *Understandable*. Individuals and organisations should be able to understand how their tax is calculated or they will think it is unfair.

- *Cost effective to administer*. If a taxation system is too complex then too much will be spent administering it and collecting the tax, thereby wasting resources.

- *Difficult to avoid paying!*

- *Non-distortionary*. It should not alter market signals in an undesirable fashion; for example, it should not discourage the production or consumption of a product below the socially efficient level.

Economics in context The UK tax system and international competitiveness

The following is based on an article by Vanessa Houlder that was published in the *Financial Times* on 21 April 2006.

In 2006, a survey of UK company directors stated that the UK tax system was so complex that it was endangering the country's international competitiveness. This was because the costs of understanding and complying with the system were making it more expensive to operate in the UK. Not only was this affecting domestic companies, but it was also putting foreign companies off the idea of locating in the UK. This was affecting investment and employment.

According to the professional service group, KPMG, the burden of complying with UK taxes simply in terms of administrative costs was around £5.1 billion per year. The Institute of Directors found that the most difficult area of the UK tax system was employment tax, with its various regulations affecting benefits in kind, business expenses, statutory sick pay and statutory maternity pay.

? Question

What other factors do you think determine whether a firm locates in the UK, apart from its tax system?

▦ A 'fair' tax system

The fairness of a taxation and benefit system can be measured in terms of the following.

• *Horizontal equity*. This occurs if people in the same situation pay the same amount of tax.

• *Vertical equity*. This occurs if taxes are regarded as fair between different income groups. Obviously, what is regarded as fair is very controversial and people will have very different opinions on what they think a taxation system should involve.

▦ Using taxation as a government policy instrument

The factors to consider when assessing the effectiveness of taxation as a government policy instrument include the following.

• Taxing people and firms can reduce their earnings but cannot directly increase their income. This can only be done if the taxation revenue is redistributed in some way. It is therefore important to consider not just what taxes are charged, but what is done with the money raised.

• There is always an incentive for tax avoidance and tax evasion. Avoidance occurs when individuals or firms take legal steps to avoid paying as much tax, for example, by finding loopholes in the system. Tax evasion is illegal and means that people are trying to get out of paying the tax that they are meant to pay.

Richard and Judy, who have a daytime television programme, won a battle with the Customs and Revenue office in 2006 to have themselves classified as 'entertainers'. Due to oddities of the tax law, this allowed them to offset their payments to their agent (around £500,000 per year) against tax and claim a rebate on the tax they had already paid since the 1990s. The twenty-nine-page ruling confirmed that they were entertainers. Jeremy Paxman, by comparison, could not claim such a rebate as he is a television interviewer. This is an example of tax avoidance rather than tax evasion (which is when individuals or firms act illegally).

? Question

What factors would the government want to consider when deciding how many resources to invest in catching people who evade their taxes?

- Increasing tax can have a disincentive effect. For example, increasing income tax can lead to there being less incentive for people to work (or at least to work more hours) because the amount that they earn is relatively little after tax. This is known as the poverty trap. On the other hand, a tax cut can have an incentive effect and, according to Laffer (see Wanniski, 1978), may increase tax revenue, as explained below.

■ The Laffer curve

Professor Art Laffer advised President Reagan in America between 1981 and 1984. He highlighted that the total tax revenue depends on the tax rate and the income being earned; if cutting the tax rate encourages people to work and thereby increase incomes then this can increase tax revenues (see Fig. 26.3).

If the average rate of tax was zero then no tax revenue would be raised. As the average rate of tax increases more tax revenue is raised. However, if the tax rate is set too high then this might discourage people from working and firms from investing, therefore reducing the income and the tax revenue being earned. Laffer argued that the US had reached a point where the tax rate was too high and acting as a disincentive to firms and households to earn more. A tax cut would encourage more earnings and lead to an increase in revenue.

What do you think?

At the moment the government can use the money raised from any tax on whatever it decides. Some economists argue for hypothecation, whereby the tax from a particular source must be used for a specific purpose. For example, road tax would have to be spent on road improvements, or the revenue from national insurance would have to be used for the health service. Do you think that hypothecation would be a good idea?

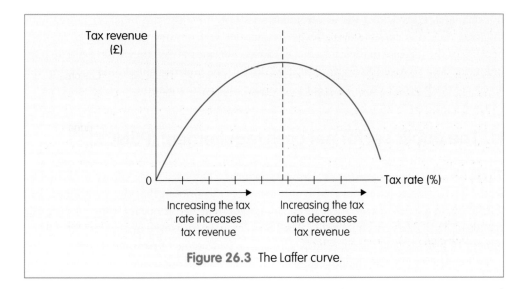

Figure 26.3 The Laffer curve.

Types of benefits

The impact of fiscal policy is not just to do with the tax system or government spending on goods and services; it also depends on the government's spending on benefits. Types of benefits include the following.

- *Means tested benefits*. These are benefits that are paid to people on low incomes, such as income support.
- *Universal benefits*. These are available to everyone, such as child benefit and state pensions.
- *Benefits in kind*. These are not direct monetary payments but provide free or subsidised goods or services, such as healthcare and education.

These payments are known as transfer payments; they are transferring money from one group to another (e.g., taxpayers to non-taxpayers) and are not in return for final goods and services.

What do you think?

What do you think are the opportunity costs of transfer payments?

Fiscal drag

Fiscal drag occurs when individuals pay more tax because their nominal incomes have increased and this has moved them into higher tax brackets, even if in real terms their incomes have not increased. Imagine that someone receives a 2% pay increase and inflation is also at 2%. In real terms this person is not better off; his or her real income has not changed. However, if the government does not move the tax brackets in line with inflation then it is possible that this person may move from one tax bracket to another because of the increase in their nominal earnings. This means that they would end up paying more tax. To avoid fiscal drag (if it wants to!) the government should move up the levels at which people enter different tax bands in line with inflation.

■ The public sector net cash requirement (PSNCR)

The PSNCR is the public sector net cash requirement. (This used to be known as the public sector borrowing requirement (PSBR).) It measures the amount that the government has to borrow in a given year to meet its spending requirements. It occurs if the government spends more than it earns in revenue. The PSNCR can be measured in absolute terms (i.e., billions of pounds) and also in relative terms, as a percentage of national income.

To finance its PSNCR the government will need to borrow money. It can do this by borrowing from the Bank of England or by selling government securities. Government securities include Treasury bills and government bonds:

- Treasury bills are short-term loans to the government (they are paid back within three months);

- government bonds are long-term loans (e.g., they are paid back several years later).

■ The national debt

The national debt is the total amount of money that a government owes. If a government has a deficit in a given year then this will increase the national debt.

What do you think?

Is the government wrong to borrow?

■ Automatic and discretionary fiscal policy

Some changes in fiscal policy occur automatically as the level of income in the economy changes. In a boom, for example, more people will be employed and more people will be spending. This will increase tax revenue. At the same time unemployment benefits will not be needed as much, so government spending will fall. Therefore, in a boom a government's fiscal position will automatically improve because income will be higher but spending will be lower, as shown in Fig. 26.4. Similarly, in a deficit a government's fiscal position will automatically worsen. With any given tax rate, less tax revenue will be generated in a slump and more will be spent on unemployment benefits.

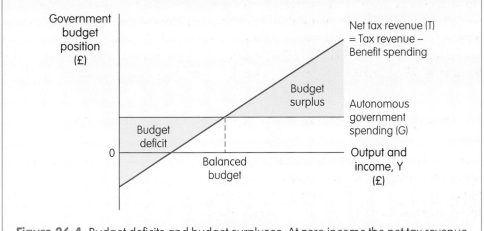

Figure 26.4 Budget deficits and budget surpluses. At zero income the net tax revenue is negative due to spending on benefits.

In Fig. 26.4 G – T shows the difference between the government's spending and revenue (the PSNCR).

Discretionary fiscal policy occurs when the government makes a deliberate attempt to change the level of economic activity. For example, it might:

- change the rate of tax;
- increase its spending in addition to any automatic changes in expenditure.

▓ Fiscal stance

A government's fiscal stance shows whether it is adopting an expansionist or deflationary policy. You cannot tell this simply by looking at the size of the PSNCR. This is because the budget position will not only depend on the discretionary decisions of the government, but will also be automatically affected by the level of national income. To identify the fiscal stance of a government it is important to remove the automatic effects of national income changing in order to measure the discretionary changes.

Automatic changes to the government's fiscal position are shown as we move along a given budget line. If the government deliberately changes the tax rate or deliberately changes its levels of spending then this is discretionary fiscal policy. This can be seen by a shift or pivoting of the line, as shown in Fig. 26.5. As we can see from Fig. 26.5(a), an increase in government spending has increased the deficit at Y2 from B – A to C – A. Also, Fig. 26.5(b) shows how a cut in the rate of tax increases the deficit at Y2 from A – B to A – C.

Now you try it

Using Fig. 26.5 show the effect of an increase in the tax rate and the effect of a decrease in government spending.

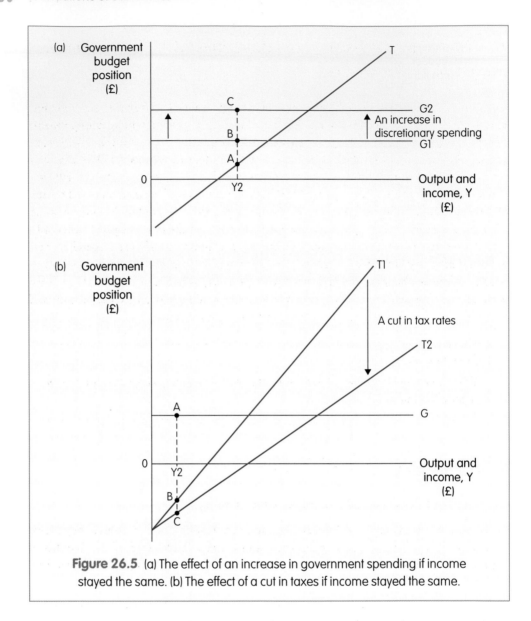

Figure 26.5 (a) The effect of an increase in government spending if income stayed the same. (b) The effect of a cut in taxes if income stayed the same.

What do you think?

Do you think the government should cut taxes?

In 2006, the Conservative Party discussed removing inheritance tax. Do you think this is a good idea?

Changing tax versus changing spending to affect the aggregate demand

When using fiscal policy a government may use changes to the taxation system or changes in government spending to influence demand. Changes in government spending directly affect the aggregate demand. By comparison, reducing direct taxes increases disposable income, but the impact on the aggregate demand will depend on how much of the extra income is spent and how much is saved. A spending of £100 by the government will have a greater multiplier effect than giving £100 back to households because some of the latter will be saved and only a proportion will be spent, for example, only £80 may be spent. Also, by using spending the government can target specific industries or regions quite easily.

On the other hand, taxes can usually be changed more quickly than spending programmes and they are likely to have a faster effect on the economy. Changes in spending usually involves changing major government projects, which can take years to bring about. Furthermore, the government may have committed itself to particular projects and levels of spending. It may not be easy to alter these commitments.

Now you try it

If the government was trying to boost the aggregate demand, what changes might it make to the taxation system?

The effectiveness of fiscal policy

The effectiveness of fiscal policy depends on the following.

- *The accuracy of government forecasting.* Intervention will depend on where the government thinks the economy is at any moment and where it thinks it is heading. If either of these estimations are wrong then fiscal policy may not remedy the problems effectively; it may even make them worse!

- *The impact of any policy changes.* The government may base a policy on a set of assumptions about the behaviour of households and firms, only to find that they do not react in the expected way or at the expected time. Not only are delays likely between the economy changing position and the government realising this, but delays are also likely when it comes to agreeing a policy response to this change. Lastly, there may be a delay in the policy change taking effect. For example, an income tax cut may not lead to an immediate increase in consumer spending; households may wait for a while before deciding to increase consumption. This is particularly likely if consumption is linked to permanent income rather than current income (see unit 24).

Economic forecasting

- In December 2005, Gordon Brown, the Chancellor of the Exchequer, had to change his prediction of UK growth. His new estimate of national income growth was 1.25% per year, which was half of his prediction in the Budget speech of the previous March.

- Highlighting the problems for a government of intervening in an economy, the economist John Kenneth Galbraith said, 'The only function of economic forecasting is to make astrology look respectable.'

? Question

If economic forecasting is often wrong, is there any point in forecasting in the first place?

- *The funding of government spending may also create problems*. It is possible that fiscal policy by the government may lead to less private sector investment. This is called 'crowding out'. Crowding out can occur because, with higher levels of government spending, the Bank of England does not need to keep interest rates as low as it otherwise would to maintain the desired level of demand overall in the economy. As a result, the higher interest rates may deter private sector investment because borrowing is more expensive. The effect of this depends in part on the sensitivity of investment to changes in the interest rate. Also, if the government attracts private finance by selling bonds then these funds will not be available for other private sector projects; these projects have been 'crowded out' as the government has the funds that would be needed to go ahead with them.

■ Supply side fiscal policy

This involves the use of fiscal policy to influence the aggregate supply in the economy, and the methods for achieving this include the following.

- In the labour market the methods include:
  - offering individuals funding to help them with training and developing their skills;
  - helping the unemployed to get back into work, for example, with retraining schemes;
  - guaranteeing a minimum wage to encourage people to work;
  - reducing income taxes to act as another incentive.
- In the goods market the methods include:
  - encouraging firms to invest with tax incentives to undertake research and development to develop new products and new production processes;
  - helping start-ups with advice and financial aid, thereby encouraging new businesses and increasing the supply of goods and services in the economy.

Now you try it

Show the effect of an increase in the aggregate supply on the equilibrium price and output in the economy.

Case Study

The US budget deficit has been very high in recent years; for example, it was around $500 billion in 2004. This is the largest in US history in absolute terms, and, at 5% of the GDP, the largest since 1993 as a percentage of the economy. The US budget deficit in 2005 was around one-quarter of the total Federal government spending, and equal to 80% of the total receipts from Federal income taxes.

The deficit was the equivalent of $1600 per US citizen for that year alone, and the accumulated deficit over ten years was equal to nearly $20,000 per person.

Given the scale of this deficit, there were fears that a loss of confidence in the government's ability to control this could cause a fall in the currency and that, in order to raise finance for the debt, higher interest rates would need to be offered. This would have an adverse effect on the domestic economy.

The Bush government stressed that it would reduce the deficit over time and argued that the impact of the deficit was to boost the economy. However, Benjamin Friedman, a professor of economics at Harvard University, argued that the effect of large budget deficits is to take a large proportion of America's savings; this prevents these funds from being put to more productive use in the private sector, who should be investing in new capital equipment, research and development, and in the training of employees.

According to Friedman, tax restraints and less spending were needed. This looked unlikely in the short term, especially with military spending exceeding all of the other forms of discretionary spending put together.

❓ Questions

- Why might the US budget deficit be so high?
- How might the US budget deficit be affected by economic growth?
- Does it matter if the US government has a high budget deficit?

Checklist

Now you have read this unit try to answer the following questions.

- ☐ Do you understand the key elements of government spending?
- ☐ Can you outline the different elements of an effective taxation system?
- ☐ Can you analyse the impact of changes in taxation?
- ☐ Are you able to assess the fiscal stance of a government?

End of unit questions

1 What is meant by fiscal policy?

2 How does the government raise revenue?

3 Can you tell a government's fiscal stance from its budget position?

4 Can cutting tax rates increase tax revenue?

5 What factors might limit the effectiveness of fiscal policy?

Key learning points

- Fiscal policy involves the use of government spending and taxation to influence the economy.

- Fiscal policy can be used to influence the aggregate supply and the aggregate demand.

- Fiscal policy acts as an automatic stabiliser on the economy; discretionary changes can also be used to try to influence the state of the economy.

- Fiscal drag occurs when the tax bands do not change in line with inflation or growth in the economy.

Reference

Wanniski, J. (1978). Taxes, revenues, and the 'Laffer curve'. *The Public Interest*, Winter.

Learn more

To learn more about the UK government's budget position visit our website at the address below.

 Visit our Online Resource Centre at www.oxfordtextbooks.co.uk/orc/gillespie_econ for test questions and further information on topics covered in this chapter.

Unemployment  »27

Reducing unemployment is often seen as one of the major economic objectives of governments. This unit examines the causes and problems of unemployment and considers how it can be reduced.

LEARNING OBJECTIVES

By the end of this unit you should be able to:

✔ explain the possible causes of unemployment;

✔ outline the costs of unemployment;

✔ examine ways of reducing unemployment.

▮ Introduction

Unemployment is a measure of the number of jobless people who want to work, are available to work, and are actively seeking employment. It can be measured in different ways, including the following.

- *The claimant count.* This is the number of individuals who are actually claiming unemployment-related benefits at any moment. This is a relatively straightforward figure to gather, but may be misleading because governments can change the conditions under which people can claim. It is therefore open to abuse by governments because to reduce unemployment they can simply make claiming more difficult!

- *The labour force survey.* This measure of unemployment is based on interviews with people to determine those who want to work but who are not employed. This is now the official way of measuring unemployment in the UK.

Of the two measures, the claimant count is always the lower of the two because some unemployed people are not entitled to claim benefits, or choose not to do so. When employment is high the gap between the labour force survey and the claimant count will tend to widen. This is because some jobless people who were not previously looking for work start to do so. By actively looking for work they are counted under the labour force survey but do not feature in the claimant count unless they also begin to claim benefits, which is not necessarily made easy for them.

◼ Causes of unemployment

There are several causes of unemployment. These include the following.

- *Cyclical (or demand-deficient) unemployment.* This occurs when demand is low throughout the economy. For example, there may be a recession with negative GDP growth. Demand for labour is a derived demand, so if demand for goods and services is generally low then this will lead to less demand for employees and more unemployment.

- *Structural unemployment.* This occurs when the structure of an economy changes. For example, an industry may lose its international competitiveness with the arrival of new global competitors. With the decline of a particular industry, some of those who are employed in it will lose their jobs. It may not be easy for these individuals to find alternative employment because they may have the wrong skills to work in other industries. They will need retraining.

- *Seasonal unemployment.* This occurs in seasonal industries, such as skiing and fruit picking. When the relevant season is over people in that industry may be unemployed (unless they find work elsewhere). This does not usually involve large numbers of people. Seasonally unemployed workers are likely to find jobs again in the following season, so this type of unemployment is not usually a major concern.

- *Frictional (search) unemployment.* This occurs when people have left one job and are looking for another. This may not be a concern if employees find another job easily. As long as people are passing through this period of frictional unemployment this is not a major cause for concern; the problems occur if they get stuck and do not find work. As time goes on it becomes increasingly difficult for employees to get re-employed.

- *Classical real wage unemployment.* This occurs when the real wage remains too high for equilibrium. This will lead to an excess supply of labour (more people want to work than are demanded because of the relatively high real wages). Real wages may be too high because employees continue to demand high wages even when prices are falling. The downward stickiness of nominal wages in this situation (because employees resist nominal pay cuts) leads to higher real wages. Real wages may also be too high if trade unions push the wages above the equilibrium rate.

What do you think?

What do you think is the major cause of unemployment in the UK at the moment?
Why might unemployment differ between countries?

Economics in context

German unemployment

In 2006, unemployment in Germany increased to over five million; this represented 12.6% of the working-age population. This was the highest it had been since the 1930s. At the time economic growth was just over 1%. To reduce unemployment the German government introduced a number of policies, including the Hartz IV programme that radically changed welfare benefits to push people back to work. In the short term this actually increased unemployment as more people became available for work.

? Question

How do you think people could be attracted off benefits and back to work?

Voluntary and involuntary unemployment

Another way of categorising unemployment is to distinguish between voluntary and involuntary unemployment.

'Voluntary unemployment' is made up of those people who are looking for work but are not yet willing to accept work at the given real wage rate. They are in the labour force but are not willing to accept a job. This is shown by the difference at any real wage between the job acceptance and the labour force curves. The job acceptance curve shows the number of people who are willing and able to accept a job at a given real wage rate. It increases as the real wage increases because people will be less willing to wait around in the labour force as the rewards of taking a job increase. The labour force curve shows the number of people in work or looking for work at each real wage; this will also be slightly upward sloping because as the real wage increases it is an incentive for more people to start looking for work. In Fig. 27.1 L2 – L1 represents voluntary unemployment.

'Involuntary unemployment' measures the number of people who are willing and able to work at the given real wage but who are not in employment. This is because there is a lack of jobs available. This is due to a lack of demand in the economy.

If, for example, the real wage is too high at W2 then L4 – L3 in Fig. 27.2 represents employees who are willing and able to work but are not demanded. This is 'involuntary' unemployment. L5 – L4 represents voluntary unemployment at this real wage.

What do you think?

A detailed analysis of unemployment would examine the level and rates of unemployment in different categories, such as men and women and between regions.

What other categories would you analyse?

Why might this analysis be useful?

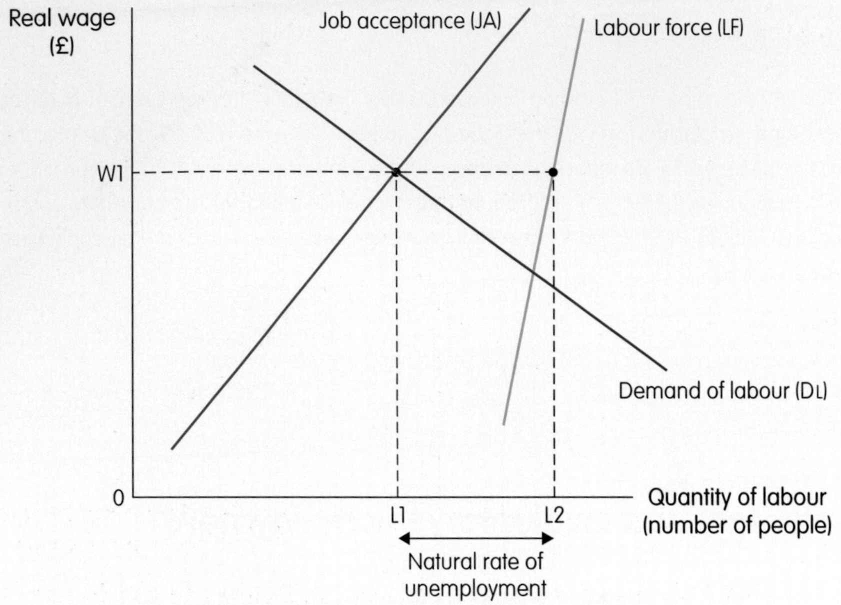

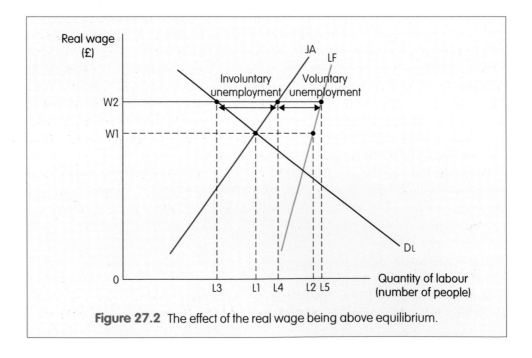

Figure 27.1 The natural rate of unemployment.

Figure 27.2 The effect of the real wage being above equilibrium.

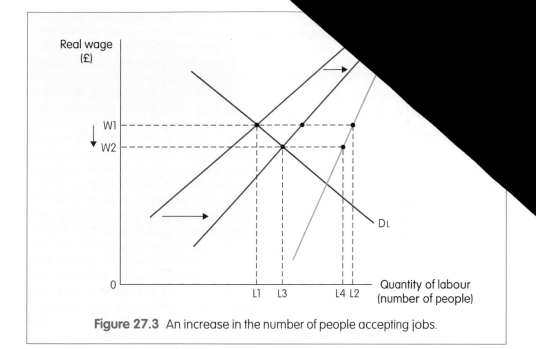

Figure 27.3 An increase in the number of people accepting jobs.

▦ The natural rate of unemployment

Even when the economy is in long-run equilibrium, at full employment there will still be voluntary unemployment. This level of unemployment is called the natural rate of unemployment (or full-employment unemployment). It represents the level of unemployment when all of those who are willing and able to work at the given real wage are working. This may be because they are simply between jobs or have no intention of working at the moment. To reduce the natural rate of unemployment supply side policies must be used. These can increase the number of people that are willing and able to accept a job at each real wage. This shifts the job acceptance curve to the right and nearer to the labour force curve (see Fig. 27.3). The natural rate of unemployment has fallen from L2 – L1 to L4 – L3 because the real wage has fallen from W1 to W2.

The natural rate of unemployment is the long-run equilibrium rate of unemployment; this means that there is no pressure for wages or prices to change. At the given real wage the economy is settled for the long term. Some economists call the natural rate the non-accelerating rate of inflation or NAIRU.

What do you think?

Do you think it is the government's responsibility to reduce unemployment?
How low should the government try to get unemployment to be? What is the best way of achieving this?

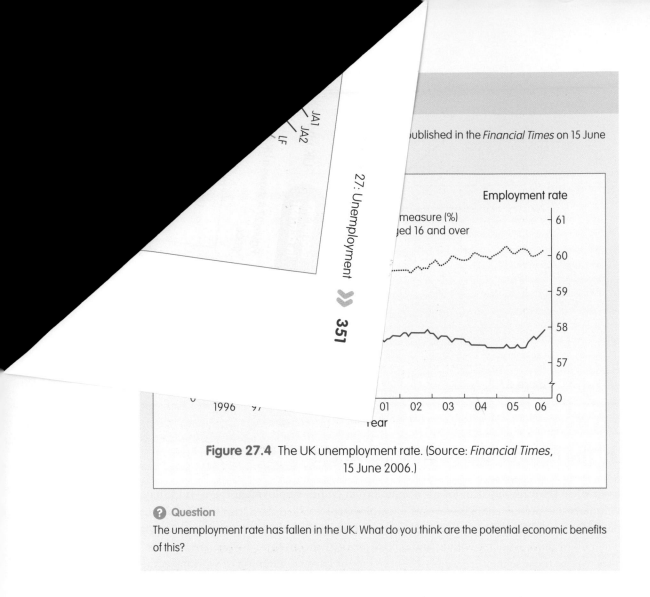

published in the *Financial Times* on 15 June

JA1
JA2
LF

measure (%)
ged 16 and over

Employment rate

61

60

59

58

57

0

01 02 03 04 05 06

Year

Figure 27.4 The UK unemployment rate. (Source: *Financial Times*, 15 June 2006.)

? Question

The unemployment rate has fallen in the UK. What do you think are the potential economic benefits of this?

■ Government intervention to reduce unemployment

Demand side policies

By using demand side policies the government can boost the aggregate demand and provide jobs for those who are involuntarily unemployed, that is, individuals who have the necessary skills and who want to work, but for whom there are no jobs available.

Demand side policies include:

- cutting direct taxes to boost spending by firms and households;
- increased government spending;
- reducing interest rates to stimulate borrowing and spending.

Demand side policies raise the level of demand in the economy; to produce more firms need to employ more labour, so the demand for labour shifts to the right (see Fig. 27.5). Voluntary unemployment falls from L1 to L2, to L3 to L4.

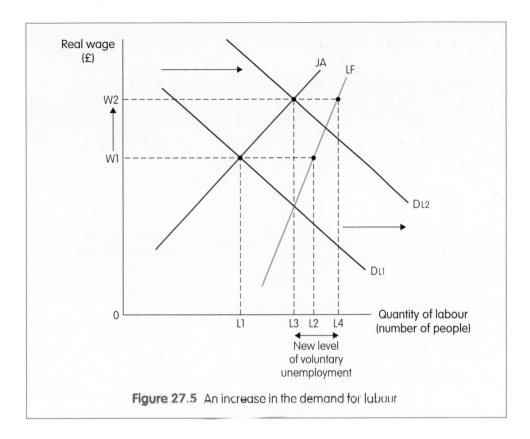

Figure 27.5 An increase in the demand for labour

Now you try it

Which organisation has control of the interest rate in the UK? What are its objectives?

Supply side policies

In the case of voluntary unemployment the problem is not a lack of jobs; it is a question of whether individuals want to or have the required skills to work. If the government intervened to increase spending to provide more jobs then this would not solve the problem. What is needed here is help for individuals to get work that is actually there already, that is, supply side policies.

To reduce voluntary unemployment the government might do the following.

- The government could invest in training to provide the skills that people need to get jobs in other industries.

- It could change the benefits and tax system to make being unemployed less of an option, that is, force people to accept a job.

- The government could reduce the tax wedge. Taxes drive a wedge between the pay that employees receive and their take-home pay. In Fig. 27.6 the equilibrium wage is W1.

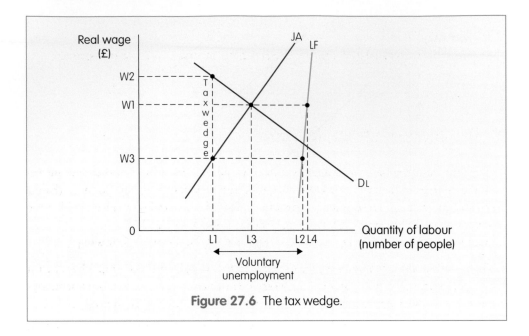

Figure 27.6 The tax wedge.

However, because the firm has to pay national insurance contributions for employees, the actual cost to the firm is W2. After tax the employee will only receive W3. At this wage the amount of voluntary unemployment will be L2 – L1. If the tax wedge could be reduced then the level of voluntary unemployment would be less (L4 – L3).

- It could provide more information so that employees know what jobs are available; this could increase the mobility of labour.

Economics in context   Supply side measures

The Labour Government that was elected in 1997 has introduced a number of supply side measures to reduce unemployment. These include:

- The New Deal, which has helped over 640 000 young people back to work;
- Working Tax Credit, which helps protect the earnings of low-income earners and helps over two million families;
- the introduction of the minimum wage to increase the incentive to work;
- offering support to lone parents to make it easier to work;
- developing a Pathways to Work scheme for incapacity benefits claimants to provide tailored support;
- providing greater information and training opportunities for jobseekers.

 Question

What policies would you suggest to reduce voluntary unemployment?

■ The costs of unemployment

Perhaps the main problem with unemployment is that it is inefficient. If there are unemployed resources in the economy then less goods and services are being produced than it is possible to produce. The economy is productively inefficient and is operating within the production possibility frontier, for example, at the point X in Fig. 27.7.

High levels of unemployment in an area are also likely to mean the following.

• There will be less income in a given region as less people are working. This in turn means less spending on local goods and services; this can then lead to more unemployment. This lowers living standards in the region due to a downward multiplier effect.

• There will be more social problems as people have more free time and lower incomes. It may, for example, lead to more crimes.

• There will be more spending by the government on benefits, such as unemployment benefits.

• There will be less income for the government from taxation. The government will earn less from direct taxation because people are not earning, and indirect taxation revenue will also fall because people are not spending as much. With less income and higher spending the government's budget position will worsen.

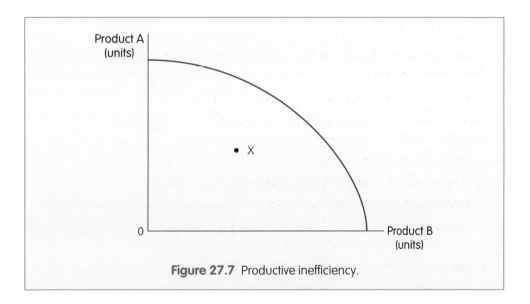

Figure 27.7 Productive inefficiency.

- Less investment may occur if firms lose confidence in the economy and so do not want to put money into longer-term projects until unemployment is seen to fall.

The costs of unemployment can be divided into the following.

- *Private costs*. These are the costs for the individual, such as lower morale and lower income.

- *Social costs*. These are the costs that affect society as a whole, for example, higher levels of unemployment deter future investment in an area.

What do you think?

Does unemployment matter? Why?

Should reducing unemployment be a priority in the UK?

Case Study

Unemployment increased in the UK in 2006. Between April and June 2006 the number of people out of work increased by 92 000 to 1.68 million. The number claiming unemployment benefit was 957 000. The UK's unemployment rate was 5.5% during this three-month period, which was up from 5.2% in the previous three months and 4.8% for the same period in the previous year. Average earnings rose by 4.3% in the year to June.

Over the previous year more than 100 000 jobs were lost in manufacturing, according to data from the Office of National Statistics. The manufacturing sector was hit the hardest because of sharp increases in production costs caused by higher energy costs. However, the number of people who were actually in work as well as the number of job vacancies increased by 7600.

Over the previous year the labour force had increased by 483 000. This was due to the growth in the working-age population, pensioners returning to work and a fall in the number of people claiming long-term sickness benefit. The growth in the working-age population was partly due to the increased immigration into the UK from other EU countries. Of those 483 000, 240 000 were in work in June 2006, while 242 000 were unemployed.

❓ Questions

- What determines the size of the labour force in an economy?
- What determines the number of people in work at any real wage?
- How can unemployment rise and the number of people working increase at the same time?
- With more unemployment you might expect wages to fall or to grow slowly, but in the UK average earnings rose by 4.3%. Can you think why this might be?
- How might the UK government reduce unemployment further?
- Do you think reducing unemployment is a priority in the UK at the moment?

Checklist

Now you have read this unit try to answer the following questions.

☐   Can you explain the possible causes of unemployment?

☐   Can you outline the costs of unemployment?

☐   Can you examine ways of reducing unemployment?

End of unit questions

1   What is the difference between voluntary and involuntary unemployment?

2   Would increasing the aggregate demand reduce unemployment?

3   What supply side policies can be used to reduce unemployment?

4   Why does the level of unemployment in an economy matter?

5   What would the opportunity cost be of trying to reduce unemployment?

Key learning points

•   There are different ways of classifying unemployment, such as structural, seasonal, frictional and cyclical, or voluntary and involuntary.

•   The appropriate methods to reduce unemployment depend on the cause.

•   Unemployment imposes both private and social costs.

Learn more

To learn more about levels of unemployment in the UK and government measures to influence this visit our website at the address below.

   Visit our Online Resource Centre at www.oxfordtextbooks.co.uk/orc/gillespie_econ for test questions and further information on topics covered in this chapter.

»28 Money

At the heart of economics is money. We earn it, we save it and we spend it! This unit looks at the meaning of money and the functions it performs. It examines the market for money and considers the consequences of an increase in the amount of money in the economy.

LEARNING OBJECTIVES

By the end of this unit you should be able to:

✔ explain the key features of money;

✔ explain the factors influencing the demand and supply of money;

✔ outline ways of controlling the money supply.

▨ Introduction

'Money makes the world go around' according to one song, but what exactly do we mean by money? Money is something that we usually want more of. It is something that we work for, that we try to accumulate and something that we measure success by. But what exactly does money do? The answer is that money performs a variety of functions, such as the following.

- *It is a medium of exchange.* This means that it is something that the various parties involved in a transaction are willing to accept as payment for this to happen. They must be confident that it will hold its value (they would obviously be reluctant to accept something that then became worthless). This in turn means that they are confident that others will accept this money in the future in return for products (otherwise it is not much use to them when they want to buy things later).

- *It is a unit of account.* This means that money must be in a form whereby it can be used to measure the value of things; for example, the value of an item may be equal to £1, £2 or £10.

Economics in context

When two pence is three pence

In 2006, the price of copper reached what was then an all-time high of $8000 per tonne. This was due to major buying by commodity brokers and traders. Every 2p piece made before 1992 is 97% copper, that is, 6.9 g of the metal. Approximately 145 000 coins would equal one tonne. The face value of these coins is just £2900. However, given the level of copper prices at the time, this meant that they were worth around £4400, that is, they could have been sold for a profit of £1500. A 2p piece was therefore worth over 3p!

 Question

The value of the paper used in banknotes or the metals in coins is usually very low and nothing like the value of the money itself (except in the unusual case above).
Why then are we willing to accept the face value of notes and coins?

In reality there are different forms of money. For example, if you are asked how much money you have then you may think of it in terms of the cash you have in your pocket or the money in your bank account. What about any shares you have? What about other forms of saving? Which of these would you count? If you own property or other assets, such as a car, then are these forms of money?

The answer is that it depends how you want to define money. Some definitions of money are 'narrow'; these concentrate on cash or other items that can be quickly turned into cash (this means that they are 'liquid'). Other definitions of money are broader. This means that they include items that are less liquid (i.e., less easy to turn quickly into cash), such as deposit accounts. The various definitions of money are all equally valid, but simply include different items; they highlight that actually defining what money is is not as simple as it may seem.

The narrowest definition of money is M0. This comprises notes and coins (in circulation and in banks' tills) plus the balances that banks hold at the Bank of England. However, notes and coins only represent a relatively small part of what most of us would include when we think about what 'money' we have. Money in a broader sense will include what is held in bank and building society accounts. The measure of money that includes these is called M4.

■ The Bank of England

The Bank of England was established in 1694. It is the UK's central bank and plays a critical role in determining how much money there is in the economy. The role of the Bank of England (and indeed any central bank) is to:

- be the banker to the government;
- manage government finances;

- be the banker to commercial banks, such as Lloyds TSB;
- hold gold and foreign-exchange reserves that can be used when trying to influence the exchange rate;
- control the issue of notes and coins;
- promote and maintain monetary and financial stability to contribute to a healthy economy.

 Web

For more information on the Bank of England visit www.bankofengland.co.uk

■ Banks and financial institutions

The 1979 and 1987 Banking Acts defined the UK banking sector as consisting of a series of financial institutions whose activities are supervised by the Bank of England. To be recognised as a bank a financial institution must be granted a licence.

Financial institutions in the UK include the following.

- *Commercial (retail) banks*, such as Barclays and HSBC. They provide banking facilities for individuals as well as businesses. They provide facilities such as current accounts and loans.
- *Merchant banks*. These specialise in receiving large deposits from and lending to businesses. They also help firms to raise finance.
- *Building societies*. These are organisations that are owned by the people who save with them, as opposed to outside investors. Many building societies, such as Halifax and Abbey National, turned themselves into public companies owned by shareholders in the 1990s.
- *Finance houses*. These organisations specialise in lending money to enable individuals to buy items, such as sofas and electrical goods.
- *Discount houses*. These organisations specialise in the short-term lending of money to the government through the Bank of England and to local authorities. To do this the discount houses obtain money from the banks by borrowing money on short notice that they then lend out.

■ The role of banks and financial institutions

Banks and other financial institutions exist to make a profit by investing and lending money. To do this they need money in the first place, which they get via savings. To attract money banks will offer interest. If you put money into a bank then it will reward you by paying you interest on your savings. The amount of interest it offers will depend on:

- how long you are prepared to leave it in the bank (the longer you can tell them that it will be left with them, the longer they have to earn profits with it; this should mean that they will pay you higher interest);

- the amount that you give them (the more money they have to generate profits, the more they can offer you).

If you are borrowing money from financial institutions then the interest rate charged will depend on:

- how much you are borrowing;
- your track record (do you have a good credit rating?; the better your rating, the lower the interest rate that banks can charge);
- how long you want it for;
- what assets you have as security (collateral) (the lower the risk you are, the lower the interest rate that banks can charge).

There are therefore many different interest rates in an economy that depend on factors such as whether you are borrowing or saving. However, they will be linked to each other; for example, if one savings rate was significantly different from another then savers would move their money there. Differences in interest rates are due to differences in the terms and conditions; for example, how long you are borrowing the money for, and whether the interest rate is fixed or can fluctuate.

What do you think?

What are the circumstances required to get a low-cost loan?

Changes in the interest rate will affect you in many ways. It will affect the amount that you have to repay on any loans or credit card borrowing, or on any money that you have borrowed via a mortgage to buy a property. It will also affect the cost of any new borrowing. If you go to the bank to borrow money and the interest rate has increased then this may deter you from borrowing. This will then reduce your spending. Similarly, changes in the interest rate affect the costs to firms of borrowing money and determine whether it is profitable to invest. Higher interest rates usually lead to less investment.

So interest rates obviously have a big impact on the level of spending in the economy. High interest rates will tend to reduce borrowing and spending by firms and households, thereby reducing the aggregate demand. Less investment will also reduce economic growth. An understanding of how interest rates are determined is therefore important. The interest rate is the cost of money (the amount you pay to borrow it) and in a free market would be determined by the supply and demand of money.

Now you try it

High interest rates can reduce the aggregate demand.
What others factors might reduce demand in the economy?

■ The market for money

The money market, like any other market, is made up of supply and demand. In a free market the interest rate will adjust to equate the supply and demand of money.

The demand for money

There are various reasons why individuals and firms want to hold money. These motives include the following.

- *The transaction motive*. People hold money because they need it to live their daily lives. To pay our bills, pay for the bus and buy a drink we need money, that is, we need money to finance our transactions. Similarly, firms need money to buy their supplies, pay their rent and reward their staff.

  The amount of transactions demand will be determined by the following.

- *Real income levels*. With more real income we are likely to undertake more transactions (buy more things) and therefore need more money for this.

- *How often people are paid*. The less frequently that people are paid, the more they hold on average. Imagine that you are paid £500 per week. When you are paid you have £500; by the end of the week you have spent it and have £0. On average you will have held £250 (see Fig. 28.1 (a)). If instead you were paid £26,000 each year (52 × £500) and spent this over the year then the average holding during the year would be £13,000 (see Fig. 28.1 (b)). The overall annual earnings are the same, but when you are paid less regularly you hold more on average.

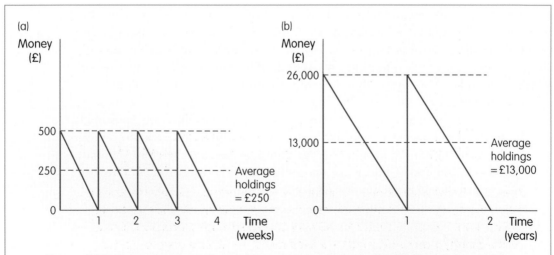

Figure 28.1 The transactions demand for money in relation to the frequency of payment. In (a) you are paid £500 per week; instead, in (b) you are paid £26,000 per year.

- *The rate of interest.* With higher interest rates households will try to reduce the amount of money that they need for transactions because of the higher returns from saving. Whilst this might have some effect, it is not likely to be much. For simplicity, we assume that the transactions demand motives are not affected by the interest rate (e.g. in Fig. 28.3).

- *The precautionary motive.* This is where people hold money just in case something happens. For example, you may hold some money in case urgent repairs are needed to your house.

  Holding money for transactions and precautionary reasons is described as holding active balances. There is a positive reason why people hold money for these motives.

- *The speculative motive.* This is where people hold money whilst waiting to invest it in other assets. If, for example, you are worried that the price of shares is going to fall then you might sell your shares and hold the proceeds in the form of more liquid assets for the short term. This level of money holdings is determined by expectations. If you think that the values of some assets are going to fall then you may hold more money now. If, however, you think that the values of assets are low at the moment then you might hold less money and invest in assets instead. This is shown in Fig. 28.2. Speculative holdings are called idle balances; you are holding money because you feel that you have to due to what you expect to happen in other markets.

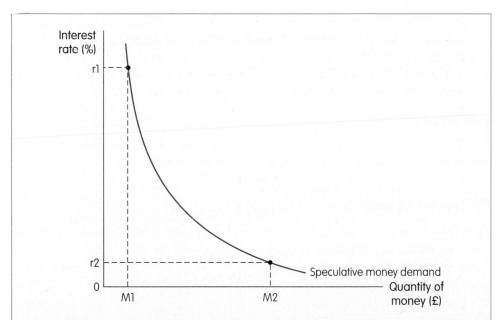

Figure 28.2 The speculative demand for money. For the quantity of money M1 and the interest rate r1, high returns are available on other less liquid assets (their prices are relatively low); firms and households will not want to hold much speculative money. For the quantity of money M2 and the interest rate r2, low returns are available on other assets (their prices are relatively high); firms and households are willing to hold high levels of money.

The relationship between interest rates and asset prices

The speculative demand for money is inversely related to the interest rate. This is due to the relationship between interest rates and asset prices. Imagine that you buy a government bond (an IOU) for £100 and the government agrees to pay £10 per year until it repays the loan in ten years. The £10 per year represents a 10% return on the £100 spending. If you had paid £200 for this bond then the return would be 5% (£10/£200 × 100). The higher price of the asset means that the rate of return is lower. The same sort of analysis can be used with other assets. Imagine, for example, that you are going to buy a house to rent out for a given amount per month. The more you pay to buy the house, the lower the rate of return from the rental income.

Asset price and interest rates (rates of return) are therefore inversely related. The more that you pay for an asset, the lower the rate of return, and vice versa. This therefore affects the speculative demand for money; when asset prices are perceived to be low (i.e., interest rates are high) individuals would rather hold assets than money, believing that they will increase in value. When asset prices are high and interest rates are low, individuals are more likely to want to hold money because they will fear that asset prices will fall in the future.

> **What do you think?**
>
> If you had £500,000 to save, what would you put your money into? What factors would influence your choice?

Liquidity preference

The liquidity preference schedule is the demand for money. It is made up of the precautionary, transactions and speculative demand, and is illustrated in Fig. 28.3.

The supply of money

The supply of money at any moment is taken as a given amount. The money supply is, therefore, shown as being completely inelastic relative to the interest rate. Changes in the interest rate are assumed to have no impact on the supply of money available at any moment (see Fig. 28.4).

The money market: the supply of and demand for money

Equilibrium in the money market is brought about by changes in interest rates. The interest rate is the price of money and it adjusts to equate the supply of and demand for money.

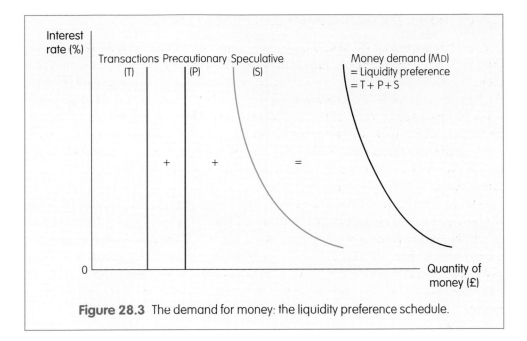

Figure 28.3 The demand for money: the liquidity preference schedule.

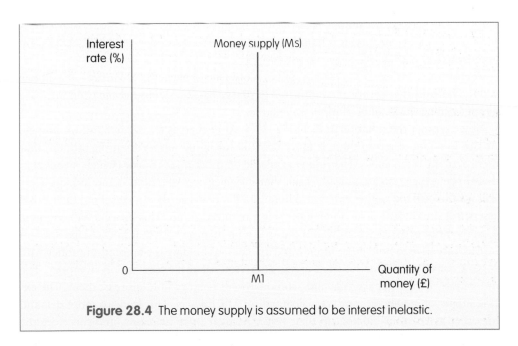

Figure 28.4 The money supply is assumed to be interest inelastic.

When analysing the money market we must also consider other asset markets. At any moment in time, households and firms will want to hold a certain amount of money and a certain amount of other assets (such as shares or property). Their decisions about how much to hold of each depend on their desire for liquidity and the returns available in each

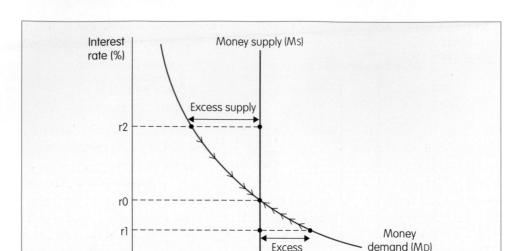

Figure 28.5 Equilibrium in the money market.

market. The demand for money is also called liquidity preference; firms and households should hold money because it is liquid and/or because the returns available elsewhere are not attractive.

At any moment there is a given amount of money available in the economy—the money supply. Imagine that we are at equilibrium at r0 (see Fig. 28.5). Households and firms are happy holding the amount of money available.

Now consider the situation at r1 in Fig. 28.5. At r1 there is excess demand for money. At this low rate of return there is more demand for liquid money than the amount that there actually is available. The return available on other assets is low (which means that their price is high), so households think that they might as well hold liquid money. They will want to sell their other assets and hold liquid money. As they start selling their other assets this drives their price down and their rate of return up. This process will continue until the price of assets is so low and the return on them so high that households have no further incentive to hold more money and are content holding the amount of money M0.

Now consider the situation at r2 in Fig. 28.5. At r2 there is excess supply of money. The rate of return on other assets is high, so households want to hold more of them. The excess supply of money means excess demand for other assets. This leads to more demand for other assets, thus bidding up their price. As their price increases (and therefore the return on them falls) this makes these other assets less attractive relative to money. With rising prices and falling returns people become more willing to hold money, thereby reducing the excess supply. This process continues until equilibrium is reached at r0, and households and organisations are content to hold the amount of money M0.

As you can see, the money market and other asset markets are completely interrelated. An unwillingness to hold the amount of money available in the economy leads to excess demand in the other asset markets. This affects asset prices and returns until people are willing to hold the amount of money available. Similarly, excess demand for money means excess supply of other assets, which again leads to changes in asset prices and returns until equilibrium is restored.

The growth of the money supply

When money is deposited in banks, the financial institutions would like to lend it all out or invest it all; in this way they can earn profits by earning or charging interest. However, they know that the depositors may come and ask for some of it back at any moment. Therefore the banks have to hold some money in reserve. The amount held depends on how much they think is going to be asked for by depositors.

The money that is not kept back can be lent out. For example, it may be lent to individuals to go on holiday or to buy a new house. The money borrowed is therefore likely to be spent on goods and services. The people who receive this spending will deposit it in their banks. Once again, a proportion will be kept in reserve and the remainder will be lent out. Again it is spent, and again a proportion will be kept back by the banks and the remainder will be lent. This process continues and is known as the 'money multiplier'. It is equal to 1/ Liquidity ratio. If, for example, the banks keep 10% in reserve then the money multiplier is 1/0.1 = 10. An initial deposit of £100 would therefore increase the total deposits, and the money supply will be equal to £1000.

The money supply may therefore grow if:

- more money is deposited in banks and lent out;
- the banks retain a smaller proportion of the money deposited and lend out more at any stage.

The effect of an increase in the money supply

The effect of an increase in the money supply can be analysed in the following series of stages.

Stage 1: lower interest rates

Imagine that the money market is initially at r0 (see Fig. 28.6(a)). If there was then an increase in the money supply then this would lead to an excess supply of money at the original rate. Households and firms will want to invest this 'excess money' into other assets. This will lead to more assets being bought, making them more expensive and reducing the return on them. As this happens these assets become less attractive to invest in (as their price has gone up), and so people become more willing to hold the additional money in the economy. This process continues until the price of the other assets is so high that people are now willing to hold all of the extra money. This happens when the interest rate is at r1 in Fig. 28.6(a).

Stage 2: the impact of a fall in interest rates on the rest of the economy

The fall in the interest rate is likely to increase the aggregate demand (see Fig. 28.6(b,c)). This is because the increase in the money supply affects each of the following.

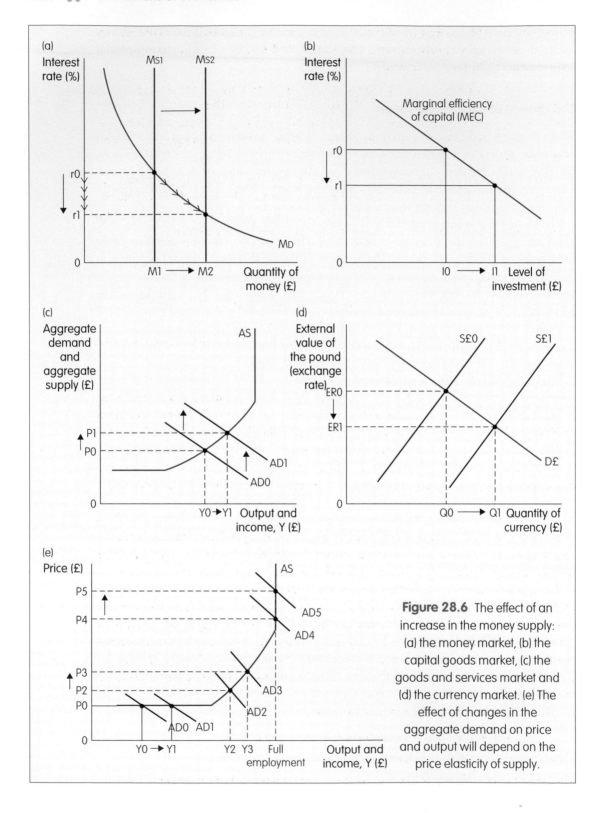

Figure 28.6 The effect of an increase in the money supply: (a) the money market, (b) the capital goods market, (c) the goods and services market and (d) the currency market. (e) The effect of changes in the aggregate demand on price and output will depend on the price elasticity of supply.

- **Consumption.** With lower interest rates it is cheaper for households to borrow money and there is less incentive to save. This should lead to extra consumption, thereby increasing the aggregate demand.

- **Investment.** With lower interest rates there will be more projects that have a higher marginal efficiency of capital than the cost of borrowing. This should lead to an increase in investment (how much depends on how sensitive the demand for capital goods is to changes in the interest rate). This will also increase the aggregate demand in the economy.

- **Exchange rates.** Lower interest rates may lead to an outflow of money from the economy because investors will seek higher returns abroad. This is likely to reduce the external value of the currency, making exports relatively cheap abroad and imports relatively expensive. This should increase demand for domestic products.

Now you try it

In addition to interest rates, what are the influences on consumption, and the influences on investment?

Stage 2b: the direct exchange rate effect

An increase in the money supply may also affect the economy in another way via the exchange rate. With more money in the economy there will be an increase in demand for foreign products and assets. This will lead to an increase in the supply of pounds in exchange for foreign currencies (see Fig. 28.6(d)). Other things being unchanged, this will decrease the external value of the pound. This should make UK exports cheaper abroad in foreign currency, thereby boosting demand for exports. This in turn boosts the aggregate demand.

Stage 3: effect on price and output

The consequences of an increase in the money supply are likely to be an increase in the aggregate demand either via interest rates boosting consumption, investment and exports or the exchange rate effect. If the economy is well below full employment then this increase in the aggregate demand means that there is a high level of unused capacity and there are likely to be high levels of unemployment. An increase in demand would, in these circumstances, lead to more output, as shown in Fig. 28.6(e) when the aggregate demand increases from AD0 to AD1. If the economy is at full employment then this means that the aggregate supply is completely price inelastic. An increase in demand will lead to an increase in prices (i.e., inflation), as shown in Fig. 28.6(e) when the aggregate demand increases from AD4 to AD5.

An increase in the money supply may therefore:

- increase output (if the economy is below full employment);
- increase prices (if the economy is at full employment);
- increase prices and output (if the economy is approaching full employment).

The effects of an increase in the money supply can be analysed using the quantity theory of money.

Now you try it

Outline the possible impact of a decrease in the money supply on the aggregate demand.

◼ The quantity theory of money

The quantity theory of money states that

$$MV = PT,$$

where

- M is the quantity of money in the economy,
- V is the velocity of circulation, that is, this measures how often money moves around or is used in any given period,
- P is the average price level of goods and services, and
- T is the number of transactions, that is, the quantity of national output sold in a year.

The quantity PT is therefore equal to the money value of the national output sold in a year (basically, Price × Quantity).

The quantity MV represents the total spending on national output and must therefore equal PT because, unsurprisingly, total spending must equal the total amount spent!

For example, if the money supply is £100 billion and each pound is spent five times then the total spending is 5 × £100 billion = £500 billion. This means that the value of goods bought is £500 billion. If 25 billion goods are bought then the average price level would be £20.

If the economy is at full employment then the number of transactions in the economy cannot increase. If the velocity of circulation is also stable then this means that an increase in the money supply leads to an increase in the price level, that is, more money in the economy leads to inflation. An increase in M leads to an increase in P.

For example, if the money supply was now £200 billion and each pound was still spent five times then the total spending would be £1000 billion. If the number of goods was still 25 billion then this means that the price level would be £40. A doubling of the money supply has doubled the price level.

However, if the economy is below full employment then this means that an increase in the money supply can lead to more output (i.e., more transactions). That is, an increase in M can lead to an increase in T. This means that the price level may not increase, that is, an increase in the money supply may not lead to inflation.

For example, MV could be £1000 billion, but if the number of transactions doubles to 50 billion then the average price level remains at £20.

Also, it is possible that the velocity of circulation may decrease. This could be because of lower interest rates, so there is less pressure to pass money on quickly (due to a lower opportunity cost). In this case an increase in the money supply might lead to a decrease in the velocity of circulation. This means that there may not be any extra overall spending in the economy, and therefore the price level may not increase.

Monetarists

A group of economists known as monetarists believe that V and T are relatively stable. They therefore think that an increase in the money supply will lead to an increase in the price level. In fact, they think that 'inflation is always and everywhere a monetary phenomenon in the sense that it is and can be produced only by a more rapid increase in the quantity of money than output' (see Friedman, 1968), that is, inflation was always due to growth in the money supply. Over time the full employment level in an economy can increase due to, for example, developments in technology. This enables some growth in the number of transactions (T), so the money supply can grow in line with this without being inflationary. However, 'excessive money supply growth' will lead to more demand and higher prices.

The monetarists argued that the cause of inflation must ultimately be the money supply. Imagine that we have a situation where

- quantity of money (M) = £100 billion,
- velocity of circulation (V) = 5 billion,
- overall spending (MV) = 5 × £100 billion = £500 billion,
- number of transactions (T) = 25 billion.

Therefore the average price level is £20.

Imagine that the price level now increases to £50, perhaps due to an increase in wages or imported components. If the money supply does not grow to accommodate this and the velocity does not change then this means that the total spending is still 5 × £100 billion = £500 billion. As the price level is £50, the number of transactions must fall to 10 billion.

The higher prices without more money supply in the economy lead to less goods being bought and probably unemployment. This will put downward pressure on wages and prices, which would force the price back down to £20. Inflation has not persisted because the money supply was controlled.

However, if the money supply was allowed to expand then the inflation could continue.

For example, if the money supply grew to £250 billion then MV would become 5 × £250 billion = £1250 billion. Also, PT = £50 × 25 billion = £1250 billion. A growth in the money supply has allowed prices to stay higher.

According to monetarist theory, the temptation for governments is to let the money supply grow if prices increase. Although this leads to higher inflation, it avoids a difficult period of higher unemployment that is necessary to bring prices down if the money supply is not expanded.

Clearly, the growth of the money supply and, in fact, controlling its growth are key elements of the monetarist approach.

According to the Bank of England,

> The amount of money in the economy and the level of prices are positively related in the long run. Without money, inflation could not exist. And, across many countries, persistently high rates of money growth have usually been associated with high inflation . . .
>
> . . . Although money and inflation are clearly linked over the longer term, the usefulness of money as an indicator of inflationary pressures in the short to medium term depends on there being a predictable relationship between money and the value of spending. For example, suppose money grew at the same rate as the value of spending over time. Then money growth of 4.0%– 4.5% per year would be consistent with annual growth in economic activity of 2%–2.5%—the historical average in the UK—plus inflation of 2.0% per year, in line with the inflation target.
>
> In practice, however, the relationship between money and inflation has not been stable. Money growth has been influenced by many other factors, including financial innovations—such as the introduction of credit cards—changes in banking regulations, and developments in international capital markets. The effects of these changes have not always been easy to predict accurately. So rules of thumb like the one above have not usually been useful guides for policy.

 Web

For more information on the Bank of England visit www.bankofengland.co.uk

---

What do you think?

According to the Bank of England, do you think monitoring or controlling the money supply would reduce inflation?

■ Factors that might limit the impact of an increase in the money supply on prices

The impact of an increase in the money supply on prices might be limited by the following factors.

• The liquidity trap: at very low interest rates (which means very high asset prices) an increase in the money supply may not lead to a fall in interest rates (see Fig. 28.7). Firms and households would simply absorb the extra money. The returns elsewhere are simply too low to appeal. The extra money is held with no impact on asset prices or interest rates; the demand for money is horizontal. The velocity of circulation falls as the money supply increases.

• The demand for money generally may not be very interest elastic, so any increase in the money supply might have a relatively small impact on interest rates (and therefore on the aggregate demand).

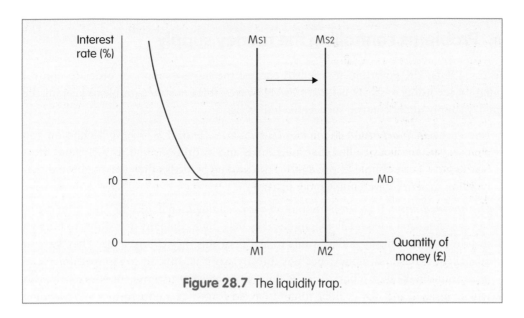

Figure 28.7 The liquidity trap.

- The impact of lower interest rates on consumption and demand may be limited. Investment in capital goods is very dependent on expectations, for example, so a fall in interest rates on its own may have a limited effect.
- The economy may be below full employment, in which case output increases and the number of transactions (T) rises.

In any of these cases, an increase in the money supply would not have a significant impact on prices and inflation.

■ Controlling the money supply

If an increase in the money supply does lead to inflation then governments will want to try to control it to achieve their objective of stable prices. A central bank may attempt to reduce the money supply as follows.

- *Requesting that banks keep higher reserves and lend less out at any stage.* The Bank of England, for example, can try to persuade other banks that this would be desirable for the economy. If the Bank of England can reduce the amount lent out at each stage by the banks then this will slow the growth of the money supply.
- *Open market operations* occur when a government buys or sells bonds. For example, to reduce the money supply the government might sell bonds. To buy these bonds households will use their money. This will usually be taken out of their banks. This reduces the amount that the banks have to lend out, thereby reducing the growth of the money supply.

Problems controlling the money supply

In the 1980s, UK governments tried to control the money supply in order to control inflation according to the monetarist view. However, there are often problems keeping the money supply under control, such as the following.

- *Knowing which definition of the money supply to control.* Whichever definition you choose, you are likely to find that individuals and institutions find ways around these restrictions. For example, if you control the lending by banks then you might find that building societies start lending more instead.

- *Disintermediation.* If controls are put on bank lending then banks may position themselves as financial advisers. For example, they may put a company that wants to borrow in contact with a business that wants to lend. For this they charge a fee. They have in effect lent a business money, but not directly, so it is difficult to control. Financial institutions make their money from lending, so whatever a government does to stop this will be resisted and ways will be found to avoid control (e.g., organising more lending via overseas banks).

Monetary policy in the UK

After disappointing experiences trying to control the money supply in the 1980s, monetary policy in the UK in recent years has focused on controlling the interest rate and using this to control the demand for money. Higher interest rates should reduce the quantity of money demanded; less will be borrowed from banks, thereby reducing the money supply (see Fig. 28.8).

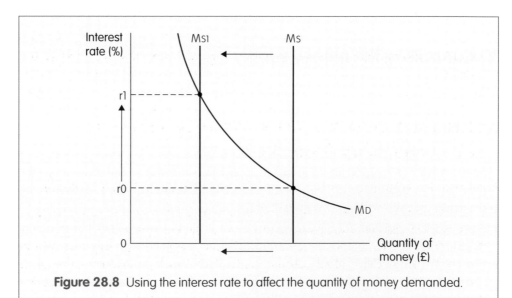

Figure 28.8 Using the interest rate to affect the quantity of money demanded.

In May 1997, the Labour Government gave the Bank of England's Monetary Policy Committee the ability to set whatever interest rates it felt were necessary to achieve given inflation targets. This was made law with the 1998 Bank of England Act. Price stability at present is defined by the government's inflation target of 2%. Prior to the creation of the independent Monetary Policy Committee, interest rates had been influenced by the government and were often used to achieve political rather than economic objectives. When an election was coming up, for example, the pressure was on to reduce the interest rate to make borrowing cheaper and therefore make the government more popular, even if it was not the right decision for the economy as a whole.

The Monetary Policy Committee meets monthly to assess the possible level of inflation and to decide on what to do about the interest rate. The Committee is made up of nine members; some are from the Bank of England, but others are outsiders who provide a different perspective. The Committee considers indicators such as:

- the growth in the money supply;
- national income figures;
- consumer confidence surveys and expectations of inflation (these are important because if people expect prices to rise then they are more likely to demand larger wage increases, and so higher inflation can be a self-fulfilling prophecy);
- lending by banks and building societies;
- consumer spending and credit;
- trends in the housing and labour markets, including average earnings, unit costs and unemployment figures;
- developments in the foreign exchange market.

If, having looked at these indicators, the Committee believes that the aggregate demand is growing too fast and pulling up prices then it will decide to raise its interest rates.

@ Web

For more information on the Monetary Policy Committee visit www.bankofengland.co.uk/monetarypolicy/overview.htm

■ The effect of an increase in interest rates by the Monetary Policy Committee

An increase in the interest rates charged by the Bank of England will do the following.

- It will increase the rates charged by other banks. Most banks will need to borrow from other financial institutions at particular times. The Bank of England is known as the 'lender of the last resort'. For example, a high level of withdrawals may leave a bank short of liquidity. The Bank of England may be called upon to lend money to other institutions. They will be influenced by the rate that the Bank of England charges because they will want to charge their own customers more to ensure that they make a profit. If

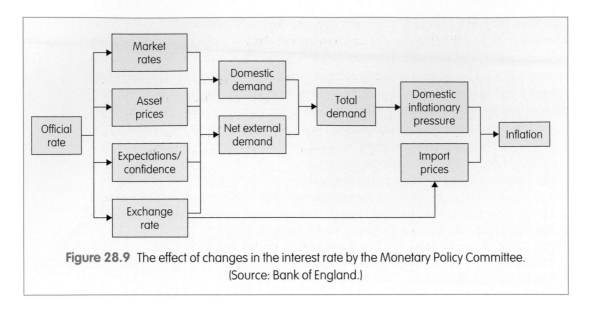

Figure 28.9 The effect of changes in the interest rate by the Monetary Policy Committee. (Source: Bank of England.)

the Bank of England therefore announces that its rate is increasing then other financial institutions will usually follow to cover any increased costs that they might have if they need funds. Higher interest rates offered by financial institutions will encourage saving and reduce consumption spending. There will also be less demand for other assets (leading to lower prices) because of the high returns from saving. Lower asset prices will reduce individuals' wealth and dampen demand.

- It will send a clear signal that it is prepared to take action to control inflation. This should lead to wage demands in line with the stated inflation target. This in itself should help to ensure that the target is hit because it discourages inflationary wage claims.

- It will lead to more demand for the currency from overseas investors, who will want to buy pounds to save in UK banks to gain higher returns. This should increase the external value of the pound. This makes UK exports relatively expensive overseas, thereby reducing the aggregate demand. It also reduces import prices in pounds, thereby reducing cost pressure. Both of these help to reduce inflation.

The effect of changes in the interest rate can be seen in Fig. 28.9.

What do you think?

Do you think that the Monetary Policy Committee should cut the interest rate at the moment in the UK?

The Bank of England and interest rates

In 2006, the Bank of England increased interest rates by 0.25% to 4.75% to keep inflation under control. This was the first increase in two years. At the same time the European Central Bank, which sets rates for members of the euro currency, increased rates to 3%, Australia raised rates to 6% and the Federal Reserve in the US raised rates to 5.25%. The Bank of England's decision reduced share prices by 1%, but led to a sharp increase in the external value of the currency. The interest rate increase was prompted by concerns over inflationary pressures caused by oil prices and rising energy costs.

 Questions

Why might share prices fall if interest rates increase?

Why might the external value of the currency increase if interest rates increase?

Case Study

In 2006, the World Bank increased its economic forecast for the Chinese economy from 9.2% to 9.5% after very rapid growth in the first quarter of the year. This followed ten years of extremely fast expansion within China as aggregate demand increased rapidly. With demand outstripping aggregate supply, there were fears of demand-pull inflation in the economy. In particular, demand for property was expanding and, even with a construction boom, property prices were increasing very rapidly.

Analysts recommended that China should tighten control of its money supply. It was hoped that this would limit spending and help to control inflation. However, there was concern that this may not be enough, especially with strong expectations of future growth leading to a high level of confidence and therefore spending. Therefore the World Bank also called for measures to limit the amount of credit given by banks to individuals and firms. In particular, it wanted a limit on the lending given to high-risk sectors, such as real estate. The Chinese banks had been lending very heavily in recent years and had offered high levels of credit to customers and firms for building and house buying. Regional governments, for example, had been investing in many construction projects. Investments in factories, property and roads rose by 30% in just the first seven months of the year.

In other countries excessive lending has led to a property bubble that has burst with terrible effects. In a boom people are tempted to borrow more and more because they are confident that the price is going to increase. Borrowing soars, but when the property boom stops households and firms find that they cannot repay their loans. In the UK this happened after the consumer spending boom of the late 1980s. When the economy slowed in the early 1990s households experienced 'negative equity'; they had borrowed so much to move to a bigger house, believing that they would actually make money when the house price increased, but when it fell they found that they had borrowed more than the house was worth.

? Questions

- Why might excessive money supply growth cause inflation?
- How might China try to control its money supply? What problems might this cause?
- How else might a government try to prevent a property bubble?
- Is buying a house better than renting one?

Checklist

Now you have read this unit try to answer the following questions.

☐ Can you explain the key features of money?

☐ Can you explain the factors influencing the demand and supply of money?

☐ Can you outline ways of controlling the money supply?

End of unit questions

1 Is money the same as cash?

2 In a free market what would determine the interest rate?

3 Does growth in the money supply lead to inflation?

4 What is the role of the Monetary Policy Committee?

5 Why do interest rates matter?

Key learning points

- Monetary policy uses the money supply and interest rates to control the economy.
- The motives for holding money include the transactions motive, the precautionary motive and the speculative motive.
- The interest rate in the UK is determined by the Monetary Policy Committee; it is used to achieve an inflation target.
- The quantity theory of money states that $MV = PT$. If V and T are constant then an increase in the money supply leads to an increase in the price level. This is known as a monetarist view of the causes of inflation.
- The interest rate affects borrowing, saving, the price of assets and the exchange rate.

Reference

Friedman, M. (1968). The role of monetary policy. *American Economic Review*, 58 (March), 1–17.

Learn more

To learn more about the UK government's approach to monetary policy over the years visit our website at the address below.

 Visit our Online Resource Centre at www.oxfordtextbooks.co.uk/orc/gillespie_econ for test questions and further information on topics covered in this chapter.

Inflation

One common economic objective of government is to achieve stable prices. This involves controlling inflation. This unit examines the causes and problems of inflation and considers how inflation may be controlled.

LEARNING OBJECTIVES

By the end of this unit you should be able to:

✔ explain what is meant by inflation;

✔ outline the different causes of inflation;

✔ explain the costs of inflation;

✔ examine ways of reducing inflation;

✔ discuss the possible trade-off between inflation and unemployment.

▨ Introduction

Inflation occurs when there is a sustained increase in the general price level over a given period. If annual inflation is 2%, for example, this means that prices are generally 2% higher than the year before. In the UK inflation is measured by the consumer prices index (CPI). This compares the price of a typical basket of goods and services of a household with the price the year before. Inflation reduces the purchasing power of a currency within its economy; it reduces its internal value. If prices are increasing in the UK then £1 will not be able to buy as much as it did before the price increase.

The consumer price index

The items in the typical basket of goods used to calculate the consumer price index are regularly reviewed to make sure that they match the current spending patterns. In total the Office of National Statistics collects around 120 000 prices every month for a 'shopping basket' of around 650 goods. When the index first began it included wild rabbits, candles and corsets. In recent years, items such as salad cream and streaky bacon have been taken out, while herbal tea, mayonnaise, salmon fillets and gym membership have been added in. Recently MP3 players and music downloads were included.

? Questions

What are the top ten items in your typical shopping basket each week?

How do you think this might vary with people in other countries, or differ from a typical shopping basket from five years ago?

@ Web

For more information on the consumer price index visit the Office of National Statistics website at www.ons.gov.uk

▨ What causes inflation?

The causes of inflation include the following.

- *Too much demand in the economy*. This is shown by an outward shift of the aggregate demand curve. If demand is growing faster than supply then this will pull prices up, causing 'demand-pull inflation'. If firms cannot meet the demand then they will increase their prices. Demand-pull inflation is characterised by shortages, low levels of stocks, long waiting lists and queues. In this situation firms will be eager to produce more as soon as they can. They may invest in extra capacity, but this can take time to come online. In the short term supply is likely to be price inelastic because firms may not be able to recruit staff easily or produce more given the existing equipment. This means that an increase in demand will affect prices more than output. Inflation caused by an increase in demand is shown in Fig. 29.1.

- *Cost-push inflation*. This type of inflation is caused by costs increasing; for example, higher wages that are not related to productivity gains, higher import prices or monopoly suppliers pushing up their prices. Faced with higher costs, firms increase their prices to customers to maintain profit margins. This shifts the aggregate supply curve to the left and causes cost-push inflation (see Fig. 29.2). An inward shift of the aggregate supply will also lead to a fall in output and to firms operating under capacity.

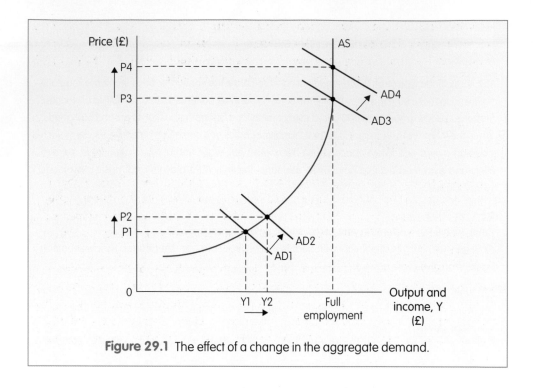

Figure 29.1 The effect of a change in the aggregate demand.

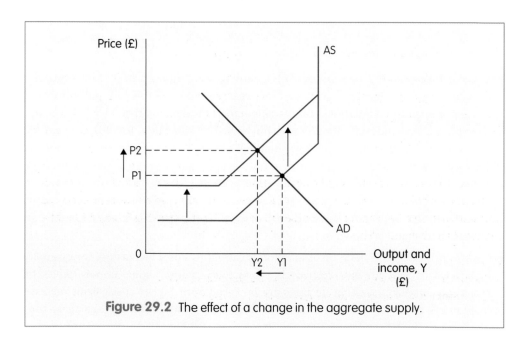

Figure 29.2 The effect of a change in the aggregate supply.

- *Monetary inflation.* According to monetarists, inflation occurs when there is too much money supply in the economy. With more money circulating this leads to more demand in the economy and then higher prices. This is a form of demand-pull inflation that is caused specifically by excess growth of the money supply (see page 370).

Economics in context   Hyperinflation

In 2002, Argentina experienced high levels of inflation; prices in general rose by 10% in one month alone. The prices of fresh eggs and vegetable oils, as well as the prices of computers and televisions, rose by between 100% and 200%. However, even this level of inflation was nowhere near the levels in the 1980s when inflation in that country was around 5000%; when inflation is this high it is known as hyperinflation.

In 2006, inflation in Zimbabwe reached 1000%! On average, goods were about eleven times as expensive in April 2006 as they were twelve months earlier. To respond to this massive increase in prices the government introduced a 'bearer cheque' worth 50 000 Zimbabwean dollars. This was fifty times the highest available banknote, but was actually only worth around half a US dollar and could only just buy a loaf of bread. The bread prices in Zimbabwe were as shown in Table 29.1.

Table 29.1 The price of bread in Zimbabwe.

	Price (Z$)
December 2004	3500
August 2005	7500
December 2005	44,000
March 2006	65,000
May 2006	80,000

In August 2006, the central bank of Zimbabwe tried to solve the problem of inflation by removing three zeros from the values of the currency. Old notes were to be replaced with new notes that had three zeros less. By August a loaf of bread had reached a price level of Z$220,000. Under the new system this was to be Z$220.

? Questions

What problems do you think are caused by hyperinflation in an economy?
Do you think that changing the currency is likely to cure inflation?

▪ Controlling inflation

To control inflation there are a variety of methods that the government may use, such as the following.

- *Reducing the aggregate demand.* To control demand-pull inflation the government will want to reduce the level of the aggregate demand in the economy relative to supply. This may be done using deflationary fiscal or restrictive monetary policies.

Economics in context **US interest rates**

In 2005 the US economy was growing rapidly. Demand was likely to grow much faster than supply, so the US Federal Reserve—the country's central bank—raised interest rates ten times in succession to reduce the threat of inflation.

❓ Questions

How does increasing the interest rate reduce the threat of demand-pull inflation?

What other policies could be used?

- *Reducing costs.* To control cost-push inflation governments may do the following.
  - Governments may introduce wage controls to prevent wages from increasing too fast. This is known as an incomes policy. However, incomes policies can lead to frustration on the part of employers, who want to offer more money to reward and attract good quality employees. Employees may also be frustrated and look for better-paid jobs abroad.
  - Governments may try to influence the exchange rate to make the external value of the pound stronger. This gives UK-based firms more purchasing power, making it cheaper to buy in supplies from abroad. However, it may affect exports adversely.

- *Setting inflation targets.* By setting clear targets for inflation and giving the relevant organisations the authority to take actions to achieve these, a government can try to convince households and business people that such targets will be met. For example, the UK government in 2004 onwards had an inflation target of 2%. Its success in achieving this target early on helped to convince individuals and groups that this was going to be the level of inflation in the future. As a result, wage claims and price increases were linked to this level of expectations. If, on the other hand, people think that inflation is going to be very high then they will demand high wages. This could cause higher prices due to cost-push inflation. This inflation could then stimulate higher wages, higher costs and higher inflation again. This is called the 'wage–price spiral' (see Fig. 29.3).

What do you think?

Do you think that the government should aim for an inflation rate of 0% in the UK?

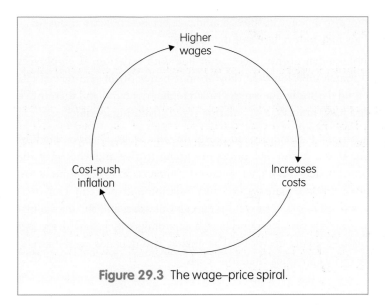

Figure 29.3 The wage–price spiral.

Why does inflation matter?

Inflation can cause a number of problems for an economy, such as the following.

- If prices are increasing this creates costs for firms because they may have to update their promotional material to reflect the higher prices. For example, this means reprinting brochures, updating price lists and changing vending machines. These are called 'menu costs'.

- With higher rates of inflation, individuals and firms may have to search more to find the best returns on their savings. This will be necessary to preserve the real rate of return (i.e., the return adjusted for inflation). The costs of searching around are called 'shoe leather costs'.

- Not all individuals will have the bargaining power to ensure that their own earnings rise at the same rate as prices are increasing. If your wages do not increase as much as prices then, in real terms, you are worse off. Your real income has fallen. The ability of an employee to bargain for higher wages in line with inflation depends on the extent to which they are in demand and/or whether they are well represented by trade unions. Inflation may therefore redistribute real incomes. Some groups may find that their earnings keep pace with inflation; others may not. This means that inflation has redistributive effects.

- Internationally, if the prices of firms in the UK are increasing faster than their trading partners then this may make the country's products uncompetitive compared to those of foreign firms. This may reduce the earnings from exports and increase the spending on imports. This will affect the balance of payments adversely. Domestically, the UK may also struggle to compete because imports will be relatively cheaper.

- Inflation may also damage business confidence because of fears about the future impact on costs. This may reduce levels of investment.

- Tax thresholds often do not increase in line with inflation. If employees gain a pay increase to match inflation then they are not better off in real terms. However, with higher nominal pay individuals may enter a higher tax band and therefore be worse off. This is called fiscal drag. Again, inflation is redistributing income.

The effects of inflation will depend partly on whether it is 'anticipated' or 'unanticipated' inflation. If you know that prices are going to rise and you have the bargaining power then you can demand higher wages to compensate, for example. However, if you are locked into a 2% pay increase and then inflation unexpectedly increases to 5% then you will be worse off in real terms. If inflation levels are regularly unanticipated then this will lead to high levels of uncertainty in the economy, which may deter investment and affect spending and saving decisions. The impact also depends on the levels of inflation; high levels are more damaging than low levels.

What do you think?

What do you think inflation will be next year? How did you decide this?

◼ Deflation

Deflation occurs when prices in an economy are falling. This may be due to the following reasons.

- Aggregate demand may be falling, perhaps because interest rates are too high or because there is a lack of household and business confidence. Deflation is often associated with a recession in the economy.

- Supply may be growing faster than demand. In certain markets, such as some consumer electronics markets, supply is increasing rapidly due to developments in technology. This causes deflation in these markets.

Economics in context   Falling prices in the UK

The chart in Fig. 29.4 illustrates how prices for various products have fallen in the UK between 2000 and 2005.

 Question

Why do you think that the prices of the products have been falling?

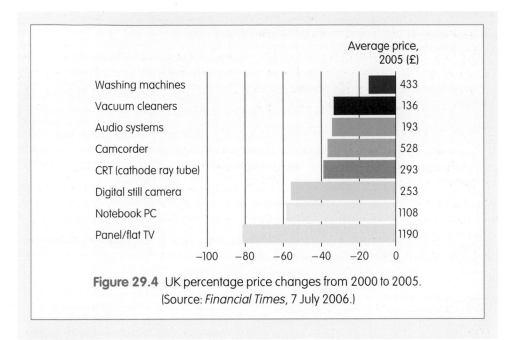

Figure 29.4 UK percentage price changes from 2000 to 2005.
(Source: *Financial Times*, 7 July 2006.)

Economics in context

Japanese interest rates

In the 1990s, Japan suffered from a collapse in the price of property and other assets. This led to a fall in demand and a fall in prices between 1998 and 2005. In 2001, interest rates were put down by the government to 0% to encourage spending. The government actively urged people to save less and spend more!

? Question

Why might demand have been so low in Japan?

Now you try it

Using the aggregate demand and supply show the effect on the equilibrium price and output of a fall in the aggregate demand.

Deflation may lead to the following.

- There may be lower profits for firms because of lower prices. This means that there are less funds for investment, which may delay the purchase of new machinery.

- There may be redundancies as firms try to rationalise their production and make it more efficient; managers will be pressurised to cut costs to maintain profit margins.

- Businesses may close because they may not be able to make profits if prices are falling.

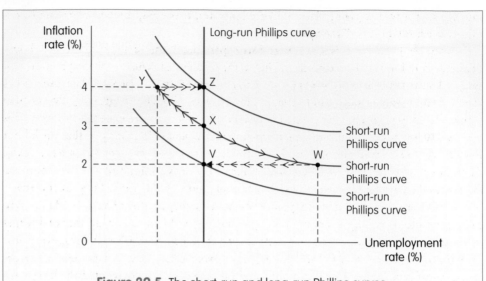

Figure 29.5 The short-run and long-run Phillips curves.

▪ The Phillips curve: inflation and unemployment

The Phillips curve shows the relationship between the rate of inflation and the rate of un-employment in both the short run and the long run.

In the short run there appears to be a trade-off between the rate of inflation and the rate of unemployment; the government can reduce unemployment below the natural rate at the expense of faster-growing prices.

Imagine that the economy is at full employment equilibrium at X (see Fig. 29.5). Wages and prices are growing in line with each other at 3% and the rate of unemployment in the economy is at the natural rate. All unemployment is voluntary.

If the government then increases spending then this will create demand-pull inflation. Prices will grow faster than wages; for example, prices may grow at 4% whilst wages are still increasing at 3%. This is because wages are often 'sticky' in the short term. Indi-viduals will have agreed their wages for a given period (e.g., for the next year) and will not be able to renegotiate them. Also, employees are often slow to realise that inflation has changed; they tend to focus on the prices of things that they buy regularly and do not appreciate the overall trend with inflation. This is called money illusion. With prices growing faster than wages, real wages actually fall. This makes it cheaper in real terms to employ people, which should lead to a fall in unemployment (the point Y in Fig. 29.5).

Over time, however, employees will notice that their purchasing power has been reduced and will want to bargain for higher wages to compensate for the inflation. If they manage to match wage increases to the price increases then, in real terms, wages and the economy will be back to where they started, except that prices and wages are now growing at a faster rate of 4%, not 3% (the point Z in Fig. 29.5). Unemployment is at the natural rate again, but with higher inflation. In the long run, therefore, there has been no trade-off between inflation and unemployment.

Conversely, if the government brings down spending in the economy then, with lower demand, inflation may be reduced, and in the short run prices will be growing slower than wages. This is again because wages are slow to change due to contracts and because it takes time for employees to notice fully changes in inflation. If prices are growing slower than wages then real wages have increased and so employees are more expensive to hire. This will lead to less people being employed and unemployment rising. Imagine that the labour market is in long-run equilibrium at X with prices and wages growing at 3% (see Fig. 29.5). Then prices start to grow at 2%, so real wages have increased. Employees are more expensive and unemployment increases; the economy moves to W. In the long run, however, because of higher levels of unemployment and because they realise inflation has fallen, employees would be willing to accept lower pay increases; this would mean that real wages were back where they were originally. All that has changed is that prices and wages are now growing at the lower rate of 2%. The economy moves to the point V. Once again, there is no trade-off between the rate of inflation and the rate of unemployment in the long run.

Now you try it

If the rate of inflation is higher than the rate at which nominal wages are growing then what is happening to real wages? Why?

What might be the impact of this on the quantity demanded and the quantity supplied of labour?

What do you think?

To what extent do you think employees are aware of the rate of inflation?

The Phillips curve suggests the following.

- There is a possible trade-off between the rate of inflation and the rate of unemployment in the short run provided that prices grow faster than wages. If the government intends to keep unemployment below the natural rate then it will always need to keep prices growing at a faster rate than wages. Obviously, if the government adopts such tactics then employees might soon realise this; therefore, to keep fooling people, the government would need to create ever-larger increases in inflation so that employees do not anticipate this.

- There is no long-run trade-off between the rate of inflation and the rate of unemployment. This suggests that efforts by the government to use demand side policies to manipulate inflation and affect unemployment levels will not work. Attempts by the government to reduce unemployment below the natural rate will in the long run simply lead to more inflation. The implication is that a long-run policy by the government would be to focus on changing the natural rate of unemployment through supply side policies (see Fig. 29.6).

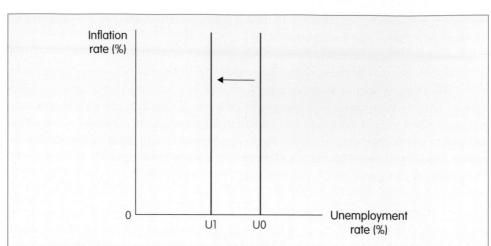

Figure 29.6 Supply side policies may be used to reduce the natural rate of unemployment.

Case Study

In the UK in 2006, inflation increased due to rising gas and electricity prices and the higher cost of fruit and dairy products. The consumer price index (CPI) rose to 2.5%, well above the government's target of 2%.

The headline rate of inflation, which is measured by the retail price index and unlike the CPI includes mortgage interest payments, rose to 3.3%.

This increase put pressure on the Bank of England to take action. The inflation figure in 2006 matched the highest level since the CPI measure was introduced in 1997. An increase in the interest rates up to 4.75% was expected, which would problems for households who were struggling to pay off mortgages, loans and credit card bills. Recent figures had shown record numbers of people becoming insolvent in the UK. Analysts were also concerned that higher energy bills were reducing consumers' disposable income and might reduce their spending.

❓ Questions

- Why does it matter if inflation has increased to 2.5% in the UK?
- How could the UK government reduce inflation to achieve its target of 2%?
- Why do different measures of inflation exist?
- Should controlling inflation be a priority in the UK at the moment?

Checklist

Now you have read this unit try to answer the following questions.

☐ Can you explain what is meant by inflation?

☐ Can you outline the different causes of inflation?

☐ Can you explain the costs of inflation?

☐ Can you examine ways of reducing inflation?

☐ Are you able to discuss the possible trade-off between inflation and unemployment?

End of unit questions

1 Does inflation mean that all prices are increasing?

2 What are the causes of inflation?

3 What are the main costs of inflation?

4 Is it possible to control inflation?

5 Can the government reduce inflation and unemployment simultaneously?

Key learning points

• The possible causes of inflation include demand-pull and cost-push.

• The appropriate cures for inflation depend on the cause.

• The Phillips curve suggests that there is a trade-off between inflation and unemployment in the short run but not in the long run.

Learn more

To learn more about rates of inflation in the UK over the years visit our website at the address below.

 Visit our Online Resource Centre at www.oxfordtextbooks.co.uk/orc/gillespie_econ for test question and further information on topics covered in this chapter.

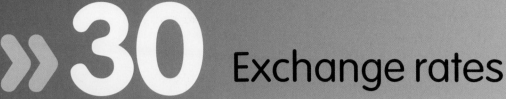

»30 Exchange rates

All economies are involved in international trade to some extent. The exchange rate is a key factor in determining the amount and value of trade between countries. This unit examines the determinants of exchange rates and the effects of changes in exchange rates.

LEARNING OBJECTIVES

By the end of this unit you should be able to:

✔ explain the determinants of the external value of a currency;

✔ distinguish between a floating rate and a fixed rate exchange rate system;

✔ explain the possible impact of a change in the external value of a currency.

■ Introduction

If you have ever gone on holiday abroad you will have had to change your pounds into another currency. The amount of foreign currency you received in return for your pound depends on the exchange rate. Sometimes you might have felt that you received a lot of money in return for your pound; other times you might feel that the money you receive does not go very far. The value of the exchange rate clearly matters to tourists and this is a very important sector of the UK economy. It also matters to any firm buying or selling products abroad.

■ Exchange rate

An exchange rate measures the value of one currency in terms of another; for example, the value of one pound in terms of dollars or yen. It measures the external value of a currency. The external value of a currency is important because of its impact on trade and its impact

evenue and import spending. An economy such as the UK's is very open to
herefore changes in the exchange rate are particularly important.

What determines the external value of a currency?

If a government does not intervene in the currency market then the value of the exchange rate is determined by the supply of and demand for this currency, that is, by market forces. This is known as a floating exchange rate system.

The demand for the UK currency will be influenced by the following.

- *Demand for UK goods and services from abroad*. To buy more UK products, overseas buyers will need more pounds and so the demand for UK currency will increase. Overseas buyers will give up their own currency and change it into pounds.

- *UK interest rates*. If UK interest rates are higher than interest rates elsewhere in the world then, all other things being unchanged, the demand for pounds will rise. Overseas investors will look to buy pounds to save in UK banks and earn higher returns. High UK interest rates will attract what is called 'hot money' flowing in to the country.

- *Relative inflation rates*. If UK goods and services are relatively expensive then this is likely to reduce demand for the products, and therefore for pounds. With less demand for the currency it will fall in value, all other things being unchanged.

- *Expectations*. If currency speculators believe that the pound will rise in value in the future then they may buy now so that their investment will become worth more. This increase in demand will in itself increase the value of the currency, all other things being unchanged.

The demand for pounds will be downward sloping. As the exchange rate increases the price of UK goods and services will become greater in foreign currencies, all other things being unchanged. This will lead to a fall in the quantity demanded of UK products, and therefore a fall in the quantity demanded of pounds. The greater the price elasticity of demand for UK products abroad, the greater the fall in the quantity demanded of pounds (i.e., the more price elastic the demand for pounds will be) following an increase in the exchange rate (see Fig. 30.1).

Example

Imagine that a UK firm produces a product for £100 and sales abroad are ten units. Imagine that the exchange rate now rises from $1.5:£1 to $2:£1. The price of the product abroad rises from $150 to $200. Originally the firm earned $10 \times £100 = £1000$. If demand is price elastic then demand falls to, say, two units. This means that earnings fall to $2 \times £100 = £200$.

If demand is price inelastic then sales may fall to nine units. The earnings are now $9 \times £100 = £900$. Clearly, the more price elastic demand is for UK products abroad, the greater is the fall in the quantity of pounds demanded given an increase in the external value of the pound.

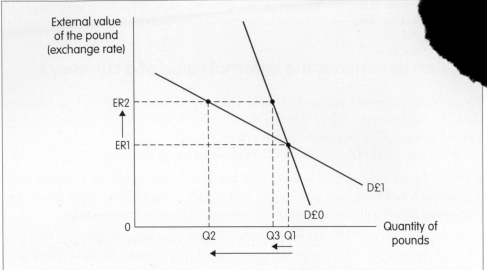

Figure 30.1 The demand for pounds in the currency market. For the demand curve D£0, the demand for UK exports is price inelastic. For the demand curve D£1, the demand for UK exports is price elastic.

A change in the exchange rate is shown by a movement along the demand curve for pounds. Changes in any of the other factors above will shift the demand curve for pounds in the currency market.

Now you try it

Imagine that a UK firm produces a product for £200. What would the price in dollars be in the following cases?

- If the exchange rate is $1.5:£1.

- If the exchange rate is $2:£1.

Suppose that the original level of sales was 500 units and then sales fell to 450 units.
Calculate the original and new value of sales in dollars.
Calculate the original and new value of sales in pounds.

The supply of UK currency to change into foreign currency will depend on the following.

- *The demand for foreign goods and services by UK households and businesses.* If UK consumers and firms want to buy more US goods, for example, then they will sell more pounds to buy the dollars they need.

- *Interest rates overseas.* If the interest rates overseas are higher than UK interest rates then the British investors may change more pounds into foreign currencies to save abroad.

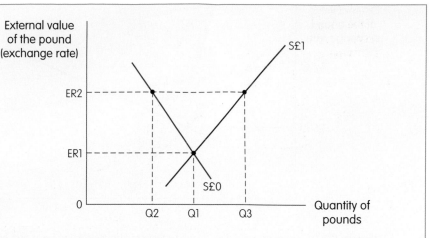

Figure 30.2 The supply of pounds in the currency market. The supply curve S£0 represents the supply of pounds if the demand for imports is price inelastic. The supply curve S£1 represents the supply of pounds if the demand for imports is price elastic.

- *Speculation.* If speculators believe that the pound is going to fall then they will want to sell now. This selling in itself is likely to lead to a fall in the value of the pound due to an increase in supply.

The supply of pounds is usually upward sloping. As the pound increases in value, less pounds are needed to buy foreign products. The price of foreign products falls in terms of pounds. This should increase the quantity demanded of foreign products. If demand for these products is price elastic then there will be an increase in the overall spending on imports, and therefore an increase in the supply of pounds. The increase in the value of the pound increases the quantity supplied, and the supply curve is upward sloping (see Fig. 30.2).

If, however, the demand for imports is price inelastic then a fall in price will lead to a relatively smaller increase in the quantity demanded. This will lead to a fall in the overall spending on imports. An increase in the value of the currency in this case leads to a fall in the supply of pounds. This means that the supply curve for pounds is downward sloping (see Fig. 30.2).

Example

Imagine that a US firm produces a product worth $300. A UK business imports ten of these. The exchange rate is $1.5:£1, so the American product costs £200 (calculated by $300/$1.50). The UK firm spends 10 × £200 = £2000.

If the UK exchange rate now rises to $2:£1 then the American product now costs £150 (calculated by $300/$2).

Suppose that demand for the import is price inelastic and the firm now buys, say, eleven.

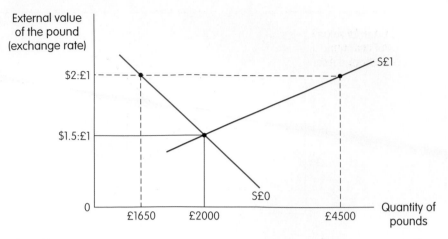

Figure 30.3 Upward- and downward-sloping supply curves for a currency. The supply curve S£0 represents the supply of pounds if the demand for imports is price inelastic. The supply curve S£1 represents the supply of pounds if the demand for imports is price elastic.

This means that it spends $11 \times £150 = £1650$. As the price is lower and the increase in quantity demanded is relatively low, the amount spent abroad (i.e., the supply of pounds) falls. The supply of pounds falls as the exchange rate rises, as shown in Fig. 30.3.

Suppose that demand for the import is price elastic and the firm now buys, say, thirty. The firm spends $30 \times £150 = £4500$. The increase in the quantity demanded is so great that, even with the lower price, there is more spending in pounds on foreign goods, and so the supply of pounds rises, as shown in Fig. 30.3.

Now you try it

The exchange rate appreciates from $1.5:£1 to $2:£1. The US price of a product is $300. A UK consumer buys twenty units initially and then, when the exchange rate changes, forty units. What happens to the amount of pounds spent on this import?

■ Equilibrium in the currency market

If the value of the pound is at ER2 in Fig. 30.4 then there is excess demand for the currency (equal to Q3 – Q2). This means that overseas buyers want to buy more pounds than others want to sell and convert into other currency. This will lead to an increase in the value of the pound. As the value (price) increases the quantity demanded will fall, whilst the quantity supplied increases (assuming that the price elasticity of demand for imports is price elastic). This process will continue until equilibrium is reached at ER1. At this value the supply of the currency equals the demand for the currency. This means that the

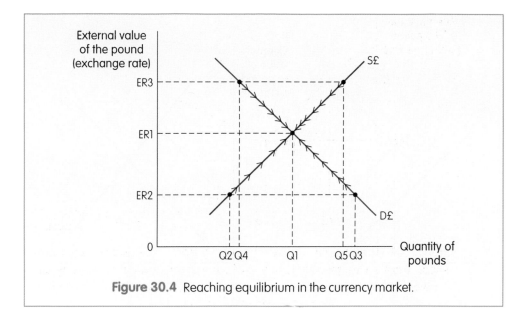

Figure 30.4 Reaching equilibrium in the currency market.

number of pounds demanded by overseas buyers equals the number of pounds sold. This is equilibrium in the currency market.

If the exchange rate is at ER3 in Fig. 30.4 then there is excess supply of the currency (equal to Q5 – Q4). This means that the sellers want to change more pounds than buyers want to buy in exchange for foreign currency. This means that the value of the pound will fall. As it does the quantity demanded of this currency will increase and the quantity supplied will decrease until equilibrium is reached at ER1.

In a floating exchange rate system the value of the currency will change to automatically bring about equilibrium, so that the supply of the currency equals the demand for the currency. The exchange rate is the price mechanism that equates supply and demand in currency markets.

■ Appreciation and depreciation of the exchange rate

An appreciation of the exchange rate means that it has increased in value. It is more expensive in terms of other currencies. For example, if the value of £1 rises from $1.50 to $1.60 then this is an appreciation of the pound. This might be because of an increase in the demand for the currency or a fall in the supply (see Fig. 30.5). If a currency has increased in value then it is sometimes called a 'strong' currency.

A depreciation of the exchange rate means that it is less expensive in terms of other currencies. For example, the pound depreciates if its value falls from $1.50 to $1.40. This might be because of a fall in demand for the currency or an increase in the supply (see Fig. 30.6). If a currency falls in value then it is said to have become 'weaker'.

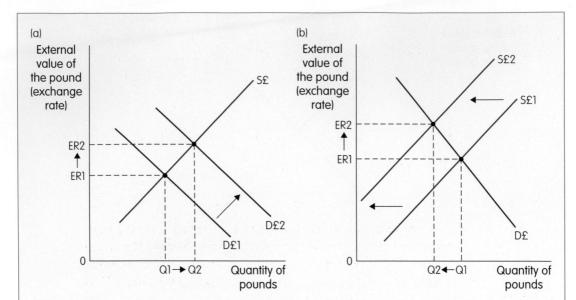

Figure 30.5 (a) The effect of an outward shift in demand for a currency. (b) The effect of an inward shift in the supply of a currency.

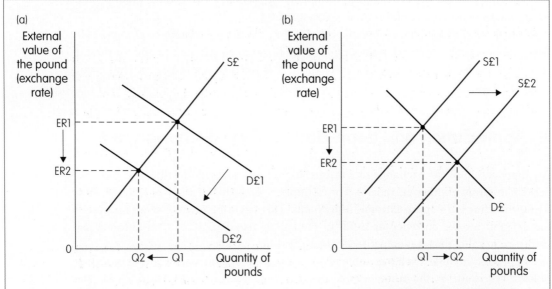

Figure 30.6 (a) The effect of an inward shift in demand for a currency. (b) The effect of an outward shift in the supply of a currency.

What do you think?

Do you think that a strong pound is better than a weak pound?

The advantages and disadvantages of a floating exchange rate system

The advantages of a floating exchange rate system are as follows.

- The value of a currency will adjust to reflect changing market conditions. For example, if UK inflation increases faster than for its trading partners then at the original exchange rate its products would become more expensive abroad. This would be likely to lead to a fall in demand for UK goods and services, and therefore the demand for pounds. This in turn will reduce the value of the currency, which will:
  – make exports relatively cheaper, which will offset the higher inflation;
  – make imports relatively expensive.
  The fall in the value of the currency should eventually restore equilibrium, so that the supply of and demand for the currency will be equal. This means that the balance of payments will balance (see Unit 31).

- There are no costs of intervention. The government will not have to use its resources to buy and sell currency. This enables the government to focus on internal domestic economic issues.

The disadvantages of the floating exchange rate system are as follows.

- The value of the currency will change regularly (literally every minute), making it difficult for firms to plan ahead. UK exporters, for example, will not know at any moment what the actual price of their products will be to overseas buyers. UK importers will not know what they will have to pay to buy in foreign products. This makes planning difficult.

- The unpredictability of the value of the currency is likely to deter investment. It may lead to resources being invested in other countries.

- Given that the value of the currency can change all the time as demand and supply conditions alter, this encourages speculation. By buying and selling currency in the belief that it will change, this leads to greater instability.

- The exchange rate may not be able to adjust to bring about equilibrium. For example, if the supply of pounds is downward sloping then the currency market may not settle in equilibrium. At ER1 in Fig. 30.7 there is an excess supply of pounds. This leads to a fall in the value of the currency. In this case the excess supply increases (e.g., to ER2). Changes in the exchange rate in this situation move the market away from equilibrium.

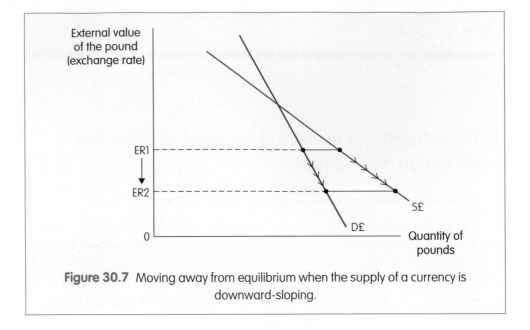

Figure 30.7 Moving away from equilibrium when the supply of a currency is downward-sloping.

The strong won

In 2006, the Hyundai Motor Company suffered a fall in profit after its exports were hit by a strong South Korean won. Over 60% of its sales were in export markets. The strong won was reducing the value of profits when converted back into the domestic currency.

? Questions

Why might the South Korean won be so high in value?

Explain why a high value for the won affects the profits of a company such as the Hyundai Motor Company.

■ A fixed exchange rate system

In a fixed exchange rate system a government intervenes to maintain the value of a currency at a fixed value or within a given range.

A government can intervene in the currency market as follows.

- The government may buy or sell its currency. If it wants to increase the value of its currency abroad then it can buy it in return for foreign currency that it holds. To decrease the value of its currency it would sell pounds in return for foreign currency. This type of intervention involves transaction costs to monitor the possible currency movements and to exchange currency.

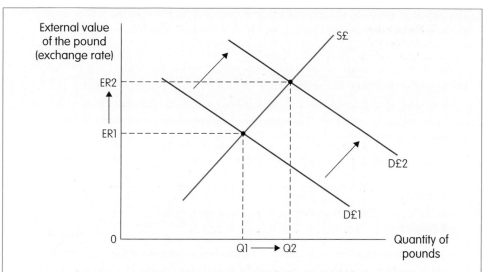

Figure 30.8 Government intervention to increase demand for a currency and increase its external value. The government buys pounds to increase demand using foreign currency reserves.

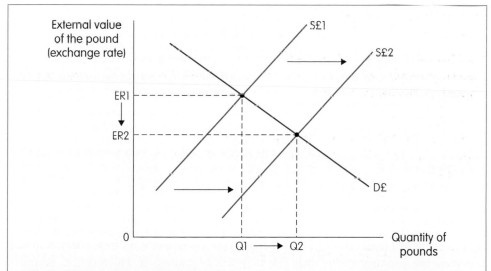

Figure 30.9 Government intervention to increase supply of a currency and reduce its external value. The government sells pounds in return for foreign currency.

Suppose that equilibrium in the market is at ER1 in Fig. 30.8. If this is below the rate that the government is trying to achieve then it could increase demand for the currency by buying it in return for selling foreign reserves.

Suppose that equilibrium is at ER1 in Fig. 30.9. If this is above the rate that the government would like it to be at then it can sell pounds in return for foreign currency.

- The government may change the interest rate. An increase in the UK interest rate is likely to attract investment (hot money) from overseas, which increases the demand for pounds; this should increase the external value of the currency, all other things being unchanged.

- The government may use reflationary or deflationary policies to affect the level of demand and spending in the UK. Deflationary policies, for example, would reduce aggregate demand spending. This would reduce spending on imports. With less spending on imports there is less demand for foreign currency, and therefore less need to change pounds. This reduces the supply of pounds.

Economics in context   Relaxing currency controls in Russia

In 2006, Russia lifted controls on its currency, the rouble, making it fully convertible with other currencies. Previously, there had been severe restrictions on the amount of currency that could be changed from roubles to other currencies and on the movement of money into Russia. The Russian government hoped that introducing convertibility would lead to a major inflow of foreign currency, but it also led to more roubles being converted. Prior to this change in policy, Russians wishing to transfer funds to a foreign bank account had to put one-quarter of the sum in an account in the Russian Central Bank, and foreigners transferring money to Russia were required to deposit a 'collateral' amount as a security against speculative buying and selling of the currency. The rouble is now like the dollar and euro, and can be converted without any restrictions.

? Question

Why would the Russian government have wanted to restrict the amount of money entering and leaving the country?

Now you try it

Outline three ways in which a government might reduce the value of its currency.

The benefit of a fixed exchange rate system is that it provides stability for importers and exporters because they know what rate they will be trading at. However, decisions to intervene to affect the value of the currency have an opportunity cost and side effects that might disrupt other policies. For example, higher interest rates might increase the value of the pound, but will also have an impact on domestic savings and borrowings. High interest rates are likely to decrease domestic demand and may cause slower economic growth and unemployment.

Also, as market conditions change the fixed value of the currency may become too high or low. This will affect the competitiveness of a country's products abroad and a country's balance of payments position.

| Economics in context | The value of the yuan |

For several years up to 2006, many governments, especially the US, complained about the value of the Chinese yuan. The Chinese currency is pegged against the dollar and many analysts argued that its value was kept too low. The yuan was fixed at 8.28 yuan to the dollar for a decade. The undervaluation of the yuan helped Chinese exporters and led to a massive trade deficit for America. China did revalue the yuan upwards by 2.1% in July 2005, but American officials did not think that this was enough. Some analysts claimed that the yuan was still undervalued by between 15% and 40%. China's trade surplus in 2006 was over $110 billion.

? Question

Do you think that the American government needs to adopt policies to improve its trade deficit? What would you recommend?

■ The exchange rate mechanism (ERM)

The exchange rate mechanism (ERM) was a system in which member European countries fixed their exchange rates against each other. The aim was to stabilise exchange rates in Europe and thereby encourage trade. The currencies of member countries were given an upper and lower limit on either side of a given central rate within which their currencies could fluctuate. Britain joined the ERM at a rate of 2.95 Deutsche Marks to £1 in October 1990.

The system collapsed on 16 September 1992 when countries could not keep their currencies within the set limits. On what became known as Black Wednesday, the British pound was forced to leave the system; it was then followed by the Italian lira. The UK government had fought against speculators who were selling pounds, believing that the fixed rate of the pound had been set too high. In a floating exchange rate system, this sale of pounds would drive the value of the pound down. However, because it was in the ERM the UK government had to try to keep the value of the pound constant; it did this by buying billions of pounds with its foreign currency reserves and increasing domestic interest rates. In the end, the UK government recognised that it could not keep intervening like this (not least because of the impact of such high interest rates domestically) and left the ERM. Speculators such as George Soros made a fortune because they had been selling pounds; once the pound fell they could buy them back much more cheaply.

■ Does a strong pound matter?

A strong pound means that the pound is relatively expensive in terms of other currencies. All other things being unchanged, this means the following.

- UK goods and services become relatively more expensive in other currencies. This may reduce demand for them and reduce UK export earnings. If the pound increases in value from £1:$1.5 to £1:$1.6, then a £100 good now costs $160, not $150, in America. This is likely to reduce the volume of and earnings from exports.

- Overseas products become relatively cheap in pounds. This may lead to cheaper costs for UK firms and therefore an increase in firms' profit margins. However, it also means that overseas final products are cheaper, which may threaten some UK sales domestically. If the pound increases in value from £1:$1 to £1:$1.5, then a $300 good now costs £200, not £300, in the UK.

The extent to which a strong pound has these effects depends on:

- how much the pound increases in value and for how long;

- the time period being considered (many prices are fixed for some periods, e.g., until brochures are updated or contracts renegotiated);

- how sensitive demands for imports and exports are to price (it may be that the quality of the products mean that demand is not that sensitive).

■ Depreciation, the J curve effect and the balance of payments

If the pound depreciates then, all other things being unchanged, UK products become cheaper abroad in terms of foreign currency, whilst imports become more expensive in pounds. The cheaper exports should lead to more sales and greater income for UK firms. The extent to which sales abroad increase depends on how price sensitive demand is for UK products abroad. If demand is price elastic then the increase in sales is greater than the fall in export prices (in %), and spending on UK exports rises relatively significantly. If demand is price inelastic then the increase in sales will be less than the increase in price (in %), and so the increase in the number of UK products sold will be relatively low; therefore the increase in UK export earnings in pounds will also be relatively low.

Meanwhile, the increase in the price of imports in pounds is likely to lead to a fall in the quantity demanded. If demand for imports is price elastic then this will lead to a larger fall in sales than the increase in price (in %); this will lead to a fall in the total spending on imports. However, if demand is price inelastic then this means that the fall in sales is less than the increase in price (in %); this leads to an increase in the total spending on imports.

The effect of a depreciation in the value of the currency therefore depends a great deal on the price elasticity of demand for imports and exports.

In the short run

In the short run UK importers and exporters may have negotiated and fixed prices with their trading partners. They may also find it difficult to find alternative suppliers abroad at short notice. The result is that demand for UK products abroad is likely to be price inelastic and demand for imports is also likely to be price inelastic. This means that the increase in exports sales is relatively low, so export revenue does not increase much; at the same time demand for imports is not sensitive to price, leading to more being spent overall on them given the higher price.

Overall, the balance of payments position is likely to worsen in the short term following a fall in the value of the pound because demands for imports and exports are likely to be price inelastic.

Over time

Over time, following a fall in the value of the pound, buyers abroad are more likely to switch to the cheaper UK products, thus boosting UK exports. This should lead to an increase in export revenue. At the same time UK firms may switch to UK suppliers rather than stick with relatively expensive foreign products. This leads to a fall in the total spending on imports. This means that in the long run, following a fall in the value of a currency, the balance of payments position should improve.

The balance of payments position will improve following a depreciation of the currency provided that the price elasticity of demand for exports plus the price elasticity of demand for imports is greater than one. This is known as the Marshall–Lerner condition.

The short-term deterioration of a country's balance of payments following a depreciation of the currency before an improvement in the long term is called the 'J curve' effect. This is because the balance of payments moves into deficit before rising into surplus. The J curve effect is shown in Fig. 30.10.

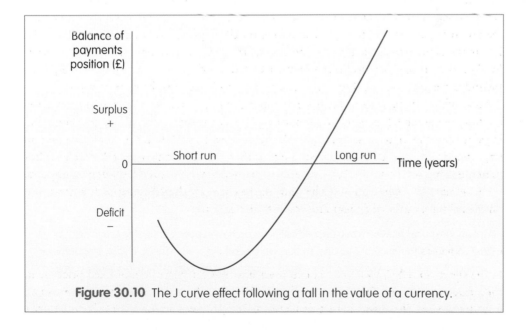

Figure 30.10 The J curve effect following a fall in the value of a currency.

The very long run

In the very long run the higher import prices may lead to cost-push inflation. This is because UK firms will be dependent to some extent on imported goods and services, and will try to pass on their higher costs to consumers. This will push up UK prices, thus offsetting the export benefits of a fall in the value of the currency. This may lead to the balance of payments position returning to its original position but with higher domestic inflation. This suggests that a fall in the value of a currency may only have limited beneficial impact over time and is not a very long-term solution to balance of payments problems.

Other problems with depreciating the currency include the following.

- *A crisis of confidence.* If a government devalues the currency or allows it to depreciate then this may trigger concerns that there are problems. This may lead to an outflow of capital on the capital account, causing a worsening of the balance of payments position.

- *A lack of capacity.* If the economy is near capacity then a fall in the currency would boost the aggregate demand and lead to demand-pull inflation. In this case it may be necessary for a government to create capacity in the economy before depreciating the currency.

▧ Purchasing power parity (PPP)

Purchasing power parity (PPP) is the exchange rate that gives one currency exactly the same purchasing power when converted into another; for example, £1000 when converted into the other currency could purchase the same goods and services. If, for example, £1000 of goods in the UK costs €1700 then the exchange rate that would lead to PPP would be €1.7 to £1. Thus we have:

$$\text{Purchasing power parity exchange rate} = \frac{\text{Consumer price index in other country}}{\text{UK consumer price index}}$$

$$= \frac{€1700}{£1000} = €1.7 = £1.$$

To maintain PPP the value of a currency must move to offset differences in inflation rates. If UK inflation is relatively high then the pound will need to fall; £1000 will buy less in the UK because of domestic inflation, and when converted into other currencies it needs to buy less there as well.

Economics in context   The price of McDonald's burgers across the world

To compare prices between countries and estimate purchasing power parity, *The Economist* magazine compares the price of McDonald's burgers around the world. This is a fairly standardised product globally, so it provides an easy means of comparing the cost of living in different countries.

❓ Question

What other products would you expect to have similar prices in different countries across the world?

Case Study

In 2006, the dollar fell in value significantly in world markets. This was said to be due to the massive US trade deficit. For many years the financial markets had been concerned about the extent to which American imports exceeded its exports. By August 2006 the trade deficit had reached $742 billion. The US also had a government budget deficit of $400 billion due to tax cuts and the costs of the war in Iraq. Much of the trade deficit was due to imports from East Asian countries such as China, Japan and Korea, who sell much more to the US than they buy.

Some analysts were worried about the short-term impact of the fall in the dollar in terms of imported inflation and then the consequent impact on US interest rates. Analysts thought US interest rates might have to increase to control inflation. This worried some companies, such as Sony, Canon and Volkswagen, who relied on the US market for their export sales; a higher US interest rate may dampen sales.

This type of problem with the dollar happened in the 1980s. At that time there was an agreement between the major economies to gradually reduce the value of the dollar. In 2006, market forces were allowed to work for themselves.

❓ Questions

Explain why the value of the dollar might have fallen. Illustrate these factors using a supply and demand diagram.

- What might be the long-term impact of the dollar falling?
- Should the US government intervene to stop the dollar falling? How could it do this?
- Why might countries such as China, Japan and Korea sell more to the US than Americans buy from them?
- To what extent do you think that the value of a country's currency matters?

Checklist

Now you have read this unit try to answer the following questions.

☐ Can you explain the determinants of the external value of a currency?

☐ Can you distinguish between a floating rate and a fixed rate exchange rate system?

☐ Can you explain the possible impact of a change in the external value of a currency?

End of unit questions

1　Is a free floating exchange rate better than a fixed exchange rate?

2　To what extent can a government control the external value of its currency?

3　Will a fall in the external value of a currency improve a country's balance of payments?

4　For what reasons might the value of a currency increase?

5　Does controlling the value of the currency conflict with other economic objectives?

Key learning points

• The value of a currency is determined by supply and demand in a floating exchange rate system.

• In a fixed exchange rate system the government intervenes to keep the external value of a currency stable.

• If a currency depreciates then the J curve effect shows that the balance of payments may get worse before getting better; the position will only improve if the Marshall–Lerner condition is met and the price elasticity of demand for exports plus the price elasticity of demand for imports is greater than one.

Learn more

To learn more about the value of the pound over time and the impact on the UK economy visit our website at the address below.

 Visit our Online Resource Centre at www.oxfordtextbooks.co.uk/orc/gillespie_econ for test questions and further information on topics covered in this chapter.

International trade    >>31

All countries engage in international trade and this has a large impact on their economies. This unit examines the reasons why international trade exists and the benefits that can be gained from it. It then considers the reasons why protectionism exists and the effects of this on different stake-holder groups.

LEARNING OBJECTIVES

By the end of this unit you should be able to:

✔ explain the theory of international trade;

✔ explain the elements of the balance of payments;

✔ outline the possible elements of protectionism;

✔ analyse why governments might protect industries;

✔ examine the possible consequences of protectionism.

▧ Introduction

Whenever you go shopping you are likely to be buying goods from all over the world. Clothes produced in China, wine from France, oranges from Spain, ham from Italy—the shops are full of products imported into the UK. You are also likely to make use of foreign services on a regular basis: your phone enquiry may be directed via a call centre in India, your bank may be based in Hong Kong and your energy provider may be from continental Europe. At the same time, UK firms are busy exporting a range of products, including music, films and education. We now live in a global village, buying products from and selling products all over the world, and where travel and tourism into and out of the UK is routine. International trade therefore has a massive influence on the UK economy.

◼ Exports

The value of a country's exports measures the value of the goods and services that it sells abroad. In the case of goods these may actually be transported abroad. In the case of services they are more likely to have been consumed in the UK; for example, international students coming to study at a British university are UK exports. Exports are an injection into the economy and are an important element of the aggregate demand.

The level of exports from a country may depend on the following.

• *The quality of the goods and services produced relative to international competitors.* This in turn will depend on a range of factors, such as the levels of investment in technology, the training of staff and the investment in research and development. It will also depend on the level of competitiveness domestically; high levels of domestic competition may force domestic firms to improve the quality of their products, which will improve their ability to export.

• *Protectionism.* Protectionism occurs if a government protects its own firms from foreign competition. The ways in which this may be done include placing taxes (called tariffs) on foreign products coming into the country or limiting the number of foreign products allowed in (a quota). Protectionist measures may reduce the export opportunities for a country. In some cases political disputes may lead to a complete ban (embargo) on products from a particular country, with the aim of putting pressure on the government there to change its policies. If other governments introduce protectionist measures then this may reduce the export opportunities for UK firms.

• *Exchange rates.* The exchange rate is the value of one currency in terms of another. If, for example, the pound is expensive to buy in terms of dollars then, all other things being equal, this is likely to reduce the sales of UK products to the USA because they will be relatively expensive. The exact impact of the price increase in dollars would depend on the price elasticity of demand for UK products. More generally, the relative price of one country's products compared to those in other countries will affect sales. The impact on sales will depend on the price elasticity of demand.

• *Customer preferences.* The tastes and preferences of overseas buyers will obviously influence levels of demand for UK products.

• *Income levels abroad.* If incomes are relatively high and growing abroad then this may increase demand for UK products. With more disposable income, foreign buyers may buy more products in general, including UK products. The amount of UK goods purchased will be influenced by the other countries' marginal propensity to import (MPM) in foreign countries. This highlights the importance of other economies to the UK. If countries abroad are in recession then this will hit UK exports and may lead the UK into recession as well. Equally, if countries abroad are prospering then this offers the UK export opportunities.

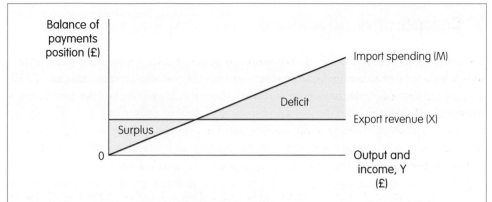

Figure 31.1 The balance of payments and national income. UK export revenue is not determined by UK national income; it is autonomous of UK income. Import spending does depend on UK income; with more income, spending on imports rises. This means that, all other things being unchanged, the balance of payments position would worsen as national income grows.

Imports

Imports are a withdrawal and reduce the level of the aggregate demand. The level of import spending into a country will also depend on factors such as the exchange rate, customer preferences and the quality of products abroad. Import spending will also depend on the UK's marginal propensity to import and the level of income in the UK. With more income there will be more spending, and this will increase the spending on imports.

The difference between the amount earned by selling exports abroad and the amount spent on imports is measured by the balance of payments. The relationship between the balance of payments and national income levels is shown in Fig. 31.1.

Economics in context   Shares of world exports

Between 1990 and 2005 the US's share of world exports fell from around 12% to under 9%. China's share rose from under 2% to over 7%. The UK's share went from around 5% to under 4%. Japan's share fell from 9% to around 6%.

Total trade as a percentage of the GDP was over 60% for China, nearly 70% for South Korea, 30% for India and around 20% for the US.

❓ Question

Why might the share that different countries have of world trade have changed over time? Does it matter?

■ Comparative advantage

In theory, an economy can be closed and not open to trade. This would mean that it would have to produce all of the products it wanted by itself. In this case production would be restricted by the resources of that one country. However, by engaging in trade it is possible to benefit from the skills and resources of other countries.

The theory of international trade is based on the concept of comparative advantage. Firms in a particular country or region have a comparative advantage in producing particular products if the opportunity cost of producing these products is less than in other regions. When producers in certain industries in one country sacrifice less than firms in other regions then they are relatively efficient at producing these products. This means that they should be able to export them. At the same time, other areas will be more efficient at producing other products, and therefore the first country can buy these in from abroad at a lower price than it could make them itself.

Example

Consider two economies, X and Y, where resources are split equally between the two products A and B. In these economies the outputs produced are as in Table 31.1, and so this two-country economy produces 7 units of A and 3 units of B in total.

Table 31.1 The outputs of two products, A and B, produced by the two countries X and Y.

	Product A (units)	Product B (units)
Country X	4	1
Country Y	3	2
Total	7	3

The opportunity costs show what is being sacrificed to produce 1 unit of A or 1 unit of B. In country X, for example, the country can produce 4 units of A or 1 unit of B, so the opportunity costs of 1 unit of A are $\frac{1}{4}$ unit of B and the opportunity costs of 1 unit of B are 4 units of A. The opportunity costs for countries X and Y are shown in Table 31.2.

Table 31.2 The opportunity costs of producing the products A and B in the two countries X and Y.

	Opportunity costs of 1 unit of A	Opportunity costs of 1 unit of B
Country X	$\frac{1}{4}$ unit of B	4 units of A
Country Y	$\frac{2}{3}$ unit of B	$\frac{3}{2}$ units of A

From Table 31.2 we can see that country X has the lower opportunity cost in the production of A and therefore should specialise in this product. Meanwhile, country Y has the lower opportunity cost when it comes to producing product B and should specialise in this product. If, instead of splitting resources, these economies now put all of their resources into one product then, all other things being equal, output in these products should double.

The production levels would now be as shown in Table 31.3. Compared to the original situation, world output has increased by 1 unit of A and 1 unit of B. Focusing on an industry in which there is a comparative advantage has led to more production of both products.

Table 31.3 The production levels for the products A and B in the two countries X and Y.

	Product A (units)	Product B (units)
Country X	8	0
Country Y	0	4
Total	8	4

The model in the above example assumes constant returns to scale, that is, by doubling the resources in an industry the output doubles. In reality, there may be further gains because, by specialising in one product, the country's firms may be more productive due to economies of scale, and output may more than double (i.e., benefit from increasing returns to scale). This would further increase the benefits of specialisation.

Now you try it

Consider two economies, X and Y, for which the outputs produced of products A and B are as shown in Table 31.4.

Table 31.4 The outputs of two products, A and B, produced by the two countries X and Y.

	Product A (units)	Product B (units)
Country X	6	2
Country Y	2	3
Total	8	5

Calculate the opportunity cost of each product for each country.

Identify which product each country would specialise in and the total output if all of the resources focus on this industry.

What has happened to the world output of A and B as a result of trade?

What do you think?

The model above assumes that resources can move easily from one industry to another. Why might barriers to mobility exist?

▪ Terms of trade

Obviously, in the example above each country ends up specialising in one product, so what is needed to enable them to consume both products is for them to engage in trade. For this to happen it must be cheaper for a country to buy products from abroad than to produce them itself, and it must achieve a profit from exporting the products that it specialises in.

If we consider country Y then it is now specialising in producing product B. Each unit of B has an opportunity cost of $\frac{3}{2}$ units of A. Provided that it can sell its units of B for more than this, its firms will make a profit.

Meanwhile, in country X 1 unit of B costs 4 units of A to produce; provided that its firms and households can buy units of B for less than this, it will be beneficial to trade.

For both countries to benefit from trade 1 unit of B must sell for more than $\frac{3}{2}$ units of A, but less than 4 units of A, that is,

$\frac{3}{2}$ units of A < 1 unit of B < 4 units of A.

The following are known as the terms of trade.

- Provided that 1 unit of B costs more than $\frac{3}{2}$ units of A then country Y will be willing to export because it will make a profit from selling them.

- Provided that 1 unit of B costs less than 4 units of A then country X will be willing to import because this is cheaper than it could produce this product itself.

For example, possible terms of trade which would prove mutually beneficial for both countries are when 1 unit of B costs the same as 2 units of A. Exporters would make a profit. Importers would benefit from buying from abroad, where the opportunity costs are lower than it would cost to produce it itself.

Now you try it

Calculate the possible terms of trade for the example shown in Table 31.4 for which you calculated the opportunity cost of each product.

Trade is therefore based on the idea that a particular country is likely to be good at some things but not others. By engaging in trade a country can benefit from the skills, abilities and resources of others. Why do something yourself if you can buy it more cheaply from abroad? Free trade should benefit all of those involved.

However, there may be problems caused by specialisation, such as the following, for example.

- Firms may suffer from decreasing returns to scale, in which case the overall world outputs may not gain as much as suggested in Table 31.3.
- Countries may become over-specialised and reliant on a limited number of products. This makes them vulnerable to changes in that market or if there were political problems with other countries supplying key products.

Economics in context   The share of world exports in goods and services

Table 31.5 shows the relative share of exports in different regions of the world and how this has changed between 1993 and 2003.

Table 31.5   The percentage share of world exports in goods and services in 1993 and 2003.

	1993	2003
NAFTA*	23	19
Europe	23	24
Japan	12	8
Brazil, Russia, India and China	10	15
Others	33	34

* NAFTA is the North American Free Trade Area; it is a group of countries, including America and Mexico, that have free trade between each other.
Source: UNICE.

 Question
Why do you think that the changes in world trade shown in Table 31.5 might have happened?

The terms of trade index

The terms of trade index measures the prices of exports compared to the prices of imports. It is usually calculated as follows:

$$\text{Terms of trade index} = \frac{\text{Index of export prices}}{\text{Index of import prices}} \times 100.$$

It shows how many exports can be bought relative to imports. For example, if the average price of exports is £200 and the average price of imports is £100, then one export buys two imports.

An increase in export prices relative to import prices is known as an improvement in the terms of trade. It means that if a product is sold abroad then more imports can be bought in return than before. However, an improvement in the terms of trade does not necessarily mean that it is good for the economy (even though it sounds like it is); this is because if exports are more expensive relative to imports then less may be sold. The balance of trade may worsen.

Now you try it

What are the likely effects of a fall in the terms of trade?

Absolute advantage

Absolute advantage occurs when one country can produce more of one product than another with the same factor inputs, or can produce a product using less resources. If one country has an absolute advantage in product X and another has an absolute advantage in product Y then trade may clearly be beneficial, with each country specialising and trading with the other.

However, even if a country has absolute advantage in all products (e.g., because it was more efficient at producing generally) then trade may still be possible, and indeed beneficial, due to differences in comparative advantage. This theory was developed by Ricardo (1817). For example, America may be more efficient than another country in all products and has an absolute advantage. However, this does not mean that trade cannot be beneficial between the two countries. Although America can produce more, there will still be some product categories where the other country would be relatively more efficient, that is, where it has a lower opportunity cost and a comparative advantage.

Example

Consider two economies X and Y that have split their resources between the two products A and B. From Table 31.6 we can calculate the opportunity costs of producing products A and B in each country (see Table 31.7).

Table 31.6 The outputs of two products, A and B, produced by the two countries X and Y.

	Product A (units)	Product B (units)
Country X	4	8
Country Y	3	2
Total	7	10

Table 31.7 The opportunity costs of producing the products A and B in the two countries X and Y.

	Opportunity costs of 1 unit of A	Opportunity costs of 1 unit of B
Country X	2 units of B	$\frac{1}{2}$ unit of A
Country Y	$\frac{2}{3}$ unit of B	$\frac{3}{2}$ units of A

Country X has comparative advantage in the production of product B and country Y has comparative advantage in the production of product A. Country X could buy in units of A from abroad for cheaper than it could produce these products itself. Country Y could buy in units of B from abroad for cheaper than it could produce these products itself.

Even though country X could produce more of both goods, trade is still beneficial due to comparative advantage.

What do you think?

What do you think the terms of trade might be in the example above?

■ The balance of payments

The balance of payments records all transactions between one country and the rest of the world.

A balance of payments surplus means that a country's revenue from exports is greater than its spending on imports. This leads to extra demand in the economy because more money is coming in from abroad than is being spent on foreign products. A balance of payments deficit means that a country's export revenue is less than its import spending. This leads to less demand in the economy because less money is coming in from abroad than is being spent on foreign products.

The balance of payments is made up of a current account and a capital account.

The current account of the balance of payments

The current account records the value of imports and exports of goods and services. It is made up of the following.

- *Visible trade*. This records the value of imports and exports of physical goods. The balance of trade measures the difference between the value of exported goods and the value of imported goods.

- *Invisible trade.* This records the value of imports and exports of:
  - services;
  - interest profits and dividends into and out of the country;
  - the transfer of money, including government grants to developing countries and the EU budget.

The capital account of the balance of payments

The capital account records the inflow and outflow of investments and other financial flows. This includes the following.

- *Long-term capital investments*; for example, money invested in new factories.
- *Short-term capital flows*; for example, deposits in overseas banks (this is money that moves around the world very quickly looking for the best returns—it is called 'hot money').
- *Changes in reserves by a central bank*; for example, when it buys pounds with foreign currency to influence the exchange rate.

■ The balance of payments and exchange rates

Floating exchange rates

In a floating exchange rate system the external value of the currency changes to equate the quantity of pounds supplied to change into foreign currency and the quantity of pounds demanded in exchange for foreign currency. This means that the number of pounds being given up is exactly equal to the number being bought, so overall the balance of payments equals zero. This does not mean that each element is in equilibrium (e.g., there may be a current account deficit and a capital account surplus), but overall the spending in pounds equals the income in pounds and the balance of payments 'balances'. Even so, equilibrium does not mean that there is no cause for concern. If, for example, there is a current account deficit but capital surplus then this may be undesirable even if the overall balance of payments does balance. This is because, although in the short term it leads to a higher standard of living due to more consumption thanks to imports, this is being financed by capital inflows into the country. These represent purchases of UK assets by overseas organisations and will lead to dividends flowing out of the country in the future.

Fixed exchange rates

In a fixed exchange rate system the balance of payments is not necessarily equal to zero. Imagine that the exchange rate is fixed at ER1 in Fig. 31.2. At this exchange rate the number of pounds demanded (Q2) is greater than the number supplied (Q1). There is a balance of payments surplus equal to Q2 – Q1. In a floating exchange rate the external value

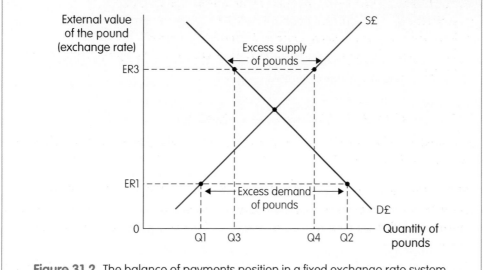

Figure 31.2 The balance of payments position in a fixed exchange rate system.

of the pound would rise. To keep it fixed at ER1 the government must sell pounds to meet the excess demand Q2 − Q1. It will sell pounds in return for foreign currency reserves. This is known as official financing. For example:

Balance of payments surplus = +£300 million,

Official financing = −£300 million (selling pounds).

If the pound is fixed at ER3 (see Fig. 31.2) then there is an excess supply of pounds equal to Q4 − Q3. The quantity supplied exceeds the quantity demanded and there is a balance of payments deficit. In this case, the government buys pounds equal to Q4 − Q3 to prevent the value falling. To buy pounds the government uses its foreign currency reserves. For example:

Balance of payments deficit = −£200 million,

Official financing = +£200 million (buying pounds).

■ A current account deficit on the balance of payments

A current account deficit on the balance of payments means that the value of goods and services exported is less than the value of goods and services imported into a country. This may lead to a fall in the aggregate demand as money is leaking out of the economy (unless the increase in imports is actually caused by an increase in the aggregate demand in the first place). Domestic employment could fall as more imports are purchased.

Economics in context — US current account deficit

In 2006, the US current account deficit was well over $750 billion—a truly staggering amount. This led to downward pressure on the dollar.

? Question

Why might the US have such a massive current account deficit?

If the pound does not fall to rectify the current account deficit then this means that the capital account must be in surplus to balance the balance of payments. This in turn may be due to the following reasons.

- *The central bank is buying currency using foreign exchange reserves*. This is possible in the short run, but in the long run the central bank will run out of foreign exchange reserves and so the value of the currency will have to change.

- *Hot money inflows*. Banks may not be able to lend this money out because it may be withdrawn at any time. Alternatively, the hot money inflows may go into buying UK shares, thereby increasing share prices.

- *Foreign direct investment*. This could create jobs in an economy and bring new technology. The investment may set up companies in the UK that then export and generate export earnings. The increased competition may also help to create greater efficiency domestically. However, the foreign investment may bring competition that destroys jobs domestically. Also, the profits earned in a country are often repatriated to the country of origin and do not remain in the domestic economy.

Economics in context — UK current account

According to the Office of National Statistics:

The UK has had a current account deficit in every year since 1984. Since the last surplus was recorded in 1983, there have been three main phases in the development of the current account. In the first phase, from 1984 to 1989, the current account deficit increased steadily to the record deficit of £26.3 billion recorded in 1989 (equivalent to 5.1% of GDP); during the second phase, from 1990 until 1997, the current account deficit declined to a low of £1.8 billion in 1997; in the third phase, since 1998, the current account deficit widened sharply, to around £22–£24 billion in 1999 to 2001 and £16–£17 billion in 2002 and 2003. A deficit of £23 billion was recorded in 2004, equivalent to 2.0% of GDP.

The profile for the current account has historically followed that of trade in goods, its biggest and most cyclical components. From the last trade in goods surplus recorded in 1982, the goods deficit increased to a peak of £24.7 billion in 1989, while the current balance deteriorated to a record deficit of £26.3 billion. From then until the late 1990s, both the trade in goods and current account deficits fell and then subsequently rose. Since 1999, however, the goods deficit has continued to grow but the current account deficit has stabilised, due to widening surpluses on trade in services and investment income.

When ranking individual countries by the size of the current account balance in 2004, the largest surpluses were recorded with: the United States of America (£17.1 billion), Ireland (£6.0 billion), Netherlands (£3.8 billion), Australia (£3.4 billion) and Saudi Arabia (£1.2 billion).

The largest current account deficit was with Germany, with imports of goods exceeding exports of goods (by £13.4 billion) being partly offset by a surplus on trade in services (£1.4 billion). The deficits with China, Norway and France are all a result of trading deficits. A trade in services deficit, mainly due to tourist travel expenditure, is the main factor in the balance with Spain. The remaining deficits are largely due to high levels of UK imports of goods from these nations.

? Questions

Why might the UK have a current account deficit?

Why does it have a surplus with some countries?

▨ Curing a current account deficit

To remove a current account deficit a government may do the following.

- *Use demand-switching policies.* This involves methods of protecting domestic firms from foreign competition, so that consumers switch to domestic firms. This should reduce the value of imports relative to exports. However, protectionism may not be possible (e.g., within the European Union) or may lead to retaliation.

- *Use demand-reducing policies.* This involves policies to reduce the total spending in the economy (e.g., by increasing taxes). With less demand there will be less spending on imports. However, these policies also lead to less spending on domestic products, which can slow the growth of the economy.

- *Use supply side policies.* These policies, such as training schemes and incentives to invest in research and development, should help domestic firms to become more competitive internationally and therefore export more.

- *Allow the exchange rate to fall.* There may be downward pressure on the currency anyway due to less demand for exports, or the government can intervene to reduce the value of the currency (e.g., by lowering interest rates). If the currency depreciates then this should make exports relatively cheaper in foreign currencies and imports relatively more expensive in pounds. This should encourage exports and reduce the volume of imports. However, the precise effect in terms of spending depends on the price elasticity of demand for imports and exports, and may need time to take effect.

Now you try it

Explain how the government might reduce demand in the economy.

What do you think?

Do you think that demand-switching policies or demand-reducing policies would be more politically acceptable?

Economics in context   The fall in the peso

In 2002, Argentina experienced a 70% fall in the value of its currency (the peso) after ending a policy of fixing it to the US dollar. This sent the prices of imported goods soaring, causing cost-push inflation. It also boosted demand for home-grown products, leading to demand-pull inflation. This highlights the dangers of a depreciating currency and the fact that, whilst it may make exports cheaper, it also makes imports more expensive, which can cause economic problems.

❓ **Question**

What are the problems caused by inflation?

▣ Protectionism

Despite the apparent benefits of free trade, not all governments believe in it or believe that it is always appropriate. There are often instances when governments try to restrict trade. This is known as protectionism. Protectionism occurs when governments try to protect their domestic firms from foreign competition. It prevents free trade and introduces barriers to trade.

The methods of protectionism include the following.

- *Tariffs*. These are taxes placed on selected goods and services from overseas. The tax revenue raised from tariffs goes to the government that placed them on overseas products.

- *Quotas*. These are limits placed on the number of products from a particular country. For example, a limit might be placed on the number of sales or the market share of new cars from a foreign country.

- *Legal restrictions*. A country may impose certain regulations or standards on products from abroad to make it more difficult for them to be allowed in.

- *Voluntary export restraints (VERs)*. These are agreements negotiated between governments to restrict exports.

Why do governments protect domestic firms?

Given the arguments for free trade, the idea of protectionism may seem odd. However, the reasons why a government may protect its domestic firms include the following.

- A government may want to retaliate against the protectionist measures of other governments.
- A government may want to protect industries that are regarded as strategically important. A government may target certain defence industries or food producers and protect these in case of times of emergency.
- A government may want to enable small and new firms to grow and benefit from the economies of scale and experience that might be needed to compete worldwide. This is called the infant industry argument.
- A government may want to protect certain selected industries to keep jobs safe within them and protect a way of life (e.g., agriculture).
- A government may want to protect jobs if a particular industry is struggling.

What do you think?
Do you think that protecting a domestic industry is the right thing to do if it is struggling?

The appeal of protectionism

Protectionism is quite popular politically because a government is seen to be taking action to protect domestic firms. Domestic producers often organise themselves into effective lobbying groups to influence government policy and try to bring about measures that will safeguard them from foreign competition. As comparative advantage changes over time, certain industries may be particularly affected and there may be high levels of unemployment in these industries as they struggle against worldwide competitors. Over time individuals will be able to transfer to other industries or retrain, but in the short term unemployment could be high. Governments, particularly if they are coming up to an election, may protect these industries to keep these people in work.

The stakeholder group that suffers most from protectionism is the consumer; consumers end up paying higher prices for goods and services that are being provided by inefficient domestic producers. However, consumers are from individual households and tend to have little effective representation in government; therefore they are less likely to influence government policy than the well-organised producers.

Economics in context | Concessions for poorer countries

In 2005, Tony Blair, the UK Prime Minister, urged America and the EU to stop protecting their own interests and make concessions to help poorer countries. A 1% additional share of global exports, for example, would generate $70 billion (£40 billion) for Africa. According to Blair, 'Self-interest and mutual interest are inextricably linked. National interests can best be advanced through collective action.' He pointed out that the previous Uruguay round of trade talks generated $500 billion (£286 billion) per year in international trade and a new agreement that cuts trade barriers by one-third could boost the world economy by $600 billion (£343 billion).

 Question

How can 'self-interest and mutual interest be inextricably linked'?

■ The World Trade Organization

The World Trade Organization (WTO) is an international body whose purpose is to promote free trade by persuading countries to abolish import tariffs and other barriers. The WTO oversees the rules of international trade. It monitors free trade agreements, settles trade disputes between governments and establishes trade negotiations. WTO decisions are absolute, and so, when the US and the European Union are disagreeing over products such as bananas or beef, the WTO decides. The WTO was set up in 1995 and is based in Geneva. It replaced the General Agreement on Tariffs and Trade (GATT). WTO agreements cover goods and services, such as telecommunications and banking, as well as other issues, such as intellectual property rights. The membership of the WTO now stands at 149 countries. China joined in December 2001.

 Web

For more information on the World Trade Organization you can visit **www.wto.org**

The effect of tariffs

In Fig. 31.3 the world price for the product is shown at a given level P1. Consumers in the country can buy as much as they want at this price on the world market. The result is that the quantity Q1 is demanded and bought. Of this, the domestic supply curve shows that at this price domestic firms can supply the quantity Q2. No more can be supplied domestically because at this price local suppliers cannot cover their costs at quantities beyond Q2. The quantity Q1 – Q2 is therefore imported from other countries. If the government now imposes a tariff on the product then this will raise the price to P2. This means that domestic suppliers can now produce Q4. With the higher price more local suppliers can

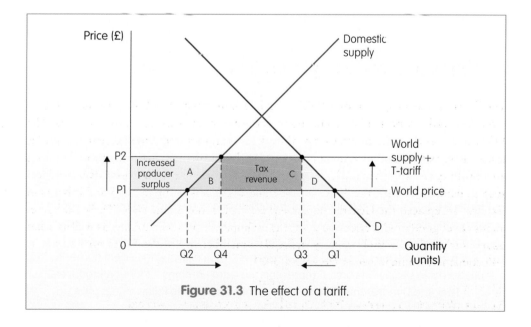

Figure 31.3 The effect of a tariff.

cover their costs and afford to supply. With the higher price the quantity demanded falls to Q3. This means that the quantity imported falls to Q3 – Q4.

The results of introducing the tariff are as follows.

- Consumers pay a higher price and buy less.
- The government earns a tax revenue, represented in Fig. 31.3 by the area C.
- Inefficient domestic producers who could not supply at the old price are able to produce at the higher price. The area B in Fig. 31.3 represents the money paid to keep inefficient domestic producers in business.
- There is more producer surplus (equal to the area A in Fig. 31.3) for local producers. This represents earnings over and above the price they needed to supply.
- The area D in Fig. 31.3 represents a loss of consumer surplus; these units were consumed before the tariff and this area shows consumers' utility over and above the price, that is, consumer surplus that is now lost.

What do you think?

Who wins and who loses from the introduction of a tariff?

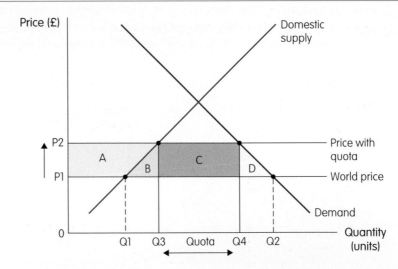

Figure 31.4 The effect of a quota. The imposition of a quota Q4 – Q3 on foreign goods increases the price of the product from P1 to P2. The area A represents the increased producer surplus for domestic producers. The area B represents the money paid to keep inefficient domestic producers in business, thus allowing inefficient domestic producers to supply. The area C represents the extra earnings for foreign producers. The area D represents the loss of consumer surplus due to the higher price.

The effects of quotas

In Fig. 31.4 there is a limit of Q3 – Q4 on the number of products sold in the country. This quantity will only be demanded if the price is P2, which is above the world price. The producer surplus of domestic producers has now increased by area A. Domestic customers have less products at a higher price in comparison to the equilibrium price and output.

The effects of subsidies

One form of protectionism is to subsidise domestic producers. This is shown in Fig. 31.5. The result is that more domestic producers can now supply the product. At the world price of P1 the quantity that domestic producers can supply increases from Q2 to Q4. The government is enabling inefficient producers to compete. The amount of subsidy paid by the government is equal to ABCP1. To finance the subsidies the government will have to raise revenue—for example, by raising taxes—which may have a negative impact on other sectors of the economy. The effect of the subsidy is to reduce imports by Q2 – Q4; the world price remains unchanged at P1.

> **What do you think?**
>
> Should governments protect their domestic firms?
> Assuming that governments should protect their firms, what do you think is the best way of doing this?

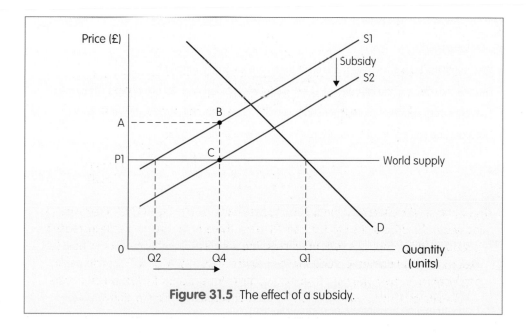

Figure 31.5 The effect of a subsidy.

Case Study

In 1999, the US government and the European Union engaged in the banana trade war. In retaliation for what it thought was unfair competition in bananas, the US imposed sanctions on a range of EU exports of luxury products, such as cashmere jumpers and handbags.

The argument was over imports of bananas into the European Union. The US felt that the EU favoured its former colonies and that this made it difficult for Latin American producers to compete. The UK and France, for example, had agreements with former colonies in Africa and the Caribbean that gave their banana producers preferential treatment. The Latin American products were marketed by US multinationals.

In 1993, the EU introduced a new banana import policy that removed trade tariffs on selected countries and gave them guaranteed quotas. The Latin American growers faced tariffs on their exports to the EU and received no quota guarantees.

The US applied to the World Trade Organisation to introduce sanctions that would amount to 100% taxes on many EU goods. This had an immediate effect on EU exports.

The dispute was finally settled in 2001.

More recently, the US and the EU argued over the extent to which the aircraft producers Boeing and Airbus were being protected. The EU claimed that Boeing, an American producer, received favourable treatment and very generous contracts from the American authorities. The US, meanwhile, claimed that Airbus, a European company, was subsidised by the EU. Airbus received 'repayable launch aid' from European taxpayers. This meant that it could develop new aircraft knowing that if it did not sell them then it would not have to pay the money back. In the case of the enormous A380, this amounted to $3.7 billion (£2 billion or €3 billion). As for Boeing, Airbus alleged that the firm's generous contracts from the American military amounted to a subsidy. These claims and counter-claims came at a crucial time when both firms were in fierce competition. Both the US and the EU protested to the World Trade Organisation. If one of them was found guilty of unfair competition then the other would be allowed to retaliate.

? Questions

- Why might the EU want to give preferential treatment to some countries?

- Discuss the effects of the introduction of significant levels of tariffs on EU luxury products by the US.

- To what extent can protectionist measures, such as those of the EU, ever be justified?

- Does anyone win in a trade war such as the Boeing and Airbus dispute?

Checklist

Now you have read this unit try to answer the following questions.

☐   Can you explain the theory of international trade?

☐   Can you explain the elements of the balance of payments?

☐   Can you outline possible types of protectionism?

☐   Are you able to analyse why governments might protect industries?

☐   Are you able to examine the possible consequences of protectionism?

End of unit questions

1   What is meant by free trade?

2   What are the opportunity costs of subsidies?

3   Is free trade a good thing?

4   Who benefits from tariffs?

5   Is protectionism ever acceptable?

Key learning points

- International trade is based on the principle of comparative advantage.

- International trade enables countries to benefit from more efficient production overseas; this can lead to more consumption and lower prices domestically.

- Protectionism can take several forms, such as tariffs, quotas and legislation.

- Protectionism can encourage inefficiency and lead to less consumption and higher prices for consumers.

Reference

Ricardo, D. (1817). *On the principles of political economy and taxation*. John Murray, London.

Learn more

To learn more about the UK balance of payments over time visit our website at the address below.

 Visit our Online Resource Centre at www.oxfordtextbooks.co.uk/orc/gillespie_econ for test questions and further information on topics covered in this chapter.

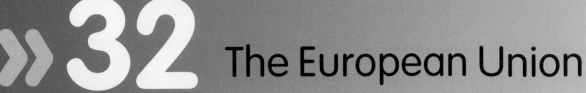

»32 The European Union

One key factor in UK trade nowadays is the European Union. Over the years this group of countries has grown in size and importance. This unit explains what is meant by the European Union and considers the benefits and disadvantages of the UK being a member.

LEARNING OBJECTIVES

By the end of this unit you should be able to:

✔ outline the key elements of the European Union;

✔ examine the benefits of belonging to the European Union;

✔ consider the issues involved in joining the euro.

▮ The European Union (EU)

The European Union (EU) is a group of countries that have joined together to form a customs union. It was created with six members in 1957, but has grown in numbers ever since. The EU is now the largest single market in the world and accounted for 40% of global trade in 2004. There are over 450 million people in this market from EU businesses.

A customs union means the following.

• Within the customs union there is free trade, that is, there are no barriers to trade, such as tariffs and quotas. Standards within the EU have been agreed between member states so that if a product can be sold in one country then it can also be sold in another member country. There do not have to be changes made to the product and no additional taxes can be placed on it.

• Member countries must stick to common agreed tariffs (taxes) placed on products from non-member countries.

The UK joined the EU in 1973 and, as the fifth largest economy in the world, it is obviously a key member. Over half of the UK's trade is with other EU countries and the government estimates that over three million jobs are linked to exports to EU members. Around 100 000 Britons work in other EU countries, and another 350 000 live in those countries.

 The growth of the European Union

By 2007, there were twenty-seven members of the EU, with more eager to join. The history of when they joined is as follows:

1958: Belgium, France, Germany, Italy, Luxembourg, The Netherlands;

1973: Denmark, Ireland, United Kingdom;

1981: Greece;

1986: Portugal, Spain;

1995: Austria, Finland, Sweden;

2004: Cyprus, The Czech Republic, Estonia, Hungary, Latvia, Lithuania, Malta, Poland, Slovakia, Slovenia;

2007: Bulgaria, Romania.

? Question

Do you know which countries now want to join the EU? Would you let them?

The advantages to the UK of being within the EU are as follows.

- Being within the EU makes it easier for UK firms to access customers in other European markets. UK firms may therefore be able to sell more products. Given that standards are agreed across the Union, UK firms are not forced to change their product for each market to meet different regulations; this makes it possible to have longer production runs and possibly gain from economies of scale.
- UK firms and households have easier access to products from other member countries. This may enable firms to find cheaper and better quality supplies and have more choice.
- There are lower costs due to the removal of technical and administrative barriers. Trade within the Union becomes easier, which should encourage investment.
- Greater competition within the EU stimulates competition and efficiency; UK firms can learn from their competitors.
- The UK can benefit from the skills, expertise and comparative advantage of other nations more easily.

  Joining a customs union can lead to trade creation and trade diversion.

- *Trade creation.* This occurs when firms and consumers can switch from higher-cost producers to lower-cost producers. With the removal of tariffs, UK firms could get supplies within the Union more cheaply than they could buy them before from anywhere in the world.

- *Trade diversion*. This occurs when firms and households switch from a lower-cost producer outside the union to a higher-cost producer within it. This can happen because of tariffs placed on non-union members that raise the price of their products. It may now be cheaper to switch to firms within the union, even though those outside were cheaper before the tariff.

Enlargement of the European Union

The EU has grown considerably since it was first created and it continues to grow in size. In 2004 the number of countries in the EU increased from fifteen to twenty-five. The surface area of the EU increased by around 25% and its population increased by one-fifth, to 450 million. In 2007, two more countries joined.

EU enlargement offers:

- more customers to sell to;
- more suppliers to buy from;
- cheaper sources of labour.

However, some UK firms are concerned about:

- the increased competition from low-cost producers;
- the potential increased tax burden—the average GDP per head of the new member countries in 2004 was about 40% of the average level in the existing fifteen EU member states.

There is also concern from some more established EU economies, such as the UK, that immigration from these countries places a burden on their economies; for example, in terms of the impact on their health and education systems. For this reason most of the existing EU members have placed restrictions on immigration in the short term. However, a European Commission report a couple of years after the EU enlargement stated that new workers from states which joined the EU in 2004 boosted the growth of economies where immigration had been allowed (such as the UK). The workers from countries such as Poland and The Czech Republic had made a positive contribution and brought valuable skills. Their willingness to work for relatively low wages also contributed to keeping inflation relatively low.

Economics in context   Immigration into the UK

About 600 000 people came to work in the UK from eight nations that joined the European Union in 2004 within the first two years of them becoming members, according to the Home Office. Around 447 000 people from Poland and seven other new EU states applied to work in the UK, but the Home Office said that the figure was nearer to 600 000 if self-employed workers, such as builders, were included.

The top ten migrant jobs in the UK in 2005 are shown in Fig. 32.1.

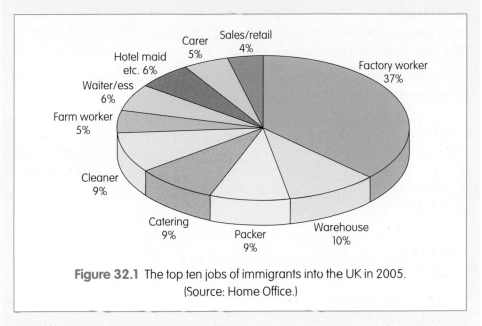

Figure 32.1 The top ten jobs of immigrants into the UK in 2005.
(Source: Home Office.)

? Question

Why might there be opposition to this migration?

What do you think?

Is the UK likely to benefit or suffer in the long term from the accession of ten new countries to the EU in 2004, or the two in 2007? What about if more countries join?

Now you try it

Would you accept any country that wants to join into the EU? Why? Or why not?

■ European Union institutions

Being a member of the EU involves agreeing to European regulations and directives and being accountable to European institutions.

The main institutions within the EU are as follows.

- *The European Commission.* This consists of commissioners appointed by each member state; they propose new policies and administer existing policies.

- *The European Council of Ministers*. This is made up of ministers from member countries. The Council receives proposals from the European Commission and can decide on all EU issues.
- *The European Parliament*. Members of the European Parliament are elected within their own countries. The Parliament discusses proposals from the Commission.

Being a member of the EU also involves agreeing to common economic policies between member states, such as the following.

- *The Common Agricultural Policy (CAP)*. This sets prices for food produced within the EU and places tariffs on imports (see the next section).
- *The EU's Monopoly and Restrictive Practices Policy*. EU competition policy applies primarily to companies operating in more than one member state. Article 85 prohibits agreements between firms, such as overpricing, that adversely affect competition in trade between member states.

Common Agricultural Policy (CAP)

The Common Agricultural Policy (CAP) is a central part of the EU. Its objectives, according to the Treaty of Rome in 1957, are:

- to increase productivity in the agricultural sector;
- to stabilise agricultural markets;
- to provide food at reasonable prices;
- to ensure the availability of food.

The CAP began operating in 1962, buying up food when the price fell below a set target level. This soon led to beef and butter mountains. The CAP also involved taxes on imported agricultural goods. The effect of minimum prices and protectionism against foreign farmers has led to very high food prices in Europe and this has created pressure for reform. Up until 1992 the scheme focused on price support; the more farmers produced, the more they received. From 1992 onwards there was a move to separate payments from production. Farmers were now paid for set aside, that is, for setting aside land rather than producing on it. In 1995, the EU also started paying rural development aid, designed to diversify the rural economy and make farms more competitive. Additional reforms in 2003 and 2004 further 'decoupled' subsidies from production levels and linked payments to food safety, animal welfare and environmental standards. Three areas—sugar, wine, fruit and vegetables—have yet to be reformed. Further reform of the dairy sector is planned after 2014.

The CAP accounts for a significant proportion of the EU budget (e.g., 46% in 2005), though this proportion has been falling for several years. Most of the CAP money goes to the biggest farmers: large agribusinesses and big landowners. The sugar company Tate and Lyle was the largest recipient of CAP funds in the UK in 2005, earning £127 million (€186 million). It has been calculated that 80% of the funds in 2005 went to just 20% of EU

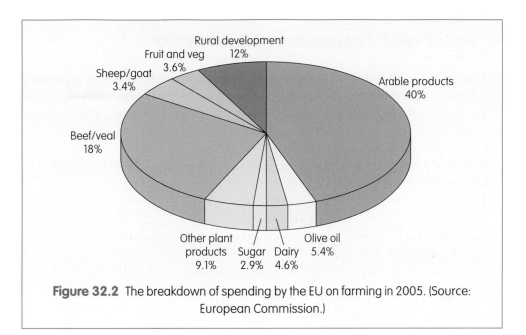

Figure 32.2 The breakdown of spending by the EU on farming in 2005. (Source: European Commission.)

farmers; meanwhile, at the other end of the scale, 40% of farmers shared just 8% of the funds. The spending by the EU on farming is shown in Fig. 32.2.

With regard to the benefits of the CAP, only 5% of EU citizens—ten million people—work in agriculture, and the sector generates just 1.6% of the EU GDP. However, it is claimed that:

- the CAP guarantees the survival of rural areas and communities—where more than half of EU citizens live;
- the CAP maintains the look of the countryside and a way of life;
- many farms would be unprofitable if EU subsidies were withdrawn.

■ The future of the European Union

One vision of the EU is that it should be an economic arrangement, continuing to offer free trade to its members but little else. However, others think that the EU should aim to be more than just an economic union and should also integrate closely in the areas of political and social policy. The nature of the relationship between countries is still being debated. In June 2004, a European Constitution was put forward to be voted on by member countries. This brought together many treaties and agreements that already existed, but some countries felt that it was also extending the power of Europe too much. This needed the agreement of all countries, but was rejected in France and The Netherlands, which put the proposal on hold.

■ The single European currency: the euro

The 'euro' is a currency that has been adopted by several EU members. It was introduced on 1 January 1999, with the notes and coins being released at midnight on 31 December 2001, when national currencies started to be withdrawn from circulation. The transition period was needed to allow time to print the thirteen billion banknotes and produce the fifty-two billion euro coins that went into circulation.

In 1997, the UK government set out five tests that would have to be met before the UK would join the euro. These were:

- that UK and European economies were converging, so that, for example, one interest rate would suit all countries;
- that the economies were flexible enough to cope if things went wrong;
- that joining the euro would encourage companies to invest in the UK;
- that joining the euro would be good for financial services;
- that joining the euro would be good for jobs.

   There is still debate over whether these criteria have been met.
   The advantages of being a member of the euro include the following.

- Firms and households do not need to change currency when visiting or trading with another euro country. This saves on transaction costs (e.g., the fee paid to change currency), which should lead to lower prices for consumers.
- It becomes easier to plan ahead. If the exchange rate is constantly changing then managers and households cannot be certain of the value of a pound; they will not know what they will get when they change their currency to go on holiday, or when they want to buy products from abroad. Equally, they will not know what the price of the products they want to sell abroad will be in terms of the foreign currency. This can add further risk to any spending or investment decision, which may prevent the decision from being made. Within the 'eurozone', all other things being unchanged, the price is more predictable, which makes trading easier and less uncertain.
- It becomes easier to compare prices. This is known as 'price transparency'. If a firm is searching for possible supplies in several countries with different currencies then managers will have to convert the prices into pounds and try to estimate possible changes in the future. It is simpler to operate and choose a supplier if the prices are all in the same currency.
- Competition between firms in the member countries will be greater because of price transparency. This may lead to greater efficiency, which should lead to a better use of resources and an outward shift of the aggregate supply.
- There may be less need to control inflation domestically. If the UK had higher inflation than other countries then this would automatically affect its price competitiveness (it

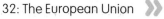

cannot be offset by a fall in the external value of the currency). This is likely to make it harder to export, which dampens demand and therefore brings inflation down again in line with other countries.

- It creates the possibility of internal economies of scale. With trade being easier due to prices being easier to predict, this could lead to higher outputs and internal economies of scale, thereby reducing unit costs.

The disadvantages of joining the euro include the following.

- *One-off changeover costs*. Changing the currency from pounds to euros would inevitably incur costs as brochures have to be rewritten, price lists updated and vending machines changed to accept new coins.

- *One-off inflationary effects*. These are likely to happen because, when changing prices, firms are likely to round up rather than down!

- *Emotional costs*. Some people are attached to their national currency and see this as a sign of independence and heritage. Changing to the euro is sometimes resisted on the basis of national pride rather than economics.

- *Loss of economic policy control*. The value of the euro will be influenced by changes in the levels of interest rates within those member countries. Decisions about interest rates must therefore be made in terms of the 'right' rate of the euro for all countries involved. At any particular moment, what is right for the euro members as a whole may not be right for a particular member; for example, a weak euro may stimulate demand generally within the zone but cause problems in an area where there is already demand-pull inflation. By joining the euro, the UK government and people would have to accept that interest rate decisions would be less UK-focused and more eurozone-focused. Interest rates are set by the European Central Bank (ECB) and not the Bank of England. The ECB is the central bank for Europe's single currency, the euro. The ECB's main task is to maintain price stability in the euro area; it would not focus specifically on the UK's economic position.

Economics in context Members of the euro currency in 2006

The euro members in 2006 were Austria, Belgium, Denmark, Finland, France, Germany, Greece, Ireland, Italy, Luxembourg, The Netherlands, Portugal and Spain.

 Question

Why do you think the UK has not joined the euro?

The following article was taken from the Foreign and Commonwealth Office website in 2006 (www.fco.gov.uk).

How can the EU deliver economic leadership?

From its founding treaties, the European Union has always recognised the interdependence of peace, economic prosperity and social cohesion. This is a vision wholly shared by the UK government. There is much to envy about US capitalism: productivity in America is significantly higher than in most European countries; innovation and risk investment is consistently higher. Global economic conditions have been difficult for the last five years, but growth rates across Europe (stuck at around two per cent) have not matched those in the US (3.5 per cent) or significant parts of Asia. Twenty million people in the EU are unemployed, and in particular nearly a fifth of Europe's young people are without work. Europe's population is ageing. Most countries face some kind of crisis in their pension provision. The single market demands some core (and high) labour standards to ensure a level playing field. But we also need to be sure that any pan-European legislation is working to support business in wealth creation rather than stifling it.

Such observations often invoke a debate about competing European social models, about a clash between Anglo-Saxon free market liberalism and a more interventionist continental European approach. This is a false contrast. There is no disagreement about the need for state intervention: as UK prime minister Tony Blair has remarked, the EU is fundamentally a political project. The question is only about where that intervention can be most effective. The 2004 Kok report (written by former Dutch Prime Minister Wim Kok) highlighted clearly what needs to be done. In the face of the rapid ascent of the Chinese and Indian economies, Europe needs to be investing in its skills, its capability to innovate, and its productivity. Some actions are clearly best handled at a European level, for instance the development of a pan-European patent reducing the cost and bureaucracy faced by European inventors. Other actions will largely be an issue for national governments. Investment in regeneration and education, for example, fall into this category. However, even then, it will be important to look at how we can use EU funding and institutions to support governments in these efforts. And our choices should be governed by the need to support retraining, new skills and entrepreneurial opportunism rather than pour money into unsustainable sectors for short-term political advantage. A high degree of social provision has become one of the core defining characteristics of the European tradition. Economic reform is about having the means to achieve that provision.

 Questions

- According to the article, what problems or challenges are there within the EU?

- What does it suggest are the priorities for the EU in the future? Do you agree?

- To what extent should policies be left to national governments and to what extent should they be determined at the European level?

- Do you think that closer integration within the EU is a good thing?

Checklist

Now you have read this unit try to answer the following questions.

☐ Can you outline the key elements of the European Union?

☐ Can you examine the benefits of belonging to the European Union?

☐ Are you able to consider the issues involved in joining the euro?

End of unit questions

1 What is meant by the European Union?

2 Why do countries want to join the European Union?

3 Should the European Union keep on growing in size? Should the UK join the euro?

4 Should the European Union intervene to maintain the price of foodstuffs above the equilibrium price?

5 Is EU enlargement a good thing for the UK?

Key learning points

- The European Union offers opportunities and threats to member countries. It offers more customers to sell to, but also more competition.

- The euro is a single currency used by most member countries that removes the problem and cost of converting currency.

Learn more

To learn more about the performance of the European Union and the UK's relationship with it visit our website at the address below.

 Visit our Online Resource Centre at **www.oxfordtextbooks.co.uk/orc/gillespie_econ** for test questions and further information on topics covered in this chapter.

»33 Developing economies

A very important world issue is that of developing econ-omies. The inequality in income and wealth distribution between countries is huge and a growing concern. This is now a big issue on the political agenda. This unit focuses on less-developed economies and the problems that these economies face.

LEARNING OBJECTIVES

By the end of this unit you should be able to:

✔ outline the features of less-developed countries;

✔ discuss how less-developed countries could increase their incomes.

▪ Introduction

Although there are some very wealthy individuals and some countries that have high incomes, the majority of the world's population actually live in poverty. This is because many people live in what are called 'less-developed countries'. There is growing aware-ness of and interest in this as a political issue, with many pressure groups trying to get gov-ernments to take more action to help these economies. According to the International Monetary Fund:

Despite progress in recent decades, the extreme poverty prevalent in low-income countries is a critical problem facing the global community. At present, more than a billion people are living on less than $1 a day. More than three-quarters of a billion people are malnourished—about a fifth of them children. One-hundred and sixteen of every 1000 children born in low-income countries die before reaching the age of five, the majority from malnutrition or disease that is readily pre-ventable in high-income countries.

■ Less-developed countries (LDCs)

There are many debates over how to decide on what is and what is not a less-developed country (LDC). One way is to focus on the average income per person and define an LDC as one where the average income is low. Other analysts include non-monetary indicators, such as life expectancy and literacy. Whatever the measure, it is clear that most of the world's population actually live in a less-developed country, whilst most of the world's income and wealth is generated and owned by developed economies. Income and wealth are therefore distributed very unevenly across the world. This has led some pressure groups to demand that developing economies are given more help by developed countries. However, even if you accept the benefits of doing this, there is still much debate about the best way of doing it.

 Economics in context — **Less-developed countries**

There are currently fifty least-developed countries on the United Nations list, thirty-two of which to date have become World Trade Organization (WTO) members. These are: Angola, Bangladesh, Benin, Burkina Faso, Burundi, Cambodia, Central African Republic, Chad, Congo, Democratic Republic of the Djibouti, Gambia, Guinea, Guinea Bissau, Haiti, Lesotho, Madagascar, Malawi, Maldives, Mali, Mauritania, Mozambique, Myanmar, Nepal, Niger, Rwanda, Senegal, Sierra Leone, Solomon Islands, Tanzania, Togo, Uganda and Zambia.

Eight other least-developed countries are in the process of accession to the WTO. They are: Bhutan, Cape Verde, Ethiopia, Laos, Samoa, Sudan, Vanuatu and Yemen.

❓ Question

Why might these countries want to join the World Trade Organization?

■ What are the features of less-developed countries?

Of course, not all LDCs are the same. For example, whilst some have stagnant economies, others are growing fast; these are often called newly industrialising countries (NICs).

However, many less-developed countries exhibit the following features.

- *High population growth rates*. For example, birth control is not widely used in many developing countries, so the birth rate is high. Children are often seen as a way of providing for the future and so large families are encouraged. Parents want more children and grandchildren to look after them when they are older. If the national income is not growing at the same rate as the population then the average income per person will fall.

- *A lack of natural resources* (such as oil and minerals) *to export abroad*. Having said this, the link between natural resources and national income is not always clear cut.

Japan does not have many natural resources and yet has a relatively high standard of living. Brazil has many resources, but the average income is much lower than Japan.

- *A lack of financial capital and investment.* A poor track record of investment means that there is limited capital stock and this reduces productivity. Industries remain labour-intensive. The focus in these economies is on day-to-day consumption rather than investment for the future; this thereby limits future growth. This is, in part, due to the lack of a sophisticated financial system (e.g., the lack of a well-developed banking system) and the lack of financial capital.

- *A lack of training and investment in human capital.* Employees in developing economies are often poorly educated and lack many skills, with the result that they are not very productive.

- *Poor health.* Low income levels mean that living and working conditions are poor. This affects the health of the workforce, which in turn affects its ability to work, its productivity and its income.

- *A lack of an effective infrastructure,* such as good roads, good communication systems and reliable energy sources. This makes it harder to produce and to move goods around.

- *Political instability.* This can deter investment from outside as investors worry that their money will be lost.

- *Export dependence.* Several LDCs rely on a single product for the vast majority of their export earnings, which makes them vulnerable to changes in market conditions.

■ Problems of less-developed countries

Some LDCs have specialised in the production of primary products, such as agricultural goods and minerals. Land is often the most abundant resource in a less-developed country. According to the law of comparative advantage, these economies should focus on production systems where land is a key factor, such as cotton or coffee. The problem with this approach is that technology has reduced the demand for some of these commodities (e.g., due to the development of man-made fabrics rather than cotton). Also, the supply of commodities has increased due to technological advances (e.g., better fertilisers have improved the supply of foodstuffs). The result of falling demand and increased supply is a long-run downward trend in the market price.

Now you try it

Using supply and demand analysis examine the consequences of increasing supply and falling demand in a market.

Another problem faced by primary producers is that of price instability. Given that the demand for products such as food is price inelastic, a change in supply and demand can lead to significant swings in price and farmers' earnings (see Fig. 33.1).

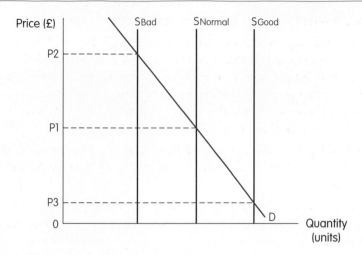

Figure 33.1 Price instability in agricultural markets. Supply and demand are both price inelastic. A shift in either one affects price more than output. Supply is particularly likely to shift with agricultural products due to good and bad harvests. When there is a bad harvest the equilibrium price increases to P2. In a good year the price falls to P3. The price fluctuates greatly with shifts in supply. Notice also how the revenue earned by farmers changes and how it can be higher when less is supplied in comparison to when the harvest is good. With a 'good' harvest the price can fall so much that farmers are actually worse off!

Other problems for LDCs include the following.

- *Low income elasticity.* Many of the products that LDCs produce are income inelastic. This means that demand is growing slower than the world economy, and therefore that these countries may also grow slower than the rest of the world.

- *Buyer power.* The big Western multinationals often dominate the markets for the products of LDCs and can force prices downwards.

- *Protectionism.* Wealthier economies often protect against competition in particular markets that threaten domestic producers.

Economics in context   Human development index

The human development index is a United Nations measure of the development of economies based on factors such as life expectancy, adult literacy rate, schooling and gross domestic product. According to the 2005 report, the top fifteen countries in the world were as shown in Table 33.1.

Table 33.1   The fifteen most developed economies in 2005.

Rank	Country	Rank	Country
1	Norway	9	Belgium
2	Iceland	10	USA
3	Australia	11	Japan
4	Luxembourg	12	Netherlands
5	Canada	13	Finland
6	Sweden	14	Denmark
7	Switzerland	15	UK
8	Ireland		

Source: United Nations Human Development Report, 2005.

? Question

What else would you include in your measure of how developed an economy is?

@ Web

For more information on the United Nations you can visit **www.un.org**

How can less-developed countries increase their income?

The following are several routes that developing economies have chosen to try to boost their income levels.

- *Encouraging foreign direct investment (FDI) into LDC economies*; for example, encouraging overseas firms to set up businesses. This may bring investment and jobs to the economy, but often the profits, in the form of dividends, leave to go to overseas investors and the skilled jobs remain in the hands of foreign staff. Several foreign multinationals have been accused of exploiting the LDCs in which they operate.

- *Debt reduction.* Many LDCs have high levels of debt as they have borrowed from foreign governments and banks over the years. There is a great pressure on Western governments to reduce or cancel this debt. Some argue for a conditional approach whereby reductions are linked to certain criteria being met, such as limits on government spending. An alternative approach, such as that promoted by the Jubilee 2000 campaign, argues for a complete end to the debt.

- *Import substitution.* This approach aims to reduce imports into the country (using protectionist measures such as tariffs or quotas) and therefore encourages buyers to switch to domestic firms. For example, a country may try to build up its manufacturing sector by protecting it for a period of time from outside competition. It may use protectionism to build up an industry to be able to compete worldwide. However, one problem with this approach is that consumers end up paying more for products than they could buy them for from abroad. Also, the country may end up specialising in sectors in which it has a comparative disadvantage (because it can do so due to protectionism), which is inefficient. Industries that are protected often fail to become efficient.

- *Export-led growth*. This approach, adopted by countries such as China, focuses on helping industries to sell more abroad. For example, an economy may try to benefit from a large supply of labour by focusing on labour-intensive industries where it can undercut on price. The problem with this is that developing economies may react by protecting themselves against these economies, and may protect their own industries using protectionism.

- *Borrowing*. This can make sense if the investment is used to generate high returns. However, in many cases the investments have not generated enough returns to pay the interest, leading to further borrowing and worsening the situation of the economy. Many LDCs already have high levels of debt and so more borrowing is either not an option or is too risky.

- *Structural adjustment*. This approach focuses on the way in which resources are being used and attempts to increase efficiency within the economy. It uses supply side measures to increase the potential output of the country. For example, supply side policies might include reducing government subsidies to different industries, privatisation and lower taxation rates. This makes sense, but it takes political will to ensure that such changes are adopted.

▧ The role of foreign aid

Some poorer countries argue that they need more aid from richer countries. Aid can come in many forms, such as money, machines, training, food or loans. The danger is that aid does not sort out the underlying problems; it may simply be a temporary relief rather than helping the economy to fundamentally improve. Furthermore, the benefits of aid may not trickle down into the economy, but remain with a select few. It can also help to maintain governments who may be slow to bring about the changes needed. Thus it is possible that the solution lies, not in aid, but in opening up markets to LDCs; some analysts believe that 'trade not aid' is the key.

> **What do you think?**
>
> Do you think that foreign aid is worthwhile?

Make Poverty History

Make Poverty History is a pressure group that, according to its website, '. . . is a movement of over 500 organisations, including Oxfam, who are working together to demand trade justice, more and better aid, and debt cancellation for the world's poorest countries.' As part of the campaign in 2005, over 200 000 people went to protest in Edinburgh during the G8 (the group of eight leading economies) Summit, over 400 000 people emailed the Prime Minister, and millions of people wore white Make Poverty History wristbands.

? Question
Why should governments listen to pressure groups such as Make Poverty History?

Market access

The key to many of the less-developed countries' problems may indeed lie in free access to world markets. At present many developed economies either limit the sales of less-developed producers to protect their own firms, or impose unfavourable terms of trade so that the majority of the profits from the products go to the wealthier nations. Under the European Union's Common Agricultural Policy, for example, developing economies' products cannot be sold in the EU; this is to protect domestic producers. In addition, the EU dumps excess agricultural products on world markets, reducing the world price and thereby making it more difficult for LDCs to generate high levels of income.

With more open economies, the following would occur.

• LDCs would be able to sell their products abroad and earn more.

• LDC nationals would be able to work abroad and earn income there. Although there has been resistance to this from developed economies who have not wanted immigration (often for political reasons), this may change in the future. This is because, with ageing populations, the more-developed economies will need younger employees and may well look to the LDCs to provide them. If individuals from LDCs were allowed freedom of movement then they could earn more abroad and at the same time create more land per worker at home. In the past there have been very successful major movements of people from one region to another. The history of America is based on migration and even today hundreds of thousands of people travel from Mexico to gain work in America.

The International Monetary Fund (IMF)

The International Monetary Fund (IMF) is an international organisation of 184 member countries. The IMF was established to 'promote international monetary cooperation, exchange stability, and orderly exchange arrangements; to foster economic growth and high levels of employment; and to provide temporary financial assistance to countries to help ease balance of payments adjustment.' The IMF's resources come mainly from the quota subscriptions that member countries pay; this also influences the amount of finance that they can receive. The IMF may, for example, lend to a member country that needs to borrow to help solve a currency crisis. The IMF is not an aid agency or a development bank, and its loans are not linked to particular projects or activities. Lending is made conditional on the country adopting various policies to correct the problems. The country and the IMF have to agree on the policies before the lending occurs. Lending is temporary. The borrowing country must pay back the IMF on schedule, so that the funds are available for lending to other countries that need balance of payments financing.

@ **Web**

For more information on the International Monetary Fund you can visit www.imf.org

■ World Bank

The World Bank provides financial and technical assistance to developing countries. It is made up of two institutions that are owned by 184 member countries—the International Bank for Reconstruction and Development (IBRD) and the International Development Association (IDA). Each institution helps the World Bank in its mission of global poverty reduction and the improvement of living standards. The IBRD focuses on middle-income and creditworthy-poor countries, while the IDA focuses on the poorest countries in the world. The World Bank provides low-interest loans, interest-free credit and grants to developing countries for education, health, infrastructure, communications and a variety of other purposes. According to the World Bank,

> Each borrower's project proposal is assessed to ensure that the project is economically, financially, socially and environmentally sound. During loan negotiations, the bank and borrower agree on the development objectives, outputs, performance indicators and implementation plan, as well as a loan disbursement schedule.

@ **Web**

For more information on the World Bank you can visit www.worldbank.org

■ World Bank and IMF initiatives

In 1996, the World Bank and the IMF launched the HIPC (heavily-indebted poor countries) Initiative to reduce the debt burdens of the world's poorest countries. The scheme provides debt relief for low-income countries that have unsustainable debt burdens; most are in Africa. In these countries, traditional approaches of debt rescheduling, debt reduction and aid may not allow them to reach a 'sustainable' level of external debt, that is, a level of debt that can be serviced comfortably through export earnings, aid and capital inflows, while maintaining an adequate level of imports.

Under the HIPC Initiative,

... debt reduction is provided to support policies that promote economic growth and poverty reduction. Part of the job of the IMF, working in collaboration with the World Bank, is to help ensure that the resources provided by debt reduction are not wasted: debt reduction alone, without the right policies, would bring no benefit in terms of poverty reduction. And policies to reduce poverty need to be supported not only by debt relief, but also by increased aid flows from the richer countries and by improved access for developing countries to industrial countries' markets.

The reforms that they have to undertake often include privatisations of industries. By 2005, nearly forty countries had started programmes under the HIPC Initiative.

Economics in context   **The International Monetary Fund**

In 1997, there was a major crisis in Asian economies. The IMF and the World Bank advised and provided funds for countries involved in this crisis. Similarly, when Argentina experienced a financial crisis in 2001 and defaulted on its debt, the IMF negotiated a new loan package. The IMF can also grant emergency loans following natural disasters, such as the 2004 Asian tsunami.

 Question

Do you think that loans are an effective way of helping less-developed countries?

What do you think?

Should Western governments give more aid to benefit less-developing countries?
How much aid would be an appropriate amount?

Case Study

In 2006, a deadlock was reached in the Doha round of world trade talks. After five years of negotiation and debate, disagreement over agricultural subsidies and tariffs led to the suspension of trade talks in Geneva. The EU and the US could not agree and both felt that the other was at fault. The head of the World Trade Organization stated that, whilst developing countries would be worst hit by a failure in trade talks, European consumers would also be affected because prices would be higher than necessary.

The key issue was how much the US and the EU were willing to reduce their barriers to agricultural exports from developing countries, including subsidies and tariffs. In return, rich countries wanted the larger developing countries, such as Brazil and India, to reduce their barriers to imports of manufactured goods.

The US and the EU faced strong resistance to any reduction in barriers from their own agricultural sectors. The US blamed the EU for being too inflexible, and vice versa; the developing countries believed that the developed nations were not serious about freeing up trade.

The danger of the failure to arrive at a common agreement is that individual countries will negotiate deals amongst themselves.

❓ Questions

- Why do you think that the developed nations seem to be reluctant to reduce trade barriers?
- What would be the effect of freer trade on the developing and developed nations?
- Why might it be dangerous if individual countries negotiated deals amongst themselves?
- Can protectionism ever be desirable?

Checklist

Now you have read this unit try to answer the following questions.

☐ Can you outline the features of less-developed countries?

☐ Are you able to discuss how less-developed countries could increase their incomes?

End of unit questions

1 What is meant by a less-developed country?

2 Do you think that developed economies should help less-developed countries?

3 How would you recommend that developed economies help less-developed ones?

4 What is the opportunity cost of giving aid? What about the opportunity cost of not giving aid?

5 Is the case for helping less-developed countries mainly a moral one or an economic one?

Key learning points

- Wealth and income are very unevenly distributed around the world.
- Less-developed countries vary in their features, but have low incomes per capita.
- There are numerous ways of trying to boost the income of less-developed countries, such as aid and trade; economists and politicians disagree about the value of each.

Learn more

To learn more about current debates regarding less-developed countries visit our website at the address below.

 Visit our Online Resource Centre at www.oxfordtextbooks.co.uk/orc/gillespie_econ for test questions and further information on topics covered in this chapter.

Globalisation

World trade is increasingly important for countries all over the globe. We buy and use products from all over the world. We travel regularly and can communicate easily and quickly on a global basis. This trend toward the greater internationalisation of business and consumption is called globalisation. In this unit we examine the causes and consequences of globalisation.

LEARNING OBJECTIVES

By the end of this unit you should be able to:

✔ understand the concept of globalisation;

✔ explain the advantages and disadvantages of globalisation.

■ Introduction

There are many different definitions of globalisation, but at the centre of them is the idea that it involves the closer integration of economies across the world. This has led to a greater movement of money, products and people across the globe. Increasingly, economies depend on each other for success. A recession in America, for example, will reduce the market for UK exports. More and more firms are operating globally and developing global brands, such as Nike and Marlboro. If you visit countries all over the world then you are likely to see a brand that you know, for example, Starbucks, Ford, Hilton or McDonald's. Some people see this as evidence of the benefits of trade. Others think it is destroying local producers and local identities, and that the power of some of the huge global corporations is too great.

To some globalisation is inextricably linked to large-scale corporations (often American) abusing their power and exploiting cheap labour and resources abroad. For these groups it has become a very emotive term and has led to riots in some cities when the leaders of the major economies have met as they protest against the power of Western firms over developing countries.

Economics in context

Levitt and globalisation

According to Levitt (1983), 'The globalisation of markets is at hand.' As new technology spread and reduced the cost of communication, the world was getting smaller. Consumer tastes everywhere were converging, creating global markets for similar products. This would create opportunities for big firms producing on a huge scale. Companies that made different products to suit local tastes were doomed. They would be undercut by 'global corporations' that offered the same products in the same way everywhere, benefiting from 'enormous economies of scale' in production, distribution, marketing and management. 'The world's needs and desires have been irrevocably homogenised', Levitt proclaimed. 'This makes the multinational corporation obsolete and the global corporation absolute.'

? Questions

Do you think that markets have become similar all over the world?

Do you think this is true for some products more than others?

Economics in context

Naomi Klein and *No Logo*

Naomi Klein's book *No Logo* is a bestseller and attacks the major multinationals for their use and abuse of power. In the book she presents some fascinating facts, such as the fact that in 1992 Michael Jordan's salary for endorsing Nike trainers was more than that of the entire 30 000-strong Indonesian workforce employed in making them.

? Question

How should American firms decide how much to pay employees in developing countries, such as Indonesia and Vietnam?

■ Why has globalisation occurred?

There are many reasons why trade between countries has increased, such as the following.

- There has been a gradual reduction of trade barriers across the world thanks to organisations such as the World Trade Organization; this has made trade easier. The entry of China into the World Trade Organization, for example, significantly increased the level of competition in several markets for UK firms and opened up a huge new market. Similarly, the growth of the European Union has created new export opportunities.

- Higher incomes and standards of living in some economies have led consumers and firms to search abroad for a wider range of products.

- Better communication systems and information technology have made it easier for firms and consumers to know and buy what is available abroad.

- There has been a growth in organisations that operate worldwide; these multinational firms may want to benefit from new markets.

- Better transport links and lower transport costs have made trade more economically viable.

Globalisation has been widening; this means that more countries have become involved. It has also been deepening; this means that a greater amount of many countries' economic activity involves international trade.

Economics in context   Lenovo buys IBM

In 2005, IBM sold its PC hardware division to China's number one computer maker, Lenovo, for £900 million. This made Lenovo the third largest PC producer in the world. Following the deal, the Chinese firm relocated its headquarters from Beijing to New York. Lenovo's chairman said that this acquisition allowed 'Chinese industry to make significant inroads on its path to globalisation'. In 2006, BMW, the German car manufacturer, agreed to sell the Rover brand to the Shanghai Automotive Industry Corp. The Chinese company agreed to pay £11 million for the name and £67 million for the design rights for several Rover cars. MG Rover went into administration with the loss of 6000 jobs in April 2005. The MG badge was sold, together with the rights to the MG range of cars and the factory in Birmingham, for £53 million to China's Nanjing Automotive. This brought MG and Rover into competition, but both were now owned by Chinese companies.

? Questions

What factors might influence the price paid for another business?
What opportunities does globalisation offer Chinese firms?

What do you think?

Tesco plc announced in 2006 that it was going to enter the American market.
What do you think will determine its success in this market?

What are the advantages of globalisation?

The advantages of globalisation include the following.

- Globalisation enables consumers and firms to benefit from goods and services produced abroad.

- Globalisation can lead to economic growth and higher standards of living.

- Globalisation can lead to greater political integration and greater stability by tying countries together.

- Globalisation can bring new technology and jobs to developing economies.

- Exporting can improve the balance of payments and boost the aggregate demand; this can lead to the multiplier effect creating more jobs.

- By accessing overseas markets, firms can sell and therefore produce on a larger scale. This creates the possibility of firms benefiting from economies of scale.

- Globalisation can export technology and better methods of production; local firms can benefit from the processes adopted by overseas firms. For example, in the UK many manufacturers learned from principles from Japan involving a commitment to quality, teamwork and the reduction of wastage.

- Greater trade can force domestic firms to become more efficient in order to remain competitive.

- Globalisation enables individuals to move abroad to find work. Many countries in Europe are suffering from an ageing population that is reducing the size of their labour forces. Globalisation can enable such countries to benefit from immigration.

- Firms that are faced with saturated domestic markets can find new markets to sell to.

Economics in context **Globalisation**

The following extract is from an article by John Kay that appeared in the *Financial Times* on 30 May 2006.

> Globalisation yields large net benefits, both for the world economy and for individual countries. But managing the process of globalisation requires that those that gain from it compensate those who lose. Without such willingness to share, we risk not only the rise of protectionism but a loss of social cohesion. Both of these problems are already evident.

 Question

How could 'those that gain from [globalisation] compensate those who lose'?

What are the disadvantages of globalisation?

The disadvantages of globalisation include the following.

- Some international firms may not invest heavily into developing economies even though they sell or operate there; they may simply exploit local economies, in which case developing economies may not benefit significantly from the growing world trade.

- Some international firms may exert great political power and abuse their power. Local and regional brands may suffer at the hands of global brands.
- The ability to produce abroad and benefit from cheaper labour and supplies may lead to a loss of jobs domestically.

Economics in context   Globalisation and workers

The following quote is from the Trade Union Congress (TUC) website in 2006 (www.tuc.org.uk). The TUC is a body that represents the major trade unions in the UK.

> The current form of globalisation . . . has brought poverty and hardship to millions of workers, particularly those in developing and transition countries. . . . There is no doubt that globalisation creates problems for workers.

? Question
What might be the response of other stakeholder groups to this view of the TUC?

@ Web
For more information about the Trade Union Congress visit www.tuc.org.uk

---

What do you think?

Do you think that globalisation is a good thing?

▇ Ways of trading abroad

Trading abroad is an important part of many firms' development. There are many different ways of trading with foreign markets, all of which differ in terms of the level of commitment and the degree of risk. The typical stages of involvement are as follows.

- *Export.* This occurs when a firm starts to sell some of its products abroad. This is a low-risk strategy.
- *Licensing abroad.* This occurs when a firm sells the right to use its technology to a foreign firm; again, this is relatively low risk. The firm will earn income from the licence, but the overseas business is taking the risk of actually selling the product.
- *Joint venture.* This occurs when a firm joins with a partner overseas. The partner is likely to have a better knowledge of the culture of the other country and so this may make it easier to operate abroad.
- *Taking over a foreign firm.*

• *Setting up production abroad.* This is the highest-risk strategy because it involves relatively high levels of investment and involves the firm operating on its own.

What do you think?

What do you think is the best way to enter a foreign market?

■ Investment into the UK

The UK has been very successful at attracting overseas investment into the country for the following reasons.

• *The UK has relatively good industrial relations.* For example, in recent years the number of strikes and working days lost through disputes has been relatively low.

• *The UK has relatively good labour markets from an employer's perspective.* For example, it is relatively easy to hire and fire people if required in comparison to other European countries.

• *Financial support from the UK government.* By providing subsidies the government hopes to attract investment and benefit from more employment and higher taxation revenues.

• *The English language.* Students in many other countries will learn English as their second or third language. This makes moving to the UK more likely than to some other countries as the managers will know the language.

Economics in context   Japanese car manufacturers

By 2006, Japanese car manufacturers were building more than half of the total number of cars built in the UK. The factories of Toyota, Honda and Nissan in Derbyshire, Swindon and Sunderland, respectively, were all expanding, whilst European- and US-owned factories were reducing their output or shutting down. In particular, Toyota had been extraordinarily successful, which had led to major expansion in the UK. The Japanese first started investing in the UK in the 1980s. They brought to the UK a range of techniques and skills, such as lean production, that were much more efficient than UK practices, and these were soon adopted by other firms. For the first decade, the UK factories of Toyota, Honda and Nissan were all loss-making as it took time to develop the brand and penetrate the European markets. Whilst the Japanese firms were doing well, Ford had closed its Dagenham assembly plant, Jaguar had closed its factory in Coventry and Vauxhall had shut its Luton works.

The output and sales of car factories in the UK in 2005 are shown in Table 34.1.

 Questions

Is Japanese investment into the UK a good thing?

Why do you think output per worker varies so much between factories in the UK?

Table 34.1   The output and sales of UK car factories in 2005.

Manufacturer	Location in UK	Output per worker	Total annual sales
Nissan	Sunderland	315	4400
Toyota	Burnaston	264	4384
BMW (mini)	Cowley	200	4500
Vauxhall	Ellesmere Port	189	3273
Honda	Swindon	187	4000
Land Rover	Solihull	176	7500
Peugeot	Coventry	127	1997
Jaguar	Three plants	84	5275
Rover	Birmingham	29	0*

* Shut down April 2005.
Source: *Financial Times*, 13 March 2006.

Economics in context   Foreign direct investment into the UK

In 2005, the UK received more inward investment than any other country. Foreign direct investment (FDI) into the UK hit a record of £91 billion. This was driven in part by the boom in takeovers of British companies. Companies such as O2, Abbey National and P&O were bought by foreign firms in that year. The UK was also spending abroad; it was the third biggest investor overseas in 2005. France was the highest.

Table 34.2 shows a number of UK companies that were subject to foreign takeover bids in 2005.

Table 34.2   The UK companies that were subject to foreign takeover bids in 2005.

Target company	Bidder	Deal value (£ million)
O2	Telefonica, Spain	17,610
BAA	Ferrovial, Spain	15,565
BOC Group	Linde, Germany	8,919
P&O	Dubai Ports World, Dubai	4,565
BPB	Saint-Gobain, France	4,389
Exel	Deutsche Post, Germany	4,032
Hilton International	Hilton Hotels Corporation, US	3,298
Pilkington	Nippon Sheet Glass, Japan	2,433

? Question

Are foreign takeovers desirable for the stakeholders of UK firms?

Tesco in South Korea

By 2006, Tesco, the UK supermarket chain, had become the second largest outlet in South Korea's $120 billion retail sector. The leader was a local firm, E-Mart. Other foreign firms, such as Wal-Mart and Carrefour, were not as successful in their entry into the market. Tesco first entered the Korean market in 1999. It entered by setting up hypermarkets that had fast-food outlets, coffee shops and restaurants in them, as well as the supermarket itself. Also, to adjust to local demand, Tesco had included in most of its South Korean stores an Internet cafe, a financial services centre and a car repair shop. At some there were community centres providing classes and even art galleries! Tesco's forty stores in South Korea earned over $4.6 billion in 2005, giving it a 17.1% share of the market. E-Mart had over 31% of the market and seventy-nine stores; Carrefour had around 7% and Wal-Mart below 4%.

Part of the reason for Tesco's success seemed to be due to its willingness to respond to the local market. The business was actually a joint venture that was 89% owned by Tesco and 11% owned by Samsung, and the majority of its employees were recruited locally from Samsung. The company had also adjusted its product mix and store layout to meet local tastes; its competitors had tended to roll out the same products as they did elsewhere and focused on keeping the price low.

? Questions

Why had Tesco been so successful in South Korea?

Should all firms expand internationally like Tesco?

Case Study

The following article was taken from the Foreign and Commonwealth Office website in 2006 (www.fco.gov.uk).

Where does the EU fit in a changing world?

Protectionism is one response to globalisation, with states using tariff barriers and other restrictions to shore up their old industries and associated jobs. (This is as much a pressure in the US as it is in Europe.)

But protectionism wilfully ignores the complex web of dependencies that shape the working of an economy in the modern world. It creates tensions that will sooner or later bite back.

The European response to globalisation has to start with the recognition of its reality: old jobs will sometimes move to new places; and internal economic policy must be directed at creating new jobs.

Commentators sometimes talk of developed nations concentrating on 'higher value' work but this is nonsensical when you look at the booming software development and professional service sectors in India, for example. What we need is distinctive work, hence the importance of innovation and flexibility.

So much for the 'internal' dimension. One of the developments that distinguishes the EU from its forerunner the EEC is its capability to manage foreign policy.

EU competence here is carefully defined to ensure that it does not intrude on national sovereignty in foreign policy proper. But there are undoubtedly areas where Europe's ability to speak as one voice gives significant benefits for all member states.

This is most obviously true in the Doha round of negotiations to liberalise world trade. There is no disputing the historical reality that the developed world has used tariff barriers to protect its agricultural sector, at particular cost to the developing world (which can least afford it). The developed world has been helping itself disproportionately to the fruits of globalisation.

Progress has been painfully slow in the Doha round, but it is progress all the same and the EU has been able to negotiate its position as an equal with the US: both sides recognise that progress depends on mutual concessions.

In the meantime Europe has led the world in debt cancellation and structural support for developing nations (in Africa in particular).

This is important partly because in the long term prosperity in those countries will create healthy demand for European goods and services, boosting our economies. But above all prosperity offers a real dividend in peace and stability: in our globalised world, terrorism and cross-border crime have become global problems.

Policing can only provide a limited measure of security (though pan-European security co-operation and intelligence-sharing is undoubtedly important) but in the longer term it is also vital that we address the despair that fuels anger and violence.

This requires economic and political action. A European voice has, for example, proved an important influence in the Middle East peace process, working as an effective member of the Quartet with the US, Russia and the UN.

At times too in this world economic and political action may need to be backed up by an enhanced military capability, complementing the security roles of the UN and NATO.

The EU project started with the gradual reduction of 'internal' barriers to trade within a small group of states. But its future will be shaped as much by its response to forces beyond its redefined borders. Globalisation is a fundamental force in the debate about the future of Europe. The debate is not just about Europe's institutions. It's about our place in the world.

❓ Questions

- According to the article, why is globalisation desirable?

- In what ways do you think the 'developed world has been helping itself disproportionately to the fruits of globalisation'?

- Do you think that globalisation is a good thing or not?

Checklist

Now you have read this unit try to answer the following questions.

☐ Do you understand the concept of globalisation?

☐ Are you able to explain the advantages and disadvantages of globalisation?

End of unit questions

1 Do you think that globalisation is likely to increase?

2 Are consumers better off with more or less globalisation?

3 Why do firms want to trade abroad?

4 Is it better to sell abroad from the UK or to set up facilities in that country?

5 What would make the UK an attractive location for investment?

Key learning points

- World trade is increasing for a number of reasons, including better communications and transport links.

- In some markets (but not all) there are global brands, such as Nike and Coca Cola.

- Some people believe that globalisation has brought many benefits, such as growth; others think that it is linked to the abuse of power by large international firms.

- When going international, firms must choose the most appropriate way of entering a market.

- The UK has been particularly effective at attracting foreign investment.

Reference

Levitt, T. (1983). The globalization of markets. *Harvard Business Review*, May–June.

Learn more

To learn more about the current issues in the globalisation debate visit our website at the address below.

 Visit our Online Resource Centre at www.oxfordtextbooks.co.uk/orc/gillespie_econ for test questions and further information on topics covered in this chapter.

Glossary of key terms

■ **Abnormal profit** Abnormal profit occurs when the total revenue is greater than the total costs.

■ **Accelerator** The accelerator shows the relationships between the level of net investment and the rate of change of national income.

■ **Aggregate demand** The aggregate demand is the total planned demand for final goods and services in an economy.

■ **Allocative efficiency** Allocative efficiency occurs when the price paid by the customer equals the social marginal cost of producing the good.

■ **Average cost** The average cost is the cost per unit. (It is also called the average total cost.)

■ **Average product** The average product is the output per variable factor (e.g., the output per worker).

■ **Cartel** A cartel occurs when there is an agreement between the firms in a market regarding the price and output to set.

■ **Change in demand** A change in demand refers to a shift in a demand curve, showing a change in the quantity demanded at each and every price.

■ **Classical unemployment** Classical unemployment occurs when the real wage is maintained above equilibrium.

■ **Community surplus** The community surplus is the sum of the consumer surplus and the producer surplus.

■ **Comparative advantage** A country has a comparative advantage in the production of a product if it has a lower opportunity cost than other countries.

■ **Conglomerate integration** Conglomerate integration occurs when one firm joins with another organisation in a different market.

■ **Consumer surplus** The consumer surplus is the difference between the price charged for a product and the utility that consumers derive from it.

■ **Consumption** Consumption shows the level of planned spending by households on final goods and services.

■ **Contestable market** A contestable market is one that is relatively easy to enter.

■ **Cost–benefit analysis** A cost–benefit analysis is an approach to investment decisions that takes into account social costs and benefits.

■ **Cost-push inflation** Cost-push inflation occurs when higher costs force producers to put up their prices.

■ **Cross price elasticity of demand** The cross price elasticity of demand measures the responsiveness of demand for one product in relation to changes in the price of another.

■ **Current account of the balance of payments** The current account of the balance of payments measures the difference in the value between the exports from and imports of goods and services to a country.

- **Cyclical unemployment** Cyclical unemployment occurs when people are unemployed due to a lack of demand in the economy.
- **Demand curve** A demand curve shows the quantity demanded at each and every price, all other factors being unchanged.
- **Demand for labour** The demand for labour shows the quantity of labour demanded at each and every wage, all other factors being unchanged.
- **Demand for money** The demand for money shows the amount of money that people want to hold at each and every interest rate, all other things being unchanged.
- **Demand-pull inflation** Demand-pull inflation occurs when the aggregate demand is greater than the aggregate supply, thereby pulling up prices.
- **Diseconomies of scale** Diseconomies of scale (internal) occur when there are increases in the long-run average costs as the scale of production increases.
- **Diversification** Diversification occurs when a firm develops new products to offer in a new market.
- **Divorce between ownership and control** A divorce between ownership and control occurs when there is a difference between the people who own an organisation and those who manage it day to day.
- **Economic cycle** The economic cycle shows the pattern of GDP growth in an economy over time.
- **Economic growth** Economic growth occurs when there is an increase in the real national income.
- **Elasticity of demand for labour** The elasticity of demand for labour measures the responsiveness of the demand for labour in relation to changes in wages, all other factors being unchanged.
- **Equilibrium** Equilibrium occurs when the quantity supplied equals the quantity demanded at the given price and there is no incentive for change.
- **Euro** The euro is a single currency adopted by most members of the European Union.
- **European Union** The European Union is a customs union. This means that there is free trade between member countries and common external tariffs against non-member countries.
- **Exchange rate** An exchange rate is the price of one currency in terms of another.
- **Expansionist or reflationary fiscal policy** An expansionist or reflationary fiscal policy attempts to increase the aggregate demand.
- **External economies and diseconomies of scale** External economies and diseconomies of scale occur when the long-run average costs of a firm change at every level of output.
- **Externality** An externality occurs when there is a difference between private and social costs and benefits.
- **Fiscal policy** A fiscal policy uses government spending and taxation and benefit rates to influence the economy.
- **Fixed costs** Fixed costs are costs that do not change with the amount of products produced.
- **Fixed exchange rate system** In a fixed exchange rate system the government intervenes to maintain the external value of a currency.

▨ Floating exchange rate system In a floating exchange rate system the external value of a currency is determined by the supply of and demand for it.

▨ Free market A free market allocates resources via the price mechanism and market forces of supply and demand.

▨ Frictional unemployment Frictional unemployment occurs when people are between jobs.

▨ Game theory Game theory is an approach to oligopoly in which each firm's strategy depends on its expectations of how the others in the market will behave.

▨ Gini coefficient The Gini coefficient measures the extent of income inequality in an economy.

▨ Gross domestic product (GDP) The gross domestic product (GDP) measures the value of final goods and services produced in an economy.

▨ Gross national product (GNP) The gross national product (GNP) equals the gross domestic product plus the net property income from abroad.

▨ Horizontal integration Horizontal integration occurs when one firm joins with another at the same stage of the same production process.

▨ Import substitution Import substitution occurs when a government uses policies to encourage domestic buyers to switch to local products and away from foreign ones.

▨ Income elasticity of demand The income elasticity of demand measures the responsiveness of the demand for a product in relation to changes in income.

▨ Inflation Inflation occurs when there is a persistent increase in the general price level.

▨ Injection An injection is spending into the economy in addition to consumption; injections increase the aggregate demand.

▨ Interdependence Interdependence occurs when the actions of one firm directly affect another.

▨ Internal diseconomies of scale Internal diseconomies of scale occur when there are increases in the long-run average costs as the scale of production increases.

▨ Internal economies of scale Internal economies of scale occur when there are reductions in the long-run average costs as the scale of production increases.

▨ Involuntary unemployment Involuntary unemployment measures the number of people who are willing and able to work at the given real wage but who are not in employment.

▨ J curve The J curve effect shows how a depreciation of a currency can make the balance of payments worse in the short run before it improves.

▨ Laffer curve The Laffer curve shows the relationship between the tax rate and the level of tax revenue.

▨ Less-developed country A less-developed country is an economy with low income and is usually associated with low life expectancy and low levels of literacy.

▨ Liquidity preference Liquidity preference (the demand for money) shows the amount of money that people want to hold at each and every interest rate, all other things being unchanged.

▨ Long run The long run is the period of time when all of the factors of production are variable.

▨ Marginal cost The marginal cost is the extra cost of producing an extra unit.

■ **Marginal efficiency of capital (MEC)** The marginal efficiency of capital (MEC) shows the expected rate of return on investment projects.

■ **Marginal product** The marginal product measures the extra output produced when another unit of a variable factor of production is added to the fixed factors of production.

■ **Marginal propensity to consume** The marginal propensity to consume measures the amount spent out of an extra pound by households.

■ **Marginal propensity to consume domestically** The marginal propensity to consume domestically measures the amount spent out of an extra pound by households within a domestic economy.

■ **Marginal revenue** Marginal revenue is the extra revenue earned by selling another unit.

■ **Marginal revenue product** The marginal revenue product measures the value of the output produced by employing an extra worker.

■ **Market development** Market development occurs when a firm offers its existing products to a new market.

■ **Market share** A market share is the sales of a firm or brand as a percentage of the total market sales.

■ **Marketing mix** The marketing mix is the combination of factors that influence a customer's decision to buy a product, such as the price, the product itself, the promotion and the place.

■ **Maximum price** A maximum price occurs when a price is set by the government and firms cannot charge more than this.

■ **Merger** A merger occurs when two or more organisations join together to form one.

■ **Minimum efficient scale** The minimum efficient scale is the first level of output at which the long-run average costs are minimised.

■ **Minimum price** A minimum price occurs when a price is set by the government and firms cannot charge less than this.

■ **Mixed economy** A mixed economy is an economy that contains both private and public sectors within it.

■ **Monetary Policy Committee** The Monetary Policy Committee is an organisation responsible for setting interest rates in the UK to achieve a given inflation target.

■ **Monopolistic competition** Monopolistic competition is a market structure in which there are many firms but each offers a differentiated product.

■ **Monopoly** A monopoly is a firm that dominates a market.

■ **Monopoly power** Monopoly power occurs when one firm dominates a market.

■ **Movement along a demand curve** A movement along a demand curve refers to a change in the quantity demanded that is caused by a change in the price, all other factors being unchanged.

■ **Multiplier** The multiplier shows how an increase in the aggregate demand leads to a greater increase in national income.

■ **Nationalisation** Nationalisation occurs when a government takes ownership of an organisation.

■ **Normal profit** Normal profit occurs when the total revenue equals the total costs.

- **Objective** An objective is a target (e.g., to increase profits by 20% over five years).
- **Office of Fair Trading** The Office of Fair Trading is a government regulator of competition policy.
- **Oligopoly** An oligopoly is a market structure in which a few firms dominate the market.
- **Opportunity cost** The opportunity cost (in the context of a production possibility frontier) is the amount of one product that has to be given up to produce more of another product.
- **Patent** A patent is a legal protection for an invention.
- **Perfect price discrimination** Perfect price discrimination occurs when a different price is charged for every single unit of the product.
- **Phillips curve** The Phillips curve shows the short-run and long-run relationships between inflation and unemployment.
- **Planned (command) economy** A planned (command) economy allocates resources via government orders.
- **Potential growth** The potential growth represents economic growth with resources fully employed, i.e. it represents an increase in the economic capacity.
- **Price discrimination** Price discrimination occurs when different prices are charged to different customers for the same product.
- **Price elasticity of demand** The price elasticity of demand measures the responsiveness of the demand for a product in relation to changes in its price.
- **Price elasticity of supply** The price elasticity of supply measures the responsiveness of the supply for one product in relation to changes in its price.
- **Price war (or predatory pricing)** A price war (or predatory pricing) occurs when one firm undercuts others to gain control of the market.
- **Privatisation** Privatisation occurs when there is a transfer of assets or services to the private sector.
- **Producer surplus** The producer surplus is the difference between the price paid to producers for products and the cost of producing the items.
- **Production possibility frontier** A production possibility frontier shows the maximum combination of products that an economy can produce given its resources.
- **Productive efficiency** Productive efficiency occurs when more of one product can only be produced if less of another product is produced. It also occurs when a firm produces at the minimum of the average cost curve, that is, at the lowest cost per unit possible.
- **Productivity** Productivity measures the level of output in relation to the inputs used; for example, labour productivity measures the output per worker.
- **Profit maximising condition** The profit maximising condition occurs when firms produce where the marginal revenue equals the marginal cost.
- **Protectionism** Protectionism occurs when a government protects its domestic firms against foreign competition.
- **PSNCR** The PSNCR is the public sector net cash requirement, which measures the amount that the government has to borrow to finance its spending in a given year.
- **Public good** A public good is a product that is non-diminishable and non-excludable.
- **Quantity theory of money** The quantity theory of money states that $MV = PT$.

- **Quota** A quota is a limit to the amount that a firm can produce.
- **Recession** A recession occurs when there are two or more quarters of negative economic growth.
- **Reflationary policy** A reflationary policy increases the aggregate demand.
- **Research and development** Research and development involves the use of science to develop new ways of producing and to develop new products.
- **Resources** Resources are inputs, such as land, labour and capital, that are used in the production process.
- **Second-Best World** The Second-Best World is one in which market failures and imperfections exist. In this situation the existence of some market failures may cancel out others. The theory of second best highlights that intervening in a market to correct one failure (e.g., removing the monopoly) may actually move the economy further away from the optimal allocation of resources.
- **Short run** The short run is the period of time when at least one factor of production is fixed.
- **Shortage** A shortage occurs when the quantity demanded is greater than the quantity supplied at the given price.
- **Supply curve** A supply curve shows the quantity that producers are willing and able to produce at each and every price, all other factors being unchanged.
- **Surplus** A surplus occurs when the quantity supplied is greater than the quantity demanded at the given price.
- **Takeover** A takeover occurs when one organisation takes control of another.
- **Terms of trade** The terms of trade measure the prices of exports from a country compared to the prices of imports into the country.
- **Total cost** The total cost equals the fixed costs plus the variable costs.
- **Total revenue** The total revenue is the value of sales (calculated as the price of a product multiplied by the quantity sold).
- **Utility** The utility refers to the satisfaction that a consumer would receive from consuming a product.
- **Variable costs** Variable costs are costs that change with the amount produced.
- **Veblen good** A Veblen good is an ostentatious good that people buy more of when the price is high.
- **Vertical integration** Vertical integration occurs when one firm joins with another at a different stage of the same production process.
- **Voluntary unemployment** Voluntary unemployment occurs when people who are looking for work are not yet willing to accept work at the given real wage rate.
- **Withdrawal** A withdrawal is a leakage from the economy and it reduces the aggregate demand.

Useful websites

The following lists some of the websites that contain useful economics information. Why not visit them and see what you can discover?

Adam Smith Institute 'The Adam Smith Institute is Britain's leading innovator of free-market economic and social policies. Since 1977, it has played a key role in developing practical initiatives to inject choice and competition into public services, extend personal freedom, reduce taxes, prune back regulation, and cut government waste.'

@ www.adamsmith.org

Bank of England The Bank of England is the UK's central bank. This website provides information on monetary policy, inflation, interest rates, the Monetary Policy Committee and the role of the Bank of England.

@ www.bankofengland.co.uk

BBC The BBC website contains numerous new stories about business and economics. Either visit the main section www.bbc.co.uk or go straight to the economics section.

@ news.bbc.co.uk/1/hi/business/economy

Biz-ed 'A Web site for students and educators in business studies, economics, accounting, leisure, sport & recreation and travel & tourism.'

@ www.bized.ac.uk

CAROL 'CAROL is an on-line service offering direct links to the financial pages of listed companies in Europe and the USA. CAROL provides direct access to companies' balance sheets, profit & loss statements, financial highlights, etc.'

@ www.carolworld.com

CIA factbook This website provides information and data on countries around the world.

@ https://www.cia.gov/cia/publications/factbook/index.html

Competition Commission 'The Competition Commission conducts inquiries into mergers, markets and the regulation of the major regulated industries.' This site provides information on ongoing and past inquiries.

@ www.competition-commission.org.uk

Confederation of British Industry (CBI) 'One of the UK's leading independent employers' organisations . . . The CBI's mission is to help create and sustain the conditions in which businesses in the United Kingdom can compete and prosper for the benefit of all.' This website has data and surveys produced by the CBI and highlights the view of many businesses in relation to economic, social and political issues.

@ www.cbi.org.uk

Department of Trade and Industry The UK's Department of Trade and Industry is: 'Working to create the conditions for business success and help the UK respond to the challenge of globalisation.' There is information on this website about innovation, employment matters, regional economic development, business sectors and the business environment.

@ www.dti.gov.uk

Department for International Development This is the website of the UK government's Department for International Development. It contains information about current government policy on development issues.

@ www.dfid.gov.uk

Europa This is the official website of the European Union.

@ europa.eu

The Guardian This is the website for *The Guardian* newspaper, and it provides access to articles and surveys.

@ www.guardian.co.uk

Institute for Fiscal Studies 'IFS® is an independent research organisation. We aim to promote effective economic and social policies through rigorous analysis of their impact on individuals, families, firms and the public finances.'

@ www.ifs.org.uk

International Monetary Fund 'The IMF is an organization of 184 countries, working to foster global monetary cooperation, secure financial stability, facilitate international trade, promote high employment and sustainable economic growth, and reduce poverty.'

@ www.imf.org

Office of Fair Trading 'The OFT is responsible for making markets work well for consumers. We do this by promoting and protecting consumer interests throughout the UK whilst ensuring that businesses are fair and competitive.' This website has information on a range of issues, such as consumer rights and competition legislation.

@ www.oft.gov.uk

Office of National Statistics This is a government website that contains information on 'Britain's economy, population and society at national and local level. Summaries and detailed data releases are published free of charge.'

@ www.statistics.gov.uk

Organization for Economic Cooperation and Development The Organization for Economic Cooperation and Development is an organisation of thirty countries 'sharing a democratic government and the market economy'. Best known for its publications and its statistics, its work covers economic and social issues from macroeconomics, to trade, education, development, and science and innovation.

@ www.oecd.org

The Times This website provides access to the articles of *The Times* and *The Sunday Times* newspapers.

@ www.timesonline.co.uk

Trade Union Congress (TUC) The TUC represents the major trade unions in the UK. 'With member unions representing over six and a half million working people, we campaign for a fair deal at work and for social justice at home and abroad.' This website provides information on employee rights, trade union objectives and initiatives, and the trade union stance on many economic and political issues.

@ www.tuc.org

The Treasury The Treasury website provides information on the UK budget, enterprise and productivity, economic data, tax, work and welfare.

@ www.hm-treasury.gov.uk

World Trade Organization The World Trade Organization is '. . . the only global organisation dealing with the rules of trade between organisations. At its heart are the WTO agreements, negotiated and signed by the bulk of the world's trading nations and ratified in their parliaments.' This website provides essential information on the World Trade Organization, its role, and developments in international trade agreements.

@ www.wto.org

Index

F